THE INSTRUMENTAL UNIVERSITY

Histories of American Education

A series edited by Jonathan Zimmerman

THE INSTRUMENTAL UNIVERSITY

EDUCATION IN SERVICE
OF THE NATIONAL AGENDA
AFTER WORLD WAR II

ETHAN SCHRUM

CORNELL UNIVERSITY PRESS
Ithaca and London

First published 2019 by Cornell University Press

Librarians: A CIP catalog record for this book is available from the Library of Congress

ISBN 9781501736643 (cloth)
ISBN 9781501736650 (pdf)
ISBN 9781501736667 (epub/mobi)

To my delightful wife, Kara

Contents

THE INSTRUMENTAL UNIVERSITY

Introduction
The Instrumental University and American Modernity

When Clark Kerr, president of the University of California, stepped to a Harvard University podium in April 1963 to present his analysis of American higher education, he emphasized the dramatic and rapid change in the sector. "The modern American university," he declared, "is a new type of institution in the world." It held a "novel position in society" because knowledge had become "the most important factor in economic and social growth." In these Godkin Lectures, published later that year as *The Uses of the University*, Kerr dubbed this new institution "the multiversity" because it engaged in a spectacular array of activities with little cohesion and no unifying philosophy. He did not deplore the multiversity, and in fact gave it a largely optimistic gloss. He joked that the multiversity could be described as "a series of individual faculty entrepreneurs held together by a common grievance over parking." He noted that "so many of the hopes and fears of the American people are now related to our educational system [that] the university has become a prime instrument of national purpose. This is new. This is the essence of the transformation now engulfing our universities."[1]

While "multiversity" is an apt term, it does not tell the whole story—or even the main story—of the postwar university. Kerr's commentary suggests a better conceptualization. According to Kerr, external constituencies such as government, industry, and foundations used the university as an instrument to achieve their own purposes—hence the title *The Uses of the University*.

A related feature of the postwar university was the proliferation of academic enterprise that prioritized instrumental rationality to shape the social order, from business and engineering schools to fields like city planning, industrial relations, and public administration.[2] Public expectations for university-based solutions to social problems increased accordingly.

Kerr did not simply notice, assess, and announce this change in American universities. He played an essential role in enacting it during twenty-two years in progressively higher leadership positions at the University of California, doing work that often influenced practices across American higher education.[3] Kerr stood at the forefront of this trend, but he was hardly alone in such activity. This book spotlights Kerr's thought and impact as part of a broader portrait of academic institution builders, including heretofore neglected figures such as Gaylord P. Harnwell, E. T. Grether, James G. March, Samuel P. Hayes Jr., G. Holmes Perkins, and Joseph Willits. These academic leaders and their like-minded contemporaries in politics and civil society attained professional standing during the Depression and World War II. The triumph of organized war research conducted in university labs convinced them that such efforts, if expanded to focus on social problems as well as military concerns, could remake American society and perhaps even the world. As they discussed goals for their institutions, these leaders increasingly spoke a mechanistic, technocratic language aimed at training managers and technicians to operate society. Kerr exemplified this sensibility when he stated that the university "not only preserves the past and prepares the future but it also increasingly helps administer the present."[4] Politicians expressed similar views. John F. Kennedy stated, "Most of the problems . . . that we now face, are technical problems, are administrative problems."[5] Since powerful postwar figures believed that the present was witnessing the realization of American modernity, it followed that for them a major purpose of the university was to administer American modernity.

In this book, I argue that Kerr and other elite Americans of his generation, inside and outside of the academy, set the American research university on a new course. They did so by creating the instrumental university. (Kerr did not use the term "instrumental university," but his ideas inspired this concept, which I employ to interpret the university's role in twentieth-century US history.)[6] With its emphasis on procedural rationality, organized research, and project-based funding by external patrons, the instrumental university would provide technical and managerial knowledge to shape the social order. Its leaders hoped that by solving the nation's pressing social problems and stimulating economic growth, the research university would become the essential institution of postwar America. Kerr and his fellows, under the spell of a postwar vision of American modernity, saw the university as an instrument that could administer society at home and abroad in order to realize that vision. This vision of American modernity was itself a historical product, growing out of the tradition of technocratic progressivism that arose in the United States in the 1910s. Four modern ideals connected to technocratic progressivism—involving industrial relations, city planning, economic development, and administration—particularly motivated the leaders who created the instrumental university. These ideals gained traction between the 1910s and 1930s, but the belief that the United States had won World War II due to its economic might and organized research enhanced their appeal and facilitated their incorporation into the broader vision of American modernity that coalesced after the war.

This transformation brought a new understanding of the research university's mission and its role in society. On this view, the university's leading purposes included promoting economic development and coordinating research from many fields in order to attack social problems. Harnwell and Kerr were among the early presidents to cite an emerging knowledge economy to justify a new strategic direction for their universities. By the late 1950s and early 1960s, they and their colleagues observed that business and universities were drawing closer together, and began to describe the university as an economic engine responsible for "innovation." Reorienting institutions to prioritize these activities had numerous consequences. One was to inject more capitalistic and managerial tendencies into universities. Another was to marginalize some founding ideals of the American research university, such as the pursuit of knowledge in academic disciplines and the freedom of individual investigators, not to mention even older ideals of liberal education. The result is that the university lost some of what made it special. It became more like other large institutions, caught up in the economics and politics of the day, rather than a place intentionally set apart from those currents so that scholars could pursue truth. This change undermined the rationale for practices that were originally tied to that special character and sapped their public support. It also weakened the landscape of American institutions by making that landscape less diverse. No other entity filled the space once occupied by the university. Consequently, Americans have fewer opportunities to consider the highest intellectual goods apart from immediate economic or social utility. Today, those who decry universities' corporatizing and market-driven tendencies often trace them to the rise of neoliberalism in the 1970s. This book suggests that a fuller explanation of these tendencies—particularly organizational changes within universities from the 1940s onward—must highlight their deeper roots in the technocratic progressive tradition.

The Instrumental University

The instrumental university's mission to promote economic development and coordinate research to solve social problems produced a proliferation of organized research units (ORUs).[7] This trend marked a break with prewar university research, which was, in the words of a 1938 National Resources Committee report, "Independent and unorganized, controlled and directed chiefly by the interests of the individual professor."[8] In that era, according to historian Rebecca Lowen, "America's universities were peripheral to the nation's political economy. They were committed to promoting the scientific method, to allowing academic scientists and scholars to discover and study 'truths' . . . the concept of autonomy from private industry and, more broadly, the world of commerce, distinguished the university from the mere technical institute."[9] But after World War II, the ethos of detachment waned as elite institutions pursued organized research on specific problems to meet the desires of patrons and perceived national needs. This research increasingly occurred in ORUs, most of which were called a "center" or "institute." A typical ORU included regular tenure-track professors (often from different academic departments but sometimes just from one), researchers appointed to the ORU rather than a department, and support staff. The term "organized" meant that these researchers worked together (under the direction of a leader) on specific problems, often funded by corporations, foundations, and government agencies. The ORU was an instrument that these patrons could use to pursue problems of interest. Although relationships between patrons and researchers were complex, the net effect of the spread of organized research was to increase the influence of patrons over the direction of university research, thus instrumentalizing the university.[10] The new organized research was often autonomous—that is, disconnected from departments and teaching, the university's academic core.[11] While autonomy was important, organization was the more salient characteristic of the postwar vision for university research. The increasing prestige of organization as a social ideal since the 1910s and the emphasis that technocratic progressives placed on organizational solutions to social problems both fed the postwar rise of organized research.

One indicator that the instrumental university model had become powerful was that leading research universities and land-grant colleges converged toward that model in the postwar era.[12] In the early twentieth century, the major genres of American higher education had been liberal arts colleges, normal schools (devoted to teacher training), technical institutes, land-grant colleges, and research universities. The latter, prominent though few in number, had made pure research—pursuing knowledge for its own sake—a central mission in the late nineteenth century. In 1900, the most formidable among them formed the Association of American Universities: older private institutions Columbia, Harvard, Pennsylvania, Princeton, and Yale; newer privates Catholic, Chicago, Clark, Cornell, Johns Hopkins, and Stanford; and state universities California (Berkeley), Michigan, and Wisconsin. These institutions were devoted to advancing specialized knowledge in professional academic disciplines. By contrast, the land-grant colleges focused on practical knowledge, particularly in agriculture and engineering. Prior to World War II, land-grant institutions like Texas A&M and Penn State conducted little research outside of those fields. They prioritized teaching, as well as public service through extension programs. After the war, they pursued research more vigorously as many changed their names from "college" to "university" and dropped the "A&M" moniker. Three of the original AAU members—California, Cornell, and Wisconsin—contained a land-grant component in addition to functioning as a research university. Each helped to drive the transition to the instrumental university among their AAU peers. Land-grant institutions retained some distinctive qualities after World War II, but the boundary dividing them from elite research universities blurred as each took on characteristics of the other.

This book describes how the elite research university transformed into the instrumental university.[13] Most of the original AAU members figure in this account, though its main archival research focuses on three, each from a different subgenre: Pennsylvania (private), Michigan (public, non–land grant), and California (public, land grant). California is a special case, because it became a system of research-intensive campuses, not all of which gained AAU membership.[14] I focus on Berkeley, the original and flagship campus, and Irvine, opened in 1965.

The technocratic progressivism that grounded the instrumental university was an intellectual disposition that portrayed technical knowledge as the key to social progress.[15] Other historians have focused—and helpfully so—on the effects of the Cold War and the federal research economy to explain why American universities changed after World War II.[16] Yet as close attention to prewar sources suggests, the federal research economy and the Cold War merely nourished an instrumental bent initially built on a decades-long quest for rational ordering of the modern world.

In this interpretation, postwar universities partook of a "high modern" impulse in American thought that sprang from technocratic progressivism in the 1910s and accelerated in the 1930s with the advent of the New Deal.[17] This quest reached its apogee in the two decades after World War II as the outgrowth of a distinctly American intellectual tradition. Hence, the postwar university was not primarily a reaction to geopolitics or immediate events. It was a product of long-germinating worldviews and visions for society. This realization demands greater attention to the intellectual history that shaped the development of the modern American university.

American Modernity

The vision of American modernity that influenced the postwar elites who transformed the research university into an instrument for administering society became so widely assumed that advocates rarely articulated it precisely. It held that the future of liberal-democratic capitalism at home and abroad depended on universities to do three things—drive economic development, provide organized social research on critical issues identified by external patrons, and expand administrative capacity in the public and private sectors. Each of these three pillars of this vision of American modernity had some traction before World War II but gained much more after 1945. Since the early twentieth century, expectations had grown that universities would produce knowledge and experts that would help to administer organizations. After 1945, new intellectual frameworks accelerated such expectations and even promoted belief that universities themselves should administer modern society. Organized research had its roots in the technocratic progressivism of the 1920s but did not really take off until after the success of government-funded organized research during the war. Of the three pillars, belief that the research university was central for economic development was the least established before the war. To the extent that such ideas had force, they were mainly limited to the land-grant colleges—and even then not really stated in terms of economic development, a concept that only gained traction in the 1930s. The technocratic progressive vision of American modernity also had an international dimension with a missionary impulse. It depicted the United States as the quintessential modern nation, charged with modernizing the world. The overall American modernity vision was widespread during the twenty years after the war, before coming under fire in the mid-1960s by challenges ranging from the Vietnam War to worries that European technological achievements were threatening American superiority in that realm.[18]

Several factors contributed to this framework's postwar influence. President Franklin D. Roosevelt's administration, through its New Deal programs and its conduct of World War II, gave new prestige to technocratic management, as many postwar leaders believed that such practices had sustained liberal democracy in the United States through depression and war. In particular, the widespread perception that the nation had won the war due to its economic might and its prowess in organized scientific research placed those attributes at the center of postwar American self-consciousness. That belief also made American modernity a bipartisan vision. Many of its key adherents—such as wartime science directors Gaylord Harnwell and Vannevar Bush, and promoters of universities' international role like John Hannah and Harold Stassen—were staunch Republicans. In addition, the United States' emergence as the preeminent global power by the end of World War II encouraged belief in American modernity. Finally, the onset of the Cold War strengthened the framework—particularly in contrast to the Soviet Union's illiberal, command economy notion of modernity—but did not create it. In fact, the vision of American modernity, by highlighting the importance of universities, shaped how Americans approached the Cold War.

University and other societal leaders working to advance American modernity in the postwar period believed in American exceptionalism. Consistent with their notion of America being uniquely modern, they often pointed to economic and especially technological superiority, rather than distinctive traditions of liberty or constitutional government, as the basis for exceptionalism. Indeed, they believed that this technological prowess was an essential guarantor of liberal-democratic capitalism. Rather than seeing technological excellence as the product of some particularly American ingenuity or experience, these leaders insisted on the transferability of technology to other nations, if only the relevant administrative and organizational conditions that had created American modernity could be duplicated elsewhere. The concept of American modernity helps to explain how Americans could think of themselves as exceptional and yet want to spread their way of life, believing that doing so would not diminish their own exceptionality. For those motivated by this vision, Americans were exceptional because they were at the forefront of a universal process of modernization. Like Henry Luce in his famous call for US internationalism, "The American Century" (1941), these leaders held that American values were universal rather than particular and thus transferable to other peoples. Americans exemplified these values and had an exceptional duty to spread them to the world. Perhaps the prime example of this mindset was "Point Four" of President Truman's 1949 inaugural address, which extolled American technology and its ability to remake the world. University leaders and faculty involved in overseas technical assistance projects subsequently launched under Point Four auspices consistently noted or assumed American superiority, in contrast to many American school teachers working abroad during this time who questioned the United States' uniqueness, its claim to represent universal values, and its alleged special mission to transform the world into its image.[19]

These overseas projects became characteristic endeavors for the postwar research university. It is well known that postwar universities expanded their study of the non-Western world and enrolled increasing numbers of international students.[20] But they also created, augmented, and staffed overseas institutions of higher learning—particularly in newly independent countries such as Indonesia and Pakistan—under the rubric of technical assistance toward these countries' economic development. Much of this work occurred via contracts with the US government under Point Four and its successors, while foundations and the UN funded similar endeavors. Many of America's elite research universities participated in such projects, which contributed to instrumentalizing the universities. A distinct vocabulary—which portrayed the university as an instrument and emphasized "using" the university—arose by the mid-1950s in elite discussions about American universities' international institution building. Kerr thus did not invent this vocabulary, but rather gave new force and broader application to ideas circulating among the elites with whom he interacted.

The American modernity vision included four modern ideals connected to technocratic progressivism—industrial relations, city planning, administration, and economic development—that propelled the rise of the instrumental university.[21] The four ideals were all related to applied social science and to Kerr's notion of administering the present. They arose prior to and independently of the Cold War, in the Progressive Era (except for economic development). The political culture and institutions of the New Deal strengthened them, but they became more fully institutionalized in the academy only after 1945. In this process, university-based applied social science motivated by a New Deal vision for domestic social change expanded in prestige and scope from the end of World War II through the mid-1960s.[22]

Each modern ideal spawned a semi-coherent body of concepts and practices that exerted influence at varying levels of the university. Industrial relations and city planning translated to inherently problem-oriented academic fields under those names, but they also had some force at a university-wide level. Economic development and administration were more protean in their institutional implications but also shaped disciplines, as the former generated the subfield of development economics and the latter acted through business administration and public administration.[23] These kinds of applied social science fields that emphasized instrumental rationality spread widely in the postwar American research university.[24] They also featured disproportionately in universities' overseas ventures, more prominently than natural science disciplines (though medicine- and agriculture-related fields were important) and certainly more than humanities. When American universities sought to transmit the American way of life to other lands, they did so through business and public administration rather than literature, philosophy, and religion. American elites believed that the former disciplines had superior capacity to promote liberal-democratic capitalism.

The New Deal state particularly influenced universities in connection with industrial relations and city planning, which have strikingly parallel histories. Each discipline corresponded to a major element in the understanding of history articulated by the most prominent postwar university presidents, such as Kerr and Harnwell, which emphasized that industrialism and urbanism steadily expanded over time to become the predominant modes of social organization. Industrial relations and city planning would provide experts to apply rational guidance to this supposedly inexorable historical process. New Deal and wartime government programs created a demand for credentialed experts in these fields, which contributed to the proliferation of university units dedicated to them in the immediate postwar years. The New Deal's National Labor Relations Act (1935) and the wartime National War Labor Board bolstered the demand for industrial relations specialists, while the National Resources Planning Board, the Public Works Administration, and the National Housing Agency and its successors propelled city planning. Members of the two nascent academic fields regularly worked for these government agencies. The fields were heavily instrumental in that they were oriented toward particular social problems, and their new prominence in the postwar university contributed to its increasingly instrumental character. The postwar era thus witnessed a burst of university activity aimed at institutionalizing instrumental knowledge that had little to do with the Cold War, although the two fields later interacted with Cold War concerns.[25]

Of the four ideals, economic development exerted the strongest and broadest influence on the university.[26] After 1945, American elites promoted continuous economic development at home and abroad. A belief that universities must join this project motivated much organized research. Several factors spurred this project: New Deal political culture and Keynesianism, residual fears from the Depression, the role of American economic might in winning World War II, the United States' new position as global hegemon in a war-devastated and decolonizing world, and the onset of the Cold War. Keynesian ideas and the rise of systems thinking (described below), combined with the experience of wartime economic management, convinced people that there was an entity called "the economy" (a newly popular term in the 1930s) that could be developed and administered, and that the university might be an instrument for doing so.[27] Patrons—especially the Ford Foundation, the most important foundation patron of the instrumental university—encouraged universities to adopt the economic development ideal.

The economic development ideal inspired postwar university leaders to trumpet the arrival of what they believed was a new phase of industrial capitalism in which their institutions were central—a nascent "knowledge economy." Scholars have given scant attention to the origins of this idea.[28] Although the term "knowledge economy" did not become popular until Peter Drucker made it the title of a chapter in his 1969 book *The Age of Discontinuity*, Kerr articulated its fundamental tenet by 1957: knowledge, considered as a form of capital, had replaced physical raw materials as the essential input for industrial production. In this view, the university became the key institution for economic development, a belief that led in later years to the expectation that the university should be "an engine of economic development." Kerr helped to formulate this idea in conjunction with other economic thinkers such as Drucker, Fritz Machlup, Theodore Schultz, and Gary Becker. University presidents such as Harnwell, although not theorists of the knowledge economy, shaped their institutions in accordance with its precepts. The notion of a knowledge economy motivated federal and state government attempts to mobilize universities for economic development by the early 1960s. Recovering the fact that universities saw themselves as central to a knowledge economy by the late 1950s suggests the prescience of Berkeley Free Speech Movement (FSM) leader Mario Savio's famous 1964 speech depicting students as raw materials. This recovery also provides a fresh angle on student movements such as the FSM by enriching our knowledge of how the universities they criticized were situated in the larger economic order. Universities did not create the knowledge economy, at least directly or intentionally, although commentators have suggested that university-based knowledge helped create the knowledge economy. Universities did, however, craft a rhetoric centered on the knowledge economy to promote their importance for society. In the process, they instrumentalized themselves in various ways.

The knowledge economy concept that Kerr and others articulated from the mid-1950s to the mid-1960s assumed that industrial production was the definitive practice for economic and social life. Kerr's knowledge economy did not constitute a vision of a postindustrial society—a concept that thinkers such as Daniel Bell and David Riesman began to discuss in the late 1950s, in which services became more economically important than the production of goods.[29] Nor was Kerr's knowledge economy a variety of postcapitalism—a mode of thought popular from the 1940s to 1970s whose proponents, mainly on the political left, saw capitalism giving way to alternative frameworks of social and economic order.[30] Kerr was committed to industrial capitalism and saw it as triumphant, not teetering on the brink of collapse. The knowledge economy was the new reality of the industrial economy, not something that eclipsed it. Kerr did espouse elements that would later be associated with a post-industrial vision—increased leisure time, reduced labor strife, business becoming more like universities with shared governance—but he saw these trends as fruits of mature industrialism rather than of a new order. More important for the long-term implications of the instrumental university, however, is that Kerr also realized that university research was increasingly adopting practices characteristic of business. The rise of the knowledge economy concept and belief in universities' centrality for economic development suggests that historians of capitalism must pay closer attention to universities.

Another characteristically modern intellectual framework—the behavioral science paradigm that broke into public view shortly after World War II—shaped the instrumental university in a different way than the four modern ideals did.[31] Behavioral science provided new conceptual tools that allowed some applied academic fields to build more robust research programs. Behavioral science can be described as an effort to integrate the insights of anthropology, political science, psychology, sociology, and sometimes economics and biological sciences to gain a deeper, theory-grounded understanding of human behavior with which to engage in social engineering. Interdisciplinarity and quantification were hallmarks of behavioral science. Its proponents aimed to break down barriers between existing social science disciplines and to make social inquiry more rigorously scientific, which meant describing the social world with statistics and mathematics.

Like the four modern ideals, behavioral science had roots prior to World War II. By 1939, when Harvard University officials appointed sociologist Talcott Parsons as chair of the Committee on Concentration in the Area of Social Science, his group was essentially promoting what would later become known as behavioral science. The committee's 1941 report, "Toward a Common Language for the Area of Social Science," called for "a single model of human behavior in societies." During World War II, team-based social science projects "gave rise to the belief that a new 'behavioral science' had taken shape, which, like the physical and biological sciences, could be a source of both fundamental laws and technological control." These problem-oriented interdisciplinary projects facilitated the postwar creation of Harvard's Department of Social Relations under Parsons's leadership. As part of this process, Parsons acknowledged the importance of organized research.[32]

Another figure from this Harvard milieu, James G. Miller, helped to institutionalize behavioral science after the war. As an undergraduate at Harvard in the early 1930s, Miller participated in a faculty discussion group centered on the writings of Italian sociological theorist Vifredo Pareto. Parsons was a member of this group, which provided ideas and networks that facilitated Parsons's vision of behavioral science. The group sought "a unified theory of human behavior" and espoused "systems theory."[33] At Chicago, Miller chaired the Department of Psychology and gathered several other faculty members in fields including medicine and statistics into the Committee on the Behavioral Sciences in 1949. Its goal was to create a unified, scientific theory of human behavior on the model of general theory in the physical sciences, as suggested by Miller's faculty club conversations with physicist Enrico Fermi.[34] Miller's committee incorporated faculty from the biological sciences, which echoed the Pareto group at Harvard, led by biochemist Lawrence Joseph Henderson.[35]

The most important step for popularizing the notion of "behavioral science" was the Ford Foundation's use of the term. It dubbed its program on individual behavior and human relations the Behavioral Science Program in 1951 under the influence of Miller's friend Donald Marquis, a psychologist at the University of Michigan. Miller and his group later moved to Michigan and established the journal *Behavioral Science*, which provided further institutional legitimation. The Ford program funded numerous projects by academics of many backgrounds.

The behavioral science paradigm fed three related movements— administrative science, the new organization theory, and systems analysis— that raised expectations for university research to solve social problems.[36] All three emphasized mathematical formalization. A key thinker behind each was Herbert Simon, a renowned social scientist who imbibed the behavioral approach to political science from his doctoral studies in that field at the University of Chicago. Simon's *Administrative Behavior* (1945) "created a new theoretical structure for administrative science" and became "arguably one of the twentieth century's ten most influential works in political science, public administration, and management."[37] The book examined how organizations influenced the behavior of their members. Simon believed that organizations, far from having the stultifying effect often associated with bureaucracies, were actually essential instruments for the extension of rationality because they transcended the limitations on the rationality of any individual.[38] Simon's work suggested the possibility of a universally valid science of human decision making. Other postwar academics embraced this ideal of a "decision science" and made it the basis for their attempt to create a general theory of administration that would transcend the settings—government, business, and educational institutions—for which universities often taught discrete types of administration. Simon established himself at Carnegie Institute of Technology's Graduate School of Industrial Administration, where he and colleague James March became key exponents of the new organization theory through their landmark *Organizations* (1958). They applied recent findings of psychology and economics to highlight human behavior and its motivation in organizations. Like Simon's earlier work, the new organization theory focused on scientific analysis of human decision making.[39] It was holistic in that it drew on mathematical biology and physiology to portray the organization as an organism, a rationally interconnected whole, a "system" that attempted to maintain equilibrium. This model suggested behavioral-functional analysis of the organizational properties that enabled the maintenance of equilibrium.[40] This "systems" approach led to yet a third influential offshoot of behavioral science in the postwar university, systems analysis, which researchers applied to all sorts of social problems from nuclear defense to urban planning.

These new modes of thinking provided a set of policy tools infused with the trappings of science and mathematics, which helped policy-oriented work in many fields gain legitimacy as a university activity. For instance, schools of business administration embraced these tools as the foundation for a new, more "scientific" curriculum and research program that raised their status within universities. As inherently instrumental units such as schools of business administration gained size and prestige, they changed the tenor of universities.

Service to Society

A leading tenet of the instrumental university was that it must solve the problems of its constituencies, whether the local community, the state, the nation, or the world. This commitment fell under the rubric of the university's "service" to society. The idea that the university should serve its various publics was nothing new; it had been a dominant theme in American higher education since the founders of Harvard in 1636 charged the college to prepare learned Christian ministers for its community. The feature that distinguished the instrumental university was not the idea of service but the *kind* of service that academic and social elites pushed it to provide. They wanted universities as institutions to provide what many of them called "direct service" by engaging public problems, often through organized research. The direct service idea formed part of Gaylord Harnwell's rhetoric portraying the urban university as a community service institution, motivated American universities' programs of overseas institution building, and helped to legitimate plans for a large-scale Public Policy Research Organization at UC Irvine.

By contrast, an older model articulated by Woodrow Wilson held that a university served society primarily by educating wise and virtuous leaders with intellectual breadth and vision. Wilson, one of his era's most influential academic leaders, became president of Princeton University in 1902. He elaborated this model in two high-profile, similarly titled speeches: "Princeton in the Nation's Service," delivered at the institution's sesquicentennial in 1896, and "Princeton for the Nation's Service," his inaugural address as its president.[41] Princeton graduates, he said, should be able to distinguish "permanent [tendencies] from [those] which are of the moment merely, [and] promises from threats, knowing the life men have lived, the hopes they have tested, and the principles they have proved." His concept thus had more in common with the nineteenth-century college and its moral philosophy framework than with the postwar instrumental university. To be sure, some resonance existed between Wilson's idea of Princeton in the nation's service and Kerr's later notion of the university as an instrument of national purpose. Wilson said that "there is laid upon us the compulsion of the national life. We dare not keep aloof and closet ourselves while a nation comes to its maturity."[42] Yet Wilson's vision for how the university would serve the nation differed from the later emphasis on organized research. Wilson valued scholarship and helped to start Princeton's Graduate School, which he believed should concentrate on "pure studies" rather than research on particular social problems.[43] Research, however, had a low profile in his speeches on Princeton and the nation's service. Instead, he focused on broad undergraduate education in liberal arts and sciences as the university's chief contribution to the nation's service. Even when he said that the university should be "directly serviceable to the nation," he believed the path to that goal was "to make our men reading and thinking men."[44]

Wilson criticized nascent scientific approaches to social change that would later dominate the instrumental university. He argued that "the scientific spirit of the age" was "doing us a great disservice, working in us a certain great degeneracy" with its ethos of experiment, "contempt for the past," and confidence in "quick improvement" and "panaceas." Wilson's problem was not with the scientist, but rather "the noxious, intoxicating gas which has somehow got into the lungs of the rest of us from out the crevices of his workshop." Wilson reflected, "I should tremble to see social reform led by men who had breathed [the gas]: I should fear nothing better than utter destruction from a revolution conceived and led in the scientific spirit." Speaking in a religious language of human sinfulness that would be foreign to the instrumental university, Wilson argued that science had not made "human nature a whit easier to reform." In light of what he viewed as the pretensions of the scientific approach to social change, Wilson concluded, "Do you wonder, then, that I ask for the old drill, the old memory of times gone by, the old schooling in precedent and tradition, the old keeping of faith with the past, as a preparation for leadership in the days of social change?"[45] For Wilson, Princeton would be in the nation's service by providing its students with a robust liberal education, not by organizing research around social problems.

Another institution making waves at that time, the University of Wisconsin, more closely prefigured the later instrumental university in its understanding of service, in part because of Wisconsin's unusual status of being both an elite research university and a land-grant institution. Charles Van Hise ascended from the geology faculty to Wisconsin's presidency in 1903, just a year after Wilson took Princeton's helm. In his 1904 inaugural address and other venues, Van Hise stated that the university should solve practical problems faced by the state's government and citizens.[46] This concept soon became known as "the Wisconsin Idea" and gained national attention. The major outworking was that professors consulted with state government agencies, which were conveniently located just a few blocks away near the other end of State Street.[47] The renowned economics professor Richard T. Ely, however, plowed a more innovative path that involved a structural change in the university when he founded the Institute for Research in Land Economics and Public Utilities.[48] Ely's biographer recognized him as "a captain of organized and cooperative research," and cited a contemporary who claimed that Ely was "the first scholar in America to surround himself with staffs of secretaries . . . the first scholar in America to be organized like a business man." Part of his pioneering work in organized research was seeking "funds from wealthy patrons."[49]

After several years of unsuccessful fundraising, Ely founded the Institute for Research in Land Economics in 1920 with assistance from the Interchurch World Movement, the Farm Mortgage Bankers Association, and a wealthy former student. By 1922 he had gifts from thirteen railroads, $10,000 from the Carnegie Corporation, and (most notably) institutional support from the university in the form of office space, a full-time secretary, and a $1,000 annual research budget. Ely retitled the unit to include utilities in 1923, and soon had several allocations of more than $20,000 each from utility organizations. During the 1920s, the institute generally employed between ten and forty people.[50] Ely had created a significant organized research unit, and one that claimed to produce neutral research on public problems rather than advocating any particular interest. The institute nevertheless became a lightning rod for criticism, including a nearly 200-page book styled as an "expose" of Ely and his institute.[51] Political forces in Wisconsin began to attack corporate and foundation support of university research. In 1925, a fearful Ely moved the institute to Northwestern University, where it flourished for several years before the Depression devastated it and Ely retired to Connecticut. The institute's move prefigured a postwar trend wherein entrepreneurial professors moved entire ORUs from one university to another. Shortly after Ely moved the institute, the University of Wisconsin briefly barred gifts from philanthropic foundations, a policy that would become unthinkable after World War II.[52] Wisconsin's ambivalence about organized research in the 1920s showed that the instrumental university had not yet taken hold. Ely's institute was the kind of instrumental ORU that later characterized the postwar university, but it was an outlier in its own time, as the criticism of it suggests.

Organized research units, though essential for the rise of the instrumental university, were not quite steamrollers. Some ORUs struggled to maintain their affiliated faculty members, while others faced an uphill battle for establishment in the face of departmental and disciplinary concerns. The structure of organized research units was one of the most discussed topics in the postwar university. Many universities developed elaborate schema of what constituted a "center" as opposed to an "institute." Faculty spent so much time discussing these issues that they became a topic for joking and sarcasm. For example, during a 1960 meeting at the University of Michigan, Professor Wilcox read an "Explanatory Ode, or How to Tell a Center from an Institute."[53] Postwar academics placed enormous expectations on organized research projects and the university units that housed them, but results were often meager. The history of these endeavors shows both the unswerving faith that postwar academics had in university-based organized research to solve every kind of social problem and the difficulties that such efforts faced.

Chapter 1 introduces the godfather of the instrumental university, Charles Merriam, and traces the remarkably parallel rise of public administration, city planning, and industrial relations as inherently instrumental academic fields. It delineates contributions to that rise from several sources: progressivism and the New Deal milieu in general, early twentieth century associational movements for planning and government reform, and the nexus of Rockefeller philanthropy and the Social Science Research Council.

Chapter 2 explores the work of Clark Kerr as a thinker and university leader. It examines the Inter-University Study of Labor Problems in Economic Development directed by Kerr, one of the largest organized research projects in American social science during the postwar years. This study proposed a new theory of industrialism that informed Kerr's thinking about universities.

The Inter-University Study provides a window into its most important institutional contexts: the Institute of Industrial Relations (IIR) at UC Berkeley and the Ford Foundation's Program in Economic Development and Administration. The chapter describes Kerr's promotion of ORUs—first at IIR, which he directed for seven years, and then across the Berkeley campus once he became chancellor. It also shows how his immersion in the administrative science movement shaped his view of the university's mission. Throughout the chapter, I uncover the sources of key ideas Kerr set forth in *The Uses of the University*.

Chapter 3 portrays Harnwell's effort to make the University of Pennsylvania (Penn) a "community service institution," in part by stimulating Philadelphia's economic development. Penn's unfolding understanding of its identity as an "urban university" and its almost overnight creation of the intellectual center of American city planning suggest the impact that both the legacy of the New Deal state and the increasingly urban setting of higher education in the postwar years had on American universities' instrumental turn. This chapter also illustrates how both Kerr's ideas about universities and the nascent concept of a knowledge economy began to play out in places around the country, such as in Harnwell's work with the University City Science Center and the Governor's Council of Science and Technology.

Chapters 4 and 5 respectively explore the international and domestic institutional arrangements that American universities created to promote economic development around the world. Chapter 4 explains the US government's university contracts abroad program, created in 1951 as part of the effort to implement Point Four. It also provides two case studies of university activities in Pakistan under government contracts: Penn's attempt to create the Institute of Public and Business Administration at the University of Karachi, and the University of Southern California's subsequent public administration program at several Pakistani institutions. The USC program self-consciously reflected on its "institution building." This case study traces the rise of that concept in the nationwide discussion of universities' overseas activities among academic, foundation, and government officials that began in the mid-1950s.

Chapter 5 examines how Samuel P. Hayes Jr., an early Point Four official who later helped design the Peace Corps, tried to "use" the University of Michigan to establish a program of multidisciplinary organized research on economic development, the Center for Research on Economic Development (CRED). The resistance he encountered from university administrators and economics department colleagues suggests that traditional academic norms did not always yield completely to interdisciplinary organized research. Yet the establishment of CRED, which had parallels at the University of Chicago,

Vanderbilt, and Yale, suggests the importance of economic development as a focus for organized research in the instrumental university. This chapter also provides an account of the new subfield of development economics and of the relationship between the economics discipline and the behavioral science paradigm.

Chapter 6 shows how the University of California at Irvine, planned under Kerr's guidance, exemplified the instrumental university in its attempt to install perhaps the most pervasive high modern social science program ever attempted on an American campus. UC Irvine's planners designed it to be a new kind of land-grant institution, in which social sciences replaced the agricultural sciences. Kerr and his colleagues placed tremendous expectations on interdisciplinary social science for leading humanity to a brighter future. This chapter tells how three related UC Irvine units—the Division of Social Sciences, the Graduate School of Administration, and the Public Policy Research Organization—attempted and failed to realize these expectations.

The epilogue treats critics of American modernity and the instrumental university, especially the sociologist Robert Nisbet, a University of California faculty member (and sometime administrator) at Berkeley and Riverside from 1939 to 1972 who knew Kerr. Nisbet lashed out at organized research in his 1971 book *The Degradation of the Academic Dogma*, where he coined the term "academic capitalism."[54] The most unfortunate consequence of the ORU's rise to prominence, Nisbet believed, was that it separated research from teaching, thus tearing asunder what he conceived as a coherent fabric of academic practice. Nisbet's thought provides a helpful framework for assessing the instrumental university's legacy for higher education and American society today.

CHAPTER 1

The Progressive Roots of the Instrumental University

Public Administration, City Planning, and Industrial Relations

The early twentieth century rise of three new academic fields—public administration, city planning, and industrial relations— laid groundwork for the instrumental university. Practitioners and educational leaders saw all three as ways for the university to manage modern society by giving it rational order. A fundamentally modern, instrumental habit of mind—technocratic progressivism—produced this vision. Technocratic progressives used terms such as social control, social engineering, planning, and intelligence to describe what they believed should be a comprehensive relationship between social scientific thought and the social order.[1] Universities, by aiming to administer American modernity through these new fields, participated in an "associational" mode of governance that characterized the American polity during this time. In that mode, civil society associations partnered with the state in governing the United States.[2]

Technocratic progressivism was one strain of a wider progressivism, a distinctive yet broad approach (or set of approaches) to American society that held sway from roughly 1900 to 1930, often called the Progressive Era. Progressivism was a response to the rise of an industrial, corporate America and the accompanying urbanization and immigration. Promising to reform the ills that characterized this new social order, progressives attended to issues such as the problems of cities, strife between corporate managers and their workers, and making government less corrupt and more efficient. These concerns led directly to city planning, industrial relations, and public administration. Progressives disagreed about whether empowering the people or experts was the better path toward their goals, but technocratic progressives venerated experts, especially as experts claimed to offer scientific solutions to social problems. Most progressives agreed, though, that stronger and more active government—even if it meant altering American constitutionalism—was necessary to carry out reforms and protect individuals from giant corporations. This trend accelerated in the 1930s under President Franklin D. Roosevelt.

Such ideas motivated a tightly connected group of elites who acted through associations, philanthropies, governments, and universities to spur the growth of the three new fields. This group included two of the most influential figures in institutionalizing social science research from the 1920s through the 1950s: Charles Merriam, who founded the Social Science Research Council (SSRC) in 1923, and Joseph Willits. Through his work at the University of Pennsylvania and the Rockefeller Foundation (RF), Willits propelled the growth of academic industrial relations and public administration, and at least grudgingly supported city planning and its associated concept of urban research. The Rockefeller Foundation was the central organization in a cluster of entities, sometimes called Rockefeller philanthropy, financed by John D. Rockefeller and his descendants. Rockefeller philanthropy was a key institutionalization of these technocratic progressive elites, and it played a leading role in establishing all three fields within universities. Rockefeller philanthropy thus helped to form the instrumental university.

Merriam, Willits, SSRC, and RF drove the expansion of organized research in the pre–World War II university. This approach to social research, which became central for the postwar university, called for the coordination and integration (terms that became important in the organized research lexicon) of social science disciplines in order to solve social problems. It held that such coordination was not only the best way to solve problems, but also the best way to advance social scientific knowledge and make it more truly scientific. This approach contrasted with an older alternative in which social investigators concentrated on theoretical questions within their own disciplines. When public administration, city planning, and industrial relations entered the university, it was sometimes in conjunction with the ideal of organized research. Industrial relations was even a kind of interdisciplinary field defined by a social problem, drawing on economics, law, political science, and sociology to address that problem.

The rise of academic public administration, city planning, and industrial relations began sporadically in the early years of the twentieth century. During those years, associational movements for government research and regional planning took shape. These movements later motivated more substantial academic endeavors. The first wave of university units dedicated to these fields appeared in the 1920s, and they expanded and proliferated in the 1930s with impetus from the New Deal. Before tracing the trajectories of the three fields separately, it is important to understand Merriam's career, which built intellectual and institutional underpinnings of these fields.

Charles Merriam was the godfather of the instrumental university. A faculty member in the University of Chicago's Department of Political Science from 1900 to 1940, and its chair for the last seventeen years of that tenure, the native Iowan exemplified the technocratic, managerial progressivism born in the early twentieth century. Through his ideas and his role in creating and growing institutions, Merriam laid a foundation for transforming the university. He was "entrepreneurial and political, an activist in the achieving of any new relationship which could promise to break through the restrictions of academic tradition."[3] Merriam founded the so-called Chicago school of political science. It produced two key figures for the instrumental university, Harold Lasswell and Herbert Simon, and generated the behavioral approach to political science, which also impacted universities. Although not a renowned theorist, Merriam is one of the titans in the history of American social science. The behavioral approach to the study of politics that he outlined from 1920 onward later (after refinement by others) became dominant in the field.[4] He took his social scientific approach into practical politics, first in associational movements for city planning and public administration, then on the President's Research Committee on Social Trends under Herbert Hoover, and finally as a powerful member of federal government bodies under FDR.

Merriam's approach to politics came to center on administration. His political theory rebelled against the Germanic constitutional approach he had learned as a graduate student at Columbia and in Berlin. He sought a "science of politics" that focused on "factual analysis" of "the methods and operations of government rather than solely . . . its forms." This approach took guidance both from Woodrow Wilson's 1887 article on administration—the first American scholarly writing on the subject—and from "John Dewey's methods of inquiry."[5] "Methods" and "operations" were part of the language of pragmatism and would enter the lexicon of the instrumental university. By the 1920s and 1930s, the central term for Merriam's political theory shifted from "science" to "administration" as the latter term gained wide usage in American thought.[6] Merriam conceived administration as a "value-neutral" practice, "the province of experts" who would scientifically determine means to carry out "political ends determined by the public."[7]

Merriam's thought fueled SSRC and its thrust to coordinate research. SSRC's structure reflected this thrust. It consisted of representatives from the major disciplinary social science associations, such as the American Economic Association and American Political Science Association. Merriam, who served as SSRC's first chairman, called for coordinating the social sciences as early as 1920, in an address to the American Political Science Association that its journal published the following year.[8] Merriam's "concept of community in social research . . . would render obsolete the traditional picture of the university as a collection of isolated monuments to contemplation whose treasured protection from the world was exceeded only by their preservation from one another."[9] By 1927, an edited collection, *The Social Sciences and their Interrelations*, testified to this new understanding of social science.[10] One way SSRC fostered its approach was by "organiz[ing] problem-oriented committees," including prominent committees on industrial relations and public administration.[11] From its founding through 1945, SSRC received a great majority of its funding from Rockefeller philanthropy.[12] Indeed, SSRC's founding was part of Rockefeller philanthropy's move to begin funding social science on a large scale, through the Laura Spelman Rockefeller Memorial (LSRM). In January 1929, Rockefeller philanthropy phased out LSRM and transferred its social science programs to a new Division of Social Science (DSS) in the Rockefeller Foundation.[13] Merriam hoped that the SSRC would achieve "such a position of leadership that governments would automatically consult the Council or local councils before starting on a problem such as city planning, housing planning, etc., where social science was involved."[14] As he wrote those words in 1929, he was helping make the vision they portrayed a reality.

Merriam played the leading role in injecting technocratic social science into the federal government during the Great Depression. The President's Research Committee on Social Trends (1929–1932), of which Merriam was vice-chairman, indicated a new relationship of social science to government and led directly to the creation of a planning agency in the federal government during the New Deal. The idea for the Committee on Social Trends began in SSRC. The committee's organizers pointedly put "research" in the title, because it was the key term for their self-conception and worldview, and the committee became a sort of proto-organized research unit. Its report, *Recent Social Trends* (1933), "demonstrated the possibility of bringing the organized research of the academic community to the service of the federal government." *Recent Social Trends* called for a "'National Advisory Council,' modeled along the lines of the Social Science Research Council, and possibly growing out of it."[15] The report also called for "more planning at all levels of government, planning that had to be based on social intelligence."[16] A few months later, the new

Roosevelt administration institutionalized the planning ideal in the New Deal state by creating just such a body, initially called the National Planning Board. It had a tenuous existence until Congress killed it in 1943, partially reflected by name changes (with accompanying structural changes) to the National Resources Board in 1934, the National Resources Committee in 1935, and the National Resources Planning Board (the name by which it is most often known) in 1939. For simplicity, I will call this entity the national planning agency.

Merriam was one of three main members of the national planning agency. Its official chair was the president's uncle Frederic Delano, but Merriam "dominated [its] activities." FDR called him "Uncle Charley." Merriam and his colleagues intended the national planning agency to bring "social science and therefore, in the [agency's] terms, 'social intelligence' to bear on the operation of government."[17] Its responsibilities included "the preparation, development, and maintenance of comprehensive and coordinated plans for regional areas" and "the analysis of projects for coordination in location and sequence."[18] This charge also stated that the national planning agency should concern itself with housing, a new interest of the federal government that would propel the study of city planning in universities.

In 1936, FDR appointed Merriam to the influential President's Committee on Administrative Management (PCAM). "Administrative management" was Merriam's term.[19] The national planning agency had proposed the creation of such a body and commissioned Merriam to write a "draft paper," *Management of the Federal Government*, in 1935.[20] PCAM engineered a shift of power to the presidency by recommending the creation of the Executive Office of the President, which Congress did in 1939. Merriam thus reached the height of his political influence under FDR, which points to the importance of the New Deal for the rise of the instrumental university. But why was FDR so interested in planning and administration?

The answer lies in ideas at the heart of the New Deal. New Deal political culture, particularly the strand that fueled public administration, was more than a proliferation of administrative agencies, more than a preference for government by experts. It was a new conceptualization of American democratic government that built from Progressive Era ideas (articulated most notably by Herbert Croly). FDR was a pragmatic juggler, but he brought to the presidency the fundamentals of this new conceptualization, even if he was not yet fully committed to them.[21] In a 1932 campaign speech, he advocated an "economic constitutional order" (he also called it an "economic declaration of rights") that reconceived both the nature of rights and the duties of government to the people.[22] In this order, each citizen had the right to sufficient economic resources for living, and the government would ensure it.[23] According to public administration scholar Brian Cook, in this "progressive conception" of democracy, government was not merely a protector of civil liberties or property rights but "would tackle the formidable social problems of modernity." Advancing democracy in the conditions of modernity thus required a more active government with "a less fettered, more energetic executive, which would formulate the most rationally organized, efficient, and thus most effective actions."[24] FDR and his advisors believed they were recasting American democracy in this way. They believed that the key to establishing this new order was making the administrative state both more robust and more closely tied to the presidency. That tie would make public administration the servant of the democratic will, since the presidency represented all the people.[25]

FDR wanted "to place public administration at the heart of a new American political system," shifting "from a government order based on *constitutionalism* to one emphasizing *public administration*."[26] Because his "expanded conception of rights was predicated on programmatic initiatives by government," it "had to be protected in ways that would sustain it beyond" his presidency. He believed that public administration was the institution that could do so. The new "rights defined by FDR were programs not 'formally ratified as amendments to the Constitution, nor . . . fully codified in statutes and policies.'" Thus public administration was necessary to fulfill and perpetuate them.[27] This new approach to government produced an "administrative constitution."[28] In this arrangement, which has endured to the present, "public administration was an *instrument of partisanship*" for programmatic liberalism.[29] The vision of this new political system led FDR to appoint PCAM to craft a program of executive reorganization. The New Deal thus boosted the prestige of public administration, a field that had been an academic pursuit in the United States for only a short time.

Public Administration

Public administration was not a completely new academic field in the early twentieth century, but the way it arose in the United States was distinctive and not connected to earlier German efforts along similar lines.[30] Scattered concern for public administration among academics can be traced at least to 1887 when Woodrow Wilson published what became a famous article, "The Study of Administration."[31] By that era, some American thinkers believed that industrial modernity must be administered. Wilson spoke of "those enormous burdens of administration which the needs of this industrial and trading age are so fast accumulating."[32] By the mid-twentieth century, American elites expected the university itself to help administer modernity. The origins of that expectation were in the Progressive Era, "a great intellectual watershed for public administration [that] served largely to reinforce the prevailing conception of administration as purely instrumental."[33] Yet scholars have said little about how this episode affected the university.

An initial push for American research universities to be concerned with public administration began around 1910, in response to a "governmental research movement" outside the university. There was some groundwork inside the university. In addition to Wilson's article, Frank Goodnow of Columbia's political science faculty (who would go on to the presidency of Johns Hopkins from 1914 to 1929) produced in the 1890s the first substantive scholarship in public administration and did much to establish it "as a university subject," albeit strictly within political science rather than in an independent unit of the university. He taught Merriam, then a graduate student at Columbia, the distinction between politics and administration that he had "systematized."[34] But neither an academic discipline nor governments spurred the creation of university units dedicated to public administration. Rather, the energy came from an associational effort, a "governmental research movement" that coalesced after 1900. This movement produced organizations such as the National Municipal League (1894) and the Governmental Research Association (1914), as well as periodicals such as *The American City* (1909), *National Municipal Review* (1912, published by the National Municipal League), and *Public Management* (1919, published by the International City Managers' Association and originally called *City Manager Bulletin*). The governmental research movement was a quintessential product of progressivism, especially technocratic progressivism. From roughly 1910 to 1915, the heyday of technocratic progressivism, there was considerable "interest in and discussion of the problem of training for the public service."[35] In this milieu, three different models of universities' relationship to public administration emerged.

First, this discussion (after the interlude of World War I) led to the creation of specific schools within universities for such purposes, such as Syracuse's School of Citizenship and Public Affairs (1924, later the Maxwell School), Princeton's School of Public and International Affairs (SPIA, 1930, later the Woodrow Wilson School), and the University of Southern California's School of Citizenship and Public Administration (1929). These units included public administration as part of a broader mission oriented toward citizenship and public affairs. Although the Maxwell School had connections to the New York State Conference of Mayors, it also functioned as a school of social science, housing the relevant disciplines at Syracuse. USC's effort did not initially focus on research. Rather, it did something like the land-grant tradition's extension service. It set up shop near the government center in downtown Los Angeles, away from USC's campus, and offered "advanced studies in the field of public administration" to people already working in that field.[36] Princeton's SPIA facilitated an interdisciplinary undergraduate major composed of courses from traditional disciplines, but it also ventured into organized research through its State and Local Government Section, Radio Research Project, Office of Public Opinion Research, and Office of Population Research.[37] An early project came in 1932, when Governor A. Harry Moore asked SPIA to survey New Jersey's finances so the state could "cope with modern conditions in a more efficient manner."[38] The leader of the 21-member faculty team that performed the survey was Harold Dodds, a professor of politics at Princeton who also served as secretary (1920–1928) and later president (1934–1937) of the National Municipal League, as well as editor (1920–1933) of the *National Municipal Review*. Dodds was faculty chair of the School of Public and International Affairs, taught upper-level public administration courses in the school's early years, and in 1931 contributed an essay to a special issue of *Survey Graphic* on city government titled "A New Deal at City Hall," alongside pieces by PCAM members Louis Brownlow and Luther Gulick.[39] He then rose to Princeton's presidency in 1933 (serving until 1957) but continued to be involved in leadership of SPIA's State and Local Government Section.[40] While he was president of Princeton, Dodds became a member of a proposed version of the group that became PCAM, but FDR did not approve that version.[41]

Dodds and his successor as president of the National Municipal League, Clarence Dykstra, ascended to leadership of important academic institutions, exhibiting the prestige of public administration within universities by the 1930s. Dykstra completed his PhD at the University of Chicago, where he knew Merriam. He taught public administration at the new Southern Branch of the University of California (UC), soon to be known as UCLA, from 1922 to 1930 while working as executive secretary of the Los Angeles City Club and director of personnel and efficiency for the Water and Power Board. He then served as city manager of Cincinnati from 1930 to 1937 and president of the University of Wisconsin from 1937 to 1945 before returning to UCLA as provost from 1945 to 1950, when the provost was the chief campus officer.[42]

A second mode in which universities engaged with public administration was the creation of early organized research units (ORUs) devoted to it. In 1914, the University of Michigan established a Bureau of Reference and Research in Government and the nation's first graduate degree in public administration, master of municipal administration. Only in 1936 did it launch a more full-fledged program, the Institute for Public and Social Administration.[43] The University of Minnesota also had a notable program, centered on the Bureau for Research in Government (circa 1920).[44] The most important of these units was the Bureau of Public Administration (BPA) at UC Berkeley. Although Berkeley created something called BPA in 1919, at that time it was classified as a "special library in the Department of Political Science"—for the most part a barely functioning adjunct to teaching, although it conducted at least one research project, on "Scientific Research in the State Government of California" for the National Research Council.[45] But in the late 1920s, Berkeley turned BPA into an ORU independent from the Department of Political Science, with its own authorization from the university regents. Samuel C. May, the bureau's first director and a member of SSRC's Public Administration Committee, led this effort.

May mobilized Rockefeller and university funding to launch a spate of meticulously planned instrumental activities.[46] LSRM awarded UC $200,000 over six years "toward its program of training and research in public administration," beginning July 1, 1929.[47] Subsequently, the regents authorized the creation of an independent BPA to absorb the departmentally based entity of the same name and launch on July 1, 1930.[48] This authorization took some work. UC president W. W. Campbell reported that he converted regents "one by one" as the university's financial problems grew, in part because of "the breaking of the Carnegie Foundation's pension system."[49] His approach suggested the pecuniary motives that universities sometimes had for accepting external funding, even for programs that did not fit with existing conceptions of the university's mission. One indication of both the ambition and nature of BPA is that May proposed to hire Hermann M. Adler to a permanent professorship at the then-astronomical salary of $9,000, to be paid $2,500 by RF, $2,500 by the state of California (for proportionate service), and $4,000 by UC—$2,000 from the Department of Psychology and $1,000 each from the Schools of Jurisprudence and Medicine. Adler was to work on one of seven initial projects of the bureau, Administration of Criminal Justice in California.[50] In its early days, BPA also pursued "the preparation of a critical guide to the literature of public administration, a study of the San Francisco Bay region, a study of the functional administrative relationships between federal, state and local governments . . . studies in personnel administration . . . and studies of legislative drafting." BPA had an advisory council with representation from different units of the university. This model of drawing together faculty from many areas of the university to focus on administering society would become widespread in the ORUs that proliferated after World War II. BPA also had partnerships outside the university. It conducted cooperative studies with the Commonwealth Club of California, the California Bar Association and Judicial Council, and the California League of Municipalities.

In addition, BPA made "a study of personnel problems" for the California Library Association.[51]

In the latter activity, BPA essentially offered research services for hire, a practice that would later become one strand in the instrumental university. John Gaus, surveying public administration research in 1930, argued that such partnerships with extra-university entities could provide compelling dissertation topics, in contrast with the "casual and insipid selections" often made by graduate students who worked purely within the framework of the academic discipline.[52] BPA brought in graduate student fellows to help conduct its studies. Most prominent among them was Herbert Simon, a graduate student of Merriam and Lasswell at the University of Chicago, who conducted BPA research by day while writing his dissertation (which eventually became the landmark book *Administrative Behavior*) at night from 1939 to 1942.[53] When Simon won the Nobel Prize in economics in 1978, some at Berkeley were upset at the lack of recognition that Simon had been "one of 'Sam May's boys.'"[54]

Columbia and Chicago followed a third model, in which organizations devoted to public administration set up outside the university but had partnerships with it. New York City was the center of the governmental research movement. The New York Bureau of Municipal Research (NYBMR) began in 1906 as the first entity in this field to be "designated as a bureau of research." Mary Averell Harriman (Mrs. E. H. Harriman), a major participant in the bureau, "proposed to several of America's major universities that she endow a school of public service to train what she thought of as a class of governmental experts." The universities declined, which could indicate that older ideals about their mission still held firm, but her efforts prompted NYBMR in 1911 to found the Training School for Public Service.[55] Both organizations developed partnerships with Columbia, and famed Progressive historian Charles Beard led each for a period, which extended across his resignation from the Columbia faculty. In 1921, the two organizations merged as the National Institute of Public Administration (NIPA), which would become a recipient of Rockefeller Foundation grants.[56] Luther Gulick led NIPA as its president from the founding until 1962. The University of Chicago affiliated in 1929 with the International City Managers' Association and the Bureau of Public Personnel Administration, which set up shop near the southern border campus.[57] Columbia and Chicago thus held public administration at arm's length and considered it not quite worthy to be the basis of a university unit.

Alongside this flurry of university activity in the 1920s, Rockefeller philanthropy—directly, and indirectly through SSRC—encouraged university research on public administration. SSRC, under Merriam's influence, launched a Public Administration Committee (PAC) in 1928. This founding was part of an SSRC expansion, which brought the total number of SSRC committees to twenty-four by 1930. In that year, however, SSRC and RF DSS began to narrow their focus, increasingly concentrating on public administration. SSRC made public administration one of four fields of concentration, alongside personality and culture, international relations, and industry and trade. SSRC's first treasurer, Edmund Day, who exemplified the Rockefeller-SSRC link by staying on SSRC until 1931 after taking charge of Rockefeller social science programs in the late 1920s, explained that the four fields of concentration "cut 'athwart recognized disciplines' and [addressed] 'striking developments in our social system and emergence of fairly definite problems.'"[58] The RF-SSRC move to focus on public administration in the late 1920s produced parallel 1930 reports. Merriam coauthored a survey of public administration for RF, while PAC commissioned Gaus, a professor at the University of Wisconsin. Gaus approvingly cited John Dewey's *The Public and its Problems* (1927) several times, and pronounced Dewey's argument about the growth of government "sound as an interpretation."[59]

Gaus's report revealed emerging principles of the instrumental university and provided an early example of how a desire for social control fueled organized research. In explaining why public administration should matter to SSRC, he described social scientists' activity in language dripping with technocratic progressive buzzwords. He said they were "working for planned and intelligent study of our society as a preliminary to understanding social change or the possibilities of social control." The public administrator would provide data that could lead to social control. Equally bracing, Gaus "stated fairly strongly . . . the case for organized research" at a time when such terminology was novel. Yet he also referred to a debate over it, with one side insisting "that thinking is done by individuals who develop ideas. To organize this process of insight and imagination is to sterilize it." Organized research, then, had a foothold by 1930, even if it became widely institutionalized only after World War II. In addition, public administration helped to popularize the terminology of "institute" that would be central to the postwar university, as exhibited in the National Institute of Public Administration and the Institute for Government Research at Washington, D.C., founded in 1916 and later merged into the Brookings Institution. Gaus also used the term "bureau man" to describe a worker in these organizations, and he noted "the estrangement between some members of the academic group of political scientists" and the bureau man.[60]

At the same time, Gaus believed that in some settings, public administration should be taught as a liberal art "rather than an excessively technical study." He reasoned that many college graduates with no professional connection to public administration would eventually "be influential in their communities," and thus be "influential consumers of the public administration of twenty years from now." Teaching public administration as a liberal art to such students would make them more aware of key issues in the field. In recommending such education, Gaus aimed to build a tradition of public administration and overcome "indifferences" and "ignorance" about it.[61] Gaus's report showed that the promoters of public administration as an academic pursuit achieved a beachhead in the 1920s.

By the time FDR took office, then, there was a burgeoning infrastructure in and outside the universities for research on public administration. His New Deal created a greater demand for such research. The economic crisis prompted FDR "to construct new national bureaucracies," but even within the Social Security Act, all titles except the one covering social insurance "were administered at the state and local levels."[62] Thus much of the focus on public administration within universities was on those levels. Early in FDR's presidency, the Rockefeller-SSRC nexus intensified the narrowing of its topical interests that had begun around 1930. In 1934, RF requested that public administration "become one of two central foci of the Council's work," alongside social security. Between 1935 and 1940, RF gave $386,000 to this work, which was "designed as a means for preventing the collapse of a liberal, democratic capitalism in the United States." These programs shaped and were shaped by the New Deal.[63]

The emphasis on public administration from FDR and the Rockefeller-SSRC nexus prompted more universities to launch units dedicated to it, particularly in major northeastern urban centers. Harvard is a case in point.[64] In the New Deal idealism of 1934, Carl Friedrich in the Department of Government proposed an institute of public administration to produce a better quality of public servant. Harvard established a Committee on Public Service Training in the spring of 1935 and brought Morris Lambie from the University of Minnesota to run it. That fall, Harvard alumnus and former Republican congressman Lucius Littauer "offered to give $2 million for a graduate school of public administration."[65] He believed it was "the best hope of avoiding disasters arising from untried experiments in government and administration" such as the New Deal.[66] Furthermore, Littauer believed that since government was becoming increasingly intrusive, there was a growing need for "well-trained bureaucrats." Harvard president James Conant, a Republican, was unenthusiastic about a separate school for public administration. He followed Littauer's wishes and established the Graduate School of Public Administration (GSPA) but took steps to keep it weak, especially by denying it a separate faculty. It drew its faculty from other schools, primarily from the Departments of Economics and Government in the Faculty of Arts and Sciences. Professor Henry Hart of the Law School was involved for a time but withdrew in 1942 because he believed GSPA was too focused on "policy."[67] GSPA also received funding from the Rockefeller Foundation in at least three installments: $66,000 in 1935, $65,000 in 1937, and $20,000 in 1938.[68]

The University of Pennsylvania and New York University also established units related to public administration in the 1930s. Joseph Willits became dean of Penn's Wharton School of Finance and Commerce in 1933 and looked for a way to encourage research oriented toward public service. These efforts bore limited fruit until Philadelphia soap manufacturer Samuel Fels agreed to give $40,000 per year for six years beginning in 1937 to fund a new Institute for Local and State Government (ILSG). Willits wanted ILSG to offer "a variety of educational, research, consulting, and conferencing services."[69] In its early years, ILSG provided research services to government entities like the Philadelphia City Charter Commission and the Philadelphia Advisory Finance Commission. Penn president Thomas S. Gates sat on both commissions. In 1943, Gates stated that ILSG was "working on projects for certain communities, which he hoped would be of *use* to the city of Philadelphia."[70] Indeed, ILSG presented its work as "combin[ing] training of students with service to towns and boroughs in the state."[71] Over time, the former took precedence as demand for credentials in public administration increased, and the curriculum emphasized procedural detail. Stephen B. Sweeney, who directed ILSG from its inception until 1967, remarked that "the demand in public service, especially at lower levels of government, is primarily for technicians."[72] In the mid-1940s, the Wharton School began offering a Master of Public Administration degree analogous to its Master of Business Administration.[73] The Fels Fund continued to support ILSG at increasing levels after Samuel Fels's 1950 death, and Penn renamed the unit the Fels Institute of Local and State Government. By 1966, the Fels Fund provided $240,000 out of the institute's $268,000 budget, which was larger than the political science department's budget.[74] The story was somewhat different at NYU. The New Deal made public administration one of the few growing fields of employment during the Great Depression. NYU, struggling to maintain enrollment, saw this emerging market for public administrators as a possible solution to its enrollment woes, and in 1938 launched a School of Public Service to tap into this market.[75]

By the late 1930s, then, many academic leaders recognized public administration as a legitimate focus for a unit of an elite research university, which indicated a changing conception of such institutions and their public purpose. Public administration's flourishing in the 1920s also suggested that progressivism—at least the technocratic variety—was alive and well in that decade, contrary to assertions by some observers that it declined after World War I.

City Planning and Urban Research

Technocratic progressivism spawned the academic discipline of city planning as part of a broader planning movement in civil society. City planning drew fuel from progressivism's belief that social change was possible, especially through scientific analysis. It emerged as a profession circa 1910, as indicated by several landmark developments: the first US conference on the subject, the National Conference on City Planning in 1909; the launch of a periodical, *City Plan*, in 1915; the first zoning laws, in New York, in 1916; and the formation of the American City Planning Institute in 1917. City planning "emphasize[d] a rational rather than an aesthetic organization of systems," and soon included a "City Scientific" movement.[76] Case studies of Harvard's School of City Planning and Princeton's Bureau of Urban Research show how city planning and the related concept of urban research initially became institutionalized in two of America's most elite research universities prior to World War II, which provided a platform for these fields in the decades that followed. Rockefeller Foundation grants were essential in creating both units. In each case, a primary impetus for creating the unit came from outside the university: from the broader planning movement at Harvard and from the New Deal state at Princeton.

The establishment of the School of City Planning at Harvard University in 1929, under a grant from the Rockefeller Foundation, created the first university unit fully dedicated to city planning. This development revealed how the broader planning movement aimed to use universities as instruments for ordering physical space in the United States. In the late 1920s, this broader planning movement was approaching a crowning achievement: a regional plan for the New York City area known as the Regional Plan of New York and Its Environs (RPNY). The group concocting this plan was the Committee on a Regional Plan of New York and Its Environs, chaired by Frederic Delano, FDR's uncle, aforementioned as chairman of the national planning agency during FDR's presidency. Delano succeeded Charles Dyer Norton, who had been RPNY's guiding force before his death in 1923.[77] The committee released its much-lauded regional plan in 1929. Many observers considered its work to be the first great regional planning endeavor in the United States and a stimulant for others. As the committee neared completion of its plan, it sponsored a Conference on a Project for Research and Instruction in City and Regional Planning at Columbia University on May 3, 1928. Attendees included the omnipresent Merriam; Thomas Adams, general director of plans and surveys for RPNY and professor in the Department of Architecture at MIT; William A. Boring, director of the School of Architecture and professor of design at Columbia; Harvard professor Henry V. Hubbard, a pioneer in landscape architecture and editor of *City Planning*, the official organ of the American City Planning Institute and the National Conference on City Planning; Frederick Keppel, president of the Carnegie Corporation of New York; as well as several city planners and the secretary of the National Conference on City Planning.[78] The regional planning advocates hoped to mobilize universities to develop formal programs of research and teaching on city and regional planning. This aspiration was a typical input for the instrumental university: an elite group concerned with a specific social problem or approach to social engineering attempted to use universities to advance its agenda.

The Columbia conference led directly to Harvard's School of City Planning. In the wake of the conference, LSRM apparently issued a call for proposals for university-based city planning programs.[79] Several universities responded, including Columbia, which the organizers of the conference had discussed as the likely site for such a program. The dean of the Faculty of Architecture at Harvard, G. H. Edgell, got wind of the preference for Columbia. Edgell was a nephew of Delano (and thus a cousin of FDR), and he asked Delano to promote Harvard's candidacy on the basis of its existing capacity for city planning education.[80] Meanwhile, Hubbard wrote to Edmund Day in late 1928 proposing Harvard's program.[81] Some of the courses that Harvard envisioned for the new graduate-level School of City Planning already existed in its School of Landscape Architecture, where in 1909 James Sturgis Pray had created the first course on city planning in an American university, motivated by a desire to improve society, especially in cities. Pray and Theodora Kimball, Harvard's landscape and planning librarian (who later married Hubbard), coauthored *City Planning: A Comprehensive Analysis of the Subject* (1913).[82] Harvard continued to offer individual courses in city planning until 1923, when the School of Landscape Architecture began the first American master's degree program in city planning. As they applied for Rockefeller funding, Harvard officials argued that separating city planning and landscape architecture would strengthen both fields.[83]

After a few months of discussions between Harvard and RF, Harvard president A. Lawrence Lowell submitted the university's formal request for $50,000 per year for ten years. He wrote that "research and instruction in the field of City Planning as a social service is likely to be of so much public benefit that a grant to be devoted to that purpose given to a properly qualified American university would be as great a contribution to the common welfare as could well be made."[84] Although American universities had long promoted their programs as having "public benefit," it is striking that Lowell went so far as to declare the university as involved with "social service." Harvard's pitch worked. RF funded the Harvard proposal while rejecting Columbia's request for a school of civic design.[85] In their justification for awarding Harvard a grant of $240,000 over seven years, the RF officers declared that "the subject of city planning is one of great public importance" but judged that American city planning had "failed to assume the comprehensive character required by more permanent public interests." They believed that "the field clearly needs the coordination of more varied and more numerous points of view," and that universities could help it reach that goal by becoming "organized to undertake work along this line on a comprehensive plan."[86]

The School of City Planning achieved few of these aspirations during the grant period. It functioned mainly as a research institute, with low student enrollment. Its most notable product was the Harvard City Planning Series, "a series of research monographs" that covered topics such as zoning, parkways, and airport locations. Although Hubbard called city planning a fine art, "the school soon leaned toward . . . the utilitarian pursuit of social goals to the exclusion of the physical appearance of cities."[87] By 1935, Day criticized the lack of progress on two objectives the foundation had stipulated: "the difficulty of effecting full integration of the work of the School with other units of the University" and "the apparent failure to broaden the financial base of the School adequately."[88] Day made the latter judgment despite the fact that shortly after receiving the Rockefeller grant, Harvard accepted a $150,000 gift to create the Charles Dyer Norton Chair of Regional Planning.[89] Hubbard became the first holder of this chair as well as chairman of the School of City Planning, which actually functioned like a department within the Faculty of Architecture. It was notable that Day criticized the lack of integration, a watchword of both the planning movement and the instrumental university. Hubbard contested Day's judgment on this issue, writing that "cooperation by the whole University, including the field of physical city planning, to the end of public service and social betterment . . . is now on the road."[90] He mentioned Harvard's new commitment to public administration as contributing to this integration.

Despite Hubbard's promise of increased integration, the foundation was sufficiently dissatisfied with the School of City Planning that it declined to renew the grant in 1936 despite much pleading from Harvard, even from President Conant. A revealing appeal came from William R. Castle, chairman of the Harvard Overseers' Committee for the School of City Planning. He wrote that Charles Eliot told him "the Government itself could take in all the men who graduate and that they are desperately needed."[91] Indeed, Harvard city planning alumni found much success on the job market during the 1930s.[92] Eliot, the executive director of the national planning agency, was the grandson of the former Harvard president of the same name, and a former Harvard professor who had taught city planning in the School of Landscape Architecture.[93] His comment to Castle suggests how new government demand encouraged universities to develop programs in this field. Harvard, however, was not willing to commit enough of its own funds to operate the School of City Planning without Rockefeller money.[94] Day remarked that "the attitude which the University has taken . . . suggests to my way of thinking that a flat rejection is in order. However, such action doubtless has to be somewhat tactfully couched."[95] The foundation's shifting priorities also contributed to this rejection. DSS was narrowing its scope to focus on international relations, economic security, and public administration, much as RF directed SSRC to do at the same time.[96] RF officers assessed the Harvard city planning project as "marginal . . . to [these] new fields of concentration."[97] As part of this reorientation, in 1937 RF eliminated "Community Organization and Planning," the category of grants under which it had classified the Harvard School of City Planning.[98]

After floundering in its first year without Rockefeller money, city planning at Harvard recovered and grew into an influential program. The RF nonrenewal coincided with two connected developments at Harvard: the hiring of Joseph Hudnut as dean of the Faculty of Architecture in 1935, and the subsequent decision to reorganize its programs in architecture, landscape architecture, and city planning into a Graduate School of Design (GSD), effective for 1936–1937. Harvard transformed the School of City Planning into the Department of Regional Planning within GSD. The new department restarted instruction in planning for 1937–1938. Hudnut had proposed that Harvard place regional planning in the new School of Public Administration rather than in GSD, because he "gave primacy to the formulation of policy and the coordination of economic and social ideas as the basic generators for plans of cities and regions." He believed planning should use "the problem method of instruction" and focus on "the successful solution of problems." Gaus, author of the 1930 SSRC report on public administration, replaced Hubbard as Charles Dyer Norton Professor of Regional Planning in 1940 and also lobbied for the School of Public Administration to play a role in educating planners, which further emphasized the connection between the two fields. The number of regional planning students was small through World War II, but some later became influential in developing city planning programs in other universities, especially William Wurster at UC Berkeley and Martin Meyerson at Penn. The latter also became a university president, first of the University at Buffalo (SUNY) and then of Penn. Only after the war, under a new chairman and Norton Professor, G. Holmes Perkins, did the Department of Regional Planning really take off, including the creation of the first American PhD program in the field. Advancing the trend of an interdisciplinary attack on social problems, Perkins formed the Council of Regional Planning, which drew faculty from "government, geography, economics, business, and sociology" in addition to planning and architecture.[99] Harvard thus played the leading role in establishing city and regional planning as a university discipline in the United States.

Another attempt at all-university coordination on a social issue appeared in a project the Rockefeller Foundation funded a few years later, Princeton's Bureau of Urban Research (BUR). Although RF had funded a *de facto* research unit in city planning at Harvard, the BUR grant was its first attempt to establish a full-fledged unit of this type in the related area of urban research. The road to this grant appears to have begun on October 11, 1940, when three Princeton officials visited the RF office of Joseph Willits, who had replaced Day as director of the Division of Social Science in 1939: Sherley W. Morgan, director of Princeton's School of Architecture and chairman of the BUR organizing committee; J. Douglas Brown, director of Princeton's Industrial Relations Section (described later in the chapter); and, remarkably, President Harold Dodds, who appears to have been a key figure in pushing the plan for BUR.[100] Indeed, he had served as chair of the organizing committee—which included Princeton faculty from various fields, as well as external members like Charles W. Eliot and Lewis Mumford, a prominent urbanist public intellectual—until turning over the position to Morgan not long before they met with Willits.[101]

Regardless of Dodds's role in planning BUR, his involvement in seeking RF funding for it seems like a conflict of interest, given that he was a member of RF's board of trustees and executive committee.[102] Perhaps Dodds attended the meeting in order to grease the wheels with Willits, because afterward Willits sent Dodds a draft of a letter addressed to Morgan for Dodds to review before Willits actually sent it to Morgan.[103] Dodds and Willits might have had a long association, as Dodds received his PhD in political science from Penn's Wharton School in 1917, a year after Willits earned his doctorate there.[104]

Dodds's reply to Willits displayed technocratic managerialism: "There is something to [the plan for BUR] and some day we are going to learn about urban civilization and how better to control it."[105] Yet Dodds stood out among mid-century academic presidents for his defense of traditional liberal education. In *Princeton's War Program and Post-War Plans*, he wrote that "there is no disposition whatsoever to jettison any part of our work in liberal education in order to conform to any present or future trend toward training for special skills . . . The mind trained to think, to carry on its own self-education, is, of course, a vocational asset . . . But vocational interest must not set the tone of the college, whose prime objective is an educated person, not a skilled person."[106] Apparently he believed that kind of education could coexist, in the same institution, with intellectual pursuits aimed at "control." Perhaps Dodds's comment shows that the belief in orienting intellectual activity toward social control was so widespread that it affected even someone who thought as he did about liberal education.

The description of the proposed BUR drew on the terminology of coordination and integration pioneered by the SSRC. The RF grant action, using language from the university's proposal, stated that BUR's "object" was "to provide a mechanism at Princeton University for the coordination and integration of information and research in the field of urban problems."[107] This framing portrayed the university as a tool. Once BUR was established and active, its leadership continued to describe it as a mechanism.[108] Morgan argued that integration was "vital to true progress" on "the problems of the American city," and depicted integration as not just between members of different academic disciplines but also between academics and practitioners.[109] To that end, BUR had both a Faculty Committee on Urban Research, which brought together Princeton faculty from different fields, and an Advisory Committee on Urban Research from outside the university.[110] The advisory committee included Eliot and Mumford.[111]

BUR provides one example of how the New Deal state fostered the instrumental university. In this case, the national planning agency attempted to mobilize universities as instruments for solving urban problems. Its Urbanism Committee, chaired by Clarence Dykstra, published a 1937 report entitled *Our Cities, Their Role in the National Economy*. Among its recommendations was the establishment of "a central agency for urban research" that would "include the stimulation of urban research in universities."[112] Princeton cited this recommendation in its proposal to RF.[113] University authorities spoke of "several years" of planning for BUR, but the exact link between the publication of *Our Cities* and the beginning of that planning is unclear.[114] Once BUR was established, the national planning agency continued to influence it. BUR's first publication, *Local Planning Activity in the United States* (1941), was based on preliminary results of a 1940 survey conducted by the national planning agency.[115] BUR's second publication, a collaboration with the School of Public and International Affairs titled *Urban Planning and Public Opinion: A Pilot*

Study (1942), commenced with an epigraph from *Our Cities*. The introduction began with a call to arms for organized research. The authors stated that "America's defense and war efforts have focused attention on the desirability of applying a greater degree of organized forethought to the conduct of local, State, and national affairs," and went on to advocate applying such methods to public works and urban redevelopment after the war.[116]

The Rockefeller Foundation funded BUR even as it expressed concerns. One of the RF proposal reviewers wondered whether Princeton was the right university for such a bureau: "Are the associations of the sponsors such as to permit them to launch the kind of university Bureau proposed by the Fed. Govt . . . in its 1937 report?" Another reviewer questioned the location: "I must confess I do not see the need for an organization at Princeton. If we were going into this field why not at Chicago?" A third reviewer, Anne Bezanson from the University of Pennsylvania, thought Princeton proposed to do too much and wondered what was concealed under the umbrella of "urban": "Why shake a waste-basket? Why not identify the one or two things that Princeton can do well?"[117] Willits emphasized the last criticism and wrote in a memo that negotiations ended in late January 1941 because the project was not ripe for RF support in its present preliminary stage of development.[118] Yet Doug Brown and Princeton vice president and treasurer George Brakeley continued to press Willits.[119] Brakeley frequently communicated with Willits, an old friend from when both were administrators at the University of Pennsylvania. Despite its misgivings, the RF mysteriously approved a one-year planning grant of $7,500 beginning April 1, 1941.[120] In May 1942, RF made an additional two-year grant of $15,000, even in the wake of a negative review of the first year by RF staffer Roger F. Evans. He cited "lack of effective purpose or direction," "lack of depth and 'bite,'" "lack of anything approaching real research or synthesis. Even the contemplated study of war impact on 12 NJ cities seems more like a Chamber of Commerce service job."[121] The provision of funding in the wake of negative reviews raises questions about the motivations of the RF officers and the conflict of interest involving Dodds.

The New Deal state shaped BUR in another way by providing its first director, Melville C. Branch Jr. He had worked for the national planning agency since 1939, mainly as "research assistant to the Local Planning Committee" and then briefly "as administrative aide to the director."[122] Just 28 years old when he joined BUR in May 1941, Branch held a BA and an MFA in architecture from Princeton. The university's hiring of such a young person with no PhD or faculty experience to direct a research bureau was a curious move. Of course, there were no PhD holders in urban studies or similar fields at the time; Branch would eventually receive the first US PhD in regional planning, from

Harvard in 1949.[123] Most likely, Princeton hired him because the faculty knew him and they coveted his connections to the federal government, which they thought might provide funding. Brakeley proclaimed that Branch "seems to me pretty hot stuff."[124] The hire was probably a recipe for instability for BUR, and that possibility only grew after the United States entered World War II. In March 1942, Brakeley told Willits that if Branch went to war, Doug Brown, Jean Labatut, and Brakeley could lead BUR until Branch came home.[125] These three men constituted the BUR executive committee.[126] Labatut, a professor in the School of Architecture and its director of graduate studies from 1928 to 1967, played a leading role in creating BUR.[127]

Willits's comments about Branch reflected his continuing hesitancy about BUR: "He is a 'planner,'—or rather, he is out of the 'planning' tradition. Ordinarily I have my fingers crossed on them. They seem to me to consist, so often, of muddy verbalisms, an unlimited desire to extend indiscriminately the regimentation of life and people, an affection for deficits, and a fondness for control as a substitute for thinking through problems."[128] This comment suggests that RF's funding of BUR was not grounded in a thoroughgoing ideological commitment to planning, at least on Willits's part. It also shows that Willits was hesitant about efforts at social control.

BUR floundered after Branch departed for the war in early 1943. The executive committee kept its pledge to continue the work and hired an assistant director, Miriam Strong, to oversee it. After a year, however, the executive committee decided to scale back the program until the war ended, and Strong left for a position with the Tennessee Valley Authority.[129] In its skeleton form, BUR focused on building a library in urban research and planning, including "the reports of various planning agencies throughout the country," and continuing its monthly bulletin, "Selected Items from the Urban Reference."[130] In June 1945, Brown, whose Industrial Relations Section was also receiving RF DSS money, wrote to Willits asking for $4,500 to help BUR stay afloat for one more year until Branch returned, admitting that "we value highly . . . the prestige of Foundation approval."[131] Willits responded with a curt note refusing the additional funds, saying that Princeton had done little with the money already granted.[132] Princeton then decided it could not support BUR "on more than the present basis for the 'foreseeable future,'" and Branch was out of a job.[133] BUR continued its minimal operations, occasionally publishing reports, until 1967, when Princeton reorganized and expanded its activities in urban planning. The School of Architecture added a degree program in urban planning and changed its name to the School of Architecture and Urban Planning. It also created a Research Center for Urban and Environmental Planning, which subsumed BUR.[134]

Princeton's BUR is instructive, its modest activities notwithstanding. By 1940, leaders of at least one elite private research university believed that such an institution should engage in organized urban research, and they had some affinity for prescriptions to that effect coming from the New Deal state. Despite all the support from campus power players Brakeley, Brown, and Dodds, the university declined to finance more than a skeleton operation of BUR when the RF grants ended. Apparently either Dodds was not as committed as he had seemed, he changed his mind about the importance of BUR relative to other programs, or wartime exigencies forced his hand. Perhaps the latter is most likely. Princeton experienced a massive conversion to a war footing in 1942, as attested by Dodds's annual reports, usually called simply *Report of the President*. His 1942 missive, however, bore the title *Princeton's War Program*, and its format was almost completely changed from the previous year's standard report. The annual issue did not return to something like its prewar version until 1947.[135] The BUR also shows that even Princeton, an institution committed to the liberal arts and still debating whether to define itself fully as a university rather than a college, undertook instrumental programs. Brown, who became dean of the faculty in 1946, led the push for the "university" self-understanding. To be sure, Princeton did not become thoroughly instrumental. Indeed, most of the programs begun under Dodds in the years surrounding the BUR experiment were unlike it: music, creative arts, humanities, American civilization, religion, and Near Eastern studies.[136]

Despite their difficulties in becoming firmly established, the School of City Planning/Department of Regional Planning at Harvard and the Bureau of Urban Research at Princeton created a beachhead for such studies in the elite research university. They also espoused a belief that would become characteristic of the postwar university: that it should pursue comprehensive, coordinated, integrated, organized research aimed at social service. Several figures associated with the Harvard program populated the faculties of the many units devoted to city planning and urban research after World War II, including the new intellectual center for the field at the University of Pennsylvania.

Industrial Relations

The academic field of industrial relations, like public administration and city planning, arose in fledgling form in the early twentieth century before successive waves of interest in the 1920s and 1930s prompted some universities to install units dedicated to it. Industrial relations did not have a clear associational background like the other two, but as with those fields, Rockefeller philanthropy and FDR's presidency fueled its growth as an academic field. In this case some funds came more directly from the Rockefeller family than through its foundations, but the RF-funded SSRC promoted industrial relations, as it did with public administration. The Roosevelt administration created a demand for industrial relations experts and research—first during the New Deal, with Social Security and the National Labor Relations Act, then during World War II with the National War Labor Board.

The appointment of John R. Commons to the economics faculty of the University of Wisconsin in 1904 in many ways marked the origin of the field that would come to be called industrial relations.[137] Commons had been a graduate student of Richard Ely at Johns Hopkins. Ely, by then at Wisconsin, spearheaded its hiring of Commons, in part by raising "two-thirds of Commons' $3,000 salary from private sources," presaging Ely's role as a pioneer of sponsored research.[138] Commons became a renowned figure in the history of American social science and is considered the founder of institutional labor economics, which along with personnel management constituted the two main approaches to industrial relations in the field's early years. His arrival at Wisconsin coincided with university president Charles Van Hise's articulation of the "Wisconsin Idea," which held that the university should solve practical problems faced by the state and its citizens. Commons and colleague Thomas Adams published a companion set of texts that became the standard for a course on "labor problems" increasingly offered by university economics departments.[139] This course and its terminology were precursors to later efforts in industrial relations.

The phrase "industrial relations" became popular after President William Howard Taft in 1912 created the Commission on Industrial Relations, on which Commons sat.[140] Scholars generally trace the takeoff of industrial relations as an academic field to the impact of labor problems brought to light by the US experience in World War I, which caused a perceived need for specialized research bureaus on the topic. Industrial relations focused on "the employment relationship and, in particular, the causes of labor problems and their resolution through improved methods of administration and organization."[141] Several events in 1919 and 1920 helped to institutionalize the concept of industrial relations: the launching of the monthly periodical *Industrial Relations*, the formation of the Industrial Relations Association of America (which soon morphed into the American Management Association), and the establishment of the Kansas Court of Industrial Relations.

The concept of industrial relations began to provide a basis for university activities shortly thereafter. The first academic unit to be concerned primarily with industrial relations research was the Industrial Research Department (IRD) of the University of Pennsylvania's Wharton School, cofounded in 1921 by Willits.[142] He earned his PhD at Wharton in 1916 with a dissertation on Philadelphia unemployment, commissioned by a mayoral committee.[143] This model for research—focused on the amelioration of a local problem, requested and supported by a patron outside the university—would prove important, as would his focus on employment.[144] After joining the faculty, he and research associate Anne Bezanson created IRD, which also became the first business school research organization in the United States.[145]

The Industrial Research Department stood out at Penn because it consistently won external funding and garnered considerable internal funding compared to the meager amounts Penn made available through teaching departments and a special research fund for individual professors. One initial funding source was the Philadelphia Association for the Discussion of Employment Problems, a group of businessmen that Willits helped to organize during his 1915 employment study. The Carnegie Corporation also supported IRD's first six years of operations. For the next six years a combination of funds from Penn and Rockefeller philanthropy sustained it. The Rockefeller Foundation then supported the department for another twenty-one years (1932–1953) through a series of three- and five-year grants ranging from $15,000 to $35,000 per year.[146] These grants were general, rather than being tied to a specific project. The latter practice would become dominant after World War II.[147]

Rockefeller philanthropy, then, formed the backbone of the IRD for most of its existence, and this relationship drew Willits steadily into the Rockefeller orbit. The beginning of Rockefeller support for IRD was related to the SSRC creating an Advisory Committee on Industrial Relations, initially called the Committee on Capital and Labor, in 1926. LSRM, as it began to support IRD in 1927, also appointed Willits to a traveling professorship in which he surveyed universities' activities in industrial research, the first of several positions connected to Rockefeller philanthropy that he would hold.[148] A year later, the committee, including Commons and Willits, created an internal report, *Survey of Research in the Field of Industrial Relations*. It defined the field as "including those problems of human behavior involved in the reciprocal relations of the worker with four types of situations: his work; his fellow-worker; his employer; and the public."[149] In late 1930, the Advisory Committee on Industrial Relations merged into a new Advisory Committee on Industry and Trade chaired by Willits. From 1933 onward, much of its work fell under the heading of social security—although, confusingly, there was a semiseparate Committee on Social Security (originally Economic Security) established in 1935, also chaired by Willits.[150] When Willits left Penn in 1939 to direct the RF Division of

Social Science, Bezanson took over as sole director of IRD until 1945, and also served as a part-time consultant for the RF from 1939 to 1950. With Willits and Bezanson in these positions, it is not surprising that the RF supported IRD for so long, nor that its support ceased as Willits neared retirement. IRD was unable to secure more funding after its last Rockefeller grant expired in 1953, and it ceased to exist. A smaller entity, the Industrial Research Unit, replaced it and did not flourish until the late 1960s.[151]

IRD helped to form the instrumental university in several ways. One was facilitating government entities' "use" of the university. Bezanson proclaimed in 1942 that IRD's "publications have been widely read, and its methods have been copied by various federal and state departments." This statement alluded to a sort of indirect government patronage. Although governments did not fund IRD, their being primary "consumers" of its "products" probably helped it stay its course, especially since Bezanson seemed proud of the government attention. IRD also provided personnel during World War II—specifically to the Office of Price Administration and the National War Labor Board (NWLB).[152] IRD's most prominent researcher, industrial relations expert George W. Taylor, became vice-chairman of the NWLB in 1942 and chairman in 1945. Taylor became one of Penn's most famous professors, dubbed the "Father of American Arbitration." His founding work in this field began when he became an IRD research associate in 1929 and a Wharton assistant professor in 1930 after earning his bachelor's and PhD degrees there under Willits's tutelage. A few years later, FDR recruited him to help run the National Recovery Administration.[153] Taylor's work, like that of the IRD overall, reflected the emerging instrumental university. External social problems strongly shaped his research agenda. The key product of his work was method (techniques of arbitration), and he served external patrons (presidents from FDR to LBJ). He also became friends with fellow industrial relations scholar and arbitrator Clark Kerr.

One year after Penn created IRD, Princeton University established an Industrial Relations Section in its Department of Economics, the first university unit to be wholly concerned with industrial relations. Princeton's was the first of five such entities created before World War II. The other host universities were MIT, Cal Tech, Stanford, and Michigan. The latter three were small and made little impact on the field. All five units owed their existence to industrial relations consultant Clarence J. Hicks, a sort of industrial relations missionary, who procured funding from wealthy industrialists like John D. Rockefeller Jr. and convinced universities to establish the units with those funds. Hicks worked from the personnel management perspective, and these units likewise adopted that approach.[154] He intended the programs as a corrective to what he perceived as "an almost universal stress in the universities on the importance and value of collective bargaining through labor unionism." He also believed that existing industrial relations courses focused too much on economic theory and did not teach students about the actual conditions of industrial relations.[155]

Princeton's IR Section operated something like an organized research unit even while based in a department, but it pursued a limited program during its first twenty years. One of its primary activities was a set of annual conferences beginning in 1931.[156] An RF staffer in attendance at the 1936 edition wrote that "representatives of about one hundred American and Canadian companies were present. The directors of the industrial relations bureaus at Leland Stanford (Paul Eliel) and the University of Michigan (John W. Riegel) were also there throughout. In addition there were a large number of so-called 'faculty' men present from other universities, from the Social Security Board, the Industrial Relations Counselors and from certain companies."[157] The IR Section built on this event by creating a similar one for younger executives in 1938, and then "one for staff personnel of national trade unions and federations" in 1947.[158] Another activity was publishing a few "research reports" each year, which generally ranged from twenty-five to fifty pages. A sample of titles includes *Collective Bargaining in the Steel Industry*, *The Seniority Principle in Employment Relations*, and *Group Purchase of Medical Care by Industrial Employees*.[159]

J. Douglas Brown, who joined the Princeton faculty the year before the IR Section's inception, became director in 1926 and served until 1955, pulling double duty for nine years after becoming dean of the faculty in 1946.[160] Brown's ascent to dean of the faculty meant that for the final eleven years of Dodds's presidency, leaders of new units discussed in this chapter held Princeton's top two positions. In Brown's final year at Princeton (1966–1967), he pulled double duty again, serving as the university's first provost while still dean of the faculty.[161] He was involved in the Roosevelt administration's process of drafting Social Security legislation, then served as the initial chair of the Federal Advisory Council on Social Security. During the first part of World War II, he led a federal government unit dealing with production.[162] Brown also served on the SSRC Committee on Social Security.[163] He received small RF grants on this topic: a $1,000 grant in 1936 for travel studies of social security, and $1,500 in 1939 for travel to do general IR research and prepare lectures to deliver at Johns Hopkins that would lead to a monograph on the economics of social security legislation.[164] The IR Section also cooperated with the School of Public and International Affairs after the latter's founding. For instance, in 1938–1939, Brown led a conference on health insurance sponsored by the school.[165]

During World War II, Princeton worked to expand the IR Section, even as it shrank the Bureau of Urban Research. It sought and secured an RF grant of $22,500 over three years beginning July 1, 1944, to hire two research assistants and two secretaries. This typical ORU move expanded the number of staff members within a university without adding permanent faculty. In conjunction with the grant, Princeton planned to enlarge the endowment of $360,000 that provided about $15,000 annual income, most of the IR Section's funding. Princeton officials believed they could increase the endowment to $600,000, providing about $22,500 in annual income, by the section's twenty-fifth anniversary in 1947. The Rockefeller grant would allow Princeton to raise the IR Section budget to that level in the meantime to enable an immediate expansion of the program.[166] Dodds told RF officials that he would pursue the endowment and not ask for renewal of the grant. Willits, in describing the grant proposal to other RF staffers, wrote that "we have been watching the six Industrial Relations sections which C. J. Hicks has had a hand in starting." Willits liked what these sections had done but wanted them to "grow better" by "find[ing] a further purpose . . . over the next decade or two." He thought that Princeton's desire "to undertake more fundamental research," even though it was "not clearly defined," showed promise in this direction.[167] On the cusp of 1945, then, units dedicated to industrial relations were flourishing at Pennsylvania, Princeton, and, to a lesser extent, MIT.

The most influential institutionalizations of industrial relations in elite research universities happened toward the end of World War II—first at Cornell and then at the University of California. UC, despite lacking a unit dedicated to industrial relations, counted two important members of the field among the economics faculty at its Los Angeles campus by the mid-1930s. Gordon Watkins belonged to the first generation of industrial relations scholars. A graduate school classmate of Willits, he earned his PhD in economics at Penn in 1918 and then published the two-volume *Labor Problems and Labor Administration in the United States during the World War* (1920).[168] Shortly thereafter, Watkins wrote *An Introduction to the Study of Labor Problems* (1922), the first textbook successful in challenging the dominance of the Commons and Adams set in the labor problems course. Watkins arrived at UCLA in 1925 and later served ten years as dean of UCLA's College of Letters and Science, then became the first provost (chief executive) of UC's new Riverside campus in 1949. Paul Dodd rose to prominence in the 1930s as Watkins's protégé. Like his mentor, Dodd earned his PhD in economics from Penn (1933). He did much of his dissertation work while serving as Watkins's associate at UCLA and credited Watkins with giving him the topic.[169] Upon completion, Dodd joined Watkins on UCLA's economics faculty, and they began to coauthor books on industrial relations. Dodd later succeeded Watkins for fifteen years as dean of the College of Letters and Science, and he eventually became president of San Francisco State University (1962–1966). The ascent of Watkins and Dodd to these key positions of academic leadership, even in a College of Letters and Science, testifies to the growing prestige of industrial relations by the 1930s.

Dodd helped to institutionalize academic industrial relations at the University of California in the 1940s. He led the internal side of a charge badgering UC president Robert Gordon Sproul to create a university unit devoted to industrial relations, while Governor Earl Warren pursued an analogous external campaign. A precipitating factor was concern that with the impending end of World War II, millions of returning servicemen searching for employment might cause economic chaos, including a crisis of mass unemployment. This subject motivated several endeavors with implications for American higher education, including the GI Bill of 1944, which swelled university enrollments in the following years, and the President's Commission on Higher Education appointed by Harry Truman, which originated from discussions in the Office of War Mobilization and Reconversion about handling the returning servicemen.[170] Scholars have rarely recognized, however, a third impact that the postwar concern about employment made on universities: it propelled the establishment of university units fully dedicated to the academic field of industrial relations.[171]

Within this environment, a New York initiative prompted the campaign at the University of California. The New York legislature in March 1944 established the New York State School of Industrial and Labor Relations at Cornell University, which took its first students in the fall of 1945.[172] Cornell became the first university in the United States to create a separate school of industrial relations, and the school was the first university industrial relations unit to be funded by a state government. Cornell's school stood out from the six academic industrial relations units that existed at the time of its founding. All of those units were privately funded and not organizationally independent, being sections of a business school or economics department.

Dodd's approach to Sproul urged consideration of something similar for California: "This type of program, supported by public funds, has a great advantage over the 'Institute of Industrial Relations' developments at such places as Stanford, California Institute of Technology, and Princeton, since in it no 'strings' whatever are attached. Perhaps you will recall that the lack of complete freedom and independence was one of my chief objections to the Princeton type of development."[173] He referred to an earlier time when a group of Southern California citizens had approached Sproul about setting up an Institute of Industrial Relations at UCLA, but Dodd and Watkins had discouraged it because they believed that taking outside funds for the purpose would make it difficult to render impartial and objective service to both management and labor.[174] Baldwin Woods, director of University Extension, also pressured Sproul in light of the New York development. He suggested that UC hold a conference to determine how it should engage with labor and industrial relations. He also visited Cornell and a Wayne State University initiative. He told Sproul that he might propose that UC do something similar, to be administered by Extension.[175]

An industrial relations program did not get off the ground, however, until Warren told Sproul that he wanted the university to do it. The men met for lunch in Sacramento just before Christmas 1944. During their college days at Berkeley, Warren and Sproul had teamed up as members of the Golden Bear marching band—Sproul as drum major and Warren as part of the clarinet section.[176] By 1944, they were arguably the two most powerful men in California. Four years later, this mix of power and friendship would find its highest display when Sproul nominated Warren for president of the United States at the 1948 Republican National Convention in Philadelphia.[177] While Sproul was slow in heeding his faculty's interest in industrial relations, he was quick to please his old friend. A few days after their meeting, Sproul wrote to Warren, "Responding to our luncheon conversation of last week, I have dictated the enclosed statement which you may find useful in preparing your recommendations to the Legislature of 1945. I hope that I have caught the spirit of what you said to me about the establishment of a division or institute of labor and industrial relations at the University."[178] Warren presented his message to the legislature almost immediately after it convened in January. He told lawmakers that "the techniques in this field are at least as important as those in the fields of business management and technological advancement for which our schools offer special training."[179] Warren was particularly concerned with developing collective bargaining techniques that could produce understanding.[180] Warren signed into law in July 1945 the bill creating the Institute of Industrial Relations (IIR) at the University of California.

The bill allowed the university to determine the exact form that the institute would take. Immediately after his lunch with Warren, Sproul asked the advice of E. T. Grether, dean of the School of Business Administration at UC Berkeley. Grether opposed setting up a "separate School of Industrial and Labor Relations as in New York state" and advocated a unit "connect[ed] with the School and Department of Business Administration."[181] The legislative bill introduced early in 1945 called for a "school" of industrial relations, but Sproul had it amended to read "institute."[182] Sproul rejected, however, Grether's suggestion that IIR be administratively connected with the School of Business Administration. Instead, in a move typical of Sproul's micromanaging tendencies, he set it up as an independent unit reporting directly to him, with two branches. Sproul named Dodd as the first director of its southern section at Los Angeles and associate professor Clark Kerr, newly hired to Berkeley's business faculty, for the same role at the northern section. The intention in keeping IIR administratively separate from the business school was to assure citizens and organized labor that it was insulated from pressure to take pro-business stances. Yet the IIR's first two northern section directors, Kerr and Grether, were professors of business administration. Setting up the industrial relations program as an institute rather than a school had other implications as well. It seems that Warren's vision was for a school like Cornell's that would train negotiators. What actually got established, however, was a research institute. Unlike at Cornell, the California unit did not grant degrees in industrial relations. Nurturing a few researchers won out over educating a larger number of negotiators.

The industrial relations units at the University of California and Cornell were the most prominent in a wave of such establishments during the immediate postwar years. State universities, including Minnesota, Illinois, Rutgers, and Wisconsin, as well as private institutions, including Chicago, New York University, and Yale, started units "expressly dedicated to research and teaching in industrial relations."[183] Kerr wrote with only slight hyperbole in 1946 that "every major university, both public and private, has established, or is contemplating the establishment of, industrial relations institutes or sections." He added that "few areas in the domestic life of the nation are vested with greater public concern than the field of industrial relations . . . these problems clearly constitute an appropriate subject of study for the universities of the nation."[184] A study of universities by the Association of Governing Boards of State Universities and Allied Institutions, which involved site visits to nearly ninety campuses in 1946–1947, included an entire chapter on industrial relations, the only academic field so represented.[185]

Other developments, too, marked the rapid institutionalization of academic industrial relations during those years. The Industrial Relations Research Association (IRRA) launched in 1947 as the first academic professional association for the field. Kerr helped organize the IRRA, became one of six members of its first executive committee, and eventually served as its president in 1954.[186] Also in 1947, the new Cornell school began publishing *Industrial and Labor Relations Review*, the first scholarly journal devoted to industrial relations. In the foreword to the first issue, former RF DSS director Edmund Day, by then president of Cornell, commented that the journal "is a logical extension of the function which higher education is assuming in the area of labor-management relations."[187] The language of "function" suggests that the surge of units devoted to industrial relations coincided with growing belief that the university should be an instrument for addressing such problems.

Both politicians and academics believed that the university's perceived neutrality qualified it to speak authoritatively into both the thorny world of labor-management relations and debates over the place of organized labor in industrial society. They believed that the university, through its research activities, could solve social problems classed under industrial relations in a nonpolitical, non-ideological way. UC officials stressed the need for impartiality when deciding on Kerr as IIR director. Grether assured Berkeley provost Monroe Deutsch that Kerr "has the confidence of employers as well as of both the C.I.O. and the A.F. of L."[188] The report of the committee charged with setting up the institute declared that "the orientation of the work of the IIR will be toward the public interest rather than toward the special interests of either labor or industry."[189] The planners intended the emphasis on research to further that orientation. Kerr later described how he saw the field at that time: "A rejection of ideology. Marxists and anti-monopolists alike were rejected; and, though to a lesser extent, so were the Wisconsin [i.e., Commons et al.] and Human Relations [Elton Mayo] schools—the one pro-labor and the other pro-management. The field became more unified in outlook and more neutrally professional in approach . . . Workable policies were of central interest. What would work among the 'bumps and grinds' of the real world; not what might work in the 'best of all possible worlds.'"[190] Yet as the next chapter suggests, Kerr was perhaps naïve to believe that his work was non-ideological.

By 1945, several of America's most elite research universities had established units dedicated to the instrumental fields of public administration, industrial relations, and city planning that emerged from the Progressive Era. One could see these fields as establishing a new model for a learned profession.[191] Whereas members of the traditional professions of law, medicine, and theology most often worked with individuals to protect or better them, the new professionals worked for the betterment or control of government and society. The three fields established their strongholds in some expected places such as UC Berkeley, an elite research university that also had a land-grant component. But they also gained ground in northeastern private universities such as Harvard, NYU, Penn, and Princeton. The last is the most surprising of this group. Princeton set up programs in all three fields despite its nonurban setting, its general aversion to professional schools, and the fact that it, along with Yale (which was largely absent from the development of these fields save a modest effort in industrial relations), remained the most "collegiate" of the original members of the Association of American Universities.[192] The New Deal state contributed to the growth of these fields, as numerous key players circulated between the Roosevelt administration and the new university programs described here.

At the same time, some of these fields' leading promoters at this stage either were not ideologically committed to technocratic managerialism or saw it as able to coexist in the same institution with more traditional understandings of liberal arts education (or both). The careers of Joseph Willits, Harold Dodds, and Gordon Watkins are instructive on this point. Remarkably, they were all born in 1889 and completed doctorates in Penn's Wharton School in consecutive years from 1916 to 1918. Like Kerr, Willits and Dodds grew up in rural Pennsylvania and attended liberal arts colleges in the state. A generation older, however, they exhibited a less full-fledged pursuit of the instrumental university. Willits remained suspicious of the planning tradition, and Dodds was a major spokesman for an older understanding of liberal arts education. When Watkins became the founding chief campus officer of UC Riverside, he built it as a small liberal arts college within the UC system.

The equivocation of these leaders notwithstanding, the creation of university units in public administration, city planning, and industrial relations before World War II formed a base for the postwar growth of the instrumental university. Public administration was central for the postwar university's international endeavors (chapter 4). City planning hit its postwar apogee at the University of Pennsylvania, which helped push the university toward a new self-concept as an urban community service institution (chapter 3). Industrial relations provided the context for the rise of Clark Kerr as the most influential leader of the instrumental university (chapter 2).

CHAPTER 2

Clark Kerr

Leading Proponent of the Instrumental University

University of California at Berkeley chancellor Clark Kerr joined a jubilant scene in Room 1135 of the Waldorf-Astoria Hotel in New York City on March 1, 1954. The Ford Foundation had just awarded Kerr and three close friends $475,000 for their joint project, the Inter-University Study of Labor Problems in Economic Development.[1] It was one of the largest grants awarded to date by a foundation for a single social science research project in the United States. The four men convened in Manhattan to decide how to use it. Kerr, John Dunlop, Frederick Harbison, and Charles Myers—the Four, as I will call them—constituted themselves that day as the board of the Inter-University Study, electing Kerr as chairman.[2] The board endured for twenty-one years and directed one of the largest and longest-running "big social science" research projects of the era. The Study spawned thirty-seven books and forty-three articles. It involved over ninety researchers from twenty-four institutions in nine countries.[3] Its signature publication, the 1960 book *Industrialism and Industrial Man: The Problems of Labor and Management in Economic Growth*, appeared in multiple editions and translations. The Study aimed at a grand theory to challenge Karl Marx and Alfred Marshall.

It was appropriate that Kerr and his associates inaugurated their board at the grandiose Waldorf-Astoria. A year earlier, a Ford Foundation official had written that he was "rather appalled by the apparent immensity of the project." In his view it was "too enormous to be practicable . . . so vast as to raise a doubt as to whether it is actually comprehensible."[4] The Four proposed "to develop the essential knowledge for a generalized concept of the labor problem in the modern world" using a new "framework for comparative analysis calling for the combined use of disciplines in social sciences concerned with labor, management, and economic development."[5]

The Four were educated as economists and thought of themselves as labor economists, but gave their primary allegiance to the interdisciplinary academic field of industrial relations. Their institutional affiliations signified their status as leaders in that field. Before his installation as Berkeley's first chancellor in 1952, Kerr had been the inaugural director of Berkeley's Institute of Industrial Relations (IIR). Dunlop was secretary of the Wertheim Committee on Industrial Relations at Harvard, Harbison was executive officer of the Industrial Relations Center at the University of Chicago, and Myers was executive director of the Industrial Relations Section in MIT's Department of Economics and Social Sciences. A few years later, Harbison moved to Princeton for a position with the Industrial Relations Section of the Department of Economics. Historians have cited Kerr and Dunlop, who did their doctoral work simultaneously at Berkeley in the 1930s, as the two most important figures in postwar academic industrial relations.[6] Dunlop served as dean of Harvard's Faculty of Arts and Sciences from 1970 to 1973 and was a serious candidate during Harvard's presidential search of 1970–1971.[7] He subsequently became US Secretary of Labor under Gerald Ford.

Investigating the Inter-University Study helps to explain Kerr's thought and its development across the entire decade of the 1950s, which encompassed Kerr's leadership of the Study from the first plans in 1950 to the publication of *Industrialism and Industrial Man* in 1960. During this period, Kerr ascended from director of the Berkeley IIR to chancellor at Berkeley to president of the multicampus University of California (UC). For his efforts in crafting the landmark California Master Plan for Higher Education in 1960, he won international acclaim—including an appearance on the cover of *Time*, which dubbed him the "Master Planner."[8] Kerr had become the face of the American university. He was also becoming its voice, a position cemented three years later with the publication of *The Uses of the University*.

Kerr was among the most important promoters of the instrumental university. His ideas shaped the American research university through his implementation of them at UC and his articulation of them in *Uses*, which then affected how other university leaders conceived of their institutions. Many of his ideas about the university's purpose came from his research in industrial relations, which climaxed in the Inter-University Study. During the postwar period, university leaders increasingly used the terminology of industrial

FIGURE 1. Clark Kerr, president of the University of California, at a dinner in his honor given by the University of California Club of New York at the Chemists' Club, New York City, November 30, 1961. Clark Kerr Personal and Professional Papers, CU-302, Carton 69. Courtesy of The Bancroft Library, University of California, Berkeley.

relations—"manpower," "human resources," "human capital"—to describe the missions of their institutions. A specific theory of industrialism generated in the Study had implications for liberal arts education that Kerr laid out in an inaugural address as UC president. Kerr's immersion in mid-century social science more broadly, especially the behavioral science paradigm and the quest for an administrative science, provided him with other important ideas about higher education. Prominent across those pursuits was his insistence on the crucial role that administration and management played in modern society (for Kerr, management was part of a larger process of administration). By the late 1950s, he came to believe that management was the key factor for economic development. Kerr's writings articulated three ways in which he believed universities should promote economic development: by producing new ideas, which would be the primary factor for industrial production in what observers would soon call "the knowledge economy"; by training specialized "manpower," especially for management; and that universities *as institutions* must help administer modern society. His thought reveals ways in which concepts of economic development and administration, especially as mid-century elites linked them, advanced the instrumental university.

Kerr and Organized Research

Kerr promoted organized research units at Berkeley, which increased the instrumental tenor of the institution. Indeed, Kerr was a major reason why Berkeley was "the country's most fertile breeding ground of organized research units, and the initiator of the acronym, ORU."[9] He joined the School of Business Administration faculty in 1945 after its dean, E. T. Grether, hired him away from his first academic post at the University of Washington.[10] As IIR director from 1945 to 1952, Kerr grew the unit by bringing new faculty to Berkeley and by connecting existing faculty to the institute. After Kerr became chancellor, IIR struggled as faculty affiliation with it dwindled, but it grew in prominence by serving as the institutional base for the Inter-University Study. Furthermore, Chancellor Kerr created several new ORUs, including the Institute of International Studies.

The record of IIR during Kerr's directorship and chancellorship reveals tensions between the impulse to use the university to solve industrial relations problems and a desire to build academic departments of distinction. The university gave one-third appointments in IIR to selected new hires in social science departments. These hires included three professors who became Kerr's main Berkeley collaborators in the Inter-University Study: Reinhard

Bendix of sociology (hired 1947), Harvey Leibenstein of economics, and Walter Galenson of business administration (both hired 1951). Available evidence does not indicate whether Berkeley hired these men primarily to build IIR or primarily to build departments, or sought to achieve both goals simultaneously. The hiring of Bendix was part of an effort by UC president Robert G. Sproul from 1946 onward to build a sociology department at Berkeley out of the previous Department of Social Institutions. The revamped department made Bendix its first hire who held a sociology PhD.[11] Since IIR had no faculty of its own, Kerr had to persuade departments to hire faculty who would be interested in working under its auspices.[12] Kerr's tools of persuasion included the one-third appointments.

Berkeley's Institute of Industrial Relations also shows that individual units did not always have continuous success, even as the ORU concept proliferated in American universities. Kerr and associate director Lloyd Fisher set up a research program that defined industrial relations broadly and welcomed a range of disciplinary perspectives.[13] This strategy helped to attract a sizeable group of faculty. IIR began to experience difficulties, however, after Fisher's untimely death from cancer and Kerr's promotion to chancellor. Kerr's good friend Grether served as caretaker IIR director in name for two years to keep the position open for Kerr if he found the chancellorship, which he believed Sproul wanted to marginalize, to be unsuitable.[14] During this time, faculty participation in IIR waned enough that Kerr asked Sproul to divert the "salary savings" to the Institute of Social Sciences, over which he as chancellor had more direct control.[15] Grether's stepping aside and the hiring of a new director in 1954 raised the question of whether IIR would maintain a broad research agenda. Bendix worried that a narrower focus would force him out of IIR due to his lack of work on collective bargaining.[16] Kerr, despite being chancellor, had no power to appoint a new director because IIR reported directly to President Sproul. After a lengthy process involving a committee, Sproul ultimately took Kerr's recommendation to hire Arthur Ross as director and Margaret Gordon as associate director.[17] The economist Ross had joined the Berkeley faculty and IIR soon after the latter's inception, and with Kerr and Fisher had launched the "California School" of industrial relations. This approach, distinguished by the manner in which it combined economic and political frameworks to analyze industrial relations situations, found its most prominent expression in Ross's 1948 book *Trade Union Wage Policy*.[18]

One element of the 1954 search for new IIR leadership points to the connection of industrial relations with broader trends in American thought. Kerr suggested Daniel Bell as a candidate for associate director.[19] The idea apparently came the previous year from Kerr's friend and IIR colleague Seymour

Martin Lipset, who would go on to fame in political sociology. Lipset had known Bell since their college days at CCNY, where they were part of the legendary intellectual circle that included Irving Kristol and Nathan Glazer.[20] Lipset told Kerr that Bell "would make the ideal replacement for Lloyd in the job as Research Director at the Institute. Bell has the same broad depth of knowledge and interest in most of the social sciences which Lloyd had . . . I told him about my idea, and he expressed considerable interest." At the time, Bell was labor editor for *Fortune*, but Lipset reported that Bell was "getting discontented with his job there and would like to return to the academic life."[21] When the search for new IIR leadership heated up in spring 1954, Kerr invited Bell to campus for a luncheon.[22] Bell remained at *Fortune* four more years, however, before joining the Columbia sociology faculty in 1958 and becoming one of the most renowned figures in American social thought for books such as *The End of Ideology*, *The Coming of Post-Industrial Society*, and *The Cultural Contradictions of Capitalism*.[23] Although Bell did not join IIR, his increased acquaintance with Kerr proved valuable. In 1955, Bell expressed interest in integrating his study of communism in the United States with the Inter-University Study, and the Four invited him to a board meeting to discuss possible collaboration.[24]

Despite solidifying its directorship under Ross, IIR continued to experience dwindling faculty participation. Less than a year after assuming leadership, Ross wrote to the IIR Statewide Coordinating Committee that "serious thought must be given to maintain the attractiveness of the Institute to its senior research personnel" in the face of competition created by money "being poured into the social sciences" through other entities. He noted that "a good scholar can undertake paid research for an organization such as the RAND Corporation, at a generous per diem rate. This is precisely what has happened in the case of two of our best scholars, to the manifest detriment of our research program."[25] Two years later, the Committee expressed "the general view that the Institutes might well lose some of their differential advantage within the next several years."[26] Indeed, in that span several professors shed their IIR affiliations and returned full-time to their departments, which led to further anxiety about the IIR being able to spend its full budget. Some Berkeley professors, then, found university organized research, if not the instrumental university model more broadly, less than ideal. The range of motives for these moves requires further investigation. Some faculty appear to have chosen larger pecuniary benefits available for participating in organized research outside the university, but others might have preferred independent scholarship to the coordinated research program that Ross advertised as a benefit of the IIR. Another possible explanation is that Grether and Ross were less effective

ORU directors than Kerr, who had greater success in rallying faculty to the institute's program.

The headwinds that caused IIR's problems during his chancellorship did not impede Kerr's promotion of other ORUs, especially in the social sciences. Among the most prominent was the Institute of International Studies (IIS), which the regents authorized in 1955 at Kerr's behest. The IIS story illustrates some forces behind structural changes that became characteristic of the instrumental university. Discussion about forming IIS began in December 1952 and carried through November 1954.[27] Kerr proposed to consolidate the existing Bureau of International Relations (established 1919) and Institute of East Asiatic Studies into the Institute of International Studies.[28] The rationale was to organize Berkeley's research in international studies to make it more attractive to patrons outside the university. He told President Sproul, "You will have heard, as I have, the complaints of some faculty members, as well as representatives of the foundations, relating to this campus for uncoordinated research efforts in the social, humanistic, and related sciences. Generous institutional grants in these fields may have gone elsewhere because of this criticism."[29] IIS, as Kerr envisioned it, would help route those grants to Berkeley: "It shall be the function of the Institute to simplify the administrative aspects of research and to coordinate approaches to foundations, governmental agencies, etc., for the support of research in international studies."[30] Kerr's emphasis on the need for coordinated and administered research revealed one of the most characteristic features of the instrumental university: the belief that the most important research emerged from teams rather than individual investigators. Kerr's gambit in establishing IIS to attract foundation money paid off. UC received two enormous block grants for international studies from the Ford Foundation, $4 million in 1961 and $7 million in 1964. The grants were third in size in those two rounds of Ford allocations, trailing only grants to Harvard and Columbia. The UC grants were to be divided between Berkeley and UCLA.[31]

Prior to this success, IIS was constantly in flux during its first few years in existence, and frequent hand-wringing memos and reports revealed much about the ideas that drove it. One such idea was that IIS would facilitate Berkeley's "proper discharge of its share of the national responsibility," as the title of a 1959 report by IIS chairman Paul S. Taylor put it. Kerr had named Taylor—an economics professor who had been Kerr's dissertation advisor in the 1930s—as chairman upon the inception of IIS in 1956. As part of a 1962 reorganization that abolished the post of chairman and replaced it with director, Kerr (by then UC president) arranged for Lipset to fill the new position. Kerr's placement of two of his most trusted friends at Berkeley to lead IIS suggests the importance that he attributed to it. Taylor's report made a four-part argument about IIS's role. First, "universities or someone else" needed to step up "to solve problems in economic, educational, social, and governmental fields," because military and scientific assistance alone would not produce "stability in Asia." Second, "university programs ought to be . . . accelerated toward a pace commensurate with the urgencies of our time." Third, Berkeley was "not meeting 'its share of the national responsibility.'" Fourth, "if University institutions are to apply their full potential" to this approach, they needed "changes in attitudes, institutions, equipment, resources, and methods that will make possible more work, and more effective work."[32] Taylor's argument implied that the university should become a political instrument, actively responsible for creating a more stable Asia—one that enhanced US prosperity and security—through work in some of Asia's polities. Kerr generalized this idea four years later in *The Uses of the University* when he called the university "an instrument of national purpose." Taylor also implied that external forces—in this case, conditions in Asia—should drive the university's agenda. Kerr's observation of these trends in an aspect of the university's work that particularly interested him might well have shaped his formulation in *Uses*.

Kerr successfully pushed for the creation of other Berkeley ORUs in the social sciences, including the Survey Research Center, the Center for Integration of Social Science Theory, and the Center for Research in Management Science. Before turning to that, however, examining the creation of the Inter-University Study is in order. Even as IIR experienced the aforementioned difficulties, it also flourished as home base for this huge organized research project.

Genesis of the Inter-University Study

The Inter-University Study and especially *Industrialism and Industrial Man* represented the apex of Kerr's career in academic industrial relations. After the publication of the latter in 1960, Kerr did little more writing in the field until picking it up again in retirement. In the interim, his fame as the leading spokesman of American higher education and author of *The Uses of the University* eclipsed his earlier reputation as one of the country's foremost industrial relations experts. During the 1950s, however, even while chancellor, he was constantly involved in directing the Study. Tracing its origins and course, then, is essential for understanding Kerr's thought during this period. Doing so also opens a window into how patrons influenced university research after 1945. In this case, the Ford Foundation promoted problem-oriented research.

This approach encouraged a shift in the behavior and goals of scholars. From the late nineteenth century through World War II, most social scientists believed they should conduct their research with detachment and objectivity on "problems that were normally defined by the state of knowledge in their fields rather than by the state of society" (although there was always tension between the goals of pure knowledge and social change).[33] After World War II, the Ford Foundation encouraged social scientists to define problems by the state of society. Social scientists such as Kerr took up this charge without much hesitation, and even advanced it apart from foundation auspices.

The Ford Foundation changed the academic landscape when it began to make enormous grants to universities, particularly for social science research, in 1950. During the first few chaotic years of the foundation's large-scale grant making, its economics program lacked direction. Thomas Carroll brought stability when he arrived in summer 1953 as associate director of the Ford Foundation and formalized the economics program as the Program in Economic Development and Administration (EDA), linking two influential modern ideals. The limited scholarship on EDA has mostly focused on its largest initiative, the $35 million effort to strengthen university business schools from 1955 through the early 1960s that "brought about a revolution in business education."[34] The Inter-University Study's road to approval during this period was rocky, mirroring Ford's internal affairs. In a foundation that frequently changed personnel and procedures while struggling to steer its newly massive ship, the personal favor of specific officers was critical for the Study to receive grants. Once the Inter-University Study did receive multiyear funding, however, it could be considered EDA's first "signature" project, prior to the more prominent investment in business education. The foundation remained closely identified with the Inter-University Study through the publication of *Industrialism and Industrial Man*, especially through Carroll's participation.

Kerr, Dunlop, Harbison, and Myers—the Four—initially formulated what would become the Inter-University Study in 1951 and submitted a grant proposal to the Ford Foundation, which had recently and suddenly become by far the wealthiest American foundation. At the suggestion of MIT president Karl Compton, the first "outsider" on the foundation's board, Henry Ford II hired San Francisco lawyer H. Rowan Gaither Jr., a Berkeley alum, to remake the foundation.[35] Gaither, though a nonacademic, shaped the postwar American university by building influential organizations. His first prominent position was during the war as assistant director of MIT's Radiation Laboratory, which became a model for organized research in the postwar American university. After the war, Gaither helped to found the RAND Corporation and served as its chairman for many years. He was also the most important figure in the first decade of the "new" Ford Foundation beginning in 1948. Gaither formed a study committee that prepared a *Report of the Study for the Ford Foundation on Policy and Program*, released to the public in 1950. The report espoused a soaring idealism about the prospects for improving human life around the world. It set forth five program areas for the foundation: the establishment of peace (I); the strengthening of democracy (II); the strengthening of the economy (III); education in a democratic society (IV); individual behavior and human relations (V). In the eyes of many, the report announced that the Ford Foundation "was going to save the world."[36] At the least, it appeared that the foundation would be devoted to a liberal internationalism that advocated American intervention in countries around the world to spread liberal-democratic capitalism and work toward peace.

Ford II conducted a long search to find a person capable of running such a well-endowed, sweeping enterprise. He settled on leading internationalist Paul G. Hoffman, head of the Economic Cooperation Administration (ECA), which oversaw the Marshall Plan. Prior to his government service, Hoffman had been president of Studebaker and chairman (1942–1948) of the Committee on Economic Development, a group of American businessmen who promoted liberal internationalism. Hoffman brought on board several associate directors, some with ECA ties, and hired as his personal assistant Joseph M. McDaniel Jr., dean of Northwestern University's School of Commerce and also a former ECA colleague. These men operated out of a flowering estate in Pasadena, California, nicknamed "Itching Palms" after the grant seekers that crowded its waiting rooms.[37]

Clark Kerr was one such grant seeker. In the late spring of 1951, the Four submitted their first proposal, "Labor Relations and Democratic Policy," asking for $500,000 over five years.[38] Kerr traveled to Itching Palms to make his case in person to associate director Robert Maynard Hutchins, fresh off twenty-two years as chancellor of the University of Chicago and perhaps the most prominent person in American higher education.[39] This meeting carried symbolism in hindsight, for it represented the coming together of two titans of American higher education in the mid-twentieth century—Hutchins on his way out of the spotlight and Kerr on his way into it.

The Four framed the project in terms of Ford's stated goals regarding world peace and in terms of American foreign policy. Their baseline assumption was that "the condition, character, and beliefs of the working classes will be among the decisive influences upon the political structure of modern nations and therefore upon the prospects for domestic tranquility and world peace." It followed that "the development of an effective American world-wide strategy demands a profound understanding of the position of the working class in a variety of societies." To that end, they proposed "a comparative analysis of working class development," using case studies in Sweden, Germany, England, France, Italy, Yugoslavia, Iraq, South Africa, India, Indonesia, Japan, and Brazil. Kerr and his colleagues depicted their work as motivated by a new American politics of international nonmilitary intervention. "The tasks of mid-century," they wrote, "appear to be the design of those forms of intervention which will provide a positive basis for democratic institutions and world peace." They referred to specific US programs to illustrate how the project would serve the American foreign policy agenda. They structured the proposal in two parts, "correspond[ing] to a vital distinction between the worker in pre-industrial society and the industrial worker," because "American foreign policy has recognized this distinction clearly in the development of the Marshall plan for [industrial] Europe and the Point Four program for [pre-industrial] Asia."

The proposal admitted a departure from the prevailing moral economy governing scholarship: "the American student and scholar reared in the liberal traditions of the first decades of the century has seldom defined his task as that of developing the skills of peaceful persuasion except as this persuasion might be accomplished by words. To go beyond exhortation and logic appeared to sacrifice that detachment with which the morals of scholarship has been identified and to lend scholarship implicitly or explicitly to the service of imperialism." Yet Kerr and his colleagues offered no justification for their departure from these "morals of scholarship." They simply asserted that "it is abundantly clear that logic and exhortation are limited instruments in developing an effective strategy of directed change," instruments that would appeal only to other intellectuals and "not be effective at the crucial levels of social action." At this point in the project, their plan for "social action" appeared to center on training consultants and staff members for labor organizations around the world, which would contribute to "an institutional structure and a resource base that will make world peace somewhat easier to realize."[40] The Four left detachment in their wake as they accelerated their social engineering. Despite the project's framing in terms of the Ford Foundation's objectives and American liberal internationalism, Ford believed it did not go far enough and declined to fund it. Ford wanted to fund "projects which will make a contribution to the maintenance of peace and . . . help to relieve present world tensions."[41] Yet the Four did not give up.

Richard Bissell revived consideration for the proposal when he joined the Ford Foundation staff in early 1952 in response to Hoffman's invitation to develop Area III, the economics program.[42] Yet another of Hoffman's Marshall Plan colleagues, Bissell later joined the CIA and gained notoriety as the chief architect of the 1961 Bay of Pigs invasion.[43] Prior to that, Bissell influenced the instrumental university through his relationships with some of its most significant figures, including those he mentored and taught while a graduate student in economics at Yale during the 1930s. In the evenings Bissell conducted a "'black market' seminar in economics for [his] friends," delivering informal lectures in his rooms. His two most important auditors were Max Millikan and Walt Rostow, then undergraduates, who would go on to be the pillars of MIT's Center for International Studies, a paradigmatic social science ORU for the postwar university. In addition to the seminar, Bissell taught for several years an official undergraduate "economics theory course on model building" that featured Keynesian macroeconomics. Economic modeling and Keynesian macroeconomics were two major frameworks adopted by many proponents of the American modernity vision. Bissell was among the first American exponents of these views, in an influential place. Rostow and future university leaders McGeorge Bundy (who would become dean of the Faculty of Arts and Sciences at Harvard and later, president of the Ford Foundation) and Kingman Brewster (who would become president of Yale) sat under Bissell's formal teaching.[44]

Bissell's advocacy for Kerr's project was critical for the foundation's eventual decision to fund it. His relationship with Max Millikan played a key role. Bissell told Millikan that Ford had asked him to survey proposals in the economic field, and Millikan, aware of the Four's project through his MIT colleague Myers, told Bissell to look up the Four's proposal that Ford had rejected the previous year.[45] Bissell immediately wrote to McDaniel asking to see the proposal.[46] McDaniel, showing quick resistance, replied, "I can assure you that the decision to reject was reached only after the project was carefully reviewed."[47] McDaniel later wrote to associate director Milton Katz, who had also rebuked Bissell: "This illustrates why it is so important for our staff members to check our files before they make even tentative commitments to people. It seems to me that knowing that the proposal had been rejected [Bissell] should have looked into our reasons before giving these people any encouragement."[48] Bissell nevertheless pressed on. He argued for the proposal to be within his jurisdiction in Program Area III, economics, rather than in Program Area I, overseas programs. By June 1952, Bissell declined to take charge of setting up a formal Area III program and instead set up an "economic workshop" to review selected proposals, including the Four's.[49]

That summer, Bissell steered to approval an updated proposal from the Four, "Utilization of Human Resources: A Comparative Analysis."[50] He favored it in part because it involved "consideration of possible action by the US Government for the purpose of influencing the development of the labor movement in other parts of the world and of encouraging the development of free rather than communist-controlled labor unions."[51] Five other proposals on the topic of international labor came in at the same time, all from prominent scholars or institutions.[52] Bissell argued successfully for the superiority of the Kerr project on several grounds: its comparative analysis, the experience of its investigators, that supporting institutions such as IIR were already in place, and that it would "result in the production of useful benchmarks for the for-mulation and guidance of US private and public policy."[53] At Bissell's behest, the Ford Foundation trustees approved an $80,000 grant to the Four for a one-year pilot study that would involve planning the larger project.[54]

Kerr's statement reporting the Ford grant to the UC regents highlighted how ideas about American modernity informed the Four's policy goals. The Study intended "to provide some framework for the guidance of American policy in those foreign areas where it undertakes to influence the development of economic institutions through loans, private investment, and technical assistance. Its major premise is that definable relationships can be discovered between foreign aid and the development of institutions compatible with and favorable to democratic practices and policies."[55] In Kerr's mind, economic development and democracy were linked, and organized research would show how economic development could be pursued in a way that would bring about democracy overseas.

The next iteration of the Four's plans brought the project closer to the shape it would take for the high point of its lifespan. This process occurred in the midst of upheaval at the Ford Foundation. Its trustees made two momentous related decisions at their February 4 meeting: to move the Foundation's head-quarters to New York City and to demand Hoffman's resignation. The official explanation was that Hoffman wanted to remain in his Pasadena home, but privately the trustees were dissatisfied with the foundation's constant chaos under Hoffman. The trustees named Gaither president and McDaniel secre-tary.[56] The Four met with Gaither, McDaniel, and Dyke Brown in Berkeley on February 9. Brown, a partner in Gaither's law firm and previously assistant director of the Ford Foundation Study Committee, was the first of Gaither's new associate directors to come on board.[57] A UC Berkeley alum, he had been a Rhodes Scholar at Oxford simultaneously with Walt Rostow.[58] After the meet-ing, the Four prepared an "Interim Report" that summarized progress and asked for more money. They submitted it via a personal delivery by Dunlop to his Harvard colleague Donald K. David, dean of the Harvard Graduate School of Business Administration and leading trustee of the Ford Founda-tion, whom Henry Ford II had asked to be involved in day-to-day affairs during the transition to the Gaither administration.[59] The Four proposed a budget of

$480,000 over three years, including $225,000 to hire ten to fifteen research associates.

The most important new thematic emphases were industrialization and protest movements. Industrialization became a central concept that held the project together through the publication of *Industrialism and Industrial Man* in 1960. The Four believed that influencing protest movements, in part by making "our political and economic principles . . . more appealing," was a key tactic for keeping communism at bay. Treating the world as a machine to be operated by social engineers, they assumed they could control the rate of industrialization in underdeveloped countries. The trick, though, was not to push industrialization so fast that it created enough social dislocation to make fertile ground for communism. They wrote that "at the conclusion of this series of studies, we plan to submit a special report dealing with the policy implications of the analysis and findings." They never wrote such a report, but the plan to do so showed the policy orientation of the project in 1953. Their policy considerations included the extent to which American techniques in management and labor were applicable to industrializing countries, the extent to which American policy should seek to influence the behavior of labor movements abroad, and the best policies with regard to intellectuals, emerging labor movements, and social welfare in industrializing countries.[60]

Initial reaction from foundation officers was icy. They "agreed that action on this proposal will be held in abeyance until the economics program takes more decided form." McDaniel recorded for the files, "I think it is fair to state that it was the consensus of those present that the chances of supporting this project are not very numerous." He relayed the decision to Kerr in a phone call.[61]

The project's prospects brightened when Thomas H. Carroll joined the foundation in September 1953 as associate director with responsibility for the economics program, Area III. Like Bissell before him, but on a larger scale, Carroll proved to be the key advocate for securing Ford funds for the Inter-University Study. Carroll was Gaither's cousin, yet another Berkeley alum, and dean of the School of Business Administration at the University of North Carolina. He had assisted Gaither with the study committee, as had another new associate director hired at that time, Don K. Price Jr. Price would leave the Ford Foundation after a few years for Harvard, where he eventually became the first dean of the John F. Kennedy School of Government.[62] Carroll formalized the foundation's economics program, and decided to call it the Program in Economic Development and Administration because he hoped people would associate it with the prestigious Committee on Economic Development.[63] Carroll built the program with the assistance of an ad hoc advisory committee chaired by Robert Calkins, president of the Brookings Institution since 1952 and formerly dean of the UC Berkeley College of Commerce (predecessor to the School of Business Administration). The committee included Kerr's colleague Robert Aaron Gordon (a Berkeley economics professor who would later write the influential EDA report on American business schools), as well as eminent University of Michigan economist Kenneth Boulding, whom Kerr unsuccessfully recruited to come to Berkeley.[64] Calkins was in the midst of transforming Brookings into a major policy research center with close links to government and the Democratic Party, shedding its nonpartisan ideal.[65]

The Four began to cultivate Carroll's favor immediately upon his start with the foundation and continued for several months. Kerr met with Carroll in New York on September 4 and reported to his colleagues, "The purposes which seemed to impress Tom most were—(1) a general strategy to give us a better basis for our tactics in conflict with Russia—what institutions, what attitudes, etc. should be encouraged . . . our final report and policy recommendations are particularly important . . . theory is acceptable but it should have practical implications. . . . Someone should go through Foundation reports to see how we can tie in our proposals to the 'constitutional principles' of the Foundation—what phrases can we use. Foundation sponsors work in which *it* is interested—it does not just receive applications!"[66] Dunlop and Kerr then met with Carroll in November.[67] A few weeks later Kerr wrote to Dunlop that "very secretly, Aaron Gordon reports that Tom Carroll seemed to have been much impressed by the presentation we made to him. He cited before the *ad hoc* advisory committee to Area 3 our approach as the type the Foundation likes to have made—that is to say, one by the leaders in a field who put behind them the over-plowed sections in their area and then ask the Foundation to help in expansion along new lines. Aaron added in his report, 'I think you'll get your money.'"[68] Dunlop drafted a new report/proposal in mid-January and wrote to the others that "I delivered twenty copies of the report and the Financial Appendix, and five copies of each of the studies to Tom Carroll . . . there was sixty pounds of material, which on a weight basis seemed to influence Tom."[69] The entire Four then met with Carroll yet again, over dinner at the Waldorf-Astoria in late January.[70] A month later, the Ford trustees approved the grant, and the Four returned to the Waldorf-Astoria to constitute their board.[71] The Four's emphasis on the Study's potential for shaping American foreign policy appears to have been a key to securing funding. In Carroll's presentation to the Ford trustees, one "reason for recommendation" was that "the project calls for empirical, on-the-spot research by some of the country's leading experts in the social sciences from which information of immediate practical importance to policy makers should emerge."[72]

The policy orientation was not mere window dressing for the foundation's benefit—it was central to the Four's purposes at that time, as indicated by their cultivation of a relationship with US Secretary of Labor James Mitchell once their project was officially off the ground with the Ford grant. Kerr wrote to Dunlop in early 1955 that

> Mitchell's consultants met with him in D.C. last week. A major item was the foreign labor program. The idea *then* was to have the four of us be the nucleus of a small advisory group—we would be consulted about the additional people—to develop ideas for Labor (& potentially and probably increasingly for State). This group could influence the development of a *Review* in the field (perhaps quarterly), the running of conferences from time to time, as well as policy. Would give us a wonderful opportunity to have our research form one source of policy; it would certainly appeal to the Ford people; might afford basis for keeping our research going with funds after the end of the three year period, etc. Mitchell wants to get going soon—talked of meeting in D.C. this spring—he planned to write Gaither for permission to bring Fred and Charlie back for a few days at Labor expense.[73]

Mitchell seeking Gaither's permission to hire Harbison and Myers as consultants implied that the Ford Foundation had some kind of proprietary authority over the two men, as if they were on retainer. This whole complex of relationships departed from the prewar "morals of scholarship" that prioritized the scholar's independence, which the Four dismissed in their initial 1951 proposal to Ford. The Four showed no hesitation to entangle their scholarship with the government's foreign labor program. The relationship with Secretary Mitchell continued to bear fruit into 1956. The minutes of a board meeting in early January recorded that "Harbison, Dunlop, and Myers agreed to contact Jim Mitchell with regard to getting information on communist tactics through the labor attaches. It was understood that the authority to proceed with this undertaking would rest with the State Department. Our strategy, therefore, is to get Mitchell to make an approach with us to the State Department on this matter."[74] A few months later, Dunlop reported to Kerr that "Fred and Charlie have been working with Mitchell on a cabinet statement on 'human resources' and economic development."[75] The Four were using the relationship with Mitchell both to collect information for the Study and to popularize its ideas.

One Inter-University Study participant, however, did express concern about the eclipse in the moral economy of scholarship furthered by the Ford Foundation and embraced by his colleagues. Walter Galenson of UC Berkeley not only conducted research as part of the Study but also team-taught with Kerr a graduate seminar based on the Study.[76] He expressed his views during a conference panel on research approaches:

> I would like to begin with a warning against overly great enthusiasm and elaborate programming of research in this field. Generally, research in an academic environment is best performed if the selection of the subject and the execution of the research are left, as far as possible, to the individual researcher. The amount of enthusiasm which must be generated to carry a project through four or five years to completion bears a direct relationship to the degree to which the individual researcher has himself conceived the idea, and to the extent to which he is "sold" on it.

These comments showed that participants in organized research sometimes soured on it, in part because they believed it was less effective than research by individual investigators. Galenson continued by criticizing overreliance on patrons to fund such research:

> I think that there has been too much foundation-directed research. Thus, at the end of the war, everyone was interested in doing research in Europe. Now, there is a movement away from Europe to research in underdeveloped areas. In part, this shift reflects the change in American interests abroad, but I suspect that considerable influence has been exerted by foundations that have given large grants for particular areas. This situation is not desirable and the results will be meager. Universities should be able to resist the siren call of foundation money in general and in this field particularly. Nor do I believe that universities should gear their research programs too closely to governmental or business needs. Government needs are unpredictable and may be terminated on short notice. The programs of business concerns are apt to change rapidly.

Finally, Galenson offered his beliefs about the proper parameters of university research:

> Universities should, therefore, keep their projects broad and focus their research beyond mundane fact-gathering which is usually the hallmark of policy-oriented research . . . the goal of the university researcher should always be directed toward *theory* for the purpose of prediction. As far as possible, theory should be at the highest level of abstraction.

He went on to criticize the theory of Marx and others for being deductive. He argued "for more inductive work" toward theory building and cited Dunlop as a model for this approach.[77] He implicitly distinguished this theory-oriented inductive work from the "mundane fact-gathering" he associated with foundation-directed, "policy-oriented" research. The advocates of behavioral science during this time were likewise calling for theory-oriented inductive work, but in some cases were also trying to show how it could be applied to policy. Galenson thus provides an example of a scholar who, through experience in doing organized research, questioned that framework and reasserted a more traditional understanding of what university research should be.

Despite such ideas from one of his closest collaborators, Kerr in the Inter-University Study's early years enthusiastically directed policy-oriented research and seemed unconcerned about the new morals of scholarship that it reflected. He worked within a Cold War framework, focusing on how to steer labor protest movements in the underdeveloped world away from communism and on creating a general strategy to inform US tactics in that area. This research exhibited instrumental rationality by seeking means to ends predetermined by US foreign policy. The Ford Foundation encouraged such approaches. Although Kerr and his colleagues took steps to tailor their activities to Ford's preferences, they showed no signs of chafing at doing so, and they made a similar move with no pressure from Ford by putting themselves at the service of the Department of Labor. By the late 1950s, the tone of the Study changed, especially because of the group's findings that management, in part because of the way it shaped labor, was a more crucial factor than labor for economic development.

Administrative Science

At the same time as Kerr was pursuing the Inter-University Study in his field of industrial relations, he was becoming steeped in another mid-century social scientific discourse that shaped his view of the university's purpose—the quest to create a science of administration or management (the preferred term varied among proponents). This movement had its roots in the behavioral science paradigm. From 1950 onward, Kerr's activities related to behavioral science and administrative science laid the groundwork for a milestone address he delivered at the University of Pittsburgh in May 1957. Little noticed by later commentators, the address unveiled key ideas that Kerr later espoused to more acclaim in *Uses*, including notions of a knowledge economy. It also showed that Kerr conceived of the university's purpose in terms of administration—that the university was an instrument for administering society.

Kerr's profile in American social science broadly (beyond industrial relations) began to develop by 1950, when he traveled the country canvassing university social science programs on behalf of the Carnegie Corporation. This tour made him "more convinced than ever" that Berkeley needed facilities for survey research.[78] Around this time, the Ford Foundation launched Area V, the Behavioral Science Program (BSP), which advanced the practice and reputation of behavioral science. Ford issued a $2.7 million grant for strengthening behavioral sciences in 1950 and allocated the grant to thirteen American universities, including $300,000 to UC.[79] At the same time as he was lobbying Ford's EDA to fund the Inter-University Study, Kerr worked for Ford's BSP as a member of the visiting committee for the University of Chicago's Ford-funded self-study in the behavioral sciences, where he interacted with behavioral science pioneer James G. Miller.[80] Shortly thereafter, Kerr made an ill-fated attempt to install Miller and his group at Berkeley.[81] BSP also funded the most prominent institutionalization of behavioral science, the Center for Advanced Study in the Behavioral Sciences (CASBS), which opened in 1954 near Stanford University in Palo Alto, California. Kerr—whose record of involvement in multifarious academic activities across the country as one of the first "jet set" university administrators was staggering—served on the CASBS board of directors from 1954 until 1961, when his heavy duties as UC president led him to shed some of his extra-university involvements.[82] By the time of his Pittsburgh address in 1957, Kerr was an important voice in American social science.

UC's handling of the Ford grant became something of a debacle, but Kerr's ideas for the money provide insight into his thought and the tenets of behavioral science.[83] The protocol for this grant differed in two ways from standard practice in postwar social science. First, the grant was general rather than tied to a specific project; universities could use it for almost whatever they wanted, and sometimes designated the funds for enterprises only tangentially related to behavioral science per se. Second, the grant was to be distributed by the university president rather than by professors working on a specific funded project. This procedure meant that at UC, Sproul was in charge of distributing the money. Stunningly, Sproul delayed deciding how to allocate the money for almost six years, despite repeated pestering from Kerr and more than thirty proposals from faculty members and committees. In one such proposal, Harold Jones, director of Berkeley's Institute of Child Welfare, wrote, "Increasingly, major universities are finding it necessary to organize research around specifically designated centers. Although no fixed pattern has emerged, the important point about all of the recently developed centers (at, for example, the Universities of Michigan, Minnesota, North Carolina, and at Chicago

and Columbia) is the provision for an integrated attack upon the difficult problems of our society, without reference to departmental boundaries."[84] This
statement exemplified a major thrust of the instrumental university.

Kerr's petitions to Sproul for this money from 1951 to 1956 focused on integration and theory, two hallmarks of the behavioral science paradigm. He
repeatedly suggested different versions of an ORU that would bring together
social scientists from many disciplines to facilitate communication toward a
unified or general theory of human behavior. The motivation for this quest
was likely related to the Carnegie Project on Theory, directed by Talcott Parsons at Harvard from 1949 to 1951 on a Carnegie Corporation grant—
especially since Kerr had just finished reviewing social science programs for
Carnegie. Parsons's project led to the publication of an edited volume, *Toward
a General Theory of Action* (1951).[85] In a 1954 petition requesting $80,000 for a
"Social Theory Fund," Kerr told Sproul, "I have the distinct impression that
the University is losing some ground in the social sciences. Both in terms of
outstanding younger personnel and quality of publication, we do not have
the strength that we deserve. It also appears to me that those institutions
which are most attractive to the younger talented social scientists are those
in which efforts are being made to develop a nuclear social theory that will
link the empirical findings of psychology, anthropology, and sociology with
the logical methods and means of analysis supplied by new trends in philosophy and the theory of political behavior."[86] Kerr's promotion of integrated
theory, then, might have been at least partly motivated by a desire to raise his
institution's prestige; in general, elevating Berkeley's status was one of Kerr's
major goals as chancellor.[87] It is also possible that his main interest was in the
theory, and he simply used the prestige argument to sell the plan to Sproul. A
year later, he illustrated for Sproul the effect that a commitment of funds
might have on faculty recruitment. Berkeley was attempting to lure Kenneth
Boulding. He agreed to come, contingent on certain issues, including Berkeley's
establishment of an Institute for Integrated Studies in the Social Sciences that
Kerr had proposed to Sproul.[88] The Institute was not established, and Boulding stayed at Michigan. By 1956, Ford Foundation officials—understandably
upset with Sproul—demanded that UC return the money. He quickly created
Berkeley's Survey Research Center and Center for Integration of Social Science
Theory, to which Ford agreed to devote the bulk of the grant, but Ford still
made UC repay over $85,000.[89]

By the time these ORUs launched in 1956, Kerr had begun to espouse ideas
from an influential postwar project to create an administrative science centered on understanding human decision making. This field had two major
inputs—Herbert Simon's theorizing and the success of operations research

(OR) during World War II. The new theoretical approach to administration, articulated by Simon's *Administrative Behavior* (1945) and institutionalized at Carnegie Institute of Technology's Graduate School of Industrial Administration after he joined its faculty, held that people created organizations "to enable them to make decisions that they could not make alone." Organizations "were means for accumulating the resources necessary for decisionmaking."[90] In a 1952 essay, Simon "call[ed] for a complete overhaul of the principles of administration in order to turn it into a genuine science."[91] Operations research emerged from efforts of the British and American militaries, especially the US Army Air Force, to use quantitative, statistical analysis in determining how to use their weapons most effectively. More generally, OR was "a body of theoretical methods for solving allocation problems." The key move in OR was to go beyond providing quantitative information that managers used to make decisions, to providing techniques for making the decisions themselves.[92] After the war, OR became an academic pursuit in the United States, particularly influencing business and engineering schools and spawning graduate degree programs at several major universities by the 1950s. Milestones of professionalization included a National Research Council Committee on Operations Research established in the late 1940s; the field's first technical book, *Methods of Operations Research*, in 1951; and the founding of the Operations Research Society of America (ORSA) and an affiliated journal in 1952.[93]

Enthusiasts for decision science began in the mid-1950s to create organizations inside and outside the university—usually under the banner of "administrative science" or "management science"—to propagate their ideas. The term "management science" recalled Frederick Winslow Taylor's "scientific management" of the 1910s. Management science perpetuated Taylor's "faith that the best government was the most technocratic one and his notion that people were factors of production," even as it was based on a new theoretical approach that arose in the 1940s. Whereas scientific management was atomistic, in that it focused on improving the efficiency of each individual part of an enterprise, management science aimed to be holistic by focusing on the entire organization as a rationally interconnected whole, often called a "system."[94] Several of Kerr's characteristics and interests inclined him toward this program. He was a theory-oriented social scientist whose faculty position was in a business school, and the Inter-University Study was increasingly focusing on the role of management in world history and economic development.

Kerr promoted decision science at Berkeley by adding to the faculty one of the field's leading figures, C. West Churchman, who came from a different academic background than most of its other practitioners. He earned all his degrees in philosophy at the University of Pennsylvania and joined the philosophy faculty there in 1939. Like many of his decision science colleagues, Churchman worked for the military during World War II, as a statistician at the Frankford Arsenal in Philadelphia. He worked on the efficacy of weaponry, the same subject that spawned operations research, and he became a leader in OR as it blossomed. During those same years, Churchman also founded the Institute of Experimental Method in Philadelphia, which attempted to apply "E. A. Singer's concept of experiment to real social problems." Singer, a pragmatist follower of William James, was Churchman's dissertation advisor. After leaving Penn, Churchman taught briefly at Wayne State, then took a position in engineering administration at Case Institute of Technology in 1950. There he built a program in OR (including the first MS and PhD programs), convened the field's first conference in 1951, and coauthored its first textbook in 1957. Churchman and other thinkers from Case, Carnegie Tech (including Simon), and the RAND Corporation formed The Institute of Management Sciences (TIMS) in 1953 as a spinoff from ORSA and started a journal, *Management Science*, the following year.[95] Churchman served as the journal's editor-in-chief and chaired the TIMS Research Committee, which proposed a management science foundation to fund basic research in the field. It used the increasingly popular conceptual distinction between basic and applied research to frame its aspirations. The committee believed that operations research constituted the applied side of management science and was already flourishing. By contrast, the basic side, research on decision making in organizations, needed an infusion of funding to spark interest.[96]

Kerr and E. T. Grether hired Churchman to be "our Herb Simon" and help launch an ORU in management science, after trying unsuccessfully to get Simon himself. Grether recalled that "when I was [dean] and Clark Kerr was chancellor, we kept an offer before Herb Simon. Clark said that if he could ever bring Simon to the campus—so the offer was always waiting, but [Simon] was never willing."[97] Berkeley first brought Churchman as a visiting professor in 1957–1958, then permanently the following year.[98] Grether recalled that as part of this process, Berkeley's Office of the Budget Committee requested "a letter from Herbert Simon about this man . . . I talked to Herbert Simon, and he wrote to Clark Kerr a 'dear Clark' letter."[99] Churchman quickly gathered several new colleagues into a Management Science Research Group within the Institute of Industrial Relations, which initially secured $100,000 from the Ford Foundation for this new group.[100] After the group operated in this manner for three years, the university established it independently as the Center for Research in Management Science within the School of Business Administration.[101] In 1963, the new center won a $600,000 grant from the Ford Foundation.[102] Shortly thereafter, Berkeley received $1.2 million from the NSF to create the Management and Behavioral Sciences Laboratory, which included a computer facility to provide "new power to understand the decision maker."[103] Berkeley's success in courting Churchman contrasted with the failure of its earlier efforts, personally directed by Kerr, to hire Boulding and Miller (who ended up at Michigan with Boulding).[104]

Meanwhile, a group of scholars at Cornell University's School of Business and Public Administration, founded in 1946, promoted a unified science of administration. Cornell was perhaps the first university to combine business and public administration in a school. The key movers in administrative science were the public administrator Edward Litchfield and the sociologist James D. Thompson.[105] Litchfield earned all of his degrees at the University of Michigan, which had one of the oldest and most prominent public administration programs, and taught in that program from 1942 to 1945. He then served as a top administrator for the US military government in occupied Germany under General Lucius Clay. Litchfield arrived at Cornell in 1950 for a visiting faculty position and became dean by 1953. Thompson came to Cornell in 1954 directly from his doctoral studies at North Carolina. Together they started *Administrative Science Quarterly*.[106] The first issue, in June 1956, revealed the founders' aspirations for this new field. Editor Thompson wrote in an editorial that the name "expresses a belief in the possibility of developing an administrative science and a conviction that progress is being made and will continue." He also contributed an article, "On Building an Administrative Science." Litchfield wrote his own piece in that vein, "Notes on a General Theory of Administration." In a serious coup, *ASQ* attracted an article from Harvard's Talcott Parsons, a founding figure of behavioral science, titled "Suggestions for a Sociological Approach to the Theory of Organizations."[107]

Litchfield's success and persuasiveness drew the attention of foundation executive J. Steele Gow, a former University of Pittsburgh (Pitt) administrator, who introduced Litchfield to Pitt's trustees. Pitt named Litchfield chancellor in 1955, to begin in 1956.[108] He brought Thompson along to direct an administrative science center at Pitt, although the journal stayed at Cornell. Litchfield launched a program to make Pitt into one of the nation's top universities, but it ended in a spectacular failure. The Commonwealth of Pennsylvania took over the university in 1965 to save it from financial insolvency—ironically a result of Litchfield's poor administration, despite *Time* dubbing him "a coldly brilliant administrator"—and he resigned in some disgrace.[109]

What is most interesting for our story, however, is that Pitt chose Clark Kerr as one of the principal speakers for a scholarly forum celebrating Litchfield's inauguration. Even more telling is that Kerr spoke on administrative science. Apparently he considered this event too significant to give a boilerplate speech;

he approached it as a platform for serious intellectual engagement. He worked on his talk for months in advance and solicited feedback from two major figures in the field of business administration, Grether and Calkins.[110]

Kerr wrote to Calkins asking for a copy of a speech on "The Economy and the University" that Calkins had given at the seventy-fifth anniversary celebration of the University of Pennsylvania's Wharton School of Finance and Commerce in March 1957. After reading the speech, Kerr wrote to Calkins, "I found your comments at Wharton the most sensible and interesting I have seen."[111] Calkins's speech argued that innovation and capable management were two critical components of economic growth. His statement that "the universities have ahead a large responsibility to train the scientists and engineers that are so necessary to economic growth" reflected the common postwar trope about specialized manpower. But Calkins broke ground when he turned to the importance of a scholarly field of administration for enabling capable management that would lead to economic growth. Although he appears to have addressed primarily business administration, he repeatedly referred simply to administration as a unique body of knowledge that warranted a place in the university distinct from other disciplines. Two related claims anchored Calkins's delineation of the field of administration. First, administration was distinct from science and indeed went beyond it: "Administration comprehends a wider range of activities and skills than the social sciences. It is more than any science, it is also a practice." He emphasized that, unlike science, administration looked toward the achievement of some particular purpose. Second, analysis of the process of decision making could be an intellectual core for administrative science researchers, "a central purpose around which to organize their work." By doing so, they "would discover a growing need for systematic operational knowledge that lies well beyond the traditional concerns of economics and the other social sciences" and thus gain territory and prestige for their field.[112] Some of these ideas likely came from Simon and his Carnegie Tech colleagues, whom Calkins cited multiple times in a similar address that he published in 1959 as *The Art of Administration and the Art of Science*.[113]

Grether responded to Kerr's query with comments on a paper Kerr had presented to the American Association of Collegiate Schools of Business in April 1956, "Business Leadership and Economic Development," suggesting how Kerr might revise the views of that paper for his Pittsburgh talk. Grether's comments indicated a belief that managers and organizational structure were keys to economic development, and therefore that universities must focus research on those issues. Grether recommended that Kerr enlarge his discussion of the centrality of managerial behavior for industrialization (presumably drawing on an emerging argument of *Industrialism and Industrial Man*, discussed below) and of how graduate education would proliferate as the complexity of the manager's role increased. Grether's letter closed with a stirring peroration urging Kerr to promote the view that decision making was more science than art. Grether attacked Harvard Business School's famous case-study method in graduate business education for relying too much on intuition rather than on "principle" and "systematic bodies of knowledge," and lauded Simon's approach: "The Carnegie group and some of us here in Berkeley feel that not all must be left to 'intuition.'" From Grether's viewpoint, Harvard taught "art" while Carnegie Tech and Berkeley taught science.[114] He had visited Harvard and Carnegie Tech, and recalled how Simon "was standing above the case, looking down at it, searching for principle; and the Harvard people kept the students inside the case and gave them vicarious business experience."[115]

Grether encouraged Kerr to "soft pedal the reference to schools of business being drawn increasingly into service type research. This, of course, is true but it likewise represents a danger. In my view, too many of the schools of business have in recent years too readily capitulated to service type research and other activities."[116] This statement harkened back to a 1940 decision by a Calkins-chaired Berkeley faculty committee on which Grether sat. That committee decided not to pursue an offer extended by the US Department of Commerce to establish at UC Berkeley a cooperative bureau of business research for the Twelfth Federal Reserve District, because it was concerned that the particular type of government involvement envisioned might threaten the university's independence. Instead, the committee wanted the university alone to establish a Bureau of Business and Economic Research, and then draw on Commerce's resources to fund individual projects.[117] Grether's comments to Kerr and the earlier decision regarding Commerce indicated the tension between research and service and suggested how a theory of administration might ease the tension. Administrative science research could be appropriate for the university and still render service, because its results would stimulate economic development.

Grether's suggestions about social scientific approaches to administration and organization indicate how Kerr's work was closely tied to some of the most important thinkers of the time on these matters. Grether told Kerr that "you might wish to enlarge your reference to education for administration in general by reference also to the newer developments in organizational theory and communications theory, all of which range outside into social science in general."[118] A year after Kerr's talk, Herbert Simon and James March gave wide circulation to these "newer developments in organizational theory" in their landmark book *Organizations.* Simon and March worked right down the street from Pitt at Carnegie Tech and could easily have attended Kerr's talk. A book that would become even more prominent, William Holly Whyte's *Organization Man*, appeared the year before Kerr's address and provided a searching analysis of how large organizations impacted American society and individuals' lives. Kerr mentioned Whyte's book in his speech, then sent Whyte a copy of the speech.[119] Kerr had a complicated relationship with the ideal and practice of "organization." Kerr frequently spoke on the danger that organizations posed to individual freedom, and Whyte's book quoted him to that effect. Yet as Mary Soo and Cathryn Carson have pointed out, in many ways "Kerr was in fact an 'organization man' *par excellence.*"[120]

In his talk at Pitt, Kerr spoke specifically about business administration and schools of business. Their major problem, in his view, was that they were largely schools of applied social science, especially economics, with nothing uniquely theoretical to hold them together. The business school had "a problem of carving out a discipline of its own which will distinguish it from Economics and which will have enough inherent possibilities to permit its followers to gain intellectual stature." Drawing explicitly on Calkins and Grether, Kerr discussed how a theory of administration might remedy this problem. He delineated three major types of business schools. The most likely type to be found in an elite research university, the Academic-Business School, focused on "basic research . . . to create a new theory of administration (not just business administration) with emphasis on decision-making . . . . The concern here is with how decisions are made, not with how to make decisions. A new discipline may be in the process of creation. If business administration is ever to have a theoretical core, it will be supplied by this source."[121] No doubt Litchfield was pleased to hear Kerr speak of such convictions to celebrate his inauguration.

In addition to showing how the quest for an administrative science was a key backdrop for Kerr's ideas about the university, the Pitt talk allows us to glimpse the initial stages of Kerr's thinking on how the university related to the emerging "knowledge economy." He set forth two of the central ideas that he would propound to significantly more attention six years later in his landmark *The Uses of the University*: that the university was becoming the crossroads of society, and that industry increasingly sought as its most important input new knowledge provided by the university. Kerr forged these ideas about the university's purpose in the smelter of his thinking about how education in business administration might further economic development.

Kerr employed the "university as crossroads" image differently at Pittsburgh than he would later in *Uses*. He told the Pittsburgh audience that the University instead of being an 'ivory tower' removed from the events and pressures of the day, is becoming one of the most important crossroads of society—a crossroads traversed not by students and scholars alone but by representatives of every industry, every profession, every level of government. From being maintained on the periphery of society, it is being drawn into the very center of our societal processes. It not only preserves the past and prepares the future but it also increasingly helps *administer* the present. Instead of the distant past and the distant future, its attention is focused more and more on the current moment of time and the players now on the stage. Business Administration is as much involved as any field in this transformation of the University."[122]

He thus used the image to describe the present state of universities. By contrast, in *Uses* he employed the image to describe the late nineteenth-century American land-grant university, which was "a dramatic break with earlier American traditions in higher education. It created a new social force in world history. Nowhere before had universities been so closely linked with the daily life of so much of their societies. The university campus came to be one of the most heavily traveled crossroads in America—an intersection traversed by farmers, businessmen, politicians, students from almost every corner of almost every state. The cloister and the ivory tower were destroyed by being thrown open to all qualified comers."[123] There is no obvious interpretation of why Kerr changed the application of the "university as crossroads" image between 1957 and 1963. But we know that during that period he was planning the UC Irvine campus (described in chapter 6) and conceptualized it as a new kind of land-grant university for economic development. Perhaps his line of thinking went as follows: the present transformation of the university that business schools were helping to drive—particularly the imperative to "administer the present" with an eye toward economic development, aided by a more theoretically sophisticated study of administration—was part of a process begun decades earlier with the dawn of the land-grant university ideal in the United States.

With respect to the importance of university-based knowledge for industry, which constituted one element of the university's new position at the crossroads of society, Kerr more closely followed the Pitt speech in *Uses*. The major exception was that in *Uses* Kerr featured the new term "knowledge industry," coined by Fritz Machlup in 1962 and thus not available at the time of the Pitt talk. The term "knowledge industry" had a jarring sound that gave Kerr's *Uses* lectures a certain resonance lacking in the Pitt talk—a resonance that UC Berkeley students used shortly thereafter to attack his leadership. At Pitt, Kerr said that "business is waiting at the [university's] very doorstep, and in some cases inside the door, for the new discoveries. The presence of a great University is becoming a locational factor for some industries, more important than new materials and markets. The University with its library, its laboratories, its training facilities, its faculty to consult, its flow of ideas is a most dynamic element in a dynamic world. No great industrial region of the future can afford to be without a great University."[124] Kerr's assertion that the university was more important than materials or markets for industry heralded the arrival of a new framework connecting universities and economic development, which Peter Drucker, another advocate of administrative science, would influentially dub the "knowledge economy" in the late 1960s.[125] Kerr was one of the first to recognize and articulate it, over a decade earlier. Drucker initiated correspondence with Kerr over a different matter in 1955. Apparently the two had never met, but Drucker wrote in some detail to praise Kerr's article, "'Industrial Conflict and Its Mediation," with "real admiration on a magnificent and pioneering job."[126] Kerr sent a pro forma reply, suggesting that he did not view Drucker as a major figure at that time.[127]

In the section of *Uses* titled "The knowledge industry," Kerr used a similar image as at Pitt, but portrayed industry acting more aggressively: "Sometimes industry will reach into a university laboratory to extract the newest ideas almost before they are born. Instead of waiting outside the gates, agents are working the corridors."[128]

Regarding ideas developing in the university, Kerr saying that industry would "extract" them is significant. Traditionally, the verb "extract" had indicated removing raw materials from the earth, not ideas from a university. Kerr's use of the verb connects his discussion in *Uses*, which only implicitly framed knowledge as replacing raw material in industrial importance, back to the Pitt talk where he did so more explicitly.

Kerr's speech at Litchfield's Pittsburgh inauguration shows us some of Kerr's most important ideas in the process of creation. It suggests how the behavioral science paradigm, the quest for an administrative science, the business school context, and his allegiance to the ideal of economic development came together to shape his view of the university. According to behavioral science, society was a system that must be kept at equilibrium by the use of "intellect" (Kerr's term from *Uses*). This process was administration, and the intellect was thoroughly instrumental. The university, as the "city of intellect," therefore had a charge to "administer the present"—in other words, to administer modern society.[129] It was a new kind of social control.

Industrialism and the University

As Kerr was promoting administrative science and using its ideas to frame the university's purpose, the Inter-University Study moved forward awash in Ford dollars, and the Four increasingly turned their attention toward writing their hallmark book, *Industrialism and Industrial Man*. Despite its foundation funding, the book aimed not to solve specific social problems or provide policy guidance (at least overtly), but to propound "a coherent and general theory of industrialization and its impact on managers and workers." It would "offer [this] framework of general explanation" by setting forth both the universal and the unique features they observed in studying industrialization in various parts of the world. These aspirations to generality were in line with the behavioral science paradigm. They called their "general" framework "the logic of industrialism."[130] According to Nils Gilman, "Kerr had inherited the term *industrialism* from the godfather of technocratic thought, Claude Henri de Rouvroy, Lecomte de Saint-Simon."[131] In Kerr and his colleagues' parlance, industrialism was "an abstraction," a vision of a society with characteristic relationships, toward which the whole world was moving through the process of industrialization. Industrialism's central characteristic was "the inevitable and eternal separation of industrial men into managers and the managed." In the Four's vision of industrialism, conflict declined and consensus developed between labor and management.[132] Given that the conflictual nature of labor-management relations sparked the founding of academic industrial relations, this vision of industrialism imagined the ultimate triumph of that field. The Four even wrote that their field was a product of industrialism, and that it "trained . . . technicians" for organizations.[133]

Industrialism and Industrial Man argued that managers and the education that produced them were the primary drivers of economic development. The Four began the Study planning to focus on "labor problems" as the title suggested, but their research led them to the view that the manager was the central figure in industrial society. As Kerr explained to Henry Luce in a July 1956 letter encouraging him to meet with Harbison or Myers, "We gradually concluded that the labor problem was largely a management problem and so the focus of our study has changed considerably."[134] In *Industrialism and Industrial Man*, the Four asserted that "management is the principal determinant of the productivity of labor." Even when the laborers were scientists and engineers in industrial laboratories, they needed to be "coordinated and directed by divisional and top managers." In advanced industrialization, "the enterprise emerges as an organization of high-talent managerial resources." Concurrently, "the largest part of the higher education system" became devoted to producing the required managers. The Four argued that education must retain "some degree of generality" due to "the rapidity of change" and to help the managers "coordinating and leading the specialists."[135]

The Four's interpretive framework, "the logic of industrialism," amounted to a philosophy of history intended to challenge that of Marx. They even paraphrased Marx and Engels in saying, "The giant of industrialization is stalking the earth, transforming almost all the features of older and traditional societies."[136] "The logic of industrialism" meant not that industrialism *had* a logic, but that industrialism *was* a logic—"the logic of the industrialization process"— that drove history forward. Industrialism was "compelling mankind to march through history at an ever faster rate." The Four argued for "the invincibility of the industrialization process" and that "countries are moving relentlessly through a transition period toward industrialism." The process was not monolithic—industrialism set "only the general direction of this march," not "the specific route of the march or the exact pace to be followed." Countries traveled "at different speeds and on different roads, but they all aspire to reach the industrial society."[137] History was the story of a convergence toward a social form, "pluralistic industrialism."[138] The Four's theory of industrialism was one version of a dominant paradigm in postwar American social science, modernization theory, which aimed to describe the transition from "traditional" to "modern" society.[139]

The Inter-University Study brought together three of the modern ideals— industrial relations, economic development, and administration—that shaped the instrumental university. The full titles of the Study and the book reflected the authors' intense concern with economic development. The Four defined economic development as the spread of industrialization and concluded that "the structuring of the labor force is *the* labor problem in economic development."[140] For that reason, the Study gave attention to how such structuring occurred. In a seminal article that emerged from the Study, Kerr and Abraham Siegel introduced the concept that a "web of rules" governed the structuring of the labor force.[141] Theodore Schultz, the University of Chicago economist who would soon pioneer human capital theory and later win a Nobel Prize, told Kerr, "I can count on one hand the occasions when I have come up against thought on labor where I have felt I was being led on to new ground." The Kerr/Siegel article was one of four that Schultz listed.[142] The Four believed that industrialism necessarily generated this web of rules as it overtook a society; they described industrialism as "weaving a web of rules." They held that "this web of rules is a universal phenomenon and many of the same rules turn up in the same industries, regardless of the contrasting nature of the societies within which they are found." The web of rules spelled out the authority of the manager and the framework for relations between the manager and the managed. It "concerns compensation, discipline, layoffs, transfers and promotions, grievances, and a vast array of matters . . . The rules also establish norms of output, pace, and performance."[143] Kerr's ideas about a web of rules resonated with a tendency in American social science of this era to portray rationality as "following rules." The era's organizational revolution shaped this tendency, which—not surprisingly—had connections to decision science.[144]

The notion of a web of rules led directly to the importance of administration, because Kerr believed that rules must be administered effectively in order to achieve full impact. In an early article, Kerr distinguished administration from policy (or rule making) and suggested that administration was primarily about how rules are applied, interpreted, and enforced.[145] Sometimes, Kerr portrayed the web of rules as created by managers, "enforced upon the many who are managed."[146] But in the early article and in *Industrialism and Industrial Man*, Kerr noted that administration was not solely a management function; workers and the government also had "a significant part in . . . administration of the rules."[147] In the article, Kerr laid out criteria for the effectiveness of administration and argued that choices about how to organize administration—in his example, whether administration of wage stabilization rules during World War II should be organized by region or by industry—had a normative element.[148] He also emphasized that the quality of administrative personnel was more important than method. These ideas suggest why Kerr believed administration was so crucial for economic development. Since the structuring of the labor force was a key to economic development, and the web of rules governed the structure of the labor force, and effective administration was required for the web of rules to function, it thus followed that effective administration was a key to economic development. From there it was just one more step to reason that if social science theorizing might improve administration, it could also spur economic development.

Industrialism and Industrial Man asserted that education was "the handmaiden of industrialism." Industrialization "requires an educational system functionally related to the skills and professions imperative to its technology." This technology was "based upon research organizations: universities, research institutes, laboratories, and specialized departments of enterprises. The methods and procedures of scientific research are likewise applied to a variety of economic and social problems." These research organizations "develop scientific, professional, technical, and managerial specialists indispensable to the operation and administration of the industrial society. The industrial society requires increasing numbers of this high-level manpower." The latter idea became increasingly prominent in the Four's thinking as the Study progressed, and the question "how should education adjust to the need for high-level manpower? . . . came to interest [them] a good deal more than [they] expected."[149] University leaders in the 1950s commonly said that their institutions should train specialized manpower to operate an increasingly complex society.[150] But the Four took this manpower trope to a new level and made it more targeted. The Four's frequent invocations of "high-level manpower" (or "high-talent manpower") usually meant managerial professionals.[151] After the publication of *Industrialism and Industrial Man*, Harbison and Myers focused their Inter-University Study work on the manpower question, which led to their book *Education, Manpower, and Economic Growth* (1964). It was "a policy-oriented work . . . a blueprint for action" for "education and manpower planners." Among those who read the manuscript was a young colleague of Harbison, William G. Bowen.[152] Then an associate professor of economics at Princeton, within a few years he would become that institution's provost, and later its president and an influential figure in American academia.[153]

In *Industrialism and Industrial Man*, Kerr implied that industrialism mandated an instrumental conception of the university. He argued that universities in industrial society were "not primarily concerned with conserving traditional values or perpetuating the classics." Rather, "The higher educational system of the industrial society stresses the natural sciences, engineering, medicine, managerial training, whether private or public, and administrative law." In this system, "the social sciences are strongly related to the training of managerial groups and technicians for the enterprise and the government." He went so far as to say that "higher education and research become two of the larger and more important industries" as skill levels increase toward the ideal of industrialism.[154] If Kerr was right about "the logic of industrialism," then the instrumental university was inevitable.

This theorizing about industrialism shaped the philosophy of education that guided Kerr as UC president, a position he assumed in mid-1958. During the first several months of 1958, the Four drafted many of the chapters for *Industrialism and Industrial Man*, including Kerr's contribution of chapter 2, "The Logic of Industrialism."[155] This chapter informed his inaugural address to the Riverside campus, "Education for the Twenty-First Century," one of several such speeches that Kerr delivered that fall during a grand tour of UC campuses. He began with the argument that two great forces, industrialization and the explosion of knowledge, were "producing changes in everyday life so drastic and fundamental, and affecting so many people, that it is no exaggeration to say we are entering a new era in the history of mankind." This statement exemplified Kerr's tendency to see world-historical forces shaping universities. Kerr believed that in the new era, "our welfare, our progress, even our survival will rest squarely upon reasoning man's ability to control and direct these forces which he has set in motion." As a result, "it is an era when the worth of intellect will be more apparent than ever before."[156] What Kerr left unsaid, however, is that his description emphasized the *instrumental* capacity of intellect—"to control and direct" rather than to discover. Five years later in *Uses*, he would call the university "the city of intellect." His description of intellect suggests that, compared to a typical view of the research university at the turn of the twentieth century, Kerr saw the university more as an agent for shaping society directly and less as an institution with special protections that facilitated the refining of knowledge in the disciplines.

The main thrust of Kerr's Riverside address examined the educational implications of five "imperatives" of "the logic of industrialization." He expected higher education to conform to these imperatives rather than standing outside of them and conceiving alternatives. Industrialism's "extreme proliferation of specialized occupational tasks," he said, meant that society would need

FIGURE 2. As president of the multicampus University of California, the nation's largest university system, Clark Kerr hired and supervised the chancellor of each campus. He is pictured with all nine chancellors circa 1963 (left to right): Dean McHenry (Santa Cruz), Herbert York (San Diego), Franklin Murphy (Los Angeles), Emil Mrak (Davis), President Kerr, Edward Strong (Berkeley), Vernon Cheadle (Santa Barbara), John Saunders (San Francisco), Daniel G. Aldrich Jr. (Irvine), Herman Spieth (Riverside). UC Berkeley Campus Events [graphic], UARC PIC 400:148. Courtesy of The Bancroft Library, University of California, Berkeley.

"enormous numbers of skilled personnel, trained in scientific, technical, and administrative techniques, and this training will have to be very highly specialized." The notion of "technical techniques" suggests the thoroughly instrumental nature of this prescription. Kerr focused on the implications for liberal education of the other four imperatives. The growth of large-scale organizations required a "tremendous array of executive talent to manage the many centers of power," and these managers "must be generalists" who receive a liberal education including "some rigorous study of the history and methodology of science" because each center related to all the rest. The next two imperatives were closely related: the increasing complexity of society, and the increasing complexity and interrelation of the whole world. The latter implied that the American university must emphasize the understanding of foreign languages and cultures, a conventional view in the postwar years. From the former point, however, Kerr made an interesting jump, informed by both his long-standing concern for preserving individual liberty and the public debate over the conformist perils of mass society that had followed the publication of *The Organization Man* two years earlier. In a society of increasing complexity, Kerr said, individuals might stick to a group for comfort. Liberal education could broaden horizons, thus helping students to place these commitments in the perspective of larger societal needs and to realize that one must protect individual rights from intrusions of private associations as well as from the state.

Kerr went further on the subject of liberal education, suggesting that university leaders must redefine it for the age of industrialism. His insistence that industrialism would continue to fuel ever-rising productivity and standards of living exhibited a core tenet of the American modernity vision, that ceaseless economic development would bring a better world. Kerr told the Riverside audience that "even before the year 2000 the four-day work week will become a reality for most of us." As a result, "universities [should] provide students with the resources and incentives to reap the rich benefits of our new leisure and the wealth of our material products. Conformity can be a problem in the cultural sphere as well as elsewhere. Mass production can lead all too easily to indiscriminate mass consumption."[157] Kerr's precise meaning was elusive, but it seems that he wanted UC to teach students how to consume material goods discriminatingly. He did not believe liberal education should cause students to question the framework of consumption and its centrality for life. That reading is buttressed by another 1958 speech, in which Kerr said, "David Riesman has noted that . . . consumption is replacing production as the channel for individual self-expression. Indeed, the individual's freedom of choice as a consumer is perhaps the most immediately effective freedom he has." Kerr observed that liberal education might "improve the quality" of such consumer choices.[158] Six years later, during the campus uprising known as the Free Speech Movement, UC Berkeley students would revolt against (among other things) the notion that the university should teach students how to be satisfied with material well-being.

After Kerr's inauguration, the Four embarked on a six-week world tour during winter 1958–1959 to promote their work. The Ford Foundation funded this journey, and Carroll's presence on the trip signified the foundation's intimate involvement in the project. The June 1956 board minutes recorded nonchalantly that "in 1959 the Board members will travel around the world together for three months during which the report will be finished," as if such a voyage was commonplace for a group of American academics.[159] By May 1957, they had decided that the tour should be a series of conferences "in various parts of the world to discuss our tentative findings with scholars, government officials, labor and management representatives in various countries and regions."[160] The actual tour, shorter than proposed, departed on December 21, 1958 and returned on January 31, 1959. In the intervening weeks, Kerr, Dunlop, Harbison, Myers, and Carroll visited Rome, Athens, Istanbul, Beirut, Tehran, Karachi, Delhi, Calcutta, Jakarta, Singapore, Hong Kong, Tokyo, and Honolulu. They wrapped up their tour on February 5 with a press conference at Kerr's sprawling home high in the Berkeley hills.[161] During the world tour, Kerr engaged in other activities related to the attempt to spread the American way of life around the world through the university. He visited the University of California's tumultuous "economics project" in Jakarta (part of a genre of university activity to which chapter 4 is devoted) and delivered a lecture in New Delhi on "University Administration in the USA," sponsored by the Indian Institute of Public Administration.[162] Also in New Delhi, Kerr invited Gunnar Myrdal, one of the most celebrated writers on international economic development during the 1950s, to join the Four.[163] These activities exhibited the prominence of Kerr and his colleagues, their continuing policy orientation despite its de-emphasis in *Industrialism and Industrial Man*, and the missionary overtones of their project to spread American modernity.

As the 1950s came to a close, Kerr had another experience that raised his national stature and probably shaped *The Uses of the University*. He served on Dwight Eisenhower's President's Commission on National Goals, which gave him a high-profile platform from which to articulate a domestic policy angle of his obsession with economic development. Kerr spoke forcefully on the need for the United States to generate a specific level of economic growth. He penned a chapter, "An Effective and Democratic Organization of the

Economy," in the commission report, *Goals for Americans*, published as a mass-market paperback in 1960. The commission worked in the wake of increasing uneasiness about the Soviet Union's rapid economic growth and of conviction among some that the United States must redouble its own efforts in order to maintain its economic advantage over the USSR.[164] The commission issued a nuanced statement that "the economy should grow at the maximum rate consistent with primary dependence upon free enterprise and the avoidance of marked inflation" but declined to set a numerical goal for growth rate, noting that "there is no merit in a statistical race with the Communist nations." Kerr believed a bolder approach was required, and added his own addendum: "I should prefer to state as our goal an economic growth rate of not less than 4 per cent, and, if reasonably possible, 5 per cent annually. Our many essential national objectives and tasks require such a growth rate and justify the measures which may be necessary to accomplish this rate of growth."[165] This statement exhibited Kerr's devotion to economic growthmanship, a key element of American modernity. This stance gave primacy to economic growth over other economic goals such as full employment, economic stability, and preventing inflation.[166]

The demand for Kerr's services intensified in the Democratic administrations that succeeded Eisenhower. John F. Kennedy made economic growth a top issue in the 1960 presidential campaign, and the Democratic platform called for a 5 percent annual growth rate. The Kennedy and Lyndon Johnson administrations made economic growth the cornerstone of an expansive vision of what the United States could accomplish domestically and internationally, a new politics that Robert Collins has dubbed "growth liberalism."[167] According to Kerr, Kennedy offered him the position of secretary of labor, and Johnson did the same for the position of secretary of health, education, and welfare. Kerr declined both positions because he did not feel he should leave the UC presidency at those specific times, but he did serve on the President's Advisory Committee on Labor-Management Policy that spanned both administrations.[168]

The President's Commission on National Goals also immersed Kerr in a robust discussion about "national goals" and "national purpose" that occupied American elites during the years around 1960.[169] Kerr might have had this discussion in mind when he crafted one of his most famous arguments in *Uses*: "The university has become a prime instrument of national purpose. This is new. This is the essence of the transformation now engulfing our universities."[170] He might also have drawn on Harold Stoke's book *The American College President* (1959), which at the time Kerr wrote *Uses* was one of the two leading books on the academic presidency, along with Harold Dodds's *The Academic*

FIGURE 3.   President John F. Kennedy, UC president Clark Kerr, and UC president emeritus Robert G. Sproul (far right) enter Memorial Stadium in Berkeley for Charter Day exercises, March 1962. UC Berkeley Campus Events [graphic], UARC PIC 04:667. Courtesy of The Bancroft Library, University of California, Berkeley.

President: Educator or Caretaker? (1962). Although Kerr cited Dodds and not Stoke in *Uses*, a couple of his descriptions were similar to Stoke's. In describing the recent transformation of the university, Stoke said that its leading characteristic was "the acceptance of education as an instrument of national policy." Unlike Kerr, Stoke critiqued this trend, arguing that "the 'power' subjects flourish in such a climate, the contemplative subjects wither."[171] The other similarity came in Stoke's and Kerr's respective definitions of the university presidency. When Kerr famously said that the university president had become "mostly a mediator," Stoke had already used the terms "broker" and "arbiter" in a similar description.[172] Both men emphasized that the president had become less of an intellectual visionary as he took on the new role. The point of this analysis is not to accuse Kerr of plagiarism, but to suggest that some of his most famous descriptions of the postwar university were adaptations of ideas circulating among higher education leaders at the time rather than his unique insights. As Kerr became the face and voice of the American university in the early 1960s, then, he channeled a number of important intellectual and political currents of the day. Above all, his commitments were grounded in a view of history that insisted the world was moving inexorably forward toward a more harmonious, more prosperous industrialism, and that the university must change along with this tide.

Governor Earl Warren, when he pushed the University of California to create an Institute of Industrial Relations, probably did not envision its signature accomplishment being a study that had as its central finding a grand theory about industrialism and sent its leaders on a round-the-world trip to promote their views. Industrial relations thinkers have often considered the Inter-University Study—like many of the ambitious projects described in this book—a disappointment. They have noted that it "is rarely cited" in current industrial relations literature, "has generated little in the way of ideas or concepts that are used in other research work," had little effect on US foreign policy, and did not produce an adequate overarching theory of industrialization.[173] Unexpectedly, the Study had its greatest influence outside industrial relations—on American higher education as a whole. The Study's ideas shaped Kerr's actions in prominent positions of academic leadership, and he articulated them to a broad audience.

The story of Kerr during the decade in which he conducted the Study suggests that the instrumental impulse in the postwar university prevailed more broadly yet less deeply than one might suspect. It was not confined only to specific academic approaches, such as empirical studies of particular problems over against theory, or only to certain structures such as ORUs over against departments. Yet problem-centered research and ORUs, while hallmarks of the instrumental university, were not always instrumental and did not always triumph. Sometimes scholars (such as many advocates of behavioral science) pursued theory for instrumental reasons, and sometimes ORUs withered. The spread of the behavioral science paradigm contributed to the creation of ORUs, especially by suggesting ways to link theory to social engineering. The rise of the new Ford Foundation—with its emphasis on problem-centered research and program titles such as "Behavioral Science" and "Economic Development and Administration"—fostered the proliferation of ORUs. All five postwar Berkeley ORUs discussed in this chapter—the Institute of Industrial Relations, the Institute of International Studies, the Survey Research Center, the Center for Integration of Social Science Theory, and the Center for Research in Management Science—received Ford money and had some connection to behavioral science. As the university increasingly became an instrument for achieving social purposes, such ORUs became abundant in the American university landscape. Kerr's promotion of these ORUs reveals that

he actively sought to reorganize UC Berkeley in light of foundation preferences, thereby contributing to the tendency for external entities such as foundations to help set priorities for university research. Such activity underpinned
his statement in *The Uses of the University* that the university's "directions have
not been set as much by [its] visions of its destiny as by the external environment, including the federal government, the foundations, the surrounding
and sometimes engulfing industry."[174] Contrary to Christopher Newfield's
assertion that Kerr "lamented" this phenomenon, the archival record shows
that Kerr advanced it.[175]

More broadly, Kerr's enthusiasm for the modern ideals of industrial relations, planning, economic development, and administration, along with his
promotion of related social scientific movements such as behavioral science
and decision science, shaped his technocratic, managerial, and thus instrumental vision of the elite American research university. For Kerr, making the university more instrumental was compatible with raising its academic quality
and in fact a pathway to that goal. As he implemented this vision in California
higher education and communicated it in *The Uses of the University*, he did
much to promote the instrumental university in the postwar United States.

CHAPTER 3

The Urban University as Community Service Institution

Pennsylvania in the Era of Gaylord P. Harnwell

When Gaylord P. Harnwell retired as president of the University of Pennsylvania (Penn) in 1970 after overseeing a transformation of the university during his seventeen-year tenure, the City of Philadelphia issued a mayoral proclamation in his honor. It lauded him for "presid[ing] over the formation of this new tradition of responsible educational participation in society" and noted that "the University [adopted] a new emphasis on social and community services which has altered the traditional role of the institution to that of more significantly involved citizenship."[1]

City officials were not alone in feting Harnwell. Five years earlier the Greater Philadelphia Movement, an elite citizen group devoted to promoting city planning, presented him its Philadelphia Award. Harnwell was a member of this group and had been chairman of its executive committee.[2] Its press release noted that "under his direction the University is more than a place of learning; it is a service institution participating in the daily life of our city."[3] These recognitions from community leaders must have pleased Harnwell, because they suggested he had achieved one of his main goals: to make Penn a "community service institution." Over against a conception of the university as a place removed from societal pressures in order to protect the scholarly search for truth, Harnwell believed that the problems of society should shape the university's scholarly agenda. In his view, the university was an instrument for achieving important social purposes.

Harnwell sounded this tone in his first presidential address to Penn's student body, at the Fall 1953 opening convocation. "A university," he declared, "is a community of men and women united in their concern with the significant problems of men and devoted to the acquisition and dissemination of knowledge relative to these problems."[4] In this statement, Harnwell staked positions in two important debates over the nature of universities. First, by using the phrase "problems of men," Harnwell alluded to John Dewey, the most prominent American thinker of the previous half century, who had died a year earlier. Dewey had titled his last substantial work, a collection of previously published essays fronted by a new introduction on the present state of philosophy, *Problems of Men*, and one of his best-known positions was that knowledge must be pursued in relation to human problems rather than for its own sake. The President's Commission on Higher Education (1946–1948) had recently given this position greater public prominence as a guiding philosophy for universities.[5] Harnwell, like the President's Commission, did not say that knowledge should be pursued to discover truth or beauty, but rather "relative to these problems." Second, by suggesting that a problem-centered approach to knowledge could unify the university, Harnwell took a position in a debate over the university's unity or lack thereof. This debate reached its zenith a decade later, when University of California president Clark Kerr coined a terminology, centered on the concept of "the multiversity," that Harnwell used to express his views more forcefully. Harnwell told the Trustees of the University of Pennsylvania (the official corporate name of the governing board; hereafter "the Trustees") in 1966 that he wanted to bring "together our diverse faculties and our cosmopolitan student body into a more closely knit community, welding a 'multiversity' into a true university—capable of responding as one, great organism to society's needs."[6] He believed that shared action could unite the university where shared belief had proven elusive.

Harnwell also echoed Dewey by locating universities in a progressive notion of history, in which they nurtured a forward march of scientific rationality that would cause unprecedented human flourishing. While Dewey did not originate this viewpoint, he was a prominent exponent of it during Harnwell's formative years. In one speech, Harnwell referenced "John Dewey's idea that education should put pressure on life," and described the current era as witnessing "the extension of rationality from the natural to the social and behavioral sciences."[7] The latter subjects were "at the point where physics was in the days of the alchemists."[8] Twenty years earlier Dewey had said that "social subjects, as far as concerns effective treatment in inquiry, [were] in much the same state as physical subjects three hundred years ago," and he spoke of the great need to extend scientific inquiry beyond physical to social subjects.[9]

FIGURE 4. University of Pennsylvania president Gaylord P. Harnwell received the 1965 Philadelphia Award from the Greater Philadelphia Movement to recognize his work orienting the university to serving its community. From the Collections of the University of Pennsylvania Archives.

This viewpoint constituted a central part of the university-based modernity that Harnwell promoted. Just months after taking office, he spoke of plans to "formulate" a "general philosophy" for social science research at the university.[10] To Harnwell, the university's role as a community service institution was the latest step in its evolution toward superior forms of its existence. A particular notion of history, one which presumed the growing importance and rigor of social science, thus framed Harnwell's idea of the university as a community service institution.

Harnwell's presidency of the University of Pennsylvania and his ideas about the university's role in society show ways in which the instrumental university took hold and reveal how terminologies to describe aspects of the instrumental university developed. Harnwell's discipline was physics, a field that experienced among the greatest demand and growth in the postwar university. He directed one of the major wartime university labs developing military technology with federal funding, an arrangement that became a model for postwar organized research. Affiliations with physics-related fields and wartime labs propelled a genre of such scientists to academic presidencies, including Arthur Compton of Washington University, Lee DuBridge of Caltech, Eric Walker of Penn State, and Martin Whitaker of Lehigh.[11] These presidents carried the ethos of wartime research into postwar universities. Harnwell integrated one element of this ethos—the notion that research should serve national needs—into his concept of the university as community service institution. As he expressed it, the scale of community to be served by university research could range from Philadelphia to the whole world. By arguing that community needs should shape the goals of universities, Harnwell contributed to an important change in how university leaders conceived their institutions during the mid-twentieth century.

While Harnwell did not originate the ideas he espoused about how a university should serve its community, he advanced them vigorously and provided an intellectual framework—based on a progressive understanding of history—to justify them. He ably articulated elements of a developing national discourse about the research university's role in society. His career thus enables us to track national trends. Harnwell was more of a pioneer in being one of the earliest university leaders to draw motivation from ideas about a knowledge economy. Even if he did not elaborate these ideas in a manner akin to a social theorist like Kerr, he stood out for translating them into action through enterprises that he led, including the University City Science Center and the Governor's Council of Science and Technology. In this work, Harnwell used the knowledge economy concept to bolster his argument that the university should be a "generator" of economic growth for its communities. Thus his ideal of the university as a community service institution, grounded in Deweyan pragmatism, fostered the instrumental university. It did so in part by pushing the University of Pennsylvania, one of the oldest and most prestigious universities in the United States, further into that mold.

Units that developed prior to Harnwell's presidency, particularly the Department of Land and City Planning and the related Institute for Urban Studies, laid important groundwork for his idea of Penn as a community service institution. Penn's city planning department became the intellectual center for that nascent academic discipline in the United States during the 1950s, and its members were important allies in Harnwell's efforts to orient Penn toward community service. One of them, Martin Meyerson, eventually succeeded Harnwell as president. Harnwell's rhetorical presentation of the university as a community service institution evolved during his presidency, especially in points of contact with important national discourses of the postwar era. The period around 1963 was particularly pivotal for Harnwell, as the University City Science Center and the Governor's Council of Science and Technology both launched and Kerr's *The Uses of the University* appeared. Taken together, these events shifted Harnwell's promotion of the instrumental university into overdrive.

Groundwork for a Community Service Orientation

By the time Harnwell became president in 1953, three University of Pennsylvania units created since 1920 had laid a groundwork that facilitated his pushing the institution toward a stronger community service orientation. The Industrial Research Department (IRD, 1921) and the Institute of Local and State Government (ILSG, 1937) shared several important characteristics: Joseph Willits exerted the majority influence in their founding, they were housed in the university's Wharton School of Finance and Commerce, they were mostly independent from teaching departments, and they attracted significant extra-university patronage. Their research tended to focus on specific current problems, mostly originating in or of special concern to the Philadelphia region, and to be coordinated efforts rather than the work of lone investigators. These attributes prefigured the postwar organized research unit (ORU) and moved the university toward being a community service institution. Patronage allowed the IRD and ILSG to plot a course independent of the university's teaching mission, since they did not rely on teaching departments for funding. Although the units were vulnerable if patronage ceased, as it did for IRD around the time Harnwell took office, the fact that they had so much more research funding than any university unit outside of the medical school gave them prestige, and the model of their organizations influenced the ethos of the university. Both IRD and ILSG moved away from Willits's vision in the post–World War II years. Although ILSG was significant for training in public administration and enjoyed high regard among Philadelphia region governments, its research activities dwindled until founding director Stephen Sweeney retired in 1967, after which it was reborn as a policy science institute.[12] Despite these struggles, the establishment and successes of IRD and ILSG put building blocks in place for Harnwell's idea of the university as community service institution.

More important building blocks came from closer to when Harnwell assumed the presidency. In 1951, Penn established almost from scratch a city planning program that quickly became the most influential in the country and shifted the intellectual center of American city planning from Harvard to Penn. Prior to 1940, city planning had little presence at Penn. In 1934–1935, the Department of Architecture established a yearlong sequence in city planning for its graduate students, but it apparently petered out after five years.[13] During the following decade, however, the city planning movement captured Philadelphia with the advent of a City Planning Commission, and those involved with the commission began to push for Penn to create a more robust academic program in city planning. The emergence of the "urban renewal" concept and the entities it spawned, such as the Philadelphia Redevelopment Authority, also shaped these developments. After a national city planning conference met in Philadelphia in 1941, civic groups urged the city government to create a planning commission.[14]

Edward Hopkinson Jr. and Robert B. Mitchell were the most important figures in implementing city planning in Philadelphia and attempting to do so at Penn in the 1940s. The lawyer and investment banker Hopkinson, titan of Philadelphia high society and influential Penn trustee, exerted decisive pressure on the city council to secure its establishment of the Philadelphia City Planning Commission in late 1942.[15] Hopkinson served as the commission's first chairman until December 1955.[16] He hired Mitchell as the commission's executive director in 1943. Mitchell, who had extensive background in the New Deal state with the Public Works Administration and the Urban Section of the National Resources Planning Board, served until 1948 when he left to assume a professorship at Columbia, where he was also affiliated with its Institute for Urban Land Use and Housing Studies.[17]

Penn's Institute of Local and State Government also promoted city planning at the university. Willits intended ILSG to provide research knowledge to local governments to help them function more effectively. To an extent, city planning fell under this same rubric. Director Sweeney created a two-course sequence in city planning during the early 1940s and continued it throughout the decade; Mitchell taught some of these courses as an adjunct lecturer while directing the City Planning Commission.[18] During the war, city planning gained attention at Penn despite wartime limits on the university's activities. In response to a 1943 National Resources Planning Board inquiry (possibly spearheaded by Mitchell), the university made an inventory of "Courses Related to City Planning," all of which were standard courses in standard fields (e.g., American Federal Government, Economic Statistics).[19] To follow up, the Graduate School of Arts and Sciences created a Committee on the Education of City and Regional Planners. Its Subcommittee on Feasible Program Under Existing Conditions, consisting of Sweeney and Professor of Political Science Charles Rohlfing, created a proposal for a one-year graduate curriculum in city planning but did not implement it.[20] The stimulating effect of the NRPB inquiry was an instance of the university's orientation toward national purpose during the war, which continued afterward.

Indeed, the movement for city planning at Penn intensified in 1947. That September, the City Planning Commission opened its Better Philadelphia Exhibition, a showcase of what city planning hoped to accomplish, which drew 750,000 visitors.[21] At a Trustees meeting the following month, Hopkinson spoke to his colleagues about the "great scarcity of men trained in both the field of city and smaller community planning." They agreed to appoint and fund an internal committee chaired by Hopkinson to investigate the possibility of establishing an Institute of City Planning at Penn.[22]

Mitchell, in providing a rationale that Hopkinson could use to sell an institute to his fellow Trustees, stated a desire to "use" the university to engrain what might be called a "culture of planning" into the local consciousness.[23] Mitchell wrote that "the movement for planning in Philadelphia, while strong in the city government at this time, and enjoying wide popular support, lacks the broad base existing in some other large metropolitan centers which have permanent schools of city planning . . . it is believed that a permanently established agency under university auspices would provide the desired continuity and greatly strengthen and renew the movement. It would be able to suggest for discussion planning ideas and objectives farther in advance of the immediately practicable than is possible for an official agency." He believed that a separate institute was needed because departmental budgets "are not flexible enough to permit special courses and much attention to planning work. Instruction in this field can not be satisfactory if merely the sum of compartmentalized courses in related disciplines."[24] Mitchell's reference to "other large metropolitan centers which have permanent schools of city planning" was odd, since very few such schools existed. Most likely he was thinking of Boston, since Harvard was then the academic center of American city planning. MIT offered a degree starting in 1933, although it did not have a department until 1947.[25] The only other program in an urban area was at Columbia, and the only other program to be established before World War II was at Cornell.[26] Programs that began immediately after the war, including the University of Illinois in 1945 and the University of North Carolina in 1946, were outside major urban centers.

The Institute of City Planning, Mitchell believed, should "apply for the first time in the planning field the principles so successfully demonstrated over the years by the Institute of Local and State Government." One of these principles was that students would begin with theory and "gradually participat[e] more and more in actual planning to solve the problems of real communities."[27] Mitchell believed that research should guide planners, and that fellows of the institute would undertake this research; he hoped for a close connection with the Social Science Research Council's Committee on Housing Research, on which he sat. Despite Mitchell's intellectual backing, Hopkinson failed to persuade the Trustees to establish the institute. The desires of government organizations outside the university, then, were not the immediate cause for Penn to start a city planning program. It took an internal movement stemming from widespread discontent with Penn's program in the related field of architecture to bring about a full-fledged planning program.

Throughout the 1940s, students and alumni of Penn's architecture program lamented the condition to which it had fallen under the guidance of George Simpson Koyl, professor of architecture and dean of the School of Fine Arts, which housed architecture, design, music, and art history. The major complaint was Koyl's insistence on adhering to Beaux-Arts classicism after the style had faded from popularity in American architecture; the complainants also believed the school was grossly mismanaged and its program incoherent. As a result, leading architecture firms now preferred Harvard's alumni over Penn's. Although these protests were to no avail for most of the decade, they finally found fertile soil in the administration of Harold Stassen, who became president in 1948. The Architectural Society, a group of architecture students, wrote to Stassen in March 1949 detailing their complaints. The document bears signs of significant attention from Stassen: heavy annotations in his own pencil and requests for comment from Chairman of the University George W. McClelland and Provost Paul Musser. Among Stassen's notes on the document are potential names for a special advisory committee of architects and educators, mostly from outside Penn, which he formed to address the concerns.[28]

Committee member Francis Henry Taylor, director of the Museum of Modern Art in New York City and a Penn trustee who sat on the Board of Fine Arts, a trustee body that played a role in governing the School of Fine Arts, lauded Stassen's approach. In replying that he would gladly join the committee, he told Stassen he feared that "unless something drastic is done, it would be better to close the School than to continue at the present rate. Living away from Philadelphia where relatively few people know of my connection with the University, I hear the unvarnished truth and it is not pleasant." He also pointed Stassen to an example for the teaching of architecture and its relationship to city planning. Taylor included with his letter a pamphlet on MIT's School of Architecture and Planning, led since 1944 by William Wurster, famed California ranch-style architect.[29] Wurster, a key figure in the rise of city planning as a university discipline coordinate with architecture, would return west in 1950 to chair the Department of Architecture at Berkeley, which had established a Department of City and Regional Planning in 1948.[30] Taylor lauded Wurster's MIT program, telling Stassen that it was "the complete expression of what a school should be at the present time . . . [it] is the only school in the country with real guts and a sense of the validity of architecture and planning in the present day. I hope that Pennsylvania can achieve something along the lines of similar objectives."[31] Penn would not only meet but exceed MIT's standard as an intellectual center for city planning and its relationship to architecture.

Taylor and his fellow committee members visited campus for research and interviews in May 1949 and produced a report the following month, which stated as its major recommendation that the School of Fine Arts needed a new dean. Stassen and the committee kept the report in utter secrecy and made only one copy in order to prevent leaks. Stassen's top advisor on the project, architect and trustee Sydney Martin, suggested that Stassen read the report aloud to the Trustees' Committee on the School of Fine Arts in order to avoid printing copies.[32] Stassen accepted the committee's recommendation, and he secured a letter of resignation from Koyl in December 1949.[33] In March 1950, Stassen announced Koyl's "retirement" and the appointment of a committee to recommend a candidate for the deanship.[34] Like the Special Advisory Committee, this committee had five members, mostly from outside the university, including Ralph Walker, president of the American Institute of Architects. Stassen named as chairman James Kellum Smith, an older alumnus of Penn's architecture program and a senior member of New York's McKim, Mead, and White, one of the most important American architectural firms.[35] The committee deliberated for months, working through a large list of names, and even created an American Institute of Architects symposium on architectural education in order to vet several candidates surreptitiously. This strategy departed from Penn's usual practice of quickly hiring an insider to fill any major vacancy. The committee was aware of this distinction. Smith commented that after reading recommendations from alumni and the profession, it seemed that Philadelphians wanted an insider and those outside the region suggested the opposite course because the school had become ingrown.[36]

The committee sent Stassen an interim report in early June 1950 with three names, all outsiders: Charles H. Warner Jr., a New York City architect who formerly taught at Cornell and Columbia; Hugh Asher Stubbins Jr., associate professor of architecture at Harvard; and G. Holmes Perkins, chairman of the Department of Regional Planning at Harvard and editor of the *Journal of the American Institute of Planners*.[37] Both Stubbins and Perkins had worked closely at Harvard with Walter Gropius, one of the world's leading pioneers of modernist architecture, who had left Germany after harassment by the Gestapo.[38] Shortly after receiving the interim report, Stassen telegraphed Harvard president James Conant, saying he had recently conducted a "preliminary talk" with Perkins "and may be having a further more serious talk with him if you will permit."[39] The archival record does not indicate why Stassen preferred Perkins, but Perkins was the only one then holding a planning position, although most of his education and experience had been in architecture. After earning his master's at Harvard in 1929, Perkins taught at Michigan for a year before returning to Cambridge, where he taught architecture at Harvard and Smith College's Cambridge Graduate School and opened a private practice in 1936. Importantly, Perkins went to Washington in 1942 to work for the newly established National Housing Agency (renamed the Housing and Home Finance Agency in 1943), part of the New Deal state, rising to acting director of the Urban Development Division. Harvard then coaxed him back in 1945 as chairman of the Department of Regional Planning.[40] To the extent that Perkins's experience in government shaped his determination to bolster the planning movement, and to the extent that Penn's city planning program under Perkins's guidance gained intellectual eminence and catalyzed the growth of city planning as an academic field in American universities, the New Deal state shaped the emergence of city planning and pushed the American university in an instrumental direction.

Stassen offered Perkins the job, and Perkins tentatively accepted in early July, on the condition that Penn establish in the School of Fine Arts a city planning program funded at $30,000 per year, including $10,000 to $12,000 for an elite professorship. Stassen agreed. Perkins told Stassen that "the profession of architecture is again becoming aware of its responsibility to society and to the community. The most effective direction that this reviving interest can take is city and regional planning . . . I am convinced that the creation of these degrees is an essential part of any program to make the school outstanding."[41] With the arrival of Perkins and city planning, Penn took a step toward becoming more like what Gaylord Harnwell would soon call a community service institution. Indeed, Perkins and his realm became allies for Harnwell in that endeavor.

Between Perkins's acceptance of the deanship and his assumption of the duties, establishing the city planning program was his top priority. Perkins wanted to work closely with Sweeney and his ILSG on "our mutual interests in city planning." In advance of one of his first visits to Penn as dean-elect, Perkins wrote that Sweeney was "the most crucial appointment and I should not wish to be rushed in discussing the problems with him."[42] Later, Perkins pressed Penn administrators to "appoint Professor Sweeney on an ad hoc committee to consider proposals for a new curriculum in City Planning."[43] The relationship got a push from the other side too. Harvard professor of government John M. Gaus wrote to James C. Charlesworth, assistant director of ILSG, gushing about Perkins's work in promoting planning at Harvard and asking Charlesworth and Sweeney to work with Perkins, "in view of the distinguished pioneering work which you people have done there at the Institute."[44] Gaus implied that by partnering with Perkins in developing the new planning curriculum, ILSG would be furthering its own work. Perkins further primed the planning engine by arranging for a special lecture before he began as dean, by Charles W. Eliot (grandson of the famed Harvard president), former director of the National Resources Planning Board and "one of the most vehement advocates of planning within the national administration."[45]

Immediately after beginning as dean on February 1, 1951, Perkins turned his attention toward hiring the elite professor of city planning for which Stassen had promised him money, and toward convincing the university to start a research program associated with the new curriculum in city planning. The two issues turned out to be intertwined. Perkins's short list for the professorship included Robert Mitchell and Coleman Woodbury, a planner who had served with the National Housing Agency and was then director of the Urban Redevelopment Study in Chicago.[46] Mitchell demanded approval of a research program as a condition for him to come. He wanted the university to provide "at least $35,000 per year in free funds beyond any research contracts or grants for specific studies beginning at once, and anticipating an increase in this free fund to over $50,000 per year as the program develops and additional funds become available."[47] Stassen agreed without even calling a committee.[48] These sums were large compared to what Penn had spent on research in the past; allocating them to this new ORU, the Institute for Urban Studies

(IUS), signaled a shift in priorities for the university. The Trustees approved Mitchell at a salary of $12,000 by mid-April.[49] Woodbury ended up replacing Perkins at Harvard, even renting Perkins's house in Cambridge.[50] Mitchell was a proponent, too, of what Harnwell would call the university as a community service institution. Reflecting on the possibilities for IUS, he wrote: "Philadelphia being on the threshold of a new phase of growth and development, the University has an opportunity to become a major force for the good of the community. Such a service can benefit the entire University program."[51] This vision of an organized research unit to tackle social problems was at the heart of the instrumental university.

Shortly after his arrival and the approval of IUS, Perkins began to court the business community for support. In so doing, he emulated on a larger scale what Harnwell had done for physics thirteen years earlier, as we will see shortly. Perkins urged Stassen "to mention the University's interest in the problems of metropolitan development in the nine-county area in your speech to the Greater Philadelphia-South Jersey Council" in May 1951. This council represented "the Chamber of Commerce's point of view in planning for regional development." Perkins also mentioned that recent discussions with Chamber of Commerce officials led him to believe they were about to embark on a campaign to raise $300,000 for research, which he hoped they would assign to IUS. Perkins believed that Stassen's talk could "establish . . . the Institute in the minds of the business communities [and] certainly facilitate the effective collaboration between us and the communities involved." Perkins also told Stassen that the first IUS project was business related: "a two-year study to observe the effects of the impact of the new steel plant of Morrisville and Lower Bucks County."[52] Perkins, it seemed, believed IUS should investigate problems of economic development. The Housing and Home Finance Agency funded this study, which suggests how the patronage of New Deal state agencies spurred the growth of university ORUs.[53]

After five years, the Department of Land and City Planning had fifty FTE graduate students, double the number of any other program in the country. Its PhD program had eight students, more than any of the other three such programs in the United States.[54] Enrollments did not tell the whole story of the department's prominence; other universities began to raid its faculty just as it had raided theirs. Perkins and Mitchell had rounded out the city planning and IUS faculty with Martin Meyerson and William L. C. Wheaton. Meyerson had been an early member of Mitchell's staff with the Philadelphia City Planning Commission, and then worked on the beginning of public housing in Chicago. During his time at Penn he cowrote an influential book on his Chicago experience, *Politics, Planning, and the Public Interest*.[55] Wheaton worked for the National Housing Agency and Housing and Home Finance Agency during the 1940s and coauthored the Housing Act of 1949 before Perkins hired him for Harvard's Department of Regional Planning, which he left for Penn in 1953.[56] Harvard tapped Meyerson in 1957 to lead its new Center for Urban Studies (which became the Harvard-MIT Joint Center for Urban Studies in 1959); he went to Berkeley in 1963 as dean of the College of Environmental Design, and Wheaton followed him there to direct the new Institute of Urban and Regional Development.[57]

For a time, however, which coincided with Harnwell's ascent to the presidency, Penn held intellectual leadership in city planning and urban research. Stassen did not plan it that way. He deferred to architectural experts outside the university in selecting a dean of fine arts. A broad intellectual current in the architectural profession—a conviction that city planning was needed to strengthen the work of architects—thus exerted the most direct force behind the advent of such a strong program in city planning at Penn. Although Stassen is generally remembered as a president who neglected the university in favor of his political aspirations, his search for and hiring of G. Holmes Perkins marked a new era of cosmopolitanism, and Perkins became one of the most important people in the university's history. The transformation of the School of Fine Arts that accompanied the adoption of a city planning curriculum exemplified the ethos of the instrumental university. It encompassed a new focus on organized research into social problems, including ones related to economic development.

At the time Harnwell became president in 1953, then, a new cutting-edge program in city planning and urban studies was thriving at the University of Pennsylvania, which built from and amplified the instrumental impulse in the earlier work of the Industrial Research Department and the Institute of Local and State Government. All of these programs engaged problems of the city through organized research, at least to a degree. Harnwell shared the view of the university's mission that motivated these organizations; he admired their leaders and sought their assistance toward his goals. Shortly after taking office he created an Executive Planning Committee on Physical Plant and made Perkins its chair and Mitchell a member. This committee spearheaded a dramatic physical restructuring of Penn's urban campus, part of a new plan to make it more permanent instead of moving the university to suburban Valley Forge as the Trustees had seriously considered for many years.[58] As we will see shortly, Harnwell also placed Willits and George Taylor of the Industrial Research Department in similar prominent positions. These appointments symbolized the importance of their work to Harnwell's idea of a university.

Harnwell Takes the Reins

Harnwell ascended to the presidency from a position of high status in several communities: Penn's faculty, the discipline of physics, and the new postwar complex of military-related patrons of scientific research. In his postgraduate training, Harnwell worked with some of the biggest names in physics—Ernest Rutherford, Karl Compton, and Robert Millikan. Penn hired Harnwell from Princeton's faculty to become chairman of the physics department in 1938, and shortly thereafter he became editor of a leading journal, *Review of Scientific Instruments*, a position from which he stepped down only after assuming the presidency. Perhaps the biggest boost to his prominence came during World War II. From 1942 to 1946, he directed the University of California Division of War Research operation at the US Navy Radio and Sound Laboratory on Point Loma in San Diego, under contract with the federal government's Office of Scientific Research and Development, which guided the country's war-related research. He oversaw a staff of 550 and an annual budget of $3.5 million. Harnwell's dramatic success in this endeavor, and its importance to the war effort, shaped his and Penn's future. It brought widespread appreciation of the power of organized research targeted at specific problems conducted by teams of investigators in university settings. It also brought federal contracts for defense research to Penn after the war. Several other institutions pursued him for presidencies or deanships, but he remained loyal to Penn. Many of these factors contributed to the Trustees' interest in Harnwell for Penn's presidency upon Stassen's resignation to join the new Eisenhower administration in 1953.[59] Three major trends marked Harnwell's first decade of leading Penn toward the ideal of a community service institution after he took office in July 1953: closer ties with industry, using language from industrial relations to describe the university's purpose, and the Educational Survey.

Harnwell had begun forging closer ties with industry as chairman of physics. When he arrived in 1938, Penn was in the midst of a university-wide discussion on this topic. It had hosted a national conference on the issue in 1936, and the administration was encouraging the faculty to move in that direction.[60] By May 1939, Harnwell had established "an Advisory Committee of business executives to advise on graduate work" in the physics department.[61] Two years later, Harnwell could report to the Trustees that Westinghouse, DuPont, and Corning Glass Works were all financing fellowships for physics graduate students.[62] Other departments did not match his record in this area.

Early in his presidency, Harnwell determined to intensify this drive for closer connections between the university and local industry. According to Harnwell, industry increasingly viewed universities, which provided ideas and personnel, as important to its "self interest." Ties with industry did not abridge the university's independence, he believed, as long as the university sought funding from many industries and not just one.[63] In his first year as president, Harnwell announced that "the university is formulating plans to broaden its service to the Philadelphia community and the Nation," which included "increased scientific research activities for industry and government."[64] This willingness to allow outside entities greater influence over university research agendas departed from the practices of the classical American research university, but developed the approach pursued by Joseph Willits three decades earlier.

Another key element of Harnwell's early presidency that shared an intellectual orientation with Willits was describing the university's purpose from a mode I call "macrothought"—thinking about the world in terms of abstract aggregates.[65] This modern thought pattern emerged from the field of industrial relations, specifically from addressing questions of employment on a macro scale, as Willits had done in the 1910s. Several federal government initiatives of the 1940s reflected the spread of macrothought: the Office of War Mobilization and Reconversion, the President's Commission on Higher Education, the GI Bill, and the Employment Act of 1946. Due in part to these initiatives, by the 1950s macrothought permeated the rhetoric of academic leaders like Harnwell and affected how universities conceived of their mission. His frequent use of a common postwar trope about the urgent national need for "specialized manpower" and the university's role in "training" such manpower reflected this mindset. By the early 1960s, his portrayal of the university's role in society shifted to different idioms, about "national purpose" and the advent of a knowledge economy in which human capital was a key ingredient for economic growth. Although the terminology was different, it still reflected macrothought. His portrayals of the university's role in society thus had a basic continuity from the mid-1950s to the early 1960s.

In arguing that the "specialized manpower" trope ultimately came from macrothought, I am not claiming that Harnwell picked it up directly from industrial relations literature or practitioners. In fact, he more likely heard it in physics circles. Talk about manpower was rampant in postwar American physics, and it became institutionalized in policy documents and branch names of entities such as the Office of Naval Research, the Office of Defense Mobilization, and the National Science Foundation.[66] Physicists' obsession with manpower continued into the late 1960s, so Harnwell's shift away from the terminology did not mirror the physicists' practice. Historian David Kaiser argued that manpower was a military metaphor, connected to the belief that physicists were now essential to US military prowess in light of the advances exhibited in World War II. My own searches suggest that the term "special-ized manpower" perhaps appeared first in 1942, and even the term "man-power" was scarcely used until World War II.[67] Still, the concept of manpower essentially came from the way of thinking about employment in the aggre-gate that Joseph Willits helped introduce in the 1910s, in connection with the military matter of World War I.

In one of Harnwell's typical enunciations of the specialized manpower trope, he cited findings of the Rockefeller-funded Commission on Human Resources and Advanced Training, itself shaped by that trope. The commis-sion's 1954 report, *America's Resources of Specialized Talent*, stated that the nation's demand for specialized manpower would continue to increase.[68] As Harnwell reported the findings, "for the next few years the total number of graduates, especially in the fields of engineering, science, teaching and medi-cine, will fall short of employers' desires."[69] Harnwell often framed the im-portance of university graduates in terms of their abilities to contribute to economic development and other community service.

Not all graduates were equally valuable, however. Throughout the 1950s, beginning well before Sputnik, Harnwell discussed the "current inability of our educational system to meet the demands for scientists and engineers."[70] He argued that "continued progress in . . . various facets of American life de-pends in the final analysis directly upon trained and educated manpower, which alone can provide the essential 'know-how' in science, technology, business management and human relations."[71] Harnwell did not speak about the need for highly trained scholars of literature and philosophy to enrich American life. Rather, the university was to produce graduates who had the "know-how" to solve social problems. By taking this position, Harnwell again echoed Dewey.

A widespread postwar belief in the increased complexity of society fueled the specialized manpower trope and provided a rationale for the expansion of higher education.[72] Society had become increasingly complex; this complex-ity called for specialized manpower; universities produced this manpower and thus must be expanded in order for society to prosper. Harnwell explained to Penn alumni that "the fact is that our society has become so complex that only the competent can begin to operate it well. We need a growing army of col-lege graduates."[73] The words "operate" and "army" are notable. One hot field of the postwar era was operations research, in which Penn launched a special master's degree program. To speak of operating a society implies that society is something inert and mechanical, pliable by an outside operator—and testi-fies to university leaders' continuing desire in the 1950s to achieve social con-trol. The army metaphor displayed the tendency to apply military concepts to the realm of employment and industrial relations.

Harnwell often spoke of "specialized manpower" in terms of graduate students, whom he considered more knowledgeable and thus more valuable than undergraduates. He even referred to "the greater social usefulness that presumably comes with the Ph.D.," which highlights his emphasis on the social utility of research knowledge.[74] A 1963 press release on Harnwell's tenth anniversary as president noted that "enrollment has grown by 2,500 students since 1953. They are predominantly full-time graduate students, for which there is an urgent national demand."[75] By implying that one of the physicist-president's great accomplishments was tuning Penn to the wavelength of national need, the press release revealed the connection between the manpower and national purpose idioms.

One cause of the surge in graduate students came from changes suggested by the Educational Survey, a project that Harnwell spearheaded shortly after taking office. Considered the most extensive self-study ever undertaken by an American university, the survey during its 1954–1959 lifespan loomed large in Harnwell's presidency and produced a flood of publications. To direct the survey, Harnwell secured the services of none other than Joseph Willits, Penn's earliest prominent supporter of coordinated research, just retired from the Rockefeller Foundation. Harnwell had a debt to Willits, who had served as a consultant to the Trustees' presidential search, preparing reports on various candidates and influencing their selection of Harnwell.[76] The survey aimed to define "what is Pennsylvania's community and, especially, its obligations to its adjacent community?"[77] More grandly, the survey's purpose was "to help formulate an expression of the University's mission in society."[78] Harnwell's declaration that the university's mission was "in society" continued his emphasis on the university addressing "problems of men."

The survey "recommended that the undergraduate years be devoted largely to general education, with most professional training being postponed to the graduate level." One rationale was that knowledge had proliferated so much that a student could no longer learn everything in four years.[79] In the wake of the survey, Penn made both the School of Education and the School of Fine Arts strictly graduate schools. The Wharton School of Finance and Commerce was an exception to this trend. The Educational Survey recommended that its four-year undergraduate program be replaced by a five-year program leading to the MBA, but Harnwell did not push this change. Wharton kept its undergraduate program and adopted the five-year program only as an experimental alternative.[80] Nevertheless, professional degrees increasingly became graduate degrees rather than undergraduate degrees, which helped to increase the number of graduate students. Harnwell also believed general education was particularly important for students in undergraduate professional schools of business and engineering, and for undergraduates who aimed toward graduate professional schools of medicine and law. He articulated the common postwar sentiment that general education would help people "to direct modern technology toward the goal of better living—not wholesale death."[81]

In his first decade, then, Harnwell took steps that pushed Penn in a more instrumental direction, even as he attended to undergraduate general education in the survey years. As the 1960s arrived, however, his speeches shed that concern and turned increasingly to how the university could meet city, state, national, and international needs more directly.

Universities as Instruments and Generators

To celebrate Harnwell's tenth anniversary as president in 1963, the Trustees created a Harnwell Chair and allowed him to name its incumbent during his tenure in office. Harnwell named as the inaugural incumbent George W. Taylor of the Wharton School, formerly the star of the old Industrial Research Department and a friend of Clark Kerr. While it is not clear why Harnwell chose Taylor, it appears that Harnwell thought Taylor represented something about the university that he wanted to underscore. In his 1964 annual report, Harnwell noted that 1963 saw Taylor receive both the Greater Philadelphia Award (representing the university as a community service institution) and the Presidential Medal of Freedom (representing the university as an instrument of national purpose).[82] Taylor's friendship and shared scholarly field with Kerr also gave the choice symbolic importance. Harnwell's elevation of Taylor ushered in a period where Harnwell increasingly interpreted the university through a historical framework shared with Kerr and adopted Kerr's rhetoric to express his goals for Pennsylvania. This period marked a watershed in Harnwell's presidency. It came in the wake of Kerr's April 1963 Godkin Lectures at Harvard, published that November as *The Uses of the University*, where Kerr said the "essence" of the university's "transformation" was that it had become an "instrument of national purpose."[83] Harnwell built his annual President's Message of February 1964, as well as other speeches, on a framework of Kerr's language and ideas. That June, Kerr awarded Harnwell an honorary degree at UCLA's commencement.[84]

Harnwell's growing reliance on Kerr's portrayal of the university drew on their shared embrace of an important change in how university leaders conceived their institutions during the mid-twentieth century—a newly vigorous belief that national needs should shape the goals of universities. Kerr's description of this shift in *The Uses of the University* became influential. At Penn's 1963 commencement, just one month after Kerr's lectures, Harnwell said that "World War II emphasized the paramount role of our universities as an essential national resource."[85] This statement echoed Kerr both by highlighting World War II as a point of change for universities and by insisting that universities' first responsibility was meeting national needs. While these views were not unique to Kerr, they did not appear in Harnwell's speeches prior to this time. Thereafter, Harnwell commonly portrayed the postwar years as a different era for universities.[86]

By fall 1963, Harnwell was following Kerr more obviously by referring to the university as an instrument of purpose. In an October 1963 speech to a statewide Convocation of Higher Education, he insisted that a private university "serves only public purposes. Such an institution, like its State-owned counterpart, is an instrument for effecting a broad social purpose." He also proclaimed, "The large modern American university . . . has expanded into a community service institution." As part of this service, the university should "conduct experimental programs in industrial innovation and expansion, and stimulate economic growth."[87] This speech was, of course, an argument for the state to keep funding private institutions such as Penn.

The strongest evidence of Harnwell's debt to Kerr was his annual President's Message of February 1964, which carried the Kerrian title *The University of Pennsylvania: An Instrument of National Purpose*. Released just three months after publication of *The Uses of the University*, Harnwell's report contained some variant of "uses" on almost all of its sixteen pages. Harnwell tried to connect this new idiom to Penn's traditions by noting "Pennsylvania's traditional usefulness" and Benjamin Franklin's belief that universities should teach "useful" things. He proclaimed that "a revolutionary era of university utility lies before us." Penn's "pursuit of useful knowledge" sought "areas of usefulness" and built "bridges of useful knowledge," which gave it a "proven capability for usefulness" and made it "a bank of useful knowledge, with generous credit facilities." Yet Harnwell believed the best was still to come; the "need for usefulness" gave Penn an "opportunity for still greater usefulness," and he looked forward to "Pennsylvania's achievement of new levels of usefulness."[88] Harnwell increasingly sought to achieve such usefulness as an instrument of national purpose in the realm of economic development, which became central to American self-conception and to federal and state policy in the postwar period.

He did so in part through an influential new way of thinking about universities and economic development that emerged in the early 1960s with the popularization of ideas introduced by economic thinkers Peter Drucker, Fritz

Machlup, Theodore Schultz, Gary Becker, and, of course, Clark Kerr. They examined the role of knowledge as a factor in capitalist production and characterized knowledge as a form of capital, which they believed was becoming a more important industrial input than traditional forms such as raw materials.[89] Kerr began to describe higher education as an industry while writing *Industrialism and Industrial Man* in the late 1950s. Machlup introduced the broader concept of a "knowledge industry" in his 1962 book *The Production and Distribution of Knowledge in the United States*, and Kerr helped popularize it by quoting it in *The Uses of the University*.[90] Others extended the analysis to the human carriers of knowledge. Drucker introduced in 1957 the concept that would later be known as the "knowledge worker" when he declared that "the majority of personnel employed even in manufacturing industries" were not "unskilled or semiskilled machine workers" but "rather people doing knowledge work, however unskilled."[91] Schultz and Becker elaborated on this kind of thinking with their "human capital theory," which held that knowledgeable workers were actually the most important form of capital for high levels of productivity.[92] Human capital theory formalized and elaborated the manpower trope, thus becoming another stage in macrothought.

Harnwell seized on these ideas to help formulate the university as a community service institution, and thus joined Kerr as one of the early university presidents to cite an emerging knowledge economy to justify the direction he was leading his institution. Harnwell's rhetoric on this theme suggests that university leaders did much to legitimate the idea of a knowledge economy. He explicitly spoke of a "knowledge industry." He did not use the term "knowledge economy," but he regularly articulated its central tenet, that knowledge was replacing raw materials in industrial production. The new vocabulary bolstered his earlier efforts to link academia with industry. By 1965, he believed that one could "see the academic and business communities being drawn closer every day, because society has come to recognize the power of education as a creator of wealth."[93] For believers in the knowledge economy concept, the university was the central institution for economic development, and industry should be located near universities rather than near raw material sources. This conclusion had profound implications for the relation of American research universities to political economy.

A related new trope that portrayed increased international and domestic economic competition also motivated university leaders to make their institutions instruments for economic development at this time. On the interstate level, California's Silicon Valley and Boston's Route 128 drew attention as new centers of American economic might, powered by "brainpower" from nearby universities.[94] Pennsylvanians worried that their state was "backward" in its reliance on older resource-based industries and its failure to get involved in the knowledge-based defense- and space-related industries. On the international level, a belief already existed that the United States must show the superiority of capitalism around the world in order to preserve its way of life against the Soviet menace. A new debate, however, erupted *within* the capitalist orbit: was the United States falling behind the economic behemoths it had re-created, Japan and West Germany? Harnwell told an audience in 1965 that "as *Fortune* magazine observed last November, 'the biggest single factor in the nation's rising productivity is the growth of the knowledge industry.' This truth is reflected in the economic geography of our day: those states which are investing the most in higher education tend to be the very states that are enjoying the richest dividends of industrial growth. I wish I could say that Pennsylvania was among them. The term 'knowledge industry,' jarring as it may be to academic ears, aptly suggests the magnitude of this business of teaching and learning."[95] This sense of competition and the knowledge economy concept shaped two of Harnwell's important ventures, the University City Science Center (UCSC) and the Governor's Council of Science and Technology, which launched in 1963 and contributed to making that year a turning point in Harnwell's presidency.

Harnwell planned UCSC, a collection of buildings near Penn's campus intended to house companies that emphasized scientific research, as the centerpiece of his plan for Penn to bolster the region's economic development. On paper, it was not Penn but the West Philadelphia Corporation (WPC) that originated UCSC. WPC, a nonprofit organization founded by Penn and several neighboring institutions in 1959 to fight the encroachment of "blight" into the area of West Philadelphia where they were located, was one of Harnwell's principal vehicles for making Penn a community service institution. Harnwell chaired the WPC board and Penn generally dominated WPC, which had connections with federal and city urban renewal efforts.[96] The WPC idea came from Martin Meyerson, who wrote a 1956 memo "on the need for the university to engage in community development activities."[97] Meyerson's role emphasizes the importance of Penn's city planning program for Harnwell's vision of the university as community service institution. In taking up Meyerson's idea, Penn followed the lead of Columbia University and the University of Chicago, which had started similar community development organizations in the preceding years.[98] The WPC's principal task was the renewal of a section of West Philadelphia that the Philadelphia Redevelopment Authority had dubbed "University City" a decade before. The Redevelopment Authority gave WPC control of the area, and WPC began to promote University City.

The idea for a science research park in University City dates back at least to a June 1959 conversation between Harnwell and Alfred H. Williams, chairman of Penn's Trustees and former dean of the Wharton School. Williams suggested that they invite research-oriented industry to locate in University City.[99] An idea to dedicate a parcel of land near campus for that purpose gained momentum, and by 1961 WPC's efforts to promote UCSC were in full swing. The city council approved the UCSC site as an urban renewal area, and the project began to attract millions of dollars in federal urban renewal grants and US Department of Commerce economic development grants.[100]

Harnwell situated UCSC in the framework of economic competitiveness in the knowledge economy: "new industries will be afforded laboratories close to the brainpower sources of the Delaware Valley. We expect [UCSC] to help win for the Greater Philadelphia area its overdue share of the new wealth, new jobs, and new tax revenues that we see being generated in other states by the new partnership of industry and institutional research talent."[101] Harnwell believed that one of the major contributions the university could make to its local community was to spur economic development by creating a space in which industries based on scientific knowledge provided by the university could flourish. This concept motivated UCSC. Harnwell explained that Penn was generating ideas that "if brought properly into conjunction with venture capital, entrepreneurs and facilities—could be developed into industries which could grow here in a city because, of course, the raw materials which we have in Philadelphia are people rather than coal or oil or steel. So that one has to have new kinds of methods of employing people in industry which can exist in a city based on novel ideas rather than on novel raw materials."[102] Harnwell's invocation of ideas over raw materials suggests how the knowledge economy concept, particularly as it shaped his thinking that UCSC could boost Philadelphia's economy, contributed to his formulation of the university as community service institution.

Harnwell recognized that the moral economy of research in a community service institution differed from the moral economy that had guided elite American research universities, and he tried to use UCSC to bridge this gap. Harnwell wanted UCSC "to use ideas that are current on the campus for the social and economic benefit of the area. In essence, the Center attempts to solve problems for outside firms and other organizations which are unable to maintain their own Research and Development facilities. You could say it offers tailor-made research for hire."[103] Harnwell believed that locating such "research for hire" in UCSC rather than in the university proper would forestall questions about the propriety of such research. The setup was rather transparent, however, and Harnwell eventually prohibited certain types of research for government at UCSC in the wake of student protests.[104]

As UCSC broke ground in 1963, a new governor of Pennsylvania drew Harnwell into promoting similar ideas on a statewide level. William Warren Scranton, a moderate Republican, implemented a massive economic development program that had been the centerpiece of his campaign. His administration created a citizen organization (100,000 Pennsylvanians for Economic Growth), began an advertising campaign in national magazines about tax and financing perks for business in "the new Pennsylvania," and launched a Governor's Council of Business and Industry and a Governor's Council of Science and Technology (GCST). The latter attempted to mobilize Pennsylvania's universities for Scranton's economic development program.[105]

Scranton asked Harnwell to help him organize GCST, and then to chair it. Scranton recalled that he selected Harnwell for the chair primarily because he believed Harnwell was the most trustworthy of those he considered qualified, although it bothered him that many at Penn treated Harnwell "like a god."[106] Deputy Secretary of Commerce Clifford Jones, who served as executive secretary for GCST, suggested that Harnwell received the chair over Penn State president Eric Walker, an electrical engineer whose standing in the scientific community neared Harnwell's, in order to counter widespread resentment against Penn State for being the consistent recipient of commonwealth largesse.[107] When Harnwell sat down to write out a vision for GCST, he noted that "a growing segment of industry in the chemical, metallurgical, electronic, pharmaceutical, fabricating and manufacturing areas is relatively independent of the proximity of particular raw materials."[108] This statement shows how important the knowledge economy framework was to his formulation of GCST. It also differed from the response of University of Illinois faculty to a 1961 request from Governor Otto Kerner to study how universities could spur economic development and draw growth industries to the state. Apparently not working from the knowledge economy framework, a faculty committee stated that "certain basic factors are far more important in attracting industry and in plant location decisions, and therefore in stimulating regional economic growth, than the advantages offered by universities."[109] The Illinois committee's response shows that the knowledge economy concept was not yet dominant, but the governor's query provides further evidence of state attempts to mobilize universities for economic development in the early 1960s.

Harnwell's advocacy for Walter Isard as a GCST member exemplified how he emphasized elements of Penn that furthered his community service institution ideal. Isard, a Penn professor of regional science, stood out as the only non-administrator social scientist on the council, which consisted of about twenty university administrators and corporation executives.[110] Isard essentially created the academic field of regional science while a professor of economics at MIT. He founded the Regional Science Association in 1954. After MIT rebuffed his efforts to start the first graduate program in regional science, he moved to Penn in the fall of 1956 and won approval of a PhD program at the end of that academic year.[111] Regional science became a full-fledged department in 1958, housed in the Wharton School, and Isard started the *Journal of Regional Science* at that time. Regional science was closely allied with city planning; indeed, Robert Mitchell, William Wheaton, and their Penn city planning colleague Britton Harris each served as president of the Regional Science Association in the 1950s and 1960s. The New Deal state gave energy to regional science as it did to city planning. Isard spent an SSRC postdoctoral fellowship year at the National Resources Planning Board in 1943–1944. While there, he "discussed with Robert B. Mitchell and G. Holmes Perkins (who later spawned the Golden Age of City Planning at the University of Pennsylvania) the implications of both location and transportation analysis for urban development and planning."[112] The basic thrust of regional science was to determine the locations of industrial and transportation structures that would most effectively promote regional economic development. More than any other academic discipline, its agenda aligned with Harnwell's idea of the university as community service institution, especially for furthering economic development. Harnwell loved to trumpet Isard's work. In a speech to the Lancaster Chamber of Commerce, for example, Harnwell noted that Isard "is studying the economic base which supports the entire Philadelphia metropolitan structure" to determine the causes and consequences of economic growth.[113] It is unsurprising, then, that Harnwell pushed for Isard's inclusion on GCST.

After a year of discussion, GCST released a report penned by Harnwell, *Science and Technology: Generators of Economic Well-Being*.[114] This use of the term "generators" was symbolically significant, and Harnwell easily moved its application from science and technology to universities: "Just as education is the largest industry in the United States, so are the educational institutions in Philadelphia some of the most important economic generators of the area."[115] The emerging vision of a knowledge economy portrayed universities as economic generators in the sense of themselves being industries with output, as Machlup indicated, but also in the sense of their output being a new kind of capital that would trigger the productivity of other industry. Cultural commentators had long portrayed the generator—and more specifically, a particular type of generator, the dynamo—as the symbol of industrial modernity. Henry Adams did so most famously, in a chapter titled "The Virgin and the Dynamo" in *The Education of Henry Adams*. Harnwell's imputation of industry's chief symbol to the university broke from the classical rhetoric of the American university. It also indicated that some early proponents understood the knowledge economy as a new feature of an enduring modern society centered on industrial production, rather than as a harbinger of a postindustrial world. Finally, "generator" is a near synonym of "engine," which suggests that Harnwell and GCST were pioneers in the movement to depict the university as an economic engine and that this movement was underway in the early 1960s.[116]

GCST sought to bolster the state's capacity for "scientifically and technologically oriented industries," and its top recommendation toward that end was to improve graduate education.[117] As Harnwell later said, GCST "appropriately put as its first priority the improvement of the Commonwealth's strength in post-baccalaureate education as the foundation upon which science-based prosperity must rest."[118] This recommendation followed Harnwell's emphasis from the 1950s on the social usefulness of graduate students. The GCST report thus shows the continuity of the older trope about specialized manpower with the newer one about the knowledge economy, both part of a larger conceptualization about industrial relations. Harnwell's work on GCST showed his acquiescence with a political program designed to mobilize universities toward ends determined by the state. It also gave him a platform from which to articulate his ideas about the university's role in economic development to a larger audience.

Placing GCST in national perspective shows how the rise of the knowledge economy concept allowed governments to mobilize universities for economic ends and thus push them in a more instrumental direction. The Kennedy administration was fixated on economic growth, and its Department of Commerce embodied notions of science-based growth. The secretary of commerce was Luther Hodges, who as governor of North Carolina during the 1950s had helped build that state's Research Triangle Park. It presupposed, like Harnwell's UCSC, that locating certain kinds of technology-intensive businesses near universities would spur a region's economic development. Kennedy's Department of Commerce also created a new position, assistant secretary of commerce for science and technology. This action institutionalized in the federal bureaucracy notions of science-based economic growth related to the knowledge economy concept. The position actually originated during the Eisenhower administration, fueled by the general post-Sputnik examination of the federal government's role in promoting science and technology (and with an eye toward a space program), with a 1960 report by the National Academy of Sciences.[119] The Council of Economic Advisers supported the recommendation, as did MIT professor of electrical engineering Jerome Wiesner when he became Kennedy's special assistant for science and technology.[120] Creating a new assistant secretary position required Congress to pass a bill authorizing it, and Hodges began talking with relevant congressional committee chairs about introducing such a bill shortly after he took office in January 1961.[121] A bill finally passed in February 1962, mostly along party lines with Democrats in favor.[122]

After lengthy deliberations within the Kennedy administration on candidates, J. Herbert Hollomon became the first assistant secretary of commerce for science and technology. Hollomon held a PhD in metallurgy from MIT and was general manager of the General Engineering Laboratories for General Electric, the company's highest research position. Wiesner was apparently influential in selecting Hollomon, who was at the time a consultant to the President's Science Advisory Committee and advising the government on technology transfer to foreign countries.[123] Since 1960 Hollomon had been pushing for the creation of a National Academy of Engineering to help engineers gain broader societal influence, and it became a reality during his time in office, in 1964.[124]

As assistant secretary, Hollomon attempted to mobilize universities as instruments for economic development through two major programs, the Civilian Industrial Technology Program (CITP) and the State Technical Services Program (STS). CITP emerged from discussions among Kennedy's economic and scientific advisors, who were troubled that the federal government had ignored the support of technological innovation in civilian industry unrelated to space and defense, thus weakening the United States in global economic competition. Kennedy announced these concerns in his 1962 budget message and economic report to Congress.[125] Hollomon then took charge of crafting CITP and persuading Congress to fund it. CITP was ill-fated from the beginning, in part due to Hollomon's lack of political experience. Part of his proposal for CITP was a University-Industry Technical Service (UITS), for which he asked $1.7 million.[126] One of the sources of this proposal was the National Association of State Universities and Land-Grant Colleges, which had been suggesting "the general concept of a university-industrial extension program similar to the Agriculture Extension Program" for over fifty years.[127] Hollomon told Congress, "Each university in the program would become a center for technical information, for demonstration projects, and for the creation of opportunities for business and industry to develop." He stated that universities had sent him more than fifty proposals requesting to participate. Hollomon also grounded his argument for UITS in the international economic competition trope. He expressed concern that "in the last ten years the rate of European economic growth, on a per capita basis, has been four times as great as our own. Foreign products are capturing markets more than ever through an increasingly effective application of technology." Universities could increase US success in worldwide markets by supplying technological information to American business.[128] Despite Hollomon's exhortations, however, Congress did not fund UITS.

After CITP as a whole fell apart in 1965, Hollomon sought to repackage UITS as an independent entity called the State Technical Services Program with specific congressional authorization. Congress complied in the State Technical Services Act of 1965, "an Act to promote commerce and encourage economic growth by supporting State and interstate programs to place the findings of science usefully in the hands of American enterprise."[129] In practice, STS "laid the basis of an extension program creating a network of information centers in universities to serve the technical needs of local firms."[130] The program made grants to a designated agency in each state that coordinated the program for that state. Universities then worked with the state agency on specific programs.[131] Sometimes the state agency was a department of commerce, as in West Virginia, but in twenty-eight states it was a university entity such as a board of regents (as in Ohio) or a state university system (such as Penn State and the University of California).[132] Grants were modest. Penn State and UC both received around $115,000 in fiscal year 1967, putting them second and third behind runaway leader the University of Illinois, which received $186,000. Other notable universities received smaller amounts: about $21,000 for Michigan and $5,000 for Vanderbilt.[133] STS focused on the dissemination of new knowledge. In correspondence with the Machine Tool and Manufacturing Research Center at the University of Cincinnati, Hollomon noted that potentially fundable activities included the publication of reports, holding conferences and seminars, and otherwise assisting industry.[134]

Hollomon wanted the program to mold participating universities into the instrumental model. He argued that universities should be a major resource in Commerce's effort to disseminate technical knowledge to spur economic development, but that some of their traditional characteristics blocked the way. He criticized universities' lack of involvement with state and local problems, their lack of communication with business and involvement with business problems, and what he perceived to be their excessive orientation toward academic disciplines rather than problems in the broader society. He also complained that university reward structures for faculty prioritized research too much and service too little, a common theme among promoters of the instrumental university.[135] University representatives involved with STS reported that it resulted in a change in some regular academic programs, facilitated better cooperation between departments and more interdisciplinary approaches to problem solving, and "provided contacts with the business community that have been beyond university influence."[136] Despite this evidence of achieving some of its goals, STS lasted just four years before congressional opponents severed its appropriations in 1969.[137] Hollomon had already resigned in 1967 to become president of the University of Oklahoma, disappointed by failures at Commerce and disillusioned with the ramping up of the war effort in Vietnam.[138]

Despite the uneven success of federal programs based on the growing belief that a knowledge economy had dawned, the fact that such programs came to life at all suggests how important the young concept had become by the early 1960s. Harnwell and other university presidents worked in a milieu where federal and state governments increasingly attempted to mobilize universities as instruments in their economic development programs. While these programs sometimes had defense- and space-related industries in view, GCST and Hollomon's projects showed a distinct concern for work not related to the Cold War. Indeed, new concerns about economic competition from noncommunist allies constituted one of several motivations for these programs. Beginning in the late 1950s, government and university officials portrayed universities as engines of economic development. This aspiration was not primarily a result of the furor over Sputnik, although the related entrance of a science bureaucracy into the Executive Office of the President probably helped advance ideas about the economic value of university research. Rather, the new portrayal of universities sprang from ideas about the role of knowledge in the American and international economies that Kerr and Drucker had identified by 1957, which soon gained wide circulation. These ideas motivated university presidents like Harnwell, corporate research director turned federal bureaucrat Hollomon, and politicians such as Scranton, Kennedy, and Hodges to spawn new initiatives mobilizing universities for economic development, thus further instrumentalizing those universities.

Direct Service to Community

By the mid-1960s, while Hollomon was mobilizing the federal government to realize his hopes for universities to provide service to their regions, Harnwell expounded a broader understanding of the service at the heart of his ideal of the university. It centered on the concept of "direct service" and capped his most complete expression of the university as a community service institution. He placed both the university and civilization in a progressive historical framework that portrayed them as moving concomitantly into a higher state of being during the postwar period. In this view, the twin advances of science and urbanization had changed the structure of civilization and consequently of the university. As Harnwell portrayed it, this change in the university was an inevitable response to larger forces rather than something he or others directed; he was simply overseeing a natural, evolutionary process. He even remarked that "in reviewing the brisk pace of expansion during my tenure [as president], I feel like William James giving his impression of the San Francisco earthquake: 'I did not start it, I could not stop it, but I was there.'"[139] In using this explanatory framework, Harnwell took a similar tack as Kerr recently had in *The Uses of the University*. Kerr portrayed the multiversity president as "mostly a mediator" rather than a figure who pushed the university in a definite direction.[140] Moreover, Kerr used this same notion of history to argue for the inevitability of the university's transformation into the multiversity. In portraying the university as simply adjusting to its environment, Harnwell and Kerr employed a Darwinian framework that American pragmatists such as Dewey had adapted to social and psychological analysis.

Harnwell portrayed the university's central activity as having shifted over time from teaching to research to service. While he embraced Kerr's argument that the post–World War II years represented a distinct era for universities, Harnwell also believed that the new era had become particularly well-defined since the mid-1950s. He told a group of journalists in 1965, "only . . . since the Second World War and in the latter part of these two decades, have we turned to the business of making the results of research and instruction more usefully effective to our immediate environment." Harnwell called this "third activity" "the utilization of knowledge."[141] Speaking in 1966, he remarked that "the past decade in particular has seen a rapid rise of the function of transferring knowledge to immediate utility at the interface between [educational] institutions and local industry and commerce."[142] Harnwell's leadership of Penn aimed to further this trend.

Harnwell's concept of "utilization of knowledge" as marking a new era of excellence in the university's evolution had several salient aspects. First, his choice of "utilization" suggests that he was working within the conceptual framework of Kerr's *The Uses of the University*. Second, universities' move toward "utilization of knowledge" entailed that "involvement in community and world affairs" was the most recent mark of the university. Third, his belief that such involvement was "indicative of the maturity attained by universities in assuming leadership and responsibility in society" shows that he conceived of the university as an organism growing toward some state of greater excellence, and thus that he conceptualized the university within a particular notion of history.[143]

Harnwell used the same notion of history to situate what he saw as a social revolution characterized by the advance of science and the growing pervasiveness of urban life. In so doing, he emphasized that the postwar era was a distinct period of human history, which entailed a different kind of university. Harnwell began to speak of the surges of science and urbanity as defining a new era of civilization as early as 1961, at the public announcement of launching UCSC.[144] A few years later, he began to use the term "revolution" to speak of these surges, which emphasized the world-historical importance he placed on them. In the WPC 1964 annual report, Harnwell wrote that "the University City Idea is based on a commitment to the pursuit and production of knowledge and the application of knowledge to all areas of life for individual and community good. Obviously this idea is not original with us. In Western Civilization, it emerged in the Renaissance, gathered force in the Industrial and American Revolutions, and is now at the center of the Scientific Revolution."[145] Here he used a framework offered by Glenn Seaborg a year earlier, which suggested that the current surge of attention to science constituted a "Third Revolution" following the American and Industrial Revolutions.[146] Seaborg, a Nobel laureate in chemistry and one of the most important figures in twentieth century American science, argued that a central facet of the Third Revolution was that economic growth required new ideas (produced by "science"); Harnwell enunciated such ideas around the same time. Seaborg was then chairman of the US Atomic Energy Commission (1961–1971), but had previously succeeded Kerr as chancellor at Berkeley (1958–1961).

While the university's relationship to the revolution of science might have been obvious, Harnwell insisted that the revolution of urbanization exerted a similar influence.[147] In 1967, he called urbanization a "social revolution which is effecting [sic] the lives of every man and woman in the United States," and cited it as "another of the external forces which is changing the shape and character of higher education." Universities, he believed, must join "the search for solutions for some of society's most pressing and emerging problems" that this revolution produced.[148]

Harnwell believed that one source of solutions in the midst of the historic tide of urbanization was closer collaboration between university and industry, about which he had been enthusiastic since his early days as chairman of physics. Here again he sounded a similar note to Kerr, who argued that business and universities were becoming more alike. As president, Harnwell spent an astounding amount of time speaking to business and trade groups such as the Corporate Fiduciaries Association, the American Society of Appraisers, and various chambers of commerce. Why? Harnwell cited urbanization.

Regarding his encounter with the appraisers, he reflected that "not many years ago, the sight of a university president speaking to such a worldly group as yours would have seemed strange to most persons whether of the business community or the academic community . . . many of us wish such meetings could have been convened a long time ago . . . the full tide of urbanization in America, and the world for that matter, is bringing together the resources of government and education with those of business and industry."[149] To be sure, the president of a major university is a civic figure upon whom such groups often call to make speeches. But many presidents decline most such invitations. Harnwell, however, being dedicated to making the university a community service institution, wanted strong ties with these constituencies. No doubt fundraising was also a goal, but the service rhetoric was not a ruse for raising money. Harnwell believed that the course of world history required universities to become community service institutions in his time.

The notion that universities should provide direct service broke with earlier understandings of the elite research university's mission. To be sure, universities throughout history have presented themselves as servants of society. As Harnwell noted, "The traditional and familiar functions of teaching and research are of themselves public service functions of paramount importance to society."[150] But during the postwar period, many university leaders began to believe that their institutions must render such service more *directly* than before, as a response to external pressures. No longer was it sufficient only to educate students who would then improve society through their professions and organizations; now universities *as institutions* must engage in serving the community around them. Harnwell framed this concept of direct service within the national purpose idiom when he said that "historically a university met society's need for the fruits of learning at arm's length, through the individuals it educated and the knowledge it put on record. Today the American university has itself become an instrument of national purpose." In his view, "the American university's function of extending to governmental, military, and industrial organizations the direct benefits of its widely diverse and highly specialized competence . . . sprang from the pressure of two world wars."[151]

Harnwell's concept of the urban university as community service institution, with its emphasis on direct service, comes into sharper relief when compared to urban universities' orientation toward their cities in earlier periods. Prior to World War II, most American universities located in urban areas were not concerned with direct service to their cities. New York University is a case in point. NYU's 1932 centennial celebration "revealed a wish to escape altogether from its own city of New York and from urban life in general." The idea "that there might be a distinctly urban role for universities was not even suggested by these speakers and discussants, whose obliviousness toward this notion—such a commonplace today—shows how easily NYU found contemporary support for its exercise in urban denial."[152] The University of Chicago was a striking partial exception to this pattern and throws Penn's postwar efforts into the boldest relief.

William Rainey Harper, Chicago's first president (1892–1906), was one of the first to declare the urban university a unique institution. In an address given at Columbia in 1902, Harper spoke of a university "which is compelled to meet the demands of an urban environment [and] to deal with problems which are not involved in the work of universities located in smaller cities," but he meant something different from what Harnwell would later intend by similar language. Harper's problems included "the care of thousands of the students, instead of hundreds; the management of millions instead of thousands of dollars; the distribution of a staff of officers made up of hundreds instead of tens." Far from Harnwell's technocratic vision of the urban university, Harper's was paternalistic: "Coeducation is one thing if considered from the point of view of an institution located in a village and having two hundred or three hundred students. It is, of course, a different thing in an institution having a thousand students and located in a small city; but it is a problem of still another kind when the institution has three or four thousand students and is in the heart of a city of one or two millions of people. The standards of life are different, and the methods of life are greatly modified.[153] Harper's focus was inward—what did the context of the city mean for the university's approach to student life, faculty, and finances?[154] Harnwell's was outward—how could the university directly address the problems of the city? Unlike Harper, Harnwell articulated and acted on a desire for the university to be a direct instrument of social change in the city.[155]

Harper's vision of the university and its role in the city met a challenge from one of his most prominent faculty members, John Dewey. Harper was committed to the ideal of pursuing specialized knowledge for its own sake, which governed the rise of American research universities in the late nineteenth century. To advance this agenda, Harper divided academic units into smaller components to reflect scientific specialties, thus becoming a pioneer in the departmental organization of universities.[156] He believed that a compulsion to orient academic work toward problems of the city might hinder such pursuit of knowledge. As Robin Bachin has noted in her study of Chicago, "University administrators posited science and the cultivation of expertise as areas that were at odds with local activism. Rather than linking scientific investigation with social reform, the university erected barriers between the two that curtailed the activities of its faculty and thwarted broader involvement with the surrounding community." Dewey took the opposite approach with his belief that knowledge should be pursued in relationship to the "problems of men." Dewey disliked Harper's push for specialization, and thought it hindered the university from being oriented toward social problems.[157] The rise to prominence of the community service institution ideal at Harnwell's Penn, then, can be seen as the triumph of Dewey's model for the university over Harper's.

Chicago faculty, particularly in sociology, did conduct pathbreaking research on the city, especially after 1915. This research, however, differed from postwar university attempts to solve urban problems in at least two ways. First, these researchers framed their work in a more departmental and disciplinary way; they did not orient it toward directly solving social problems. Sociologists conducted such research because the city of Chicago provided an ideal laboratory for collecting evidence from which to formulate a "science of society." Second, external patrons rarely funded these research projects directly. Much of the funding did come from a foundation, the Laura Spelman Rockefeller Memorial, but it came as lump sums to the university's Local Community Research Committee—which distributed the money internally— rather than attached to a particular project that the foundation favored.[158] The University of Chicago also pursued research aimed at the problems of the city in a limited way through its social work school, a formerly independent institution that it absorbed in 1920.[159]

By the 1960s, direct service had become the hallmark of Harnwell's concept of the university as a community service institution. He believed the university "must make a strong commitment to the improvement of life at the levels in which its direct intervention might be a contributing factor for improvement, a goal once accomplished through the traditional educational functions involving medicine, law, education, finance, engineering, and the sciences." Direct service was the "proper role and posture for the American institution of education in the last third of the 20th century. In acting with its communities in mind, it will not only be responding to the imperatives of the present but will be shaping the society of the 21st century."[160] Nor was such service optional. Harnwell insisted that "experience has shown that the facilities of our institutions can be employed effectively in serving the community in a pragmatic, direct manner, and with that knowledge we cannot refuse the responsibility to do so. The college or university, as a nonpolitical, nonprofit establishment, is in a position to experiment with programs of innovation and to provide a medium for action on the part of the private citizen, the philanthropic foundation, and the government."[161]

In articulating these views, Harnwell altered a rhetoric regarding the unique position and privileges of the university that had shaped the formative period of the American research university. Harnwell drew on that earlier rhetoric in emphasizing the nonpolitical, nonprofit character of the university but had a different rationale for cherishing it. In the earlier period, professors had prized this character as ensuring their unfettered pursuit of truth. Harnwell, by contrast, highlighted how those qualities afforded universities the freedom to experiment with programs for community service. He broke with the earlier understanding in other ways too. He described the university as a "medium for action" by various elements of society rather than strictly a purveyor of knowledge to those elements. He said that universities must respond to "the imperatives of the present" by becoming community service institutions, implying that such imperatives should set the agenda for university activities. "If in spirit and in fact a university is called upon to probe both the heavens and the ancient past," he wrote in 1964, "it is all the more concerned with the civilization of our own planet today." In this view he echoed Kerr's statement that universities' major task was to administer the present.

This conviction had implications for universities' involvement in the political order, which Harnwell outlined in a stunning statement: "This interest [in the present] coincides as never before with the practical aims of American foreign policy: the events of the past decade have found universities such as Pennsylvania in a timely position to help the United States bring about a more stable and hospitable world in which to pursue its destiny. Quite within the natural range of our intellectual mission, we find our University a major exporter of American knowledge and ideals to nations new and old—nations only now discovering the 20th century and nations on the frontiers of freedom."[162] Indeed, Penn teams undertook major institution building projects in Pakistan, Turkey, and Iran during the Harnwell years.

Harnwell believed the direct service paradigm demanded that Penn have a special status. He claimed that "more exacting responsibilities [for solving social problems] devolve upon a few major universities," and defended this statement at length:

These are institutions that can mobilize great concentrations of brainpower and facilities in each of many fields—in medicine, law, the physical sciences, the life sciences, economics, and the other applied social sciences . . . These are institutions that are large enough, versatile enough, sound enough, and close enough to the centers of population to exert a direct influence on society. In a day when American know-how has become a prime instrument of foreign policy, these are institutions capable of exporting American knowledge—and with it American social and economic concepts—to wherever the line of freedom needs bolstering. Pennsylvania is one of those few institutions.[163]

Harnwell did not cite a need for Penn to export literature or philosophy as part of its direct service to the world. In his view, American modernity was based on scientific method; the disciplines he listed were useful in that sense.

Harnwell was not concerned that such direct public service threatened the character of the university. Indeed, he believed the opposite. He argued that "there is no reason to believe that the trend of education's practical involvement with society will not continue nor that it should be curtailed because of the risks that some see to educational integrity."[164] He also believed that "far from diluting the quality of their academic pursuits, this sharing of knowledge between educational institutions and every segment of government, industry, and society as a whole has strengthened the institutions themselves. The research is more relevant to the live, contemporary problems that confront society."[165] The implication that a university's strength could be measured by the extent to which its research engaged social problems illuminates Harnwell's idea of the university as community service institution.

Harnwell continued to sound the theme of direct service to urban society until the end of his presidency. He told a 1968 audience that Penn had "established a Chair of Urbanism and Human Resources as a part of our *planned effort* to enlarge University programs concerning the urban environment and its problems, a major step in our developing concentration on the city as the primary social organization for man."[166] Human resources was a concept that emerged from industrial relations in the 1940s, which suggests that ideas from industrial relations still shaped the instrumental university in the late 1960s. Penn also in 1968 established the Center for Urban Research and Experiment (CURE) to be available to agencies throughout Pennsylvania and the three-state region for consulting and long-range studies.[167] The first director of CURE was none other than Robert B. Mitchell, who had come to Philadelphia a quarter century earlier to direct the new City Planning Commission.

Gaylord P. Harnwell helped to reshape the American university and its relationship with the political and economic order after World War II. His self-presentation as one who rode along with natural evolutionary changes in the university was not entirely accurate, but neither did he forcefully reorient a reluctant faculty. Rather, he articulated a sentiment latent in the Penn faculty, one which already motivated several university endeavors. Although not always an original thinker on the university's mission, he synthesized important ideas of his day into a consistent and compelling rhetoric for the university to take a particular orientation. As one of the first presidents to explore implications of the emerging knowledge economy for the university, Harnwell shaped the thought of those who would follow on an issue that would become one of the most important in American higher education. Harnwell's rhetoric for the instrumental, urban university led the University of Pennsylvania to a new understanding and practice of its mission. This change had important ramifications because of Penn's standing among American universities. Although never in the very top tier of research institutions, Penn had been since the late nineteenth century one of only a handful of American universities that held the advancement of pure knowledge through research as a primary mission. Its instrumental turn, in which knowledge pursued in order to address urban problems also became a primary concern, contributed to the larger movement of American universities in that direction. In 2006, the Carnegie Foundation for the Advancement of Teaching revised its widely utilized Carnegie Classification of Institutions of Higher Education, first developed under the direction of Clark Kerr in 1970. Among the revisions was a new category, the Community Engagement Classification.[168] The University of Pennsylvania was among the inaugural class of institutions to receive this designation.[169] Harnwell would have been pleased.

Despite Harnwell's success in advancing the community service institution ideal, however, the grandest piece in his plan, the University City Science Center, never lived up to his initial expectations for its scale or impact. To be sure, UCSC had some success; by 1976 it hosted 60 firms and 4,000 jobs, and as of 2009 nearly 100 companies employing over 7,500 people called it home. Yet numerous disappointments characterized UCSC. Its first president, Jean Paul Mather, resigned in 1967 in frustration over UCSC's inability to meet its ambitious goals.[170] UCSC never came close to filling its buildings with science-based companies, and it rented much of the space back to Penn for administrative and research use. Moreover, UCSC did not bring prosperity even to its immediate vicinity, much less the larger neighborhood. The area just blocks north and west of UCSC's mid-rises continued to be characterized by dilapidated buildings and frequent crime. These situations suggest the limits of universities' ability to be direct agents of social change, and urge caution for visionary leaders who hope to "use" the university in this way.

CHAPTER 4

"Instruments of Technical Cooperation"

American Universities' Institution Building Abroad

University of Pennsylvania president Gaylord P. Harnwell's 1959 federal tax return raised eyebrows among IRS auditors. Harnwell had claimed a deduction for a trip to Africa as a business expense, and the IRS was skeptical. What business did the president of an American university have in Africa?

Harnwell laid out his rationale in a letter to his lawyer. "The business of being President of the University," he wrote, "is a hard one which requires long hours, much gargling, and a cast iron digestion. If you are not bright-eyed and on your toes, you don't get an increase in salary; and if you are a real sluggard and make no effort to better yourself, you are apt to find yourself in the bread line. So I beaver away at all sorts of activities which may appear to be extraneous to the Internal Revenue Service but which are in fact directed toward my professional betterment and as an incidental by-product are of benefit to the University." He continued: "I could see in 1959 that to get ahead in my profession I had better busy myself about African education."[1] He saw Africa entering a period of rapid decolonization and nation building, creating a need for higher education institutions. He thus believed that in order to maintain his stature among university presidents, he needed to be at the forefront of American efforts to assist in creating African universities.

Harnwell's 1959 visit to colleges in Kenya and Uganda was part of a string of four such international trips in five years. In 1956, he took a round-the-world trip highlighted by keynoting the inaugural festivities of the Institute of Public and Business Administration (IPBA) at the University of Karachi (KU) in Pakistan, a unit that a team of Penn faculty had created under a contract with the US government. The voyage also included a stop at Kanazawa, Japan, where Penn had a sister relationship with a university.[2] In 1958, Harnwell ventured to the Soviet Union and later chronicled his visit in a 1960 book, *Russian Diary*. Lastly, in 1960, Harnwell led a team of Penn faculty to Shiraz, Iran, where they began the planning of a new American-style university for the shah, which they dubbed Pahlavi University to honor his family name. Once again Harnwell wrote a book about his exploits, *Educational Voyaging in Iran*. Two years later, Harnwell smoked cigarettes with the shah on Penn's campus and awarded the dictator an honorary degree with a citation claiming that the shah "excited the admiration of all who cherish freedom and human dignity."[3]

Harnwell represented a new educational internationalism among American university leaders in the postwar era.[4] While his activities seemed extreme, many other presidents made such trips, albeit less frequently. Harnwell was correct that overseas adventures and attention to global needs more broadly had become a standard part of the postwar university president's job. How did the conviction that American universities had a duty to build institutions abroad take root and grow to widespread acceptance?

The instrumental university model influenced institutions' enthusiastic embrace of such work. American research universities believed their overseas efforts could help bring about the promises of modernity in the host countries. The influence of external patrons on university activities perhaps reached its zenith in universities' international projects. The three major patrons for such activities were the US government, the United Nations, and foundations (especially the Ford Foundation).[5] Overseas adventuring was also a key site where the vocabulary of the instrumental university developed, prior to Clark Kerr popularizing it in *The Uses of the University* (1963).

My argument about universities' overseas institution building opens at least three new vistas for understanding postwar US development and modernization programs. Each vista highlights the prominence of institutions in the thought of development policymakers and theorists. They believed that universities *as institutions* were essential delivery mechanisms for development, that public administration was critical for bringing American-style modernity to developing countries, and—especially by the late 1950s—that institutions were central to the development process because of their role in adapting Western technologies to non-Western cultures. Historians of modernization have largely neglected these tenets.[6] Yet modernization meant

FIGURE 5.   University of Pennsylvania president Gaylord P. Harnwell welcomed the shah of Iran, Mohammed Reza Pahlavi, to campus in April 1962. Harnwell participated in many overseas educational ventures, including building a university for the shah in Shiraz, Iran. From the Collections of the University of Pennsylvania Archives.

not only massive infrastructure projects, psychological adjustment of individuals, and grassroots democratic community development, as existing accounts have emphasized. It was also fundamentally about creating large-scale organizations that would be the backbone of modern social life. Many proponents of modernization said it entailed the creation of an organization society. American experts believed that emerging organizational societies must be administered properly in order to promote economic development. The university was the key instrument for administering American modernity abroad because it exemplified the modern social fabric and trained those who would administer society. Public administration experts such as Harlan Cleveland and Edward Weidner—who directed foundation-funded organized research projects on American universities' international institution building, at Syracuse and Michigan State respectively—must be seen as central figures in the intellectual history of development, alongside more typical choices such as Gabriel Almond and Walt Rostow. Moving beyond development and modernization to our understanding of postwar US foreign relations in general, I argue that American universities became at least moderately influential diplomatic actors in the 1950s.

A key building block for all of this activity was the US government contract program with American universities for international projects, which began in the early 1950s and grew rapidly. Two case studies of institution-building endeavors in Pakistan under government contracts—the aforementioned University of Pennsylvania project in public and business administration and a subsequent University of Southern California effort in those fields—reveal forces that instrumentalized the private research university. Pakistan was among the countries hosting the largest number of American university projects. Penn and USC were among the private research institutions most active in overseas work on government contracts, a role associated with land-grant universities. Academic and foundation officials who evaluated university work overseas typically cited high-level institutional support as the characteristic most vital for success. Penn and USC displayed such support, in different ways. At Penn, it came from President Harnwell's personal commitment to international work. While the involvement of USC's top leaders was less clear, unlike Penn it established an administrative unit to coordinate overseas work. These case studies point to larger issues in the character and public purpose of postwar American research universities.

Overseas Contracts for Universities

The origins of American universities' extensive overseas institution-building work in the 1950s lay in the Point Four program of international technical assistance that President Harry S. Truman announced in his 1949 inaugural address.[7] Truman called it "a bold new program for making the benefits of our scientific advances and industrial progress available for the improvement and growth of underdeveloped areas." He stated that "the United States is pre-eminent among nations in the development of industrial and scientific techniques." Economic resources were limited, "but our imponderable resources in technical knowledge are constantly growing and are inexhaustible."

In articulating a messianic vision of science and depicting the United States as a scientific, modern nation, Truman echoed *Science: The Endless Frontier*, a 1945 manifesto penned at Franklin D. Roosevelt's request by his chief wartime science advisor Vannevar Bush, director of the Office of Scientific Research and Development (OSRD). Truman also framed his speech with an ideology of economic development and the Cold War context. He believed that "greater production is the key to prosperity and peace. And the key to greater production is a wider and more vigorous application of modern scientific and technical knowledge." Such a program would combat "hunger, misery, and despair" and thus prevent spread of communism into the southern half of the globe.[8]

The ensuing attempt to create legislation implementing Point Four revealed more clearly how the economic development ideal shaped the program. A Democratic bill introduced in the House promoted "a cooperative endeavor for assisting in the development of economically underdeveloped areas of the world." A competing Republican "bill to establish a program of foreign economic development" proposed a "Foreign Economic Development Administration" in the State Department. On the first day of hearings for the compromise resolution, Secretary of State Dean Acheson told Congress, "The bill now before you establishes economic development of underdeveloped areas for the first time as a national policy."[9]

Despite this unity on the economic development ideal, the US government had difficulty providing a stable organizational home for the Point Four impulse. The Truman administration took a year and a half to get legislation through Congress, which appropriated a meager $35 million to a new Technical Cooperation Administration (TCA) in the Department of State under the Act for International Development of 1950.[10] Nevertheless, the United States opened technical cooperation offices in sixteen African and Asian countries, most of which would soon bear the name United States Operations Mission (USOM) for their host country. Moreover, the impetus for the US government to provide international development aid gathered steam in subsequent years. The Mutual Security Act of October 1951 created the independent Mutual Security Agency (MSA) in the Executive Office of the President to coordinate all assistance—military, economic, and technical—to foreign countries that had strategic significance. The MSA absorbed the Economic Cooperation Administration (ECA), which had administered the Marshall Plan (economic assistance), and the Mutual Assistance Program, which gave military assistance to poor countries on the condition that they aligned with the United States in event of war with the USSR and accepted US military advisors in their country. The Mutual Security Act specifically preserved TCA, but henceforth TCA had administrative responsibility for technical assistance only in countries not considered strategically significant, whereas MSA administered technical assistance in strategic countries and oversaw funds for all technical assistance. The Mutual Security Act increased the technical assistance appropriation to $211 million but mandated that all technical assistance must strengthen the security of the United States.[11] Nevertheless, the number of countries in technical cooperation agreements with the United States had increased to thirty-five by January 1953.[12]

Dwight Eisenhower became president that month and appointed Harnwell's predecessor as University of Pennsylvania president, Harold Stassen, as director of mutual security, in charge of the MSA. Later that year, Congress created the Foreign Operations Administration (FOA) to combine the functions of TCA and MSA, but the Mutual Security Act continued to govern foreign assistance. Congress renewed it each year until 1961, which produced annual struggles over the size of the foreign aid budget and balancing military, economic, and technical aid. Stassen became director of foreign operations, head of FOA—thus gaining full oversight of technical assistance—and kept the post until March 1955. The Mutual Security Act of 1954 broke up FOA effective July 1, 1955, sending military assistance to the Department of Defense and shifting technical assistance back into the State Department under the new International Cooperation Administration (ICA), which assumed the university contract program. The program found its final home in the Agency for International Development (AID) after John F. Kennedy persuaded Congress to create AID with the Foreign Assistance Act of 1961, which superseded the Mutual Security Act.[13] These agencies were large; the 1956 ICA staff telephone directory alone contained about 1,200 names.[14]

The university contracts abroad program began sometime in the early years of Point Four, with influence from the field of agriculture and the Association of Land-Grant Colleges and Universities (ALGCU). The program's origins are murky. Dean Rusk, speaking in 1958 as president of the Rockefeller Foundation to a gathering of university and ICA officials discussing the program, remarked, "The university contracts abroad are a highly intelligent, I think one could almost say, a brilliant invention of the greatest promise in the technique of technical assistance . . . if there is sitting in this room tonight the person who, in his heart, knows he invented it, I extend to him my deepest congratulations."[15] Universities did respond quickly to Truman's Point Four address. John A. Hannah, president of Michigan State College and president of ALGCU, "formally offered the assistance of the universities to President Truman, on behalf of" ALGCU.[16] Hannah, a leading proponent of the instrumental university, advocated universities' international engagement and later served as administrator of AID under President Nixon. Truman appointed Hannah to the International Development Advisory Board created by the Act for International Development in 1950 to advise Truman on implementing Point Four. The board's report said nothing about a university contract program.

Hannah and other Point Four framers later recalled the influence of Henry G. Bennett, president of Oklahoma A&M College from 1928 until 1950, when he became assistant secretary of state and administrator of TCA.[17] A month before perishing in a plane crash during an inspection trip to a Point Four project in Iran in December 1951, Bennett gave a plenary address on Point Four to the ALGCU annual convention. He told the group he was "convinced that one of the soundest ways we can help in the long run is to assist the other countries to develop institutions like our Land-Grant Colleges . . . we should not try to transplant our own institutions intact to foreign soil, but rather to help other people develop the kind of institutions that suit their own particular needs."[18] According to Hannah, Bennett believed that involving American universities in technical aid "was a possible way of getting away from the suspicion of host governments toward the United States, for while individuals and governments might be suspicious of our government, or of economic imperialism, American colleges and universities, were not suspect."[19] Three others, all agriculture specialists, joined Bennett in the initial planning of the university contract program.[20] One of them, Stanley Andrews, an Arkansas farm editor, was director of the US Department of Agriculture's Office of Foreign Agricultural Relations (OFAR) from 1949 to 1951. OFAR had already "engaged in some university contracting and was planning more under the authority of the Smith-Mundt Act" of 1948, but the establishment of TCA altered these plans.[21] Andrews was involved in Point Four from the start. After Truman's address, Secretary of Agriculture Charles Brannan sent Andrews on a round-the-world trip toward developing a pilot program for Point Four aid, which resulted in two Cornell professors going to Thailand. Andrews worked closely with Bennett (whom he had already known for twenty years) and became TCA administrator himself after Bennett's death.[22]

Given this context for the government's early contracts with universities for technical assistance abroad, which began in 1951, they unsurprisingly focused on building agricultural institutions. The first three projects chosen (although not the first three formally begun) had strong connections to Point Four framers. Bennett's Oklahoma A&M worked with the Imperial Ethiopian College of Agriculture and Mechanical Arts; Hannah's Michigan State with the National University of Colombia for its agricultural colleges at Palmira and Medellin; and the University of Arkansas with the agricultural school in Divisa, Panama. Arkansas was the home state for Andrews and two leading congressional allies of Point Four, Senator J. William Fulbright and Representative Brooks Hays.[23] Another early agricultural contract joined the University of Arizona with the Agricultural College of Iraq at Abu Ghraib. OFAR jointly administered some of these contracts with TCA, while MSA operated others.[24] The first public administration project also began in 1952, the University of Michigan's work to build the Institute of Public Administration at the University of the Philippines.[25]

Whoever invented the university contracts abroad program, Stassen made it a force. Stassen asked the ALGCU if he could address its annual convention in November 1953. There he proposed a formal university contracts abroad program and outlined its details, including a model contract that he offered to review with university officials after his talk.[26] His rationale for the program rested on a similar presupposition to the modernization theory that emerged later in the 1950s—that the course of American history could be repeated in other countries. The university contracts program, he believed, would "translate to the world scene to a very major extent" the role that land-grant colleges played in the development of the United States.[27] Stassen subsequently issued a directive to all FOA mission chiefs to "get university contracts," a minimum of one per mission.[28] In other words, each mission chief should find an institution in the host country that would request a contractual relationship with an American university. This order typified Stassen's unilateral style of running FOA. His underlings "called such directives 'SSS' (Stassen says so) policies."[29] Thus the government—albeit under the guidance of a former university president—made the major push for the contract program.

Several factors motivated this push, according to John M. Richardson Jr.'s summary of an interview with Stassen in the mid-1960s. Stassen believed university contracts could "circumvent" government bureaucracy and institutionalize "channels for growth and development that would be flexible and responsive to the needs of individual countries." He "hoped that an increased emphasis on contracts would foster Congressional support for long-term commitments in the foreign assistance program at a time when conservative elements in Congress were challenging the basic idea of aid" and "that expanded university participation would be a way of improving the quality of personnel in the foreign assistance program."[30] In addition, the university contract program fit both the Eisenhower administration's desire to use "nongovernmental, contract personnel instead of government direct hire personnel in foreign assistance programs" and a congressional mandate for Stassen to reduce FOA personnel by at least 25 percent by January 1, 1954.[31]

In just over two years at the helm of MSA/FOA, Stassen expanded the number of university contracts from eight to at least sixty-six and gave

FIGURE 6.   Harold E. Stassen is sworn in as US deputy representative to the United Nations Disarmament Commission by White House administrative officer Frank K. Sanderson while President Dwight Eisenhower looks on, August 5, 1955. Stassen joined the Eisenhower administration at its inception and built the university contracts abroad program before transitioning to this post. Photo originated by the National Park Service and provided courtesy of the Eisenhower Presidential Library.

the program its enduring structure.[32] By 1956, it constituted about 20 percent of the roughly $120 million US technical aid budget.[33] The program stagnated during the two-year reign of Stassen's successor John Hollister, Robert Taft's one-time law partner and a former representative from Ohio, but then grew continuously through the mid-1960s.[34] In early stages the program lacked a consistent formal name. It was sometimes called the Inter-College Exchange (ICX) Project or the Inter-College Contract Program, but these names were used intermittently. The ICA produced an annual map showing the scope of the program (see figure 7). As of September 30, 1957 the ICA had eighty-three contracts with fifty-six American universities in thirty-nine countries with a total value of $60 million over the multiyear life of the contracts. The program ranged across Central and South America, Africa, the Middle East, South and East Asia, and even Western Europe.[35] India and Pakistan had the greatest number of contracts with ten and six, respectively.

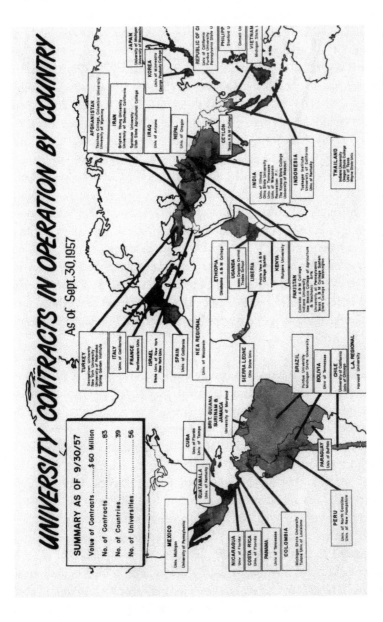

Figure 7. This map published by the US government's International Cooperation Administration provided a snapshot of its university contracts abroad program in 1957. The map illustrates that American universities were diplomatic actors around the world. From the Collections of the University of Pennsylvania Archives.

The scope of this program suggests that American universities became more significant actors in US foreign relations during this period, a reality that historians have been slow to recognize. In addition to Penn and USC, American universities with ICA contracts in 1957 included Harvard, Wisconsin, Tennessee, Purdue, Michigan State, Maryland, California, Chicago, Tulane, Florida, Tampa, Kentucky, Michigan, Buffalo, North Carolina, New Hampshire, Northwestern, Wyoming, Columbia, Texas A&M, Illinois, Rensselaer Polytechnic Institute, Ohio State, Kansas State, Missouri, Utah State, Syracuse, BYU, Arizona, SUNY, NYU, Oregon, Washington State, Colorado State, New Mexico A&M, Indiana, Georgetown, Nebraska, Oklahoma A&M, Rutgers, Prairie View A&M, Penn State, Tuskegee Institute, Massachusetts, Minnesota, Peabody College, Cornell, Stanford, Texas, Oregon State, and Wayne State.[36] In other words, the American university community as a whole was involved. As a result of the ICA university contracts abroad program, thousands around the world encountered the United States—and US government assistance—through American university personnel and institutions. As Hollister told a group of university leaders in 1956, "In a few weeks, one person, by his activities in a certain country, can perhaps destroy everything that we may try to do there."[37] University employees and entities carried out US foreign policy and affected the relations between the United States and other countries more broadly, in part by conveying ideas about and instilling practices of American modernity.

Most fields and projects of FOA/ICA contract work were instrumental, as expected from a program under the banner of technical assistance. A June 1955 policy document stated, "The technical fields in which these contracts may be underwritten by FOA are those which are directly related to a country's economic development program, such as agriculture, home economics, general and vocational education, public health, engineering, public administration, and business management."[38] Public administration was central in the thought of liberal internationalist elites during the 1950s and 1960s, as illustrated by the UN technical assistance program. The UN emphasized public administration as early as 1948, when the General Assembly ordered the planning of an international center for training in public administration. After that plan fizzled, in 1951 the UN established a Division for Public Administration and launched its first effort to assist public administration in a member state, Brazil.[39] One UN document encapsulated typical attitudes about administration in this era, stating, "Administrative improvement is the *sina qua non* in the implementation of programmes of national development."[40] UN publications with titles like *Administrative Roadblocks to Co-ordinated Development* attested to the importance policymakers gave to the linkage between administration and development.[41]

Even within public administration and the other technical assistance fields the US government sometimes pushed foreign universities to be more instrumental. In Japan, for example, "ICA and USOM criticize[d] what they consider[ed] the 'ivory tower' tendencies of Japanese universities in devoting too much of their research time and budgets to problems of 'pure theory' which do not interest the business or farming communities."[42] Unsurprisingly, land-grant institutions were thus heavily represented among ICA contractors around the world. The presence of elite private universities such as Penn, USC, Harvard, Chicago, Northwestern, Columbia, NYU, Georgetown, and Stanford, however, suggests the wide appeal of the instrumental university.

The critical mass of universities engaged in overseas adventures spawned a cottage industry of analyses of this new phenomenon by various committees and research projects. Among them, the most important was the American Council on Education Committee on Institutional Projects Abroad (CIPA), which existed from 1954 to 1960 on a Ford Foundation grant. CIPA aimed to assist American universities in their overseas work, especially by acting as a liaison with the US government. Members included prominent presidents like Harnwell and Hannah, as well as several professors involved with overseas projects. CIPA sponsored an annual Conference on University Contracts Abroad, where university, government, and foundation officials gathered to discuss overseas projects.

The language of the instrumental university germinated in these discussions of university projects abroad, as four examples suggest. First, at the 1955 CIPA conference, Representative Brooks Hays (D-AR) gave an address titled "Educational Cooperation, Instrument of National Policy."[43] The second example comes from the Institute of Research on Overseas Programs at Michigan State University, created in 1957 to conduct a sweeping research project funded by the Carnegie Corporation of New York. It examined the impact of American universities' overseas institution-building programs, both abroad and on the universities at home. The brochure circulated to promote this project probed the benefits of patrons asking American universities to help them meet their goals overseas: "From the point of view of the foundation, government agency, or overseas group, what can it expect to see achieved through the *device* of the American university? In other words, in comparison with other alternatives, what is the potential of the American university as an *instrument* of education and social action in this area?"[44] Characterizing the university as a device or instrument was original to this era. Such usage became more pronounced in the third example. CIPA chose for its November 1957 Conference on University Contracts Abroad—at which Vice President Richard Nixon was the keynote speaker—the title "Blueprint and Experience: Universities as Instruments of Technical Cooperation."[45]

Fourth, conversations about universities' overseas work also generated talk about the university's "uses." The Ford Foundation convened an elite Committee on the University and World Affairs in 1960, chaired by former University of Minnesota president J. L. Morrill and including the presidents of the Rockefeller Foundation and Carnegie Corporation of New York as well as top-level academic, business, and government leaders. Members discussed the propriety of external entities such as governments "using" the university for their ends. The committee noted "a traditional academic reluctance to think of society as *using* universities." Yet the committee argued that the very nature of the university actually required that it be used as an instrument for affecting society, within specified limits: "It is misused when it is made to serve as an agent of other institutions, when it is closely supervised, or when too many demands are made on it. When it is not used, however, or when it resists being properly used by society, it turns in on itself and suffers depreciation in its own and the public regard."[46] Moreover, "too much stress on the freedom of scholars to pursue their own interests would leave serious gaps in American competence of the kinds that only the universities can supply."[47] The committee also invoked the concept of "direct service."[48] These discussions show that Kerr did not invent the notions of the uses of the university and the university as an instrument. Rather, he gave new force and broader application to ideas circulating among elites concerned with universities' international activities, with whom he interacted regularly.

Beyond these general notions of the university as an instrument, discussions of university overseas programs established the more specific idea that the university could be an instrument for economic development. The FOA/ICA enunciation of this idea, building from Truman's Point Four rhetoric, gained broad recognition; everyone spoke about the university contract program in terms of economic development. CIPA member Walter H. C. Laves, chair of the Department of Government at Indiana University, told the first Conference on University Contracts Abroad in 1955 that establishing "educational institutions abroad is an essential aspect of economic development . . . the device of the contract is a master stroke of statesmanship as . . . universities are economically mobilized for carrying out this aspect of our foreign relations."[49] Montana State College president Roland R. Renne remarked to the same gathering, "The primary purpose of participation of American universities in institutional contracts abroad is to assist in the strengthening of economies of the free world."[50] The Committee on the University and World Affairs wrote in 1960 that ICA "treats the university by and large as a source of specific, purchasable services for economic development."[51] The economic development ideal thus encouraged academic personnel to make the university an instrument. Case studies of Penn and USC projects in Pakistan provide a closer view of how the US government university contracts abroad program instrumentalized the elite American research university.

The University of Pennsylvania in Pakistan

In March 1954, FOA asked Penn's Wharton School of Finance and Commerce "to enter into 'a sisterhood relationship' with the University of Karachi in Pakistan in order to assist that school in the establishment of an Institute of Public and Business Administration." Dean C. Canby Balderston commissioned Professor of Political Science Norman D. Palmer, a specialist on the politics of India, for a two-week survey trip "to investigate the proposed relationship in Karachi and to work out contractual details."[52] Palmer, a Yale PhD who spent fourteen years teaching at Colby College, moved to Penn in 1947 when the university began what would become a renowned program in South Asia Regional Studies.[53] At the time of FOA's request, Palmer was less than a year removed from spending the 1952–1953 academic year on a Fulbright fellowship in India, where he helped set up the Department of Political Science and International Affairs at the University of Delhi, visited eighteen universities, and observed the activities of the US technical cooperation mission.[54] He had also just published the first edition of his influential international relations textbook.[55] Palmer recalled, "I had recently come back from India with my family, when I was asked by the university if I'd like to go to Karachi and discuss the proposals. I thought it over deeply—for about 10 seconds—and said 'sure.'"[56]

Pakistan particularly interested the US government at this time.[57] Since Mao's victory in 1949 and the outbreak of the Korean War, the United States had sought to balance Chinese power in the region and build a defensive perimeter against Soviet encroachment. Realizing India's neutral inclinations and fearful the Soviets would court Pakistan, the United States pushed for Pakistan's allegiance. In April 1953, the two countries signed a technical cooperation agreement. The following month, Secretary of State John Foster Dulles visited Pakistan, India, and nine other countries in the region.[58] He criticized Egypt and India, but praised Turkey, Iraq, Syria, and especially Pakistan, where he was "immensely impressed by the martial and religious characteristics of the Pakistanis."[59] This report led the National Security Council to adopt a northern tier strategy, which held that the countries Dulles praised "could form a more effective defensive ring to encircle the Soviet bloc."[60] By early 1954, Eisenhower pledged military aid to Pakistan, and on May 19 the two countries signed a Mutual Defense Assistance Agreement. Right at this time, FOA asked at least four American universities to consider contract work in Pakistan. By the end of 1955, Pakistan had joined two American-inspired security pacts, the Southeast Asia Treaty Organization and the Baghdad Pact, solidifying its position as a US ally.

Three characteristics of Palmer's trip suggest the importance the US government placed on Pakistan. First, Palmer's April 12–24 stay in Karachi occurred rapidly after the March request from FOA. Second, his trip occurred on the heels of three similar tours. These surveys most likely became the State College of Washington project at University of the Punjab, the Texas A&M College project at the University of Dacca, and the Colorado A&M College project at the University of Peshawar, each of which covered multiple fields.[61] The former two contracts were the third and fourth largest in dollar amount among FOA contracts with American universities at the time, which further emphasizes the importance of Pakistan to US officials.[62] Third, Palmer met with an extensive range of people, especially in the Pakistani government, which suggests that US government personnel did significant legwork in arranging these contacts on short notice. He talked with high-level officials in the Ministry of Education, Ministry of Finance, Cabinet Secretariat, Planning Board, and State Bank of Pakistan, as well as several prominent businessmen and numerous University of Karachi faculty, including Vice-Chancellor A. B. A. Haleem. He spent time with the top American officials in Pakistan: Ambassador Horace Hildreth, who had been governor of Maine and president of Bucknell University before taking the diplomatic post for Eisenhower's first term, and Ralph Will, director of technical cooperation and head of mission at USOM/Pakistan. He also met with the leaders of the Pakistan offices of two American non-state entities, the Ford Foundation and the US Educational Foundation.[63] On the way home, Palmer stopped in the Philippines to visit the University of Michigan effort to build the Institute of Public Administration at the University of the Philippines and Stanford's project in business administration in Manila.[64]

Two people with whom Palmer visited played a special role in launching the project. One was Philip Newman, a British economist then serving as chairman of the KU Department of Economics and Commerce. He apparently lobbied for Penn to get the contract, especially with Vice-Chancellor Haleem.[65] The other person was Al Wilson, who at the time of Palmer's April visit was education and training officer at USOM.[66] Wilson wrote that he "served as mid-wife to the idea" of IPBA.[67]

Palmer concluded from his visit that "there is unquestionably a desperate need for assistance in the fields of public and business administration here" and recommended that Penn help KU establish an institute of public and business administration along the lines of a plan he sent to Vice-Chancellor Haleem the day of his departure. He told Balderston that KU was "a sad excuse for a University" but that throughout Pakistan, "The attitude toward Americans, of course, is excellent." He learned that Cornell, Indiana, and probably other universities had expressed interest in the kind of relationship that FOA and KU were asking Penn to consider. His plan called for five faculty and one librarian to arrive in Karachi around October 1, another two or three faculty around January 1, and that this group would formally launch the institute on July 1, 1955 and continue to staff it for two years. Palmer believed the institute would "be a real contribution to the objectives of the United States in the world and to the development of Pakistan . . . it will also be a frustrating and tough assignment."[68] Subsequent events proved him more correct on the latter point than on the former.

Balderston, at Palmer's urging, sold the program to Penn's administration. Balderston's pitch to Provost Edwin Williams included a key argument: Palmer and Director of Project Research and Grants Donald Murray had determined that the arrangement "should be of financial benefit to the University." He told Williams that FOA and KU favored Penn because they knew the reputation of Wharton, its Institute of Local and State Government (ILSG), and the South Asia Regional Studies program. The government's selection process for universities was murky; it later claimed that "universities are selected on the basis of a suitable location or specialty. The University of Wyoming, for example, is doing work in Afghanistan, which is somewhat similar to the State of Wyoming in terrain and resource pattern."[69] Penn was one of twenty-seven universities being asked to do such work around the world, and Balderston highlighted that Harvard, Michigan, and Stanford were among those already on board.[70] In other words, Penn could rest assured that this new kind of endeavor for American universities was suitable for an institution of its stature and not just for land-grant colleges. Williams approved, and Harnwell sent Penn's acceptance of the project and a proposed budget to FOA in late May.[71]

After deliberations over the summer, Penn signed a contract with FOA on September 24, covering the period from August 15, 1954 to June 30, 1957. The contract provided $800,000—$300,000 in each of the first two years and $200,000 for the final partial year. The bulk of the money paid salaries, but a sizeable chunk was overhead—20 percent of salaries paid for off-campus work and 45 percent of salaries paid for on-campus work, such as Palmer's role as campus coordinator.[72] Overhead was one of the key concepts in the system of federal government grants and contracts to fund university work that emerged after World War II. Technically it covered indirect project costs, but in practice universities could use it for anything they wanted, which made some grants and contracts a financial boon for universities.[73] This provision is probably why Penn thought the Karachi project would benefit the university financially. Observers at the time believed Harvard took overseas contracts "mainly to collect the administrative overhead allowance."[74] It is difficult to track what happened with the overhead money from the Karachi contract. Some of it really was used for indirect costs, such as paying accounting professor Rufus Wixon $1,200 to manage the project's budget from Penn's campus after he returned from a two-year stint in Karachi.[75] The contract also stated that "services will be performed under the general direction of the Director of the US Operations Mission in Pakistan."[76] The notion that Penn was performing services signified an instrumental concept of the university. Giving ultimate authority over Penn activities to the USOM director—in contrast to the American academic tradition of freedom from government control—would come back to haunt Penn.

Two possible reasons for Penn undertaking the work in Pakistan warrant further examination: Stassen's influence and the potential financial gain. The latter is especially salient because the university, and the Wharton School in particular, were in the midst of heated discussions about a budget crisis right when the FOA request arrived. Harnwell inherited this crisis and began to address it immediately. In an October 1953 letter to faculty announcing the 1953–1954 budget, he identified a $1 million deficit in Penn's $27 million budget. He wrote another letter in January instructing persons in charge of unit budgets to make cuts in current expense and equipment budgets.[77] The Wharton School was up in arms over a directive (probably given to other schools also) to cut its overall expenditures, including salaries, by 10 percent for 1954–1955.[78] March 1954 featured a dizzying array of meetings between the Wharton faculty, chairmen, Dean Balderston, Provost Williams, and President Harnwell, along with a barrage of documents analyzing the situation and Wharton's future.[79] As Balderston bemoaned how Wharton's low salaries made it difficult to retain faculty, he made a statement that would seem shocking today: "The Wharton School's salary scale should be moved up so that it at least equals that of the College."[80] He speculated about "the savings of $19,650 if Dr. Hess and Dr. Palmer go on leave."[81] At this early stage of the Pakistan project, Balderston likely envisioned Palmer taking leave in conjunction with it. Perhaps, then, Penn administrators thought they could offload senior faculty salaries onto the FOA contract for Pakistan and replace them with instructors, thus helping solve the budget crisis.

Is it possible that Stassen offered contracts to Penn in part to ameliorate university budget problems he helped create? There is no direct evidence regarding the Karachi project, although Palmer and Stassen corresponded in early June.[82] But Stassen definitely secured the other FOA contract Penn entered around the same time, for collaboration between its School of Veterinary Medicine and Mexico's Ministry of Agriculture and associated Cattle Research Institute, which lasted until 1958.[83] Penn professor Geoffrey Rake "went directly to Stassen who agreed, without consultation with his staff, to allocate $18,000 to the project."[84] While this amount was a fraction of other FOA contracts (and thus unlikely to affect Penn's budget substantially), the project had joint funding from corporate sources: pharmaceutical company Squibb de Mexico, with whom Rake consulted, and its American parent Olin Mathieson Chemical Corporation.[85] This project was not the only example of joint funding under the Stassen regime. Dean G. Holmes Perkins led a team from Penn's School of Fine Arts that spent several years beginning in 1955 creating the Middle East Technical University of Architecture and City Planning in Ankara, Turkey. The UN initiated and funded this project, but as of May 1955, FOA was on the brink of signing a three-year, $300,000 contract with Penn for joint support before unknown factors—possibly related to Stassen's departure from FOA and its transformation into ICA—scuttled it.[86] As with Harnwell, the desire for professional prestige drove Perkins to engage in overseas institution building. He recalled that UN consultant "Charlie Abrams recommended three universities that could do it. We were number one, Harvard was number two and the University of California was number three. Having just come from Harvard, I couldn't afford to let Harvard have the job. I didn't want it, but I took it."[87]

Stassen also attempted to create another project for Penn under Perkins's leadership. He wrote Harnwell in November 1954 to follow up on a conversation at a recent Wharton dinner. Stassen suggested an FOA contract for Perkins and the School of Fine Arts to study "whether it might be possible to design a type of village construction, organization, and plan, with the use of indigenous materials" in "undeveloped non-Communist areas" of the world.[88] Perkins met Stassen in Washington in early December to discuss the issue, then took William Wheaton along for a December 21 meeting with FOA official George L. Reed.[89] Although it is unclear whether anything ever came of this proposal, it exhibits Stassen's proactive outreach to universities and Penn's interest in international work.[90]

Whatever Penn's motivations for the Karachi project, it assembled a seven-man faculty for IPBA (five in business administration, two in public administration). Only three were tenured professors, including Chief of Party G. Wright Hoffman, nearing age sixty, professor of insurance and marketing and director of Wharton's Securities Research Unit; and Associate Chief of Party Rufus Wixon, chairman of accounting. The others included one instructor and three from outside Penn.[91] Palmer thought about including a sociologist, but "the people in FOA told [him] quite positively that they were interested in programs of *technical* assistants [*sic*] only."[92] The contract put strict controls on faculty appointments, which later led to friction between the government and the university. It stated that FOA must approve personnel, and that they must be terminated upon written request from FOA, the government of Pakistan (GOP), or KU. Like every FOA contract, this one stipulated that all Penn personnel involved in the project, whether in Pakistan or on the home campus, must obtain security clearances. Universities disliked this provision. University of Chicago economist T. W. Schultz lambasted the rule: "Why the universities of the United States allow these clearances to stand . . . is beyond me. It implies weakness on the part of our universities or a willingness to see their own personnel and work impaired in many and sundry ways."[93]

Despite these government strictures, Penn's contract did provide that each professor would be paid a salary considerably higher than his regular academic salary, probably as an incentive to lure faculty to Pakistan. FOA considered at least part of the additional salary an "overseas differential" (not to be confused with overhead, which went to the university) of the same amount it paid to its own employees stationed in Pakistan.[94] Another reason for the higher salaries was that faculty on overseas contracts were paid on a twelve-month rather than an academic year basis. Hoffman made $14,300 in Pakistan after earning $9,900 at Penn, while Wixon's Pakistan salary was $14,000.[95] Each man's salary in Pakistan was higher than that of any professor at the University of Pennsylvania, where the top professorial salary in 1952–1953 (including department chairs and directors) had been $13,450.[96] Hoffman landed in Karachi on October 24, and several colleagues soon followed.

IPBA officially opened on July 1, 1955, and classes began a couple of weeks later. The fall semester ran from mid-July through early December, and the spring semester from mid-December through early April. The institute featured full-time graduate programs leading to the MBA and MPA degrees, in-service training of shorter duration, and a research element that included the Management Services Program, which helped business or public officials with specific programs that needed expertise. Both the MBA and MPA required a bachelor's degree for admission and twenty-eight credits for completion, including a thesis, broken down to four three-credit courses and one two-credit course each year. These requirements were less stringent than most comparable degrees in the United States. The curriculum was basic, with both tracks sharing a first-year core of statistics, accounting, and economics.[97]

Early reviews of IPBA were mixed. Roger F. Evans, assistant director of the social science division of the Rockefeller Foundation, wrote in August 1956 that "in all my travels [I] have seen [no project] that has made quicker progress or shown greater promise."[98] Some reports from the inside were less sanguine. Wixon wrote to Palmer in the middle of IPBA's first semester that the students were "somewhat of a disappointment. All of us are going very slowly and certainly the level of what we are doing is more that of the first two years of undergraduate work rather than graduate, but at least a third of them are having difficulties. They are not accustomed to daily preparations and also like to come to class when they feel like it." Wixon's comments pointed to the clash of values that occurred when American professors entered the realm of Pakistani higher education.

This clash of values, with its implications for the acceptance of IPBA among Pakistanis, played out in a number of ways. From the beginning, Penn personnel criticized the Pakistani examination system. At the university level, there was one exam per course at the end of the term, given by an outside examiner. The course's instructor neither prepared nor evaluated the exam. Penn faculty believed that this system inclined the students to a dismissive attitude toward the courses.[99] Penn felt like it had to implement practices foreign to Pakistani students such as requiring attendance and giving exams designed by the professor covering what was actually taught. The Central Superior Services (civil service) exam was another problem, because it did not recognize the field of public administration and thus there was little motivation for aspiring civil servants to seek an MPA at IPBA. According to USOM, "prior to the opening of the Institute there were no courses in public administration in Pakistan and no curriculum of business administration comparable to more than a commercial business college in the United States (existing courses in Commerce hardly appear directly comparable in subject-matter content.)" Central Superior Services made only a slight concession to the Americans, allowing a 200-point public administration option within the 1,200-point exam.

Near the end of the institute's second year in April 1957, USOM evaluated IPBA as the most successful out of the five "Mission ICX Contracts" in Pakistan (by this point Indiana University had joined the three other American institutions mentioned earlier). USOM praised IPBA for its high academic standards, such as its higher thresholds for earning a first-, second-, or third-class degree than was the area norm, and hoped that it could raise the standards of sister institutions. On the basis of this evaluation, ICA extended Penn's contract through June 30, 1959. Nevertheless, IPBA remained small and the full-time two-year master's programs had little traction among Pakistanis. They enrolled only sixty-two students, with just twenty in public administration.[100] In addition, ICA around this time registered broader concerns about the US aid program for Pakistan in a report for the State Department. ICA believed that the US emphasis on building Pakistan's military "was proving counterproductive to the establishment of a viable state structure," especially by diverting the most talented young Pakistanis to the military. ICA recommended a reorientation of American aid, including a reduction of military support.[101] ICA was interested in state building, and believed that American universities creating institutions to develop public administration in countries like Pakistan could be important instruments for achieving that goal.

Even in light of the positive evaluation and contract extension, difficulties beyond low enrollments rumbled under the surface. Penn was having trouble getting its faculty on board with the Karachi project, and ICA bureaucracy was becoming ever more niggling. In September 1957, Carroll K. Shaw became chief of the Near East and Asia Branch of ICA's Public Administration Division. He immediately began frequent correspondence with Palmer, and he traveled to Karachi in November to inspect the project. His strict adherence to ICA rules, particularly about travel and equipment for the Penn faculty in Karachi, annoyed Palmer. In an early letter, Shaw wrote that "we should not stretch regulations to suit the personal convenience of individuals."[102] Palmer fired back with a three-page, single-spaced letter stating that "on the contrary, I believe that we should stretch regulations to the maximum extent possible to suit the convenience of individuals . . . unfortunately, ICA's interference with our conduct of the project, down to the smallest details, and ultra-technical interpretations by the Office of Contract Relations make it very difficult for us to carry out contract objectives or to maintain the morale of the excellent people whom we have in Karachi."[103] Palmer, an original member of CIPA, had already spoken out publicly on this issue two years earlier (just a year into Penn's contract), when he told the Conference on University Contracts Abroad that "whether they intend to do so or not, officials of FOA-ICA place innumerable obstacles in the way of the interuniversity programs, and . . . the basic relationship between ICA and the American universities is an intolerable one from the point of view of the universities."[104] John B. Fox, director of overseas relations at the Harvard Graduate School of Business Administration, lauded Palmer's remarks, commenting that "it was nice to hear someone who felt that something more than white wash was needed."[105] The many hours that Palmer spent haggling with Shaw and other ICA officials were hours he could not spend preparing inspiring lectures for undergraduates or pondering original research.

Shaw also weighed in on an issue Penn was already aware of: despite the high salaries for teaching at IPBA, Penn had difficulty convincing its faculty to make the typical commitment of two years to Karachi. Harnwell became agitated by this problem at least by May 1957. He wrote to C. A. Kulp, who had become Wharton dean in 1955, "I have read with great interest the recent Karachi reports . . . I have also had extremely favorable reactions from various Foundation representatives, and it was a pleasure to be able to congratulate [Palmer and Hoffman] upon what is being accomplished in Karachi in the name of the University of Pennsylvania. It is all redounding greatly to our credit." Yet he was concerned "that not many of our own faculty have caught the spirit of enterprise which has characterized the men carrying on the Karachi Institute." Harnwell wondered if some professors recruited from outside Penn to staff IPBA would be "qualified" for a visiting position at Penn afterward and could enrich the campus with their international experience.[106] He also took concrete steps to reward service in Karachi. He wrote to Provost Jonathan Rhoads praising Wixon's work in Pakistan and hoping that it would be recognized in considering salary and rank when Wixon returned to campus that fall.[107]

Less than a year later, ICA seized on this issue. Shaw wrote a long letter to Harnwell in early March 1958, saying that they should begin thinking about extending the contract beyond June 1959 but that ICA wanted Penn to commit more regular faculty as a condition of contract extension. Things were looking up at IPBA since the introduction of evening courses in Fall 1957. Shaw believed that an "overwhelming . . . response in the form of applications from key officials . . . has made necessary a reconsideration of the Institute's curriculum and future staffing needs. This development has greatly increased the impact of the project in Karachi." Finally ICA officials saw something that had purchase with the Pakistanis, and they wanted to encourage more of it.

Shaw told Harnwell he had written directly to the president because the issue of insufficient faculty participation needed to be addressed at a university policy level. Shaw waxed philosophical about how this issue related to ICA's big picture for university contracts. One of ICA's goals, he wrote, was to spark cooperative relationships between American and foreign universities. American universities "can modernize and improve [foreign universities'] educational policies, curriculum, course content, teaching methods, and materials. The ICA contract is regarded as an instrument through which the American university is assisted in assuming this important role; we hope that the cooperative relationship thus established may continue long after the contract may terminate, or ICA go out of business." Shaw said that the American university must show sincere desire including the devotion of faculty resources; Harnwell wrote "dead on!" in the margin. Shaw believed that the lack of participation by regular Penn faculty meant that Penn was not achieving ICA's goal of "cultivation of continuing institutional relationships." He suggested that he come to Philadelphia to meet with Harnwell or a designate.[108]

Predictably, Harnwell sprang into action in response to Shaw's letter. He asked Rhoads, Willis J. Winn (who had taken the Wharton deanship earlier that year after Kulp's untimely death), and Palmer to meet with him within a week to plan a response and set policies to promote faculty participation. He added that "it is of great concern to me" to have strong faculty support "and that the administration shall recognize by exceptional promotion and salary increases the participation of members of the faculty in these activities."[109] After the four men met, Palmer planned a visit to Penn for Shaw on April 21. Palmer told Harnwell that everyone involved in the Karachi project was "deeply grateful to you for the personal interest which you have showed from the outset in all phases of this work."[110] Apparently the personnel committee told Shaw that it would meet with department chairmen to inform them that service in Pakistan would be counted favorably in considering promotion or merit increases.[111] Whether that ever happened is unclear.

This account of Penn's interaction with ICA over faculty participation in overseas contract work highlights several issues regularly featured in the broader conversation about university contracts abroad: the notion of a sister relationship between the American and foreign universities, how to prompt more regular faculty of the contracting university to serve on overseas projects, and the commitment of the entire university—rather than just a few people directly involved—to an overseas project. Palmer publicly questioned the viability of sister relationships, asking "in heaven's name, how is this continuing, lasting pattern of international cooperation to be carried on once the almighty dollar is somewhat removed from the scene?"[112] An early CIPA document prepared for discussion at the 1955 Conference on University Contracts Abroad reported several reasons for the difficulty in recruiting faculty, including "the preferred two-year period of service which raises uncertainties regarding positions and promotions upon return," "the timing of ICA approval of appointments not being predictable or geared necessarily to the academic year," and "the time-consuming and blanket ICA security clearance."[113] The Committee on the University and World Affairs linked faculty recruitment and institutional commitment. It recognized that "whether or not effective service abroad counts toward tenure and promotion" was a key factor determining the participation level of core faculty in overseas work. The committee urged "a long-range, university-wide approach, under the highest auspices, to the total complex of substantive activities and administrative arrangements in the international field." Such an approach would encourage central policymaking about the value of service under contracts abroad for faculty career advancement.[114] Penn stood out for Harnwell's personal commitment to overseas projects, but the university did not have a dedicated office to coordinate such work.

Despite Penn's willingness to break academic norms and change policies to meet ICA demands, several events in 1958 led to Penn's undoing as operator of the IPBA. First, there was a new five-year plan in conjunction with an expected contracted renewal by ICA. Second, an October 1958 coup brought Mohammad Ayub Khan to power in Pakistan and changed GOP priorities. Third and most importantly, a series of bizarre and belligerent diplomatic moves by USOM/Pakistan director James Killen brought Penn's involvement to an end.

The sparring between Penn and ICA that led to their final rupture began in discussions over contract renewal in fall 1958. The official ICA document that all parties needed to sign in order for the work to go forward was the Project Proposal and Approval Summary (PPA). This particular PPA was framed by the purposes of a five-year plan for IPBA released May 8, 1958 and jointly prepared by the Penn party in Pakistan, the Pakistani faculty of IPBA, and the Public Administration Division of USOM.[115] The plan called for Pakistani funding and staffing to cover an increasing share of IPBA work over time and to become complete when US assistance ceased at the plan's conclusion. Penn was initially hesitant to sign the PPA for a number of reasons. It wanted more assurances from the GOP—on issues such as funding, legal status, land, and status of Pakistani faculty—before renewing the contract.[116]

Killen reacted negatively to Penn's approach to the PPA, as indicated by an internal ICA document. He made a cryptic comment that Penn would not be worrying about the GOP funding commitment if it knew of current GOP deliberations on the subject in Karachi, which had delayed GOP signing of the PPA. He was upset with Penn personnel in Karachi for not responding to his query about what they wanted the legal status of IPBA to be. He claimed that IPBA's public administration courses were "seriously deficient" because they were too theoretical, US-oriented, and ignorant of GOP workings, which led to reduced acceptance of IPBA among Pakistanis. Speaking about the apparent difficulty of IPBA graduates in finding GOP jobs, Killen stated that he "does not believe that the graduates can be stuffed down the government's throat." He was also upset that Hoffman, without notifying USOM, submitted an IPBA budget through KU which was approved by the GOP; the GOP later balked at the "higher" budget set out in the PPA. "Everyone concerned is irritated over this latest manifestation of inexcusable unilateral action," Killen wrote of Hoffman. This incident suggests the difficulties that constrained American universities working overseas under the oversight of both the United States and host country governments.[117]

Penn's response to Killen's histrionics showed its own stridency in trying to maintain as much authority as possible to guide its program in Karachi. Writing to Shaw's subordinate, Palmer noted his disbelief of Killen's claim that the Penn party in Karachi would not respond to Killen on the desired legal status for IPBA, because they were discussing it very explicitly with Killen's subordinates when Palmer was in Karachi. He also blasted Killen's statement about public administration courses' neglect of Pakistani context as "definitely untrue" and "absurd."[118] Winn entered the fray too. He wrote to G. W. Lawson Jr., chief of ICA's Public Administration Division and Shaw's supervisor, in early February lauding Hoffman and said he was unable to find a suitable successor among senior Penn faculty. He insisted that Hoffman be reappointed for a two-year term and implied that it was a *sina qua non* of Penn extending the contract.[119]

Things heated up in March, following a late February letter from Lawson questioning whether Penn was devoting adequate resources to IPBA. Palmer responded that "we have not underestimated the importance of the project." He seemed worried that Lawson was unfamiliar with Penn's structures for backstopping the project and gave an extended description. He claimed that he and his secretary devoted up to two days a week to IPBA work. He provided extensive detail about the involvement of senior Wharton faculty and many offices of the university, and seemed especially concerned to emphasize involvement of the ILSG and its director Steve Sweeney.[120]

Arthur Adams, president of the American Council on Education, then brokered a meeting between Penn and ICA officials at the ACE offices in Washington, D.C., on March 17, 1959. Richard A. Humphrey, the executive secretary of CIPA, also assisted with the negotiations.[121] Harnwell, Winn, Palmer, and Wixon represented Penn, while Killen, Lawson, and Shaw came from ICA.[122] That a president of an elite university and even a dean of a top business school like Wharton would devote an entire day to such a meeting shows the intensity of Penn's institutional commitment to overseas institution building and perhaps suggests, as Harnwell did to his tax lawyer, the perceived importance that had come to be attached to international work for the professional status of university administrators.

Killen, in from Pakistan, was a terror at this meeting. Palmer and Harn-well both wrote to Adams the very next day about Killen. Palmer noted that "after Mr. Killen's original interjection, I thought for a while that the confer-ence might break up before it really started," while Harnwell commented that Killen had behaved in "unwise and undiplomatic" ways.[123] Harnwell later said that during the meeting Killen boasted of his long experience as a labor nego-tiator and wanted Arthur Adams to leave the meeting taking place in his own building. He also reported that Killen had "insulted us generally and imputed quite improper motives to us in connection with the undertaking."[124] Winn wrote to a friend that he was "truly embarrassed" by Killen's behavior.[125] Killen did report discussions by President Ayub with provincial administra-tors and GOP top officials in which they decided to hold in abeyance plans for civil service training academies in East and West Pakistan to see if things could be centralized at IPBA.[126]

As a result of this meeting, Lawson prepared at Harnwell's request a mem-orandum for Winn detailing the needs for an expanded program in public administration.[127] In many ways, Lawson's memo epitomized the kind of thinking that instrumentalized the university. He wrote that "both of these governments [East and West Pakistan], and the central government have be-come increasingly aware in recent months of the need for administrators who have been trained in modern management techniques." The governments had thus requested that ICA provide more extensive training in public administra-tion. Lawson believed that "the Karachi Institute needs a much stronger American faculty in public administration, consisting of well-recognized and experienced experts under the leadership of an authority on education in pub-lic administration." Courses should introduce "specialized officials [of civil services] to sound principles of modern management applicable to their own fields of specialization." He called for IPBA faculty to conduct research on specific Pakistani government protocols, which would have constituted exactly the kind of administered research that opponents of the instrumental univer-sity feared. Lawson acknowledged that the desired expanded services were more "on the job" training and less academic, but insisted that "the times in Pakistan demand a program which will have an immediate impact upon gov-ernmental administration."[128] According to the ICA plan outlined by Lawson, the University of Pennsylvania would be an instrument for administering mo-dernity in Pakistan rather than independently developing its program of research and teaching.

Also following the ACE meeting, Palmer invited the ICA contingent to Penn's campus to meet other faculty who might be involved in ramping up the IPBA efforts in public administration and "try to get down to cases regarding the future of the Institute and the work in Pakistan." This invitation appears to have been a last-ditch effort to placate Killen and show that Penn could construct a larger, more service-oriented program in public administration. Palmer told Lawson that the ICA contingent could spend time at ILSG, including with members of its Government Consulting Service, and also with Harnwell.[129] The group visit apparently never happened, but Shaw came on his own March 26 to meet various Wharton faculty. He indicated that ICA wanted one leading figure in public administration to head the program, two or three others in public administration, one or two in-service specialists, and perhaps a couple of others with expertise in consulting or research and development.[130] This collection of personnel represented a leap from the one or two professors of public administration, not leaders in the field, whom Penn had provided at any given time since IPBA's inception.

Meanwhile, Killen circumvented Wharton and made a stealth visit directly to President Harnwell on April 6.[131] He told Harnwell that Penn's overall performance had been unsatisfactory, a judgment which contradicted all previous evaluations by ICA. He wanted to remove Penn from the project but feared that Harnwell "would raise hell." Harnwell replied that he would not.[132] He suggested that Killen go across campus to talk with members of ILSG, including James Charlesworth, professor of political science and assistant director of ILSG, who Penn wanted to take a leading role in the expanded work. Killen did so, and apparently finding them unsatisfactory, returned to Washington to have ICA terminate Penn's involvement in Pakistan.[133] Yet he had told Harnwell that Penn should prepare a proposal for an expanded program in public administration in Pakistan and send it to him personally and unofficially because he would make the decision and his time in the country was short.

Not knowing of Killen's move to terminate, Harnwell had Winn craft the proposal, which Winn wrote as a formal response to Lawson's March 23 letter. It went out to Lawson April 14 under a cover letter from Harnwell apologizing for the delay and explaining they had been awaiting further directions from Killen that never came.[134] The centerpiece of the plan that Winn outlined in this document was that Charlesworth would go to Karachi for two months over the summer as a consultant to plan the new program. Charlesworth was "one of the leading American authorities in public administration" and had served as secretary of administration for the Commonwealth of Pennsylvania. Winn promised to play an active role and visit Karachi at some point; every indication is that he was actively "deaning" IPBA from afar.[135] That the dean of the Wharton School took time to write a five-page, single-spaced letter to the ICA, let alone travel to Washington to meet ICA leaders and promise to visit the project in Pakistan, is yet more evidence of how much Penn invested high-level university resources in IPBA.

The formal verdict that ICA would not extend Penn's contract arrived in a typically terse letter from Edward Kunze, ICA director of contract relations, dated April 20. Just over a page long, the letter provided no overt explanation for the cancellation, citing only "careful assessment of the many factors involved." Kunze admitted that Penn had done an admirable job in business administration. "However," he wrote, "the Government of Pakistan has now requested that the Institute substantially expand its work in the field of public administration, with heavy emphasis on education and training for all levels of civil servants, and to provide expert consultative services, both at the Center and in the Provinces." Kunze implied that Penn was not up to the task of this expanded, more service-oriented program in public administration.[136] Word about ICA's termination of Penn's work spread quickly. Ross M. Trump, dean of the School of Business and Public Administration at Washington University in St. Louis, wrote Winn on May 12. He had heard about the unpleasant ending and asked for details, concerned about his own contract in Korea.[137]

Despite his words to Killen, Harnwell did "raise hell"—at least in the form of a long letter to Senator Joseph S. Clark (D-PA), who as mayor of Philadelphia had worked with Harnwell on several issues and still lived near him in the city's elite Chestnut Hill section. Harnwell's letter, dated just a week after Kunze's, asked Clark to investigate ICA. He told Clark that his observations of ICA liaison work between American and foreign universities, from this project and as a member of CIPA, "convinces me that it is basically unsuccessful and as often does harm as good." He denounced Killen as "exceptionally limited in his intellectual view, inexperienced in this sort of work, and regrettably inept in dealing with the people he encounters."[138] It took Clark and his staff four months to make contact with the appropriate people in ICA, and they reported to Harnwell that they were unable to learn much.[139] Harnwell quickly shot back that "the work will go for very little; the taxpayers' money has been largely wasted." He lamented that "the immediate pressures to which government officials are exposed are almost irresistible, and certainly the ICA personnel give no evidence of rising above these or having any well considered policy or broad purpose in their university programs which is either appropriate for the long-term needs of the countries or to the universities in accomplishing such tasks."[140] For Harnwell, then, there were limits to the instrumental university.

Harnwell also drafted a letter to Kunze that was never sent, demanding to know the reasons for the termination and the respective roles played by ICA, USOM, and Pakistanis. He implied that the Pakistanis liked Penn's work and must not have been involved.[141] This impression might have come in part because President Ayub Khan had been a student in an IPBA course prior to his presidency and Winn described him as "an enthusiastic booster."[142] Harnwell wrote directly to Khan expressing deep regret at the termination and telling him that "the decision to sever our ties with the project represents the unilateral action of the ICA."[143]

Harnwell was not the only one at Penn to be upset. Hoffman unloaded on Killen in a five-page, single-spaced typed letter that was part lament and part plea for his vision of IPBA's future. He spoke of "the role which you are playing in this unfolding drama . . . likely to end as a tragedy." Remarking on his "disappointment" and "bitterness," Hoffman mused that "perhaps I'm generating steam for another Ugly American story!" Like others from Penn, he complained of the obfuscating ways of ICA staff. He cited Lawson's visit to IPBA, during which Lawson came to his house for lunch and a full afternoon with the faculty, played golf with him another morning, "yet not one word to me regarding his mission. I am now told that neither Philadelphia nor Washington had any clear idea of the character and direction of events ahead. So we drift." Hoffman argued for keeping the institute as a formal education institution, not just for providing in-service training or revamping the GOP. He asserted that the institute compared favorably to other university contracts in Pakistan and to US public administration work in Tehran, Saigon, Bangkok, and Manila, all of which he had visited.[144]

A group of Penn faculty—apparently those then in Philadelphia who were or had been involved in the project—also composed a long statement of public protest (probably drafted by Palmer), although there is no evidence that they actually released it. In fact, Harnwell, after quoting it at great length in his initial letter to Senator Clark, commented that "these remarks are clearly too intemperate for any public release."[145] They began by asserting that Penn "holds ICA—and particularly the ICA Mission in Pakistan—solely responsible for the many unfortunate consequences which this decision will produce." They continued to bash ICA at length, blasting ICA's unwillingness to allow universities the scope and latitude they needed to work effectively, "the manner in which ICA is crippling the university contract program and the cavalier treatment which it is according to American universities." The faculty stated that "this is a matter for deep public concern" and predicted perilous consequences "unless the great American universities make concerted protest against this kind of arbitrary treatment by ICA."[146] The irony of this protest is that Penn brought the situation upon itself when it signed a contract with ICA. By submitting itself to government control, Penn ensured that with IPBA, it would not have the freedom that had been a hallmark of the American university.

Stunningly, Harnwell accepted another ICA contract, for work in Iran, almost immediately after the Pakistan debacle.

A few words are in order about the fate of IPBA. Almost immediately, ICA asked some of the Penn faculty if they would like to continue the work as independent contractors.[147] ICA also negotiated with other American universities to take over.[148] Hoffman wondered if the University of Southern California was among them—he reported to Palmer that Dr. Henry Reining, dean of USC's School of Public Administration, arrived in Karachi with an unknown mission the day before Hoffman returned to the United States.[149]

The University of Southern California in Pakistan

USC did in fact replace Penn as ICA contractor for business and public administration in Pakistan. By the spring of 1960, ICA had decided to split the two programs but contract with USC to assist both efforts.[150] ICA signed a letter of agreement with USC in July 1960 and a contract on March 24, 1961.[151] USC pursued two important conceptualizations of its work more explicitly than Penn had: a social scientific approach to administration, and a reflective commitment to institution building. Similarly to Penn, however, USC believed that abrupt and unwarranted actions by the US government ultimately limited the efficacy of its program. The contract stated that USC should achieve "the modernization of public administration educational programs carried out by appropriate Pakistan institutions" in order "to advance the managerial capacity of present government administrators" and "to increase the supply of professionally and technically competent administrators."[152] The language of technical and managerial approaches to social problems was typical of the instrumental university. American officials from both government and university believed they could bring modernity to Pakistan by building institutions devoted to public administration.

USC was a leading American institution in public administration and had a School of Public Administration, which had created an International Public Administration Center (IPAC) to coordinate its efforts in overseas technical assistance programs and training programs at USC for foreign nationals. IPAC began in 1954, the same year that the US government's university contracts abroad program came to life.[153] Perhaps the most significant IPAC overseas program prior to beginning work in Pakistan was its effort to assist the Institute of Administrative Affairs of the Law Faculty of the University of Tehran, Iran, from 1954 to 1961.[154] From 1959 to 1965, USC contracted with ICA to support public administration education in Brazil, initially sending eight professors spread across four Brazilian institutions.[155] With respect to educating international students in Los Angeles, one notable venture was the Program for Executive Development for Officers of the Superior Civil Service of Pakistan (CSP), which USC conducted from 1957 to 1960 under contract with the US and Pakistani governments. In this "program specifically designed to fit central and provincial government needs," eighty-eight Pakistanis came in groups of fifteen to twenty for six months of training per group.[156] This experience likely made USC a strong candidate when ICA started looking for a university to replace Penn in Pakistan.[157]

USC's insistence that public administration must be understood on a social scientific basis tracked with some of the more extreme technocratic and "high modern" notions of administration that arose during the 1950s. According to USC faculty on the Pakistan project, administration "learned outside of the social sciences context" taught techniques "useful only at a mechanical level of administration" that would not equip a person "to assume broader managerial functions." USC also sought to understand administration as a generic process. Its curriculum aimed to "strip away, so to speak, those parts of the administrative process which are cultural adaptations, in an attempt to understand which elements are universally human."[158] USC sounded similar themes in its Brazil program, which adopted "a problem-solving orientation . . . whereby Brazilian needs could be scientifically identified." It considered Brazilian undergraduate curricula insufficient in social science and required Brazilian trainees pursuing graduate degrees in Los Angeles to take a special two-semester course in social science.[159]

USC's educational philosophy dovetailed with that of some Pakistani leaders who advocated technocratic public administration. M. W. Abbasi, principal of the Administrative Staff College and a senior CSP officer, wrote that "the old concept was that public servants needed to be trained only on the post or just once on recruitment . . . some 35 years ago it would have seemed ridiculous to talk of the theory or science of public administration . . . at Cambridge and Oxford it was not included in training courses . . . the Civil Service Commissioners drew up a large syllabus for trainees which covered many subjects including Phonetics but not Public Administration." Abbasi believed that the advent of the welfare state, with its focus on "economic planning and development," had made administration "so complicated" that regular in-service training was necessary.[160] He further emphasized the importance of the development paradigm for educating Pakistani administrators by noting that "everything is being done at these [educational] institutions to make the participants development-minded."[161]

USC's commitment to institution building was such that it set up a new collection of institutions in Pakistan rather than continuing public administration work through IPBA. The most prominent were the National Institutes of Public Administration (NIPA) in Karachi, Lahore, and Dacca. They were considered "mid-career training institutions," intended for government officers with eight to fourteen years of service.[162] Their curriculum was "heavily slanted towards development economics, development administration, and management processes."[163] By September 1961, just nine months after the first USC personnel started their work in Pakistan, each NIPA had a Pakistani director culled from CSP ranks with twelve to fifteen years of experience. The GOP assigned these directors, and USC claimed that it and USOM had no say in the matter. The director of NIPA Lahore, a Mr. Inayatullah, had earned an MPA from Harvard's Littauer School in 1956 under a Ford Foundation grant. The director of NIPA Dacca, A. M. Sanaul Huq, had studied at the London School of Economics, while the director of NIPA Karachi, Masrury Hasan Khan, had participated in the executive development program on USC's campus.[164] NIPA Lahore quickly began publishing a *Public Administration Review*.[165] USC also established a more traditional academic unit offering graduate degrees, the Department of Administrative Science at the University of the Punjab in Lahore. It envisioned a similar department at the University of Dacca but encountered opposition from the university's vice-chancellor and was only able to create a limited curriculum rather than a full-fledged department.[166] In addition, USC helped set up agencies within the central government to bolster administration, including a National Administrative Training Council headed by a cabinet minister and a joint secretariat in the Establishment Division to coordinate government activities and a national training policy for all these institutions. At the project's height, sixteen USC faculty members were in Pakistan. USC's effort, then, was larger and more comprehensive than Penn's work at IPBA.[167]

USC reflected on its work of institution building and called its final report on the project *Institution Building in an Emerging Nation: Pakistan*. USC's goal was "to get something started . . . which will take root and eventually become a self-sustaining activity, native to the political and social environment, no longer in need of infusion of aid and assistance abroad."[168] USC intended that "the institutes for the training and education of public administrators will not merely exist as an organizational entity, but as a true 'institution' which is protected and valued by the society in which it functions."[169] True institutionalization meant the "indigenization of project leadership and resources."[170] The key test would be the extent to which the institutions flourished after USC left

Pakistan. In thinking about "institutionalization as a process that happens to an organization over time," the USC program cited UC Berkeley sociologist Philip Selznick's *Leadership in Administration* (1957), a study that began during his association with the RAND Corporation and summarized his work since the mid-1940s.[171] Selznick distinguished between organizations and institutions. The term "organization," he wrote, "refers to an *expendable tool*, a rational instrument engineered to do a job. An 'institution,' on the other hand, is more nearly a natural product of social needs and pressures—a responsive, adaptive organism."[172] Many scholars consider Selznick the founder of the institutional school of organization theory.[173]

The USC team's nod to Selznick suggested how its theorizing about institution building drew on a broader emerging framework in American academic and public policy discussion.[174] Selznick did not use the term "institution building." It apparently emerged in the writings of Harlan Cleveland, dean of the Maxwell School of Citizenship and Public Affairs at Syracuse University and a veteran of US and UN aid agencies, who served a term on CIPA simultaneously with Harnwell from 1958 to 1960.[175] Cleveland seems to have originated the phrase in 1956 in *The Theory and Practice of Foreign Aid*, a ninety-three-page typescript prepared for the Special Studies Project of the Rockefeller Brothers Fund.[176] He argued that the first few years of the Point Four program had showed that such American aid must center on institution building—"the development of social institutions that provide a conduit for tangible benefits from a government to its people, and for participation by people in their own government." American representatives abroad, he said, discovered that Point Four "wasn't a technical or economic program, it was aid in building organizations, influencing political decisions, charting procedures, making up budgets, getting human beings to work effectively together, and teaching the elements of large-scale administration."[177] This perspective reinforced American policymakers' belief in the importance of public administration for the developing world.

Cleveland elaborated his ideas in two subsequent volumes produced under the auspices of a grant from the Carnegie Corporation of New York for a research project he directed, Education and Training of Americans for Public Service Abroad. *The Art of Overseasmanship* (1957) was an edited collection of pieces first presented at a March 1957 Conference on Americans at Work Abroad that gathered leaders from academia, business, foundations, and government to discuss the Carnegie project and determine how Americans could "best be prepared for effective work overseas." The participants asked, "What is the 'Factor X' that makes overseas service different from working in the comparable job at home?"[178] Cleveland's answer was that "whatever other skills and qualities may be required, an American in a responsible position abroad evidently has to be unusually good at the building of institutions—much better at it than would normally be required in a comparable job in New Orleans or Minneapolis. This generalization is distilled from a dozen years of United States and United Nations aid programs, and stems directly from the nature of foreign aid operations."[179] He cited as examples of successful institution building an Italian public agency that processed UN cotton donations and two efforts sparked by the Marshall Plan: the counterpart funds program and the Organization for European Economic Cooperation. These examples indicate that when Cleveland spoke of institutions he meant not the narrower concept that Selznick denoted with that term but more like what Selznick meant by organizations. Cleveland also sounded the theme that technology transfer alone was insufficient and possibly dangerous. Institution building was necessary to bring positive social transformation from technology: "people must be trained in techniques and in administration, and effective organizations must be set up to control the imported miracles."[180] *The Overseas Americans* (1960) constituted the Carnegie project's culminating effort; it repeated some of Cleveland's earlier points about institution building, fortified with new examples from extensive research on Americans serving overseas.[181] As the Carnegie project concluded, Cleveland took a position as assistant secretary of state in the Kennedy administration.[182]

The Overseas Americans subsequently became a training manual for Peace Corps volunteers, and "institution building" entered the lexicon of government aid programs. By 1960, the Committee on the University and World Affairs could refer to "the primary ICA objective of institution building," which spurred the ICA policy that American contract faculty should spend less than 30 percent of their time teaching to "concentrate on planning and advising on curriculum, organization and methods."[183] In 1963, AID administrator Hollis Chenery wrote in a policy memo that "institution building" should occur when a given country is at a middle stage of development.[184]

The "institution building" concept also permeated the UN by the early 1960s. The terminology was in use in official UN publications by 1961, when a handbook called institution building one of the main tasks of a public administration specialist.[185] An important discussion came in a 1962 article in *Technology and Culture* by Arthur Goldschmidt, director for special fund activities in the UN's Department of Economic and Social Affairs.[186] Goldschmidt viewed institutions as technologies for "speeding up development" by introducing and adapting other new technologies to specific cultural contexts.[187] He followed Selznick in speaking of institutions' "adaptive" capacities, but it is unclear whether he did so overtly. The importance of this adaptive work meant that institution building was not mere technology transfer. Goldschmidt believed that "the major point on which success or failure in technical assistance has hinged has been the existence or strength of the necessary institutions in the country being assisted, or the ability of the program to create them."[188] He exhorted social scientists "to discover ways to develop institutions for introducing change . . . We must know more about the birth, growth, health, and decay of institutions. We must know more about their interrelationships, their effect on one another, and how they may be affected from outside." Goldschmidt used the language of the instrumental university when he mentioned "the assumption that the land-grant colleges were the most likely instrumentalities for creating counterparts in their own image in the less-developed world."[189] The USC program mentioned Goldschmidt's views, but it is not clear how extensively it drew from them.

The Ford Foundation gave the "institution building" concept perhaps its greatest impetus by funding an Inter-University Research Program in Institution Building starting in 1963, headquartered at the University of Pittsburgh and involving Indiana, Michigan State, and Syracuse.[190] The program aimed to create "a theoretical framework of the process of institution building in developing societies." One of its publications, *Technical Assistance and Institution Building*, attempted to determine "whether or not the reporting on the results of technical assistance efforts can be structured to fit into the [theoretical] framework . . . so as to provide both evaluative and predictive data." To do so, the authors developed a coding system for translating reports into mathematical statements that could be processed by computer. Approximately half of the publication consisted of tables and charts to support quantitative analysis. The authors wanted to assess the impact of "variables" and "to isolate the inputs of technical assistance to institution building projects and assess their actual and theoretical contributions." This work typified the high modern milieu in that it attempted to force description of social life into a mathematical model.[191]

Despite USC's connection to this broader discussion about institution building and its large profile in Pakistan, it felt the sting of US government betrayal just as Penn had. Around the beginning of 1963, AID told USC that the project, originally scheduled for ten years, would be cut to three years and the contract would be allowed to expire in just a few months, on October 31, 1963.[192] The impetus for this decision came from new leadership in the AID Mission (successor to USOM) in Pakistan, just as Penn's troubles had started when Killen took the helm of USOM/Pakistan.[193] These incidents suggest that the director of a US mission exerted preponderant influence over the character of technical assistance in that country while the central office of ICA/AID had less power in such matters. USC managed to win a reprieve, however, especially when the GOP rallied to the program and dramatically increased its funding of the institutions. Wesley E. Bjur noted that this GOP response actually made the AID decision in part a blessing in disguise, because "in terms of institution building theory, [a major financial commitment from the host government] is an extremely significant moment in the indigenization of an innovative organization."[194] The number of USC faculty dropped from sixteen to nine for the 1963–1965 period, then to two for the final two years before the program disbanded in 1967.[195] USC faculty and officials from both governments worried about whether the Pakistani institutions would thrive after the contract ended. An AID evaluation team of two AID staff and one Pakistani wrote that "the possibility of maintaining a capable staff in the institutions after the AID support ceases appears small at this juncture."[196] They discussed whether it would be possible for USC to maintain a liaison to keep the staff of the Pakistani institutions updated on developments in the literature and profession.[197] Ultimately, most of the institutions that USC created did survive.

The experiences of USC and Penn in their Pakistan projects under contract with the US government suggest how the new impulse of overseas institution building contributed to instrumentalizing the elite American research university and eroding its traditional moral economy. Indeed, the vocabulary of the instrumental university sprang from discussions of universities' institution building abroad. The US government and universities both contributed to this instrumentalizing process. The government saw universities as instruments of technical cooperation, essential delivery mechanisms for the development and modernization programs that were increasingly central to its foreign policy. This reliance on universities as instruments for reshaping the globe—bringing American modernity to the world—illuminates the importance that both academic and political leaders attributed to institutions and "institution building" for development schemes. For the universities' part, individual institutions seeking money and prestige saw contract work abroad as a means to those ends.

The control that US government agencies exercised over contracting universities disrupted the traditional moral economy of those schools. When institutions such as Penn and USC eagerly took on government contracts, they gave up the freedom associated with the special character of the American research university, which protected scholars from political pressures so they could take a long-term view in their teaching and research. These case studies of Penn and USC in Pakistan show that universities working under government contracts abroad were subject to the whims of the political process, demands for immediate impact, and bureaucratic rigidity. The many committees and reports that evaluated the university contracts abroad program almost unanimously stated that universities must have more freedom from government control and short-term impulses in order to plan programs for the long term.

Early technical assistance policymakers such as Bennett and Stassen, themselves recruited from university presidencies, turned to universities in an attempt to depoliticize technical assistance. These men were committed to the vision of American modernity. In planning economic development work abroad, they mirrored the impulse to have nonpolitical universities provide technical solutions for problems of industrial relations and city planning. While these policymakers considered how university participation might benefit the US government and American foreign relations, they seem not to have pondered the possible negative consequences for universities. Ironically, the university contract program that they created helped to erode a characteristic of the university that they admired in the first place—its nonpolitical nature. While overseas experience might have enriched faculty members' scholarship and teaching when they returned home, the academic core of teaching and fundamental research suffered at contracting universities as professors and administrators expended energy on the overseas work and on wading through the accompanying mass of red tape spun by AID and its predecessors.

Government officials were not the only ones to blame for universities' plight. Far from the humanitarian ideal proposed by early framers like Bennett, many university participants had less than noble motivations. University officials such as Harnwell and Perkins admitted that they accepted overseas projects for reasons of prestige, professional standing, and inter-university competition. Some universities pursued contracts primarily in hope of financial benefits and sent few of their regular faculty to work on overseas projects.

The size of the AID program of university contracts for overseas institution building peaked in the mid-1960s. It declined slowly from 123 contracts in operation during late 1966 totaling $199 million over their lifetime to 105 contracts for $189 million in mid-1970, then more rapidly to 62 contracts for $102 million by mid-1973 and 47 contracts by mid-1974.[198] This decline did not indicate that AID had diminished its use of universities, but rather that it had changed its methods for doing so by introducing other kinds of grants and contracts. Indeed, the total number of universities receiving funds for all AID projects (not just overseas institution building) increased from 72 in December 1963 to 134 in June 1974.

This diversification and expansion of AID-university projects was partly a response to a 1964 report, *AID and the Universities*. AID commissioned Carnegie

Corporation of New York president John W. Gardner to write the report, which became the most influential assessment of AID-university relations. Gardner held that a major problem in the AID-university relationship was universities' lack of commitment "on an institution-wide basis, to regular involvement in overseas activities." In an attempt to remedy this situation, the Johnson administration successfully lobbied Congress in 1966 to add Section 211(d) to the Foreign Assistance Act. It authorized AID to grant foreign assistance funds to universities "to strengthen their capability to develop and carry out programs concerned with the economic and social development of less developed countries." Appropriations began in 1968, and totaled $42.8 million under fifty-four grants to forty-five universities by the end of 1975.[199] Even before the 211(d) program, AID in 1962 had begun research contracts with universities "based on unsolicited proposals" responding to a general call for "innovative solutions." Awards under this program totaled $83 million through 1975.[200] AID also used universities in a fourth way, through contracts for technical services, including training of AID personnel. This program had more new contracts than any of the other three between 1967 and 1975.[201] The result of all these programs is that despite the decline of the Stassen-era university contract abroad, total AID spending on university grants and contracts remained fairly constant between 1967 and 1975, ranging from $37 million to $55 million (except for one year) and having no discernible pattern of increase or decrease.[202] Indeed, a 1996 report shows that AID was still funding universities' overseas institution building. For example, the University of Eastern Washington had a five-year, $350,000 grant to "establish a collaborative capacity-building relationship with Univ. of Cape Coast in Ghana."[203]

The expanded AID program had various impacts on universities. The next chapter looks at one example. It centers on Samuel P. Hayes Jr., who as an advisor to President Kennedy drafted the legislation authorizing the AID-university research contracts that began in 1962. His efforts eventually led to the University of Michigan receiving one of the early AID research grants and moving closer to the instrumental university model.

CHAPTER 5

A Use of the University of Michigan

Samuel P. Hayes Jr. and Economic Development

For Samuel P. Hayes Jr., the fall of 1960 was a dream come true. After four long years of battling his reluctant faculty colleagues at the University of Michigan, they were finally on the verge of establishing his pet project, the Center for Research on Economic Development (CRED), which he believed would coordinate a university-wide effort toward the improvement of life in "underdeveloped" countries. Even more exciting, Democratic presidential candidate John F. Kennedy's chief speechwriter, Archibald Cox, asked Hayes in September to prepare a memorandum explaining the possibilities for "an International Youth Service," an idea that people within the campaign had bandied about.[1] What happened beginning October 14, however, was beyond Hayes's wildest hopes. Kennedy's motorcade rolled in to Ann Arbor around 2 a.m. that Friday. A crowd estimated at 10,000 had gathered outside the Michigan Union, the campus landmark where Kennedy was to spend the night. Kennedy had not planned to make an address but spoke extemporaneously for three minutes to the crowd. Many observers considered this speech the spark that launched the Peace Corps, though he did not mention the idea formally. He asked the crowd, "How many of you who are going to be doctors are willing to spend your days in Ghana? Technicians or engineers, how many of you are willing to work in the Foreign Service and spend your lives traveling around the world? On your willingness to do that, not merely to serve one year or two years in the service, but on your willingness to contribute part of your life to this country, I think will depend the answer whether a free society can compete." The speech electrified the crowd.

Four days later, Kennedy advisor Chester Bowles, who would become under secretary of state in the new administration, spoke at the university on a proposed "U.N. civil service, which would send doctors, agricultural experts and teachers to needy countries throughout the world." Graduate students Alan and Judy Guskin immediately wrote a letter to the student newspaper pledging to do such work in underdeveloped countries, and implored fellow students to write similar pledges to Kennedy and Bowles. Hayes was thrilled. He contacted the Guskins, and together they held a meeting where 250 students signed a petition saying they would volunteer. Hundreds more signed within the following days. Kennedy formally announced the Peace Corps idea at a November 2 speech in San Francisco, and on November 6, two days before the election, the Guskins and other students drove to Toledo, Ohio, to present Kennedy their petitions during his stopover there.[2] Sargent Shriver, Kennedy's brother-in-law, who served as the Peace Corps' first director, wrote in his memoir that "it might still be just an idea but for the affirmative response of those Michigan students and faculty. Possibly Kennedy would have tried it once more on some other occasion, but without a strong popular response he would have concluded the idea was impractical or premature. That probably would have ended it then and there. Instead, it was almost a case of spontaneous combustion."[3] Shriver began setting up the Peace Corps the day after Kennedy's inauguration, and by later in 1961, the Guskins were serving in Thailand with the Corps.[4]

Hayes advised Shriver on setting up the Peace Corps and wrote a pamphlet for the public, *An International Peace Corps: The Promise and the Problems*, an expanded version of his earlier memo.[5] By May 1961, Hayes was on leave from the university for six weeks in Washington serving on the President's Task Force on Foreign Economic Assistance, which created the new US Agency for International Development (AID). Just as he returned to Ann Arbor in mid-June, the university's regents passed the bylaw establishing CRED. Life seemed good for Sam Hayes.

The simultaneous establishment of the Peace Corps and CRED symbolized the common intellectual framework that motivated both endeavors in Hayes's mind. For Hayes, they were instruments to promote economic development. But Hayes saw economic development as more of a psychological, sociological, and political problem than an economic one. As a result, he believed the Peace Corps should be much more than a technical assistance program, and CRED must be a university-wide effort rather than a Department of Economics initiative. In *An International Peace Corps* he argued that "economic growth is a manifestation of a social process. It is a kind of external symptom of something going on deep within and pervasive throughout the whole society."[6] In his view, Peace Corps volunteers would nurture this ambiguous social process.

Hayes's most important theoretical contribution to the formulation of the Peace Corps was the idea that volunteers would constitute "middle manpower."[7] Sounding a bit like Harlan Cleveland (a leading development theorist described in chapter 4), he argued that in many foreign places, existing capital and technology would lead to greater development "if a missing element could be provided." The "missing element [was] middle manpower"— "men and women with enough education and training to undertake the wide range of operational tasks between the heads of organizations and their unskilled or semiskilled laborers." The Peace Corps would "help provide this missing element in the socioeconomic structure of those nations that need it and want it to speed up their own development."[8] Hayes's argument displayed confidence that social scientists like him could break down an identifiable development process and then engineer social change by inserting resources at just the right spot. His approach testifies to the centrality of the manpower trope in shaping the thinking of postwar American elites. It also reflects Hayes's immersion in three related patterns of thought—the behavioral science paradigm, the new organization theory, and the administrative science movement— that gained prominence during the postwar period and provided tools to those like Hayes who sought to administer American modernity. In his view, Peace Corps volunteers—cast as middle managers and social engineers— would foster economic development in impoverished countries.[9]

The establishment of Michigan's interdisciplinary Center for Research on Economic Development, with its focus on organizing researchers from a variety of disciplines around a social problem with political cachet, exemplified the instrumental university. It also displayed the power that the ideal of economic development exerted in the postwar United States. Even the opposition that some members of Michigan's Department of Economics exhibited toward Hayes's interdisciplinary and service-oriented plans attested the power of the economic development concept. These economists wanted to focus on economic development for academic reasons related to economic theory or intradisciplinary competition. This opposition provides a window into how academic norms motivated resistance to the instrumental university's problem-solving impulse. Hayes's doctorate was in psychology rather than economics, and his emphasis on psychological and sociological roots of economic development contributed to friction with some economics colleagues. The uneasy alliance between Hayes and the Michigan economists reflected a larger disjunction between behavioral science and economics in this period.[10] That the Department of Economics gave him even a modicum of acceptance (as a nontenured professor) despite his holding a doctorate in a different field shows how important the economic development ideal had become. Department members agreed about the need to focus on economic development, but disagreed about the purpose, scope, and structure of the work.

Hayes's quest to create CRED drew almost exclusively on his interest in international economic development, as opposed to the emphasis on domestic economic development that drove other university activities in this era. The United States, holding new preeminence in the world order, wanted to increase the material wealth of emerging countries around the world, former European colonies for which it had previously exhibited little concern. Universities began to engage with materially poor countries because American elites within and outside the government began to care about such countries, to believe that university-produced knowledge about the economic development of these countries would be valuable, and to provide funding for universities to pursue such knowledge. Much of that funding came from foundations, and this exploration of Michigan's research on economic development examines how patronage shaped the instrumental university. Examining the rise of the subfield of development economics and then of Hayes's early career—especially his engagement with behavioral science and US government international development programs—lays the groundwork for analyzing the struggle to establish CRED at Michigan.

Development Economics and Behavioral Science

The subdiscipline of development economics emerged in the 1940s within the discipline of economics as a result of how politicians and economists drew on the new Keynesian theory and responded to the wartime political environment. Responses to World War II fueled development economics for a number of reasons. The Western Allies articulated war aims, in part to counter Hitler's New Order and Japan's Greater East Asia Co-Prosperity Sphere. The Atlantic Charter that enunciated those aims internationalized Franklin D. Roosevelt's promise of "freedom from want."[11] Wartime programs, "by demonstrating the power of government action in mobilizing economic resources . . . generated a climate of optimism about what could be done to make a better world, abroad as much as at home."[12] The war's physical destruction prompted a focus on building industrial infrastructure in damaged areas, and the war triggered political restructuring that gave new prominence and voice to countries moving from colony to independent status. American and British planning for postwar reconstruction established "economic development of underdeveloped countries [as] an accepted objective of national and international policy of the developed countries."[13]

Two seminal works launched development economics, both written during the war in the context of British organized research units. The authors had emigrated from Germanophone states in the 1930s. The Austrian Paul Rosenstein-Rodan taught at University College London and the London School of Economics, and had written on such abstract subjects as marginal utility and time.[14] But as part of a wartime study group on the problems of "underdeveloped countries" at the Royal Institute for International Affairs, he published "Problems of Industrialisation of Eastern and South-Eastern Europe" (1943).[15] This article became known for its "big push" theory, which held that an underdeveloped economy could make a big push into industrialization by coordinating investments across sectors.[16] It also launched the concept of a "dual economy"—the notion that many countries actually had two parallel economies: an emerging industrial economy and an entrenched subsistence agriculture economy featuring a large surplus of labor.[17]

Kurt Mandelbaum wrote from a similar framework in *The Industrialization of Backward Areas* (1945), part of a research project on international reconstruction initiated by a joint committee of Nuffield College and the Institute of Statistics at the University of Oxford.[18] Before leaving Germany for the UK, Mandelbaum had been involved with the Frankfurt School and had often written under an assumed name due to fear of Nazi persecution.[19] He sometimes went by the Anglicized "Kurt Martin" in the UK. Most of his book consisted of a highly quantitative model of a hypothetical industrializing economy in southeastern Europe. Mandelbaum argued that in "over-populated" countries a surplus population was "being driven into rural and urban occupations of very low productivity."[20] He believed that these "uneconomically employed" people must move from agricultural to industrial work.[21] The book tried to explain how a country might generate the requisite demand and capital for industrial expansion to accommodate such an employment pattern; it envisioned planned, large-scale industrialization. Both Rosenstein-Rodan's and Mandelbaum's works assumed that industrialization was all good and the sure path to a superior state of human existence. They unhesitatingly dubbed less industrialized countries "backward."

Keynesian macroeconomic theory was in ascendancy after the publication of John Maynard Keynes's *The General Theory of Employment, Interest, and Money* (1936). This theory rejected "monoeconomics"—the view that there was only one economics, applicable at all times. Keynes said there was one economics at full employment and another "very different system of analytical propositions and of policy prescriptions . . . that took over when there was substantial unemployment of human and material resources." Keynes's focus on the implications of unemployment was novel in economics, and he elaborated a theory of macroeconomic equilibrium with unemployment. Development economists applied a similar principle to argue that underdeveloped economies had to be treated as a different system: "different kinds of economies require different kinds of economics."[22] Only in light of new political circumstances did British and American scholars attend to the economic health of less industrialized countries rather than considering them primarily as markets or sources of raw materials; only then did they extend the Keynesian insight and propose that a separate economics might apply to these countries. In addition, Keynes's belief that state intervention and planning could be successful influenced development economics.[23]

Practitioners of development economics increasingly tethered the field's separateness to the concept of underemployment. Mandelbaum and Rosenstein-Rodan focused on underemployment as the crucial characteristic of underdevelopment, which gave them an affinity with Keynes's focus on unemployment. Ten years later, W. Arthur Lewis gave fullest expression to the belief that rural underemployment was the principal characteristic of underdevelopment, and this concept became "the crucial theoretical underpinning of the separateness of development economics."[24] Indeed, Lewis became the new field's most celebrated scholar with his seminal 1954 article "Economic Development with Unlimited Supplies of Labor" and 1955 book *The Theory of Economic Growth*.[25] A professor at the University of Manchester, Lewis teamed with Mandelbaum, who arrived from Oxford in 1950, to make Manchester a major center for development economics.[26] Lewis's article was the dominant paper in the field, containing one big idea that was the center of discussion for long after its publication. He argued that in a less developed country's dual economy, the traditional sector has an unlimited supply of labor that sets labor supply conditions for the capitalistic sector.[27] Lewis would eventually win the 1979 Nobel Prize in Economics for this work.[28]

While most of the important works in the early years of development economics emerged from the British context, the field started to gain a foothold in the United States as well. The earliest prominent American university organizations concerned with economic development, however, tended to be interdisciplinary rather than exclusively the province of economists. The University of Chicago founded in 1952 its Research Center in Economic Development and Cultural Change, the first American university unit to focus primarily on economic development. The center immediately began publishing a journal, *Economic Development and Cultural Change*, which became an important venue for ideas regarding economic development. Once again the leading figure was an Austrian émigré economist, Bert Hoselitz. He edited the journal—which his colleagues proclaimed to be "in large measure the lengthened shadow of Bert's intellectual vigor"—almost continuously until his retirement in 1978.[29] The interdisciplinary center featured sociologists and anthropologists and focused on the "non-economic" factors in economic development, such as the role of elite social groups.[30] Hoselitz's *Sociological Aspects of Economic Growth* (1960) was translated into approximately twenty-five languages.[31]

Also in 1952, MIT founded its interdisciplinary Center for International Studies (CIS) under the direction of economist Max Millikan, who had recently worked for the new Central Intelligence Agency. Here economic development was one of several topics among the practical policy concerns that formed its research agenda. Millikan brought Rosenstein-Rodan from the UK and hired his old Yale buddy Walt Rostow, an economic historian who had worked in the State Department when its staff formulated the Marshall Plan. These two advanced a theory of economic development that "would provide the base on which the CIS would build its superstructure of political and sociological claims."[32] CIS became one of the quintessential postwar American organized research units (ORUs), and Hayes often talked of emulating it in his plans for Michigan's Center for Research on Economic Development.

Hayes's background suggests specific ways that the behavioral science paradigm and the US government's new programs to spark economic development in foreign countries contributed to the instrumental university and its organized research on economic development. His arrival at the University of Michigan from a series of posts outside academia symbolizes the way that external forces shaped the postwar university. Hayes spent time at two of the institutions where the new behavioral approach to social science had gained the strongest foothold. He earned his PhD in psychology at Yale in 1934 with a dissertation on voting behavior.[33] As a graduate student he served as a research assistant in Yale's Institute of Human Relations, one of the most important among the few pre–World War II university ORUs.[34] He also spent a postdoctoral year in 1937–1938 at the University of Chicago, where Charles Merriam, Harold Lasswell, and Herbert Simon were building the behavioral approach. Other than the Chicago year, Hayes spent time teaching in small colleges, conducting survey research for marketing and advertising firms, and working for various government agencies during World War II.

Hayes played a role in shaping the US government's early efforts in international technical and economic assistance. He faced a choice in 1948 that symbolized options available for his generation of behavioral social scientists. He turned down an offer to join the new RAND Corporation, a California think tank with close military ties (described in chapter 6), in order to work for the State Department. State initially "loaned" Hayes to the new Economic Cooperation Administration (ECA), set up to implement the Marshall Plan. When President Truman announced the Point Four program in 1949, the State Department chose Hayes to organize its implementation as executive secretary of the interdepartmental Advisory Committee on Technical Assistance.[35] Hayes then focused on Southeast Asia, first as deputy chief of a two-month joint ECA–State Department mission to Indochina, Malaya, Singapore, Burma, Thailand, and Indonesia in 1950, then as chief of the ECA Special Technological and Economic Mission to Indonesia in 1951–1952.[36] Upon his return to the United States, he became assistant director of the Mutual Security Agency for the Far East. Harold Stassen, who became director of the Mutual Security Agency following President Eisenhower's inauguration in early 1953, fired Hayes and most of his colleagues in a political changing of the guard typical for new presidential administrations.[37] The timing of this firing was critical for bringing Hayes to Ann Arbor, since it occurred precisely as renowned University of Michigan social psychologist Rensis Likert sought a director for a new extra-university organization.

Likert influenced the use of statistics and surveys in American social science, and was one of the preeminent organizers of social science in the postwar era as director of the University of Michigan's Institute for Social Research (ISR). ISR was one of the country's largest and best known ORUs, with a budget of over $850,000 by 1950–1951, almost three times the combined budgets of Michigan's psychology and sociology departments.[38] No less an observer than Clark Kerr commented on its eminence, writing University of California president Robert G. Sproul from a 1950 visit to Ann Arbor that "the work now going on at Michigan is, I think, the most significant now taking place in the social sciences anywhere."[39] ISR was a kind of super-ORU, charged with organizing the activities of several smaller ORUs that constituted it. The original two constituents, the Survey Research Center and the Research Center for Group Dynamics, were both groups of scholars who migrated to the University of Michigan in the late 1940s: the latter from MIT and the former, including Likert, from the US Department of Agriculture.[40] Another migrating group of scholars who arrived in 1955 further strengthened Michigan's reputation as a national center for behavioral science. Psychiatrist James G. Miller, who probably coined the term "behavioral science," brought a group largely from the University of Chicago to establish the University of Michigan Mental Health Research Institute and the journal *Behavioral*

Science.[41] During this same era, ISR "popularized" the term "behavioral economics," which also had connections with Herbert Simon.[42]

Despite ISR's success, Likert and his colleagues still believed that behavioral science research lacked sufficient funding and needed to improve the communication of its findings to practitioners in business and other organizations. To those ends they set up the Foundation for Research on Human Behavior in 1952, and in 1953 they won a $206,000 grant over three years from the W. K. Kellogg Foundation. Shortly thereafter they hired Hayes as director. The foundation's early work included a seminar on "Psychological Surveys in Business Forecasting" for executives of thirty-five major firms, which attempted to teach them how survey research could help them to predict consumer behavior. The foundation began to receive contributions from corporations such as Proctor and Gamble and Inland Steel, and to make research grants, "only for quantitative, problem-oriented research which promises to be of value both in operating situations and in the advancement of basic scientific knowledge of human behavior."[43] The emphasis on quantification reflected the behavioral science paradigm, and the emphasis on problem-oriented research reflected the typical ORU attitude, even though this ORU was outside the university—but barely.

The foundation's publications later in the 1950s show that the foundation and Hayes were immersed in behavioral science and the new organization theory, and committed to the belief that such research provided sure guidance for social life. Likert and Hayes edited *Some Applications of Behavioural Research* (1957), a volume of foundation-sponsored research published by UNESCO. The book aimed "to demonstrate by concrete examples how the social sciences have contributed and can contribute to a better organization of certain social behaviors."[44] Vision-casting chapters by Likert and Hayes sandwiched chapters reporting on the foundation's work in specific areas from 1954 to 1956. Their introduction cast the foundation as a "unique" organization "devoted to promoting the support of behavioural research by business concerns and to encouraging the application of behavioural research in business, government, and other organizations."[45] Basically, the foundation was a piece of social machinery dedicated to gaining money for behavioral science research, spreading its results, and bolstering its legitimacy. The volume, the editors said, "stresses the sciences which make empirical studies of individual behavior. This includes social psychology, much of the other types of psychology, sociology and cultural anthropology, and part at least of political science and economics."[46] Hayes wrote that "we must . . . train a far larger corps of scientists . . . competent in behavioural research."[47] He framed what he saw as the central problem—the underutilization of behavioral research—in economic terms:

there was a limited "demand" for behavioral research because "the potential consumers do not seek it out, and the producers do not effectively promote it."[48] Raising the demand for behavioral research was a chief goal of the Foundation for Research on Human Behavior.

Using the University of Michigan

Hayes maintained his interest in international economic development during his time directing the Foundation for Research on Human Behavior, and began to use the University of Michigan to pursue this interest. He soon became the central figure in the university's new program of economic development activities. The story of this program provides one example of how a mingling of instrumental and more traditional academic impulses shaped the university. Enthusiasm for modern ideals such as economic development did not always lead to purely instrumental activities. In this case, the belief that attention to economic development spawned a new area of economic theory—development economics—encouraged interest in economic development research among theoretically inclined economists who did not overtly pursue an instrumental approach. Further, the concept of economic development was malleable enough that academic economists could turn it toward raising their department's prestige. Hayes wanted the university to function as a service institution to bolster economic development around the world. Members of the economics faculty wanted to advance economic thought and raise their department's prestige through increasing the number and qualifications of its graduate students. The faculty saw Hayes's economic development program as a way to meet those goals, and so eventually embraced a version of it suitably modified by their own academic commitments.

Shortly after Hayes gained formal affiliation with the University of Michigan in 1955, he began to push the Department of Economics and the university as a whole to create new structures related to economic development. Initially, the department hired him to teach Economics 147, "Economic Development of Underdeveloped Countries," on a part-time basis.[49] He continued as a part-time lecturer for the 1955–1956 and 1956–1957 academic years. Hayes's campaign for new structures spanned five years, from his first proposal in fall 1956 to the establishment of CRED in summer 1961. It began with two proposals written during 1956–1957, one to establish a Center for Economic Development and the other to establish a Michigan International Seminar for Research and Training in Economic Development. The center proposal was broader and provided a template for the discussions and proposals that followed over the next five years. It proposed expanding research, coordinating courses, coordinating with agencies engaged in economic development work, establishing an interdisciplinary PhD program and a development economics emphasis within the economics PhD program, training foreign visitors in economic development techniques, and loaning university faculty to assist foreign countries' economic development efforts. The proposed effort was large scale, even grandiose, calling for at least sixteen new FTE faculty positions, "ten clerks and secretaries," and a $300,000 annual budget.[50]

Hayes rallied support among several significant economics faculty who participated in his proposal. Most prominent was the eminent Kenneth Boulding, whom UC Berkeley almost lured from Michigan in 1955.[51] The editors of the new *Administrative Science Quarterly* attested Boulding's status as a sort of guru among social scientists, especially those concerned with unified theory, by selecting him to write a review of their first two volumes to assess their success at building a science of administration.[52] Wolfgang Stolper would become CRED's key figure once it was actually established. In the 1930s at Harvard, Stolper had been a PhD student of Joseph Schumpeter, one of the most important theorists of economic development and indeed one of the most important economists of the twentieth century. Charles Remer, an economic historian of Japan, had been chief of the Far East Division of Research and Analysis for the Office of Strategic Services, the US intelligence agency, during World War II.[53]

One important context for the proposals was a burgeoning relationship between the Michigan economics department and the Ford Foundation. In 1956, Ford's Economic Development and Administration (EDA) program gave Michigan $100,000 "over a period of five years to support problem-oriented research by members of the faculty of the Department of Economics."[54] In October 1956, EDA officials began discussion with the economics department about an economic development program.[55] Program officers Lloyd Reynolds and Kermit Gordon "indicated that the Ford Foundation is eager to induce a major University to set up a program in economic development on a substantial scale" and encouraged Michigan to submit such a proposal.[56] They solicited such proposals from six universities at once, hoping to get them all approved together. Hayes's December 1956 Center for Economic Development proposal presumed that funding for the $300,000 annual budget could be secured from the Ford Foundation and/or the International Cooperation Administration.[57] Rather than submit the proposal to Ford, the department spun off one element of the proposed center into a proposal for a Michigan International Seminar for Research and Training in Economic Development. Michigan's proposal alone requested roughly $1 million over ten years, and the six together asked for over $6 million, more than EDA's entire budget. Despite EDA pleading with the Ford Foundation board, the board denied the requests.[58]

The economics department's decision to submit to the Ford Foundation a more targeted proposal rather than Hayes's grandiose center concept points to a rift between Hayes and the department over the purposes of a program in economic development. This rift simmered just under the surface for most of the five-year process leading to CRED. The department relegated Hayes to a consulting role on the seminar proposal submitted to Ford, whereas he was the primary author on the center proposal. Whereas the center proposal was emphatically interdisciplinary and focused on building a large research program, the seminar proposal was exclusive to the Department of Economics and focused on building a large PhD program. The seminar proposal emphasized meeting the department's needs. Most prominently it would have "the tremendous advantage of solving [the] most urgent problem: the attracting and financing of first rate graduate students on a scale which would otherwise be quite impossible." The department, then, sought to use the "hot" issue of economic development and Ford's desire to fund a university program in the field to increase the number and quality of graduate students and thus bolster the department's status. The proposed seminar would have included ten international and five American graduate students, fully funded with three-year fellowships. It would have addressed "general international economic problems, problems of specific economies as related to economic development, problems of integration and so forth" with "institutional, statistical and theoretical studies." Its proponents noted that "the best way to deal with the problems of economic development is to train good foreign economists." In this assertion, they exhibited a somewhat traditional view of how the university might serve society. Hayes, by contrast, exhibited a more fully instrumental view in his hopes that a center could engage directly with specific problems of specific places. The seminar proponents nevertheless exhibited an industrial perspective on learning when they noted that "great care would be taken to set up the mechanism required in securing first rate material from abroad."[59] The reference to foreign graduate students as "material" resonated with the ascendant concepts of human capital and the knowledge economy discussed in chapter 3.

More than a year after the Ford Foundation rejected the seminar proposal, the department formulated a new plan for an economic development program in spring 1958 to present to Roger Heyns, the new dean of the College of Literature, Science, and the Arts (LSA). LSA had a remarkable run of deans in the 1950s and 1960s, with three out of four deans going on to lead major universities. Heyns's predecessor Charles Odegard, a medieval historian, became president of the University of Washington in 1958. The psychologist Heyns became vice president–academic affairs (VPAA) at Michigan in 1962, then Clark Kerr hired him as chancellor of UC Berkeley in 1965, following the Free Speech Movement and Martin Meyerson's interim chancellorship. Two deans after Heyns, geologist Frank H. T. Rhodes also became VPAA at Michigan and then president of Cornell. Finally, Harold Shapiro, who joined Michigan's economics faculty in 1964, skipped the deanship but succeeded Rhodes as VPAA and became president first of Michigan, then of Princeton.

Department of Economics chairman Gardner Ackley presented the new plan for economic development activities in a meeting almost immediately after Heyns took office in late June, which suggests that Ackley believed the new dean would be friendly to such efforts. Ackley, who would later head President Lyndon B. Johnson's Council of Economic Advisers, told his faculty that Heyns "evidenced sympathetic interest in our proceeding in this direction."[60] After the meeting, Heyns wrote, "Economics Department is unique for its lack of work of this sort. Objective observer would say the Department had its head in the sand on this matter."[61] This reaction suggested that the conviction that studying and promoting economic development was an important university function had spread in academic leadership circles.

The department tailored its new plan to the Ford Foundation's preferences, even as it expressed reluctance about some of the service work that Ford wanted universities to provide. As part of Ackley's preparation to sell a plan for economic development studies to Heyns, Hayes met with officials from three of the five divisions of the Ford Foundation on May 23, 1958. Ackley followed Ford's indications from this meeting almost exactly in the plan he presented to Heyns. Ackley proposed three major activities: the seminar, which the Ford officials told Hayes they were willing to reconsider; an all-university study committee; and a project in Pakistan.[62] The study committee idea emerged from the Ford officials' belief "that much of the value of the grants to some universities had been lost, because of the lack of integrating activities." Ford wanted different parts of universities to come together for an integrated attack on specific economic development problems that produced concrete, practical results. Ackley accepted Hayes's suggestion that in light of Ford's desire for integration, there should be "an all-University *self-study and planning committee on economic development* [to] consider how the University as a whole could get the most out of its present activities bearing on economic development." This proposal was akin to the program Hayes hoped to realize in a center, as opposed to the department-centered seminar proposal. Ford's insistence on integration helped to push a reluctant department to propose moving toward that ideal, which was a hallmark of the organized research approach that characterized the postwar university.

The Ford officials also told Hayes they were looking for a university to "backstop" the new Ford-funded Institute for Development Economics in Karachi, Pakistan, and wondered if Michigan might be interested.[63] Ackley included this project in the department's plan, but said that the department was "extremely reluctant" to assume such service activities and wanted to do so only if they could be connected with "a major new program of research and advanced training." He continued to search for funding that would not be tied to direct service activities. He wrote fruitlessly to the Rockefeller Foundation that "while it appears to be relatively easy to obtain financial support for the service activities, the agencies involved in such programs are generally not prepared to support the core activities of research and training. Nor, under present circumstances, can the University of Michigan provide any support. This is why we turn to the Foundation."[64]

Ackley also followed Ford's preferences in de-emphasizing the center, which Hayes was again pushing with a revised proposal. The Ford officials told Hayes they would not fund a center, but would consider funding specific research projects that a center might conduct once established.[65] Hayes even suggested that the Karachi project could be a "first step" toward the center.[66] Ackley, however, kept the center on the back burner in his proposal to Heyns, saying only that the proposed study committee would make a recommendation on the advisability of creating the center.[67] Hayes courted faculty from different areas of the university to participate in a center. George Cameron (Near Eastern Languages and Literature) and Bill Schorger (Anthropology/Near Eastern Languages and Literature) worried that the proposed center would detract from departments.[68] Ackley's memo outlining the department's plans did not mention these concerns, saying that "no obstacles have been raised" in conversations with faculty outside economics, even though he mentioned Cameron and Schorger by name. It is not clear whether Ackley simply glossed over the concerns Hayes reported or whether Hayes did not tell Ackley about the concerns.[69]

Hayes's approach and his focus on the center continued to rile the economics faculty during the drafting of the new plan. Richard Musgrave, lead author of the previous year's seminar proposal, registered the most thorough statement of concern. The German-born Musgrave, who came to the United States in 1933 and earned his PhD at Harvard, later came to be known as "the father of modern public finance" and the most important German political economist in the second half of the twentieth century.[70] Musgrave told Ackley that he had "a feeling that [Hayes] was primarily interested in a big field and policy operation, rather than in the academic core, and this is why I inserted myself when we did the first memo on the seminar. I wonder whether he is the right person for a program which is primarily centered on the seminar, and I have some question whether in the absence of this project we would have wanted to add him to the staff, taking purely academic distinction into consideration." He added a handwritten note, "what if the program does not work?" implying that Hayes would be unsuitable as an economics faculty member in that instance. Musgrave also criticized Hayes's notions of an interdisciplinary center and of direct involvement in overseas projects. The latter, "though highly useful and commendable as a public service, will be more of a liability than an asset to the Department" and might force it "to take lots of students in Ann Arbor who are not well qualified and who would only swell the ranks of marginal graduate students." Musgrave concluded that the key issue was "that we should insist as a department to get something out of this which will add to our *academic* distinction and scope. Harvard and MIT managed to do this. We should insist on a similar pay-off, and *not* accept the service-type of function without the *academic* counterpart, meaning by academic not the ordinary training function but a high level operation such as the seminar."[71] Musgrave's phrase "get something out of this" shows how he wanted to use the economic development issue to garner resources toward strengthening what he believed were the proper academic goals of the department. Shortly after writing this letter to Ackley, Musgrave left Michigan for Johns Hopkins.[72]

Hayes and Musgrave show us two different ways in which new postwar expectations for effecting social change (in this case, economic development) shaped universities. On one hand, people like Hayes wanted to use the university to engage with specific projects and to create new university structures (ORUs) to facilitate such engagement. On the other hand, people like Musgrave wanted to accommodate the new demand for economic development work within traditional university structures and notions of faculty roles, and to turn the new patronage toward academic goals. Resistance to the instrumental university, then, did not always mean the repudiation of imperatives such as economic development, but sometimes meant accommodating such imperatives within traditional academic structures and norms.

Despite the flurry of activity and Heyns's favorable reaction to the department's plan for economic development studies in summer 1958, nothing came to fruition until summer 1959, when the department hired Hayes as a half-time untenured professor for 1959–1960 for the sole purpose of building an economic development program. Administrators arrived at Hayes's salary of $8,333 by starting with a base salary of $20,000 (what he earned as director of the Foundation for Research on Human Behavior), reducing it to an academic year (ten-month) basis, and halving it to reflect his half-time status.[73] By giving Hayes the equivalent of a ten-month base salary of $16,667, they put him just below the highest paid professors in the College of Literature, Science, and the Arts. This salary suggests the value that the department placed on Hayes and the economic development program. The department had money to spend lavishly on Hayes because the highly paid Boulding had taken a year's leave of absence to work with W. Arthur Lewis on development economics.

Despite the department hiring Hayes to direct its economic development studies, the tension between department priorities and Hayes's all-university vision had not abated. In a letter to Heyns in summer 1959 requesting approval to appoint Hayes to lead a study committee on economic development activities in 1959–1960, Ackley again emphasized that any service activities must be rooted in a new, substantial program of research and teaching. Even as he allowed that such a committee might be all-university, he wrote that "our primary interest in the study is to get recommendations regarding the Department's program; if it should also be able to make useful recommendations regarding the total program of the University in this area, so much the better." He mentioned that although economic development must be studied by multiple disciplines in order to be understood, "nevertheless, within the discipline of economics a great deal of attention has been centered in recent years on what has come to be called 'development economics.'" He also noted that "we were delinquent in not having a program in this area" and "we believe we should be active in this field." These comments indicated the department's increasing unease about how its lack of attention to development economics might be hurting its standing among economics departments.[74]

Once Hayes was hired, an unforeseen twist occurred. Rather than starting the study committee, he began working on two linked proposals: to start a PhD program in development economics offered by the Department of Economics, and to win fellowships for prospective graduate students in that program under the provisions of Title IV of the National Defense Education Act, signed into law in September 1958.[75] Although the overall NDEA emphasized fields of study believed to be important for national defense, the graduate fellowships were intentionally open to all fields.[76] The focus was preparing teachers rather than researchers; NDEA framers believed that simply increasing the supply of college teachers, whatever their field, constituted a contribution to national defense. Some scholars have erroneously stated that the bulk of the fellowships went for study in science and engineering fields; in fact, 50 percent of fellowships awarded in the program's first five years went to humanities and social sciences, almost equally divided between the two.[77] The National Defense Fellowships were designed to support the first few years of either a new doctoral program or the expansion of an existing program, with the stipulation that the university was prepared to take over funding the program once the fellowships expired. The program awarded 1,000 fellowships to begin in 1959–1960 and 1,500 to begin in each of the succeeding five years. These numbers were substantial, given that the total number of US doctorates awarded in 1957–1958 was roughly 9,000.[78]

Winning the fellowships was the key to starting the PhD program and meeting the department's goal of securing funding to attract graduate students. As Hayes wrote in the NDF application, "Because of the heavy costs of initiating the proposed new doctoral program in economic development, it is not planned to undertake it unless at least six fellowships are made available under Title IV of the National Defense Education Act. Our request is for ten fellowships."[79] They got seven fellowships and started the program. Each fellowship was good for three years and paid a stipend of $2,000 for the first year, $2,200 for the second year, and $2,400 for the third year, plus $400 per dependent. The most important provision, however, was that *the university* received $2,500 per year per fellowship, ostensibly "for the costs reasonably attributable to each fellow pursuing a course of study."[80] In reality, the university could use the money mostly as it pleased. The National Defense Fellowship program, then, was a cash cow for universities. Ackley wrote to Boulding that "the University will receive $17,500 in matching money next year, of which $14,000 can be used for salaries, additional books, clerical assistance, and so forth."[81] Michigan used the money to hire Hayes full-time for 1960–1961, to add three courses on economic development (two graduate, one undergraduate), and to start a faculty seminar.[82]

The establishment of a doctoral program was the first success from Michigan's plans for institutionalizing economic development efforts, and it also became a stimulus finally to launch CRED, thanks to some innovative financial thinking. The problem was always how to ensure continual funding. The doctoral program and CRED, Hayes and his colleagues decided, could fund each other. Initially, the National Defense Fellowship payments to the university would provide seed money for CRED. By the time the fellowships expired, CRED would be up and running and winning grants and contracts; extra monies from those instruments would replace the lost NDF money to fund the doctoral program. This plan partially became reality. A faculty seminar funded by the extra NDF money began in 1960–1961 and took charge of planning CRED. Yet it took a grant from the Ford Foundation in April 1961 to get CRED off the ground. Only then, after months of delay, did the administration submit the CRED proposal to the regents, who established it on June 16, 1961.

The first year's budget was $65,581—$40,000 from the Ford Foundation and $25,581 in matching money from the National Defense Fellowships.[83]

Two days after the regents established CRED, Hayes returned from his stint in Washington, where he had drafted a provision in the legislation establishing the Agency for International Development that authorized "greatly increased research on development, to be carried on partly within the new AID organization itself, partly at research centers in this country, and partly at research centers abroad."[84] He should have been a happy man. But trouble brewed. Despite the apparent triumph of establishing CRED, Hayes was dissatisfied with restrictions the university had put on the center's scope and on his power and salary as director. The regents had established CRED as a university-wide organization, with an executive committee that included members of the School of Business Administration, the School of Natural Resources' Department of Conservation, the Law School, the Institute of Public Administration, and the Institute for Social Research. For administrative purposes, however, CRED was a unit of the College of Literature, Science, and the Arts, and Hayes reported to Heyns.[85] Hayes believed the latter part of the arrangement limited CRED's possibilities. He told Heyns that he was considering alternative positions in Washington and elsewhere. Heyns responded to Hayes that the university would support CRED "so long as its activities are of the essentially scholarly character that you and your colleagues have contemplated." He also denied Hayes's request to be paid at a level equal to the directors of other large research centers on campus, saying that CRED must show that its "activities will in fact justify so large an allocation of time and expense to their administration." Heyns insisted that Hayes would be paid on released time from the Department of Economics, rather than on a new FTE line specifically for CRED as Hayes requested.[86] Distrust of Hayes and his program lingered.

As CRED got underway the following fall, Hayes wrote a "preliminary statement" of its activities with a strong emphasis on its university-wide character. The statement noted CRED's focus on "studying the management of planned change." It also had strong behavioralistic overtones, particularly in noting that CRED sought to obtain more quantifiable data of noneconomic aspects of growth.[87] Another document stated that CRED would establish its own research program, and that it would "carry out specific research projects proposed by business concerns, government agencies, foundations or individuals, if this research is related in appropriate ways to CRED's own program."[88] Hayes, then, was pushing his agenda. But after just one year of

CRED's existence, perhaps frustrated by university officials' continued resistance to his ideas and desired status, Hayes left the University of Michigan to become president of the Foreign Policy Association, a nonprofit organization devoted to educating Americans about international issues.

Despite Hayes's departure, CRED began to take on the kind of large-scale projects on specific places, funded by grants and contracts from external patrons, toward which he had worked. By the mid-1960s, for example, CRED was engaged in a collaborative project with the Nigerian Institute for Social and Economic Research analyzing the long-run factors in that country's development, funded by $400,000 from the Ford Foundation. Wolfgang Stolper, who replaced Hayes as director, spent a year in Nigeria creating economic policy for the new government and wrote a book on his experience. CRED also embarked on a study of agricultural productivity in Pakistan, funded by $640,000 from an AID grant under a program Hayes had helped establish.[89] These activities and their funding signaled that CRED had arrived as a significant organized research unit, and had moved the University of Michigan toward the instrumental university model, despite opposition from faculty such as Musgrave and the hesitation of administrators such as Ackley and Heyns. Although CRED never became as grand as Hayes envisioned, Musgrave's fears about a field and policy operation under university auspices were realized. However much CRED enriched the university with overhead from grants, it is still the case that university resources such as the dean's office now spent time overseeing CRED that could have been spent on undergraduate education or facilitating independent research by department-based faculty. The ascent of the Center for Research on Economic Development at the University of Michigan was one of many signs of the rise of the instrumental university in the postwar United States. Notwithstanding his disillusionment, Hayes successfully used the University of Michigan as an instrument for promoting economic development, and thus left his mark on the American university.

CHAPTER 6

Founding the University of California at Irvine

High Modern Social Science and Technocratic Public Policy

As a US Army helicopter bearing President Lyndon Baines Johnson hovered over massive piles of dirt just off the Pacific coast in Orange County, California, on June 20, 1964, the stage was set for an under-recognized symbolic meeting.[1] LBJ had arrived to dedicate the site for the Irvine campus of the University of California (UC), one of three new campuses that America's largest university built mostly from scratch in the 1960s. As president, LBJ visited an unusually large number of universities. They were an important piece of his Great Society program, which he announced at the University of Michigan just a month before his visit to Irvine. LBJ's presence at Irvine signaled the kinds of programs the new campus would emphasize. This early part of his presidency was "the era of big promise," a period of great expectations for social change guided by technocratic experts in his administration. A similar grandiosity characterized many efforts at UC Irvine. The rapidly expanding federal state under LBJ created a demand for universities to create programs on public policy, as Irvine did.

Joining LBJ on the platform at Irvine before 12,000 spectators was America's best-known university leader, UC president Clark Kerr. The national spotlight would shine upon him even more brightly, albeit ominously, several months later during the Free Speech Movement at UC Berkeley, the first major student uprising of the 1960s. Kerr's proximity to LBJ at the Irvine groundbreaking was nothing unusual. Johnson once offered Kerr a cabinet

FIGURE 8.   President Lyndon B. Johnson (center) headlined the site dedication for the University of California, Irvine, on June 20, 1964. He is flanked by (from left) Vice-Chancellor for Academic Affairs Ivan Hinderaker, Chancellor Daniel Aldrich, UC President Clark Kerr, and Governor Pat Brown. University of California, Irvine, University Communications photographs. AS-061. Special Collections and Archives, The UC Irvine Libraries, Irvine, California.

post (see chapter 2), and Kerr must have figured he had pull with LBJ, whom he invited to the University of California *three times* in 1964.[2] The launch of UC Irvine under Kerr's leadership exhibited key elements of the instrumental university and the vision of American modernity that informed it. Indeed, academics' faith in their ability to further this modernity through social engineering reached its peak during the years that Kerr and associates were planning the new campus.

Two elements of UC Irvine's early years stood out for how they illustrated the instrumental university. First, Kerr wanted to use the Irvine campus to redefine the land-grant university. Whereas the traditional land-grant institution focused on agricultural experimentation, the new iteration would analyze human behavior scientifically in order to engineer social life. Kerr's belief in the connection between social science theory and practical programs for economic development led him to think that UC Irvine could be a new kind of land-grant institution—still committed to furthering California's economic growth, but through social science rather than agriculture. A study of

UC Irvine enables us to explore a thoughtful attempt to enlarge the land-grant tradition, and to consider the importance of that tradition in the formation of the instrumental university. Second, UC Irvine attempted to institutionalize a scientistic approach to social science and its application to public problems. UC Irvine leaders believed that that mathematical social science could provide universally applicable theoretical knowledge about human behavior, and thus facilitate rational social organization. This mode of thinking, similar to what David Harvey and James Scott have called "high modernism" and what Hunter Heyck recently dubbed "high modern social science," emerged from the behavioral science paradigm and its offshoots in administrative science, the new organization theory, and systems analysis.[3] According to its proponents, such knowledge would contribute to expert-crafted policy and enable efficient administration of organizations, which would lead the world into an American-led liberal-democratic capitalist golden age. Herbert Simon was a key figure in developing this mode of thought. UC Berkeley, under Kerr's chancellorship during the 1950s, attempted to institutionalize Simon's approach to social scientific inquiry about administration and decision making (see chapter 2). UC Irvine took that quest to another level, making high modern social science the centerpiece of multiple units of different types.

By the time UC Irvine leaders began academic planning for the new campus in the early 1960s, the practice of applying the kind of social science promoted by Simon to public policy problems had achieved widespread support among American elites, due in large part to the RAND Corporation (which Simon served as a consultant) and the Department of Defense. RAND, a policy research organization founded after the war in Santa Monica, California, emerged from wartime research by the Army Air Force on the efficacy of strategic bombing. Featuring "a certain style of mathematical-economic reasoning, an interest in organizational theory, and a commitment to what came to be known in political science as rational choice," RAND became not only the most influential institution for strategic thought but the leading policy think tank overall in the postwar period. Systems analysis, a mode of reasoning that involved quantifying all possible elements of a situation and running multivariate equations to suggest the best course of action, became RAND's signature methodology.[4] Robert S. McNamara institutionalized this approach in the Department of Defense after John F. Kennedy named him secretary of defense in 1961. McNamara hired the Oxford-educated economist Charles J. Hitch, chairman of RAND's Research Council, as assistant secretary of defense and comptroller. Together they became known for the "McNamara-Hitch approach to public service," which involved an attempt to quantify whenever possible and to use the techniques of systems analysis for all decision making. They believed that this method would result in the most rational, scientific course of action and thus be best for the country. Their approach later became widely reviled, however, first by the military, then by opponents of the Vietnam War.

Three related Irvine units housed attempts to extend the type of inquiry that Simon and RAND developed and McNamara's Department of Defense installed: the Division of Social Sciences, the Graduate School of Administration (GSA), and the Public Policy Research Organization (PPRO). They constituted perhaps the fullest attempt by an American university to institutionalize the behavioral science paradigm and its various offshoots, in part because the effort covered multiple levels: a basic arts and sciences unit (Division of Social Sciences), a professional school (GSA), and an organized research unit geared to public problems (PPRO). An emphasis on "analysis" ran through all of these programs. Each aimed to make the university more fully a tool for administering modern society and promoting economic development. At the same time, UC Irvine recruited top people from around the country for its faculty, in order to make the Irvine campus worthy of UC's reputation as an elite research university. The three units under consideration failed in many ways to reach the lofty goals their founders set. Yet the hopes that fired their creation reveal the power that high modern social science and the instrumental university model had among academic elites in the early 1960s. In addition, the creation of PPRO signaled that elite universities had accepted public policy research as a legitimate activity. Social scientists' affinity for the high modern framework facilitated this acceptance of public policy research.

These UC Irvine programs overlapped with Kerr's intellectual commitments despite Kerr playing a direct part in only one of them, and even then largely as a formality. In the first two Irvine projects—developing a general science of administration, and focusing social science on interdisciplinarity, mathematical modeling, and theory—Kerr had engaged in similar endeavors before planning the Irvine campus, yet contributed little directly to Irvine starting them. In the third project, PPRO, Kerr expressed initial enthusiasm for the idea (though it was not his), but later failed to give sufficient backing to it, perhaps because other difficulties threatened his position as president. There are several possible explanations for why these Irvine enterprises overlapped with Kerr's thought despite his limited role in their origins. The most obvious is that Kerr appointed Irvine's chancellor and approved the chancellor's selections for other top administrators. Another is that it suggests the widespread allegiance of academic leaders to a set of similar ideas, such that the candidate pool for Irvine administrators would largely share Kerr's worldview. Finally, the overlap might indicate that Kerr's innovative academic planning program for UC created an atmosphere that encouraged programs of a certain bent even if Kerr was not creating the programs directly.

The Land-Grant Tradition

Kerr set the overall focus for UC Irvine when he determined that it should be a "general campus" of the university. The primary mission of every general campus was to offer education in the liberal arts and sciences. But Kerr decided that Irvine should also have another, more distinct mission: to redefine and fulfill the role of a land-grant university for the late twentieth century. The University of California's history provides important context for understanding this decision. The university started in 1868 from a merger between the College of California and the land-grant Agricultural, Mining, and Mechanical Arts College. The new land-grant UC began with a single campus in Berkeley and added a "southern branch" at Los Angeles in 1919, later known as UCLA.[5] Each was considered a "general campus" because it offered a wide array of degree programs in the arts, sciences, and professions. The university also launched other branches: the Medical Department at San Francisco (1873), the University Farm at Davis (1905), the Citrus Experiment Station at Riverside (1907), and the Scripps Institution of Oceanography at La Jolla (1912). Davis and Riverside were particularly tied to UC's mission as a land-grant institution because they carried out research on specific problems important to the farmers and growers who constituted California's economic backbone and made it the top state for agricultural production.

Massive demographic and economic shifts in the state after 1940 prompted dramatic changes to the University of California. Industry based on the physical sciences and engineering encroached on agriculture's economic centrality, and suburbanization overtook ranches and groves. California's population leaped from seven million in 1940 to almost sixteen million in 1960. In response, Davis and Riverside added undergraduate liberal arts colleges in the early 1950s, and Kerr elevated them to general campuses in 1959. UC had taken over Santa Barbara State Teachers College in 1944 and transitioned it to a liberal arts college; it too became a general campus, UC Santa Barbara, in 1958. Meanwhile, the regents pondered how to handle the upcoming "tidal wave" of university students in the baby boom. At the October 1957 meeting where they elected Kerr as president, they also authorized three new general campuses to open in the 1960s. After Kerr assumed responsibility for planning the campuses upon his ascent to the presidency in 1958, each campus took on a particular theme. UC San Diego, built from the Scripps Institution, would harness that resource for a focus on research in the sciences. UC Santa Cruz would focus on innovative approaches to undergraduate liberal arts education. UC Irvine would experiment with how UC could redefine its land-grant mission to fit California's new era, especially by incorporating the social sciences.[6] Kerr believed UC Irvine offered a prime opportunity for carrying out this work, in part because the campus was located on the former Irvine Ranch, a massive piece of land that developers were turning into one of America's great experiments in planned suburbanism, the new city of Irvine.[7]

There was little question that Kerr intended the activities of the Irvine campus to focus on the economic development of its region. In the first announcement of its academic program, Kerr wrote that "Irvine will enroll its first students in September, 1965. These 'pioneers' will have an opportunity to share in the exciting beginning of a great new University campus, located in a part of the State that is growing rapidly in population and economic importance. The Irvine campus will be the focus for this region, serving many of its needs, and influencing its development."[8]

Among the fields that Kerr wanted to emphasize at Irvine, not surprisingly, were architecture and city planning. A 1961 document from his office suggested that "the new campus in Orange County should be given priority in future development in architecture and planning, which will probably be required in the late Sixties when the new campus is more fully developed. Students and researchers would profit from observing, and in some cases participating in the unique development of the campus and the entire Irvine Ranch area. The site could become a renowned center for these fields, similar in status to oceanography at La Jolla."[9] What *is* surprising is that these plans did not come to fruition. Although a faculty committee to create a School of Architecture and Environmental Planning began in fall 1967, and important faculty in the Graduate School of Administration and Public Policy Research Organization had city planning backgrounds, UC Irvine did not establish architecture and city planning programs in that era.[10]

Kerr's desire for UC Irvine to extend the land-grant tradition propelled his decision to appoint Daniel Aldrich as chancellor of the new campus in January 1962. Analyzing publicity photographs of Aldrich surveying the land that would become the Irvine campus, Robert Kett and Anna Kryczka commented that "Aldrich's gestures and affect convey[ed] the optimism and hubris that undergirded the technocratic imagination at work on the Irvine Ranch."[11] Aldrich, a soil chemist, had been statewide dean of agriculture for UC and thus ensconced in the academic field most identified with the land-grant tradition.[12] It would be his job to implement Kerr's dream of shaping that tradition to fit a new suburban area being built from scratch. To assist him in that task, Aldrich tapped Ivan Hinderaker as vice-chancellor for academic affairs (VCAA) at Irvine. According to Hinderaker, Dean McHenry, Hinderaker's colleague in UCLA's political science department and a good friend of Kerr, prompted Kerr to push Hinderaker for the position. Hinderaker, a specialist in public administration with a PhD from the University of Minnesota, had taught at UCLA since 1949 and was department chair from 1960 to 1962. For 1962–1963, Hinderaker was part-time academic affairs assistant to Aldrich while still a professor at UCLA; he began as Irvine's VCAA full time in July 1963. He spent only a year at Irvine—Kerr named him chancellor of UC Riverside starting in July 1964—but it was a critical year, because he hired the deans who would shape UC Irvine.[13]

From the beginning of his chancellorship, Aldrich was thinking about programs that might characterize an updated land-grant university for economic development. When Kerr became president, he began to create university-wide ten-year academic plans. Responding to a draft of such a plan being discussed in 1964, Aldrich suggested adding a proposal for "industrial sabbatical leave," which would draw "to the University scientists and engineers from industry for intellectual refreshment and renewal." He hoped such a program would "refurbish the intellectual equipment of our industry and enhance its position in the state's economy."[14] The most dramatic proposals actually enacted at Irvine, however, involved social sciences rather than physical sciences.

The Social Sciences

The behavioral science paradigm powered UC Irvine's peculiar program in the social sciences. The program emphasized several of the leading characteristics of behavioral science: "value neutrality, objectivity, quantification and mathematization, the operational definition of terms, and a combination of careful empirical data-gathering and rigorous formal theorizing (typically via formal model-building)."[15] It also resonated with Kerr's attempts at Berkeley in the 1950s to create units to support integrated social science theory.

The presence in California of the Center for Advanced Study in the Behavioral Sciences contributed to the direction that social science took at UC Irvine. The center annually brought a contingent of scholars for a year in residence. James G. March's visit to the center in the late 1950s was his first acquaintance with California, and it was love at first sight. March was one of the leading exponents of the new organization theory, which had found its most prominent institutional home in the Graduate School of Industrial Administration (GSIA) at Carnegie Institute of Technology in Pittsburgh.

Carnegie's Herbert Simon discovered March as a PhD student at Yale and brought him to Carnegie with a postdoctoral fellowship. March stayed and rose quickly to professor, particularly on the strength of the landmark book *Organizations* that he and Simon published in 1958.[16] After several years at Carnegie, March returned to California as founding dean of social sciences at UC Irvine. Hinderaker wanted to get "names" or "brains"—promising young scholars—rather than someone to implement a specific concept like problem-centered research. To a certain extent, an ethos of "it would be interesting to try X" rather than one of "we must do Y" characterized the early planners of UC Irvine. Some of the academic emphases at Irvine thus arose seemingly by chance—or perhaps better put, were simply those intellectual tendencies then carrying the greatest prestige in American academia.[17]

Nevertheless, March promoted a sharply defined version of social science in his plans for UC Irvine's Division of Social Sciences. According to this view, social science would progress to the status of true science only as it became ever more sophisticated in its quantitative methods. He believed that "the skills required in the social and behavioral sciences are far from unique to those sciences . . . such skills are highly correlated with (or identical to) the skills involved in mathematics and natural sciences."[18] He also proclaimed himself as having "the instincts of a missionary with respect to social science."[19] The prospect of installing a program leading toward a truly scientific social science at a brand new UC general campus thrilled March. He wrote to Hinderaker that "the thought of developing a completely new school without prior commitment, past history, or existing entangling alliances is exhilarating. The thought of doing it with the potential resources of Irvine is enough to make a country boy's mouth water."[20] March acted the part of a social science missionary; in the early years at Irvine he "wore Nehru jackets and pretended like he was a guru," according to faculty colleague Ken Kraemer.[21]

March installed an interdisciplinary organization for the Division of Social Sciences in part as a gambit for raising Irvine's prestige. He believed the division "should specialize by problem area rather than by traditional academic disciplines."[22] There would be no departments. He told Hinderaker that "the major subunits within the Division will be the Research Centers. Each Center will be comprised of a group of faculty and students interested in a specific problem area. New Centers will be added and old ones eliminated as interests, experiences, and opportunities change."[23] Whereas others who promoted problem-centered organization saw such a structure as ideal for attracting grant money, March was more concerned with theoretical questions and making UC Irvine an elite institution. He argued that "there is no serious possibility of becoming a major institution with a conservative strategy. As long

FIGURE 9.   James G. March (left), founding dean of social sciences, and Samuel McCulloch, founding dean of humanities, look over the University of California's new Irvine campus, circa 1965. The modernist architecture resonated with the overall plan for the campus. University of California, Irvine, University Communications photographs. AS-061. Special Collections and Archives, The UC Irvine Libraries, Irvine, California.

as the division is conservative, Harvard, Chicago, Stanford, etc., can win without exerting themselves. It will be necessary to gamble on staff, on research emphasis, on educational programs."[24] At the same time, however, March linked quantification and interdisciplinarity to a desire to use the university as an instrument to solve social problems. UC Irvine's first catalog exhibited this commitment, explaining that "important new problems confront society; and social scientists have a responsibility to assist in the development of solutions to these problems."[25] A few years later, in a "planning report" for Aldrich, he mentioned a focus on "applied problems" alongside quantification and inter-disciplinarity as key movements shaping social science at Irvine.[26]

March's vision for social science had implications for how the division would teach undergraduates. He espoused leading tenets of behavioral science when he told Hinderaker that "the division should be a leader in the application of modern techniques for empirical investigation and theory building . . . the social sciences should be heavily laced with mathematics, statistics, and computer methodology."[27] This program would begin with the freshmen in their Introduction to Analysis course, which they took in place of traditional discipline-based introductory courses. Again there were overtones of social science at Berkeley in the 1950s under Kerr; a 1955 faculty conference on strengthening the social sciences at Berkeley suggested that all students be required to take an integrated social science course.[28] March's curricular ideas were also similar to those espoused by Kerr at Aldrich's inauguration in 1966. Kerr said Irvine's academic program was "designed to counter the current tendency toward fractionalization of knowledge, to discourage premature specialization by undergraduates, and to promote the broad-ranging approaches which are proving to be so beneficial to the solution of so many current questions."[29] Perhaps he was beating a rhetorical retreat from the intellectual disarray of the multiversity, for which Berkeley students had criticized him during the fall 1964 Free Speech Movement. Yet in the end, the motivation for "broad-ranging approaches" was still "the solution of so many current questions" (a characteristic of the instrumental university) rather than a more traditional understanding of liberal education, such as forming students toward a vision of human personhood. On the surface, then, March's decision to have the freshmen take a single yearlong course on general social science analysis, rather than discipline-based introductory courses that might lead to a sequence of courses in that discipline, aligned with Kerr's desire to reduce premature specialization.

Nevertheless, March intended Introduction to Analysis to funnel incoming students into a specific style of social science, if not into a particular discipline. He even announced that he and his colleagues were "committed to the development of a new breed of social scientist." March believed that social science was lacking in analytical rigor, in part because other fields of study siphoned away most of the students best suited for the kind of social science he had in mind. These students simply did not enroll in social science classes when they arrived at the university, because what little social science they experienced in high school—March called it "the pedantic tradition of social studies"—usually lacked analytical rigor and thus did not engage them. The students who were attracted to social science, by contrast, often had what March called "antianalytical" reasons for that attraction. They were drawn to the study of human beings and social problems, and in March's view they inappropriately associated social sciences with "a rejection of things, quantities, abstractions." In sum, March believed, "The students we have are either inept at the skills we need or persuaded those skills are irrelevant; the students with the skills we need are strongly committed to a competitive field long before we have access to them at college or graduate school." March intended Introduction to Analysis to address this problem. The course, then, was intended to get the "right" kind of students interested in social science. It aimed to "expos[e] the excitement of analytical social science to significant numbers of students already committed to the natural sciences, engineering, and mathematics" and simultaneously to "discourage an interest in social science on the part of those with weak analytical ability or interest." March believed this "early exposure to modern behavioral science" was essential.[30]

To achieve these goals, March employed a revolutionary pedagogy centered on modeling social situations. In his view, traditional introductory courses emphasized the skills of reading, organizing, and labeling, which were "fundamental" skills in general, but "secondary" or "minor" with respect to social science; they were not "the major skills needed for imaginative theoretical social science." In their place, Introduction to Analysis would teach "those things with which every proper social scientist should feel comfortable": "a basic ability to abstract from reality to a model," the ability to derive "implications from a set of assumptions in a model," "competence in testing the derivations of a model through concrete empirical predictions," and "a small collection of generally useful basic social science models." These models included individual and collective choice, exchange, adaptation, diffusion, and structure. March believed that "by the end of the year a student should be able to apply any of these basic models to any reasonably well-defined social or behavioral situation for which it is relevant." In order to teach these skills, March eliminated required reading and made problem sets the major work for students in Introduction to Analysis. This "deliberate attempt to break away from reading as the primary mode of study" intended "to dramatize and enforce a rejection of the classic pedantic style."[31] March believed that reading of the type usually required in introductory social science courses did not promote the kind of analytical thinking he sought to develop in students. His problem sets, by contrast, would do so. March and his Irvine colleague Charles A. Lave wrote a textbook, *An Introduction to Models in the Social Sciences*, that was essentially a collection of problem sets related to different modeling approaches. They dedicated the book to Chancellor Dan Aldrich in gratitude for his support.[32]

Perhaps as a way of softening the hard scientistic edge of his pedagogy, March portrayed model creation as an art form. He wanted UC Irvine freshmen "to develop the *artistry* of thinking analytically about social science." He specifically distinguished this approach, which emphasized his preferred "logic of invention," from teaching scientific methodology and its "logic of criticism."[33] March believed that analytically oriented students would experience aesthetic pleasure in the work of model-building and thus be drawn to his kind of social science analysis.

In his conviction that thinking in models was the essential analytical skill for theoretical social science, March followed his mentor Herbert Simon, who exerted perhaps the dominant influence on social scientists' adoption of mathematical modeling techniques for human behavior after World War II. The Dutch physicist turned economist Jan Tinbergen brought the concept of a model into economics in the 1930s, as a method of providing a simple and mathematical representation of a complex real national economy. The subsequent adoption of the modeling strategy throughout economics contributed greatly to the field's mathematization.[34] Tinbergen's student Tjalling Koopmans also influenced the movement. He introduced critical ideas in a 1949 presentation at a conference sponsored by the Cowles Commission, a Chicago-based economics research organization, and funded by RAND.[35] Simon, an associate of Koopmans at the Cowles Commission, came to believe that the construction and testing of models was the essence of all thought.[36] A volume of his modeling-related papers from the 1950s, *Models of Man, Social and Rational: Mathematical Essays on Rational Human Behavior in a Social Setting*, exhibited that belief. In writing those papers, Simon "found mathematics indispensable" in enabling him to deal "clearly and precisely" with "several important technical questions whose solution is required as a foundation for a rigorous and testable theory of human behavior in groups and organizations."[37] Two titles further attested the strength of association between Simon and modeling in the social sciences. He called his autobiography *Models of My Life*, and his friends dubbed a memorial volume *Models of a Man*.[38]

In the early years of the Division of Social Sciences at Irvine, then, March installed a program based on the behavioral science paradigm, particularly as Simon developed it, with implications ranging from the pedagogy for freshman courses to graduate research. March's presence at UCI also helped to foster the growth of two units that represented more applied social science, the Graduate School of Administration and the Public Policy Research Organization.

Graduate School of Administration

March's attempt to craft UC Irvine's Division of Social Sciences by the precepts of the behavioral science paradigm had a counterpart at the professional school level in the Graduate School of Administration. Vice-Chancellor Hinderaker, who like Kerr was a devotee of administrative science, played the leading role in developing GSA, which institutionalized the quest for a general science of administration. Hinderaker included a Graduate School of Administration in the original academic plan for UC Irvine, which he wrote in December 1962.[39] But whereas the Division of Social Sciences took shape only after March was hired, Irvine administrators planned GSA and its intellectual framework from the beginning of their work—although Kerr's staff had created a skeletal plan (without GSA) before Aldrich or Hinderaker were even on board.[40]

Hinderaker's decision that Irvine would have a unified Graduate School of Administration offering a single degree, Master of Administration—rather than a Graduate School of Business Administration offering an MBA and a Graduate School of Public Administration offering an MPA—stemmed from his embrace of the vision for American modernity. The belief that one universal, generalized practice of administration could be applied with equal effectiveness in business, government, education, and health care institutions manifested characteristic tenets of modernity: aspirations toward universal theory and a desire to abstract and generalize from all particular, local, and individual circumstances. The push for generalization created rules that could be applied universally without needing particular knowledge of a local situation, which allowed rule-driven bureaucrats to administer things of which they had no specific knowledge. The emphasis on "administration" and "management" as scientific practices which aimed to eliminate arbitrariness, irrationality, and political influence reflected a belief that rational control of organizations would facilitate greater efficiency and productivity. The emergence of unified schools of administration such as UC Irvine's in the American research university during the 1950s and 1960s indicated the strength of the American modernity vision. Unified administration schools also constituted another institutional manifestation of the behavioral science movement, which held that an interdisciplinary theory of human behavior would spawn a unified theory of administration.

The dramatic change in university business schools that began in the 1950s and accelerated in the 1960s also shaped Irvine's GSA. This change brought business schools into closer connection with the social sciences and increased their scholarly legitimacy, since they now claimed to be doing something "scientific." As a result of this reorientation, business-related disciplines rose in academic prestige, and many such schools changed their name to include either "administration" or "management." These new-style business schools often created PhD programs and thus elevated themselves to a higher level of prestige within the university.[41] Yet the essential questions that drove programs in administration or management—"how to"—differed from the central questions in other areas of the university—"what is" or "why." To the extent that these programs grew, became prominent, and began to constitute a larger percentage of the university's research conducted and doctoral degrees granted, they accelerated the university's instrumental turn.

While he was in the process of planning GSA, Hinderaker published an article, "The Study of Administration: Interdisciplinary Dimensions," that set out his views on the unified school of administration model. He believed that such schools would produce benefits by bringing together three fields that others often scorned for being insufficiently academically rigorous: business administration, educational administration, and public administration.[42] These fields took shape during the 1910s in a milieu that emphasized the need for credentialed expertise to administer organizations. In the postwar era, Hinderaker said, business administration had been doing a kind of public soul-searching, which he believed would benefit the other two disciplines as well. The unified school would move public administration away from political science, which Hinderaker believed would enable public administration researchers to take advantage of new methodologies for studying organizations and management. Others agreed. Lloyd D. Musolf, director of the Institute of Governmental Affairs at UC Davis, who noted the influence of "the McNamara-Hitch approach to public service" on his program, believed that public administration had to embrace quantitative and statistical analysis of decision making (often using computers), systems analysis, and organization theory approaches. This move, he thought, would distance public administration from political science.[43] Hinderaker argued that "the core material for the study of administration . . . should include work in organizational theory, drawing primarily on research from such disciplines as sociology and psychology; in politics, where political science can make its most important contribution; in managerial economics; and in quantitative methods, not only because it is important to understand what quantification can be used for but to learn also its limits."[44] Despite Hinderaker perhaps taking a softer line on quantification than March did, these comments showed that behavioral science and the new organization theory formed a critical backdrop for the development of GSA, as they did for the Division of Social Sciences.

Hinderaker also believed that GSA's transgression of disciplinary boundaries aligned with a proper university goal of solving social problems. He told political scientists that "we should be giving more thought to the manner in which department boundaries can be lowered to facilitate an interdisciplinary attack on other problems which the world has every right to expect colleges and universities to deal with in a realistic and effective way. Certainly, environmental planning, or urban planning, or resource planning represents one such type of area. The stakes here, for society as a whole and for us as individuals, are worth sacrificing a little of our own disciplinary pride."[45] Hinderaker likely was thinking about Irvine as he listed those specific problems, since early discussions of Irvine's focus mentioned them.

When Hinderaker left Irvine in July 1964 for Riverside (where he launched another generic school of administration), he had not yet hired a dean for Irvine's GSA. Jack Peltason, dean of the College of Liberal Arts and Sciences at the University of Illinois, succeeded Hinderaker as VCAA at Irvine, then followed Aldrich as chancellor (1984–1992) and eventually became UC president (1992–1995). Peltason hired Richard Snyder, the chairman of political science at Northwestern University, as dean of GSA at Irvine.[46] Snyder, Benjamin Franklin Professor of Decision-Making at Northwestern, was immersed in the discipline of political science. Yet his scholarship focused on human decision making. His early book *Decision-Making as an Approach to the Study of International Politics* (1954), reprinted as *Foreign Policy Decision-Making* (1962), became influential across a disciplinary spectrum. As colleagues described his view, "For Snyder, the heart of politics is the making of human decisions that are embedded in cultural, social, and organizational settings. The hope of humanity lies in improving decision processes."[47] This attribution of messianic powers to decision science was typical of its promoters. Snyder's emphasis on the study of decision making likely endeared him to Irvine leaders seeking a dean for a school whose existence was predicated on the possibility of creating some kind of unified science of human decision making. Snyder recruited as associate dean a member of UC Berkeley's psychology department, Lyman Porter. An important figure in the emerging field of organizational behavior, Porter had just coauthored *Managerial Thinking: An International Study* (1966) with funding from the Ford Foundation. After consultation with March, Porter led the development of GSA's PhD program during 1968–1969.[48]

Two of Snyder's earliest faculty appointments, Henry Fagin and Kenneth Kraemer, suggested a bond between administrative science and city planning as these fields rose to prominence in the postwar American research university. Fagin and Kraemer worked on topics that drew on both fields and blurred the line between them. Fagin was a professional city planner, yet many of his scholarly papers discussed administration.[49] After a one-year stint teaching city planning at Penn in the early 1950s, where he interacted with the intellectual leaders of the field, he led large-scale planning projects in New York and New Jersey for the next decade before returning to teaching, at the University of Wisconsin. He also served as a visiting professor in UC Berkeley's political science department in 1958.[50] Kraemer earned his PhD in city planning at the University of Southern California, where the program was housed within the School of Public Administration. He was familiar with UC Irvine because of a consulting assignment with the Irvine Company in 1966, and the GSA concept attracted him. He admired Fagin's scholarship and was thrilled about Fagin's move to Irvine—so much so that he traveled to Wisconsin to implore Fagin to get him hired at Irvine.[51]

Despite this initial energy, GSA came unraveled after a few years, and it did not develop a unified science of administration. Snyder lasted just two years as dean. George W. Brown, a former RAND researcher who was developing a computer center at UCLA, replaced him but also had a short tenure. Stability came only after Porter became dean in 1972 and transformed GSA into a pure business school, as reflected by name changes to the Graduate School of Management (1980) and the Paul Merage School of Business (2005). Although the early faculty had a strong leaning toward public administration with Snyder, Fagin, and Kraemer, the number of students interested in public sector work soon dwindled, and many faculty members aligned with public administration departed. There were constant tensions between the business and public cohorts of faculty. These factors led to Porter's dismantling of GSA.[52]

In his article that laid the intellectual groundwork for GSA, Hinderaker worried about how the different "value systems in private and public organizations" (e.g., the different role of pecuniary concerns in each sector) might impede the creation of a unified science of administration.[53] He was right to be worried; such value disagreements proved fatal for GSA.[54] Critics such as Dwight Waldo, director of UC Berkeley's Institute of Governmental Studies (successor to the Bureau of Public Administration) from 1958 to 1967, had doubted the program to create a science of administration since its beginning. Waldo, ranked by many as one of the leading thinkers about public administration in the field's history, argued in *The Administrative State* (1948) that the field of public administration, far from having the capacity to be a value-free science, constituted a normative theory of government. He carried on an often-acrimonious debate on this issue with Herbert Simon in the *Public Administration Review* during the late 1940s.[55] UC Irvine GSA's failure to achieve its goals raises questions about the relative power of value, as opposed to technique and method, in constituting academic disciplines. To the extent that its failure also reflected the triumph of specificity over generality, it points to the limits of the push for generalization by social scientists in the high modern framework.

GSA was built on Hinderaker's belief that high modern social science, with its push for integrated theory, could help solve social problems, and that the direct solution of social problems was a proper role for universities. These views also motivated another UC project, the Public Policy Research Organization, which only became linked with Irvine shortly after Hinderaker's departure in the summer of 1964.

Public Policy Research Organization

Of all the endeavors that the University of California pursued in the 1960s, few were grander in concept and feebler in practice than the Public Policy Research Organization. Birthed by Berkeley's Institute of International Studies (IIS), and located at Irvine because of its land-grant emphasis and its adminis-tration's lobbying with Kerr, PPRO aimed to be the exemplar of a new genre: the university-affiliated policy research organization. The founders of PPRO adored RAND and explicitly set it as a model for their enterprise, intellectu-ally and structurally, including procedural details regarding salaries and over-head. They wanted to bring RAND-style analysis of public problems into a university setting, and believed that doing so was essential for crafting the best public policy and enriching the life of the university. The PPRO planners were not alone in such a quest. Simultaneously, the federal government's Office of Economic Opportunity (part of LBJ's War on Poverty) launched the Institute for Research on Poverty at the University of Wisconsin, which it conceived as an "academic RAND."[56]

PPRO exemplified the trend toward an instrumental university. PPRO plan-ners believed that by organizing teams of researchers who would perform scientific analysis of public problems around the world, the organization could help realize the promises of modernity. According to the planners, a structural innovation along the lines of PPRO would enable the university—not the pub-lic, through its elected representatives—to make the key decisions that deter-mined public policy. Universities would become the central and indispensable social institution—not only because of the students they educated or the knowledge they conveyed, but because they administered modern society directly. In these ways, the plans for PPRO crystallized a mindset that reached an apex in the mid-1960s. Proponents of this view wanted to change academic structures so that universities could rationally manage society through public policy.

PPRO also exemplified the instrumental university in its effort to combine the elite research university and land-grant traditions. PPRO planners sug-gested that the unit was an example of updating the land-grant model for twentieth-century conditions by drawing on the social sciences. Doing so would infuse the land-grant ethos more broadly throughout the university than in the past, when it primarily influenced agriculture, engineering, and home economics. At the same time, PPRO drew on the elite research univer-sity tradition in its effort to gather the best people in the country and allocate the majority of their time for research. Yet the notion of public policy as a legitimate academic pursuit was out of step with the elite research university tradition. PPRO planners further tapped the land-grant tradition in wanting their organization to have a looser connection with the university than a typical ORU arrangement. They wanted PPRO to be semi-independent so it could have its own norms that encouraged policy research. Battles over issues such as faculty ranks and salaries in PPRO exhibited the tensions that this approach often caused.

The ideas that gave rise to PPRO help to explain why the study of public policy increasingly became accepted as a legitimate university activity during this era. Such work was rare before World War II, with some exceptions under the heading of "public affairs" in units that chapter 1 described as part of the rise of public administration. By contrast, the concepts of public policy, policy analysis, policy research, and policy sciences came into vogue only after World War II and especially in the 1960s. In some quarters these ideals also replaced or warred with public administration.[57] The 1960s witnessed an explosion of policy research activity in universities. The number of university units devoted to public policy roughly sextupled (appropriately) during the decade, from about 55 in the early 1960s to over 300 in 1971.[58] Factors of supply and demand drove an increase in policy research in general, much of it housed in independent think tanks. On the demand side, the growth of the executive branch of the federal government since the New Deal, the post-WWII expansion of American power around the globe, and especially the proliferation of social programs in the Great Society created a market for policy analysis.[59] On the supply side, the kinds of social science promoted by Herbert Simon and Harold Lasswell promised a greater capacity for policy analysis. The use of new techniques such as operations research, systems analysis, and decision science made policy research seem like a rigorous, scientific enterprise that could be appropriate for the university in addition to providing solutions to policy problems.

The rising prestige of this high modern social science, which promised advances within the traditional disciplines as well as reliable tools for guiding policy, is a major reason that universities were willing to create so many units devoted to policy research. Universities could have left such work to the think tanks, fearing that policy research contravened the university's nonpartisan character. On this score, the scientific imprimatur of the new techniques helped reassure academics that such policy research was not partisan. Yet policy research still had to overcome the traditional academic norms that portrayed disinterested research, unrelated to present policy questions, as the proper mode of university investigation. The story of PPRO illuminates some of these broader issues concerning policy research in the university in the 1960s, particularly the enthusiasm and expectations for a particular style of policy analysis and how a university location could enrich it.

The two members of the university who launched the PPRO idea are remembered very differently. Roger Revelle was already the most famous ocean-ographer in the United States by 1964, though the peak of his renown would come later amid public interest in the greenhouse effect and global warming, a topic he had introduced in a seminal 1957 paper on ocean temperatures.[60] Revelle made his name at the Scripps Institution of Oceanography, part of UC's far-flung empire. When UC inaugurated Kerr as president in 1958, it also made him commander-in-chief of the institution's fleet of seafaring vessels in a ship-board ceremony. In the years immediately following Kerr's inauguration, the university built a full-fledged general campus, UC San Diego, around Scripps. Revelle, who had directed Scripps, did more than anyone to make UCSD a real-ity. Kerr nevertheless named Herbert York chancellor because he believed Revelle to be politically incautious and hot-tempered. Kerr believed that York could not be fully effective with Revelle hanging around UCSD, so he named Revelle university dean of research, which gave Revelle an office in Berkeley. The university-wide offices were located in University Hall at the northwest corner of the Berkeley campus, where Kerr's penthouse office afforded a majestic view across campus to the hills rising from its eastern edge, the hill-side emblazoned with a golden "C" to symbolize the university. Revelle later recalled that university dean of research "was essentially a non-job, but it was a job [he] dreamed up" when Kerr gave him a blank check. He did believe, however, that the position would allow him to push the "rugged individual-ists" among the faculty into cooperative research. From University Hall, Rev-elle began to plot a public policy organization.[61]

Across campus at the foot of those hills, an ambitious young researcher at the Institute for International Studies was also thinking about a public policy organization. Kathleen Archibald, a former Miss Canada and a Washington University graduate student in sociology under the noted Alvin Gouldner (a key early contributor to *Administrative Science Quarterly*), was working at IIS as a research assistant and coordinator of the International Security Program.[62] Like Herbert Simon a quarter-century earlier, Archibald had come west to work at a Berkeley ORU while writing her dissertation. Like Simon, she had grand ideas about the possibilities of behavioral science. Unlike Simon, she would fade into obscurity after a moment in the limelight. Archibald believed that a separate policy research organization, still within the university but not subject to its rules for ORUs, might solve some problems she had encountered when IIS considered taking on a Pakistan project funded by AID.[63] Revelle had worked on a separate Pakistan project beginning in 1961 as assistant secretary of the interior for research and development, a position in which he collaborated with Jerome B. Wiesner, science advisor to President Kennedy.[64] Revelle's assistant wrote to Kerr's assistant that Revelle would be bringing to University Hall his "Pakistan library," many items of which were "personally stolen by the [US delegation] from politicians in Pakistan when they were there."[65] While it is not clear whether Revelle was involved in the Pakistan project Archibald was trying to secure, it is possible that they met through their mutual interest in Pakistan. In his oral history, Revelle did not specify how he got connected with Archibald, but commented that she was "a big, beautiful woman . . . who really wanted to [create PPRO]. I worked with her quite a bit."[66]

By whatever means, Revelle's and Archibald's ideas for a policy research organization came together in the spring of 1964. Archibald's boss, IIS director Seymour Martin Lipset, was a close friend of Kerr. Revelle and Lipset convinced Kerr to appoint an all-university committee to study the proposition. The star-studded committee featured members from eight of the nine UC campuses (excepting Santa Cruz, which was still in preliminary stages), including Lipset, Aldrich, eminent economist Seymour Harris (who had just arrived at UCSD from Harvard, where a year earlier he introduced Kerr before the latter's *Uses* lectures), Revelle as chair, and Archibald, who had an unusual prominence in the committee's activities, as executive secretary. Kerr's letter to the committee, actually drafted by Revelle, proclaimed that he had "become increasingly aware of the opportunities and responsibilities of universities to provide expert advice on public choices between and among policy alternatives."[67] Ironically, the committee's first meeting was held the day that LBJ dedicated the Irvine campus site, which meant that Aldrich missed the meeting.[68]

Another important figure in the founding of PPRO was Albert Wohlstetter, one of the most famous American defense policy analysts of the postwar period, known for his strongly quantitative approach.[69] Before embarking on that career, Wohlstetter worked for the National Housing Agency in 1946–1947, then spent several years with a company that tried unsuccessfully to mass produce the "Packaged House" designed by leading modernist architect Walter Gropius.[70] These connections suggest Wohlstetter's intellectual alignment with the leaders of academic city planning. Wohlstetter gained his fame as a senior policy analyst at RAND, where he worked from 1951 until 1963, when RAND president Frank Collbohm fired him for allegedly mishandling a classified document.[71] Wohlstetter then served as Ford Rotating Research Professor at UC Berkeley for 1963–1964, the same position Henry Fagin had held several years earlier.[72] During that year, Wohlstetter participated in the Institute for International Studies and became acquainted with Archibald. That activity included a conference that she organized on the role of game theory in social analysis, which drew participants such as Harvard's Thomas Schelling, Wohlstetter's competitor for top civilian nuclear strategist; future *Pentagon Papers* leaker Daniel Ellsberg; Anatol Rapaport, a core member of James G. Miller's behavioral science group, first at the University of Chicago and then at the University of Michigan Mental Health Research Institute; and leading rational choice theorist William Riker.[73] Some evidence suggests that Wohlstetter was involved in the earliest discussions of PPRO with Archibald, Revelle, Lipset, and Kerr.[74] More evidence, including various usages of cloaked language, indicates that Archibald hoped PPRO would hire Wohlstetter as one of its major stars. She wrote in July 1964 that "if such an organization is to be established, decisions should be made as rapidly as possible because the situation will not for some time be as propitious as it is now and will be over the next four months."[75] It appears that during that time Wohlstetter was weighing the options for his future and Archibald wanted UC to hire him as a senior scholar in PPRO before someone else did. It is possible that Wohlstetter's presence around the IIS and Archibald's discussions with him contributed greatly to her vision for PPRO.

Archibald's draft proposal of June 1964 outlined the intellectual basis for establishing PPRO. Her central goal was to improve the quality of policy research, which she assumed was necessary for "the general public welfare." In her view, policy research would reach its highest state only if located in the university, which had heretofore been hostile to it on the grounds that it did not fit with the university's central mission of teaching and basic research. Policy research in nonuniversity, nonprofit organizations, she believed, "had a problem in attaining and maintaining both independence and significance. In general, they do not have the stability to stand firm in the face of pressures from clients; pressures to do only work that comes up with conclusions supportive of the views or positions of the client and/or to do short-term rush projects to meet immediate needs." To solve this problem, she crafted an argument explaining how both policy research and the university could change to embrace each other, to their mutual benefit. If the university could create a policy research organization "with a looser connection to the traditional university structure," it might allow "the significant minority of faculty members who wish to spend some of their time on policy-oriented work" to do so, and even attract top scholars from elsewhere who also sought such an opportunity, without conflicting with the central mission of the university.[76]

Archibald intended the proposed policy research organization primarily to extend the work she was involved in with the Institute of International Studies; it would not be a general policy research organization. A major purpose of the organization would be "significant research relevant to problems of American policy, particularly long term problems of international policy." She also clearly had RAND in mind. She mentioned that RAND's statement of purpose had become the standard for similar entities, how RAND's handling of salaries and overhead might be a model, that the proposed organization might compete with RAND for personnel, and that "proximity to RAND and SDC would be a possible advantage of a Los Angeles location."[77] SDC was System Development Corporation, an offshoot of RAND where C. West Churchman was research director and Gaylord Harnwell a board member.

PPRO planners attempted to emulate endeavors that they considered exemplary in the realm of "big science." PPRO, presumably, would be a leading model for a kind of "big social science" that they envisioned. One way it could do so was in its link to the university. "Perhaps the proposed organization may be most easily conceived of," Archibald wrote, "if we consider the University of California, for this purpose, as a consortium of universities, something like the Associated Universities, Incorporated, which operates the Brookhaven National Laboratory and the Greenbank National Observatory for Radioastronomy."[78] Even more telling was that the PPRO planning documents abounded with references to UC Berkeley's Radiation Laboratory (popularly known as the "Rad Lab"). Directed by Nobel laureate physicist Ernest Lawrence, inventor of the cyclotron, this unit was the home of celebrated research in high energy nuclear physics beginning in the 1930s. Teams of researchers conducted this work, and most observers deemed the Rad Lab the initiator and exemplar of the new trend of "big science" that provided a template for wartime research activities and the postwar system of national labs, including Brookhaven.[79]

One measure of the scope envisioned for PPRO was the proposed level of funding. Archibald hoped to secure a five-year foundation grant of around $2 million "to establish the organization." During those years, the new entity would seek "other long-term grants and contracts."[80] These numbers were small in comparison to larger research organizations in the physical sciences but were sizeable for the social sciences.

After writing the draft proposal, Archibald made a thirteen-day trip to Washington, D.C., and Cambridge, Massachusetts, to meet top policy scholars—mainly to get their feedback on whether they saw such an organization as desirable but also to discern whether any of them might be interested in moving west should the organization be established. She met with a number of luminaries. In Washington, her meetings included Robert Calkins, still president of Brookings; Charles Hitch and Henry Rowen, former RAND stalwarts then at the Department of Defense; and Assistant Secretary of Commerce for Science and Technology J. Herbert Hollomon. Her Cambridge meetings included two high-profile policy scholars: Carl Kaysen of Harvard, a RAND consultant and former deputy special assistant for national security affairs to President Kennedy, and Max Millikan, director of MIT's Center for International Studies.[81] Her trip stirred some excitement among these thinkers. Calkins wrote to Kerr, "I am pleased to see that the multiversity is rapidly becoming a reality on varied patterns in California." He elaborated, "Word has reached me that you have appointed a committee to explore the question of establishing an institute of policy research. I have long thought that a 'Brookings of the West Coast' was desirable and eventually would need to be established. RAND is first-rate, but not broad enough in the scope of its work. The subject is a big one and there are special problems to consider."[82] Calkins offered to talk with Kerr about PPRO on an upcoming visit to Berkeley. It is not clear whether that happened, but three years later Calkins was back in California for good as a vice-chancellor at the new UC Santa Cruz.

Archibald reported that, in general, reactions to the proposal had been similar to those of Calkins: "We can be confident as to both the desirability and feasibility of such an organization from the point of view of national needs and Government interests." The interviewees told her that the proposed organization "could attract first-rate people . . . could easily become the ranking institution of its kind in the country, and . . . as a structural innovation, might well become a prototype followed by other universities." Archibald followed that summary with a caveat that she was "typically . . . more a negativist and 'wet blanket' than enthusiast, so it does reflect quite solid feelings of confidence."[83] Despite her alleged pessimism, the notion that PPRO was something unique and utterly important permeated the planning process.

It might not have been coincidental that UC Berkeley academics hatched the PPRO idea the same year that Harvard began planning for the Kennedy School of Government, which would have similar emphases on policy analysis but a broader program and a much larger budget, given its $10 million initial endowment from the Kennedy family.[84] Under Kerr's leadership, Berkeley prioritized competing with Harvard for the title of best research university in the United States. The uptick in government patronage and the emphases of intellectual life in the early 1960s both favored programs such as PPRO and the Kennedy School, but the competition for prestige among universities might have played an additional role. Although it is not clear whether PPRO planners were aware of Harvard's plans for the Kennedy School, they certainly measured UC against Harvard. They remarked that "the lack of policy-oriented work is a weakness in the social sciences at the University of California, particularly when compared to a place like Harvard University," and that UC "has neither the flexibility nor the kind of hospitable environment that has allowed places such as Harvard and MIT to include [people studying policy implications of basic research] as members of the intellectual community."[85] Harvard hired Revelle away from UC in the midst of the PPRO planning, although Revelle served as founding director of Harvard's Center for Population Studies rather than in the Kennedy School.

The key intellectual figure at the Kennedy School was Richard Neustadt, who had earned his BA at UC Berkeley in 1939. After receiving his PhD at Harvard in 1951, Neustadt taught public administration at Cornell in 1953–1954 as one of Edward Litchfield's first hires as dean, then went to Columbia as a professor of government in 1954 before returning to Harvard to build the Kennedy School in 1965. At Harvard, as at UC Irvine, efforts in public administration and public policy were linked. The Kennedy School subsumed Harvard's Littauer School of Public Administration; PPRO would eventually link closely with UC Irvine's Graduate School of Administration. Neustadt was like the Californians in that his primary goal was to analyze decision making. He was unlike them, however, in his methods. The most striking feature of Neustadt's approach, which also marked his difference with the Californians most sharply, was his emphasis on the case study as a vehicle for analyzing common features in past decisions. He also used interviews with persons involved in these decisions.[86] The PPRO planners, by contrast, favored quantitative methods, mathematical modeling, operations research, and systems analysis. This methodological divergence in the two universities' public policy institutes mirrored what their business schools had been practicing for at least a decade. Harvard Business School famously pioneered the case-study method in graduate business education. As we saw in chapter 2, longtime UC Berkeley business school dean and Kerr confidant E. T. Grether looked upon this method with disdain, believing that it relied too much on intuition rather than the principles and systematic knowledge he believed his school taught.[87]

The agenda and invitation list for a conference hosted by the ad hoc committee on September 27–28, 1964 in the picturesque village of Sausalito at the northern terminus of the Golden Gate Bridge exhibited the intellectual proclivities of the proposed PPRO and its aspirations to grandeur. The conference's purpose, Archibald explained, was to "bring together four or five top people to act as consultants in drawing up the blueprint for an ideal setting for policy research and analysis. These should be people who could be seriously considered for appointments as senior staff members, and, in effect, we would be implicitly, though not too transparently, asking them what it would take to bring them to the new organization." The list of possible invitees read like a who's who of the policy thinkers then in vogue in government circles:

Secretary McNamara (a UC Berkeley alum) and his lieutenants Hitch and Rowen from the Department of Defense; defense strategists Wohlstetter and Schelling, a future Nobel laureate in economics; from MIT's Center for International Studies, Millikan and leading modernization theorist Walt W. Rostow, who at the time served as director of policy planning in the State Department; plus Calkins and several others of less renown.[88] Hitch, Rowen, Wohlstetter, Schelling, and several others actually attended the conference—including Neustadt, who was just then negotiating his move to Harvard.[89]

Three days after the Sausalito meeting ended, UC Berkeley students protesting restrictions on "political speech" began a massive sit-in, surrounding a police car in front of Sproul Plaza on campus. The Free Speech Movement had begun. In its course, students derided Kerr as a technocrat. Little did they know that UC was just then planning its ultimate technocratic endeavor, PPRO.

When James March arrived at Irvine in summer 1964, he and Aldrich got excited about the possibility of locating PPRO at UC Irvine, albeit for different reasons. For March, it would contribute to his social science program and raise UC Irvine's overall prestige; for Aldrich, it might be the centerpiece of his plan to plot a new course for the land-grant university. With Aldrich and March in key positions and a charge in place to extend the land-grant tradition, UC Irvine was disposed toward policy research prior to Revelle and Archibald creating the PPRO idea. Once Aldrich and March were physically together at Irvine and PPRO was on the table, the push to locate it at Irvine began. March believed that theoretical work and policy research not only could but should inhabit the same space; policy work was "a place for doing basic, theoretical research."[90] Only weeks after his arrival, March wrote to Aldrich that "Irvine should make a major effort to get involved in policy research and policy activities as soon as possible and on a basis differentiated from the other campuses. If we are just one of the minor campuses tagging along with Berkeley, we will not make the kind of name for ourselves that we want to. We can, at present, move much more decisively and quickly than Berkeley or UCLA. I think we should propose to the [PPRO] group essentially that we will take charge." Aldrich wrote "AGREE" in huge capital letters next to this point (much larger than his other "agree" annotations on the same letter), and that is exactly what they did.[91] March not only got himself appointed to the ad hoc committee but also became its vice-chairman, a position of heightened influence with Chairman Revelle off to Harvard. Aldrich elaborated his agreement in a reply, telling March, "It is my hope that Irvine will plan immediately to develop policy research capability within the Division of Social Sciences and the Graduate School of Admin, and that the Irvine campus can become an example of how a campus of the U of C can respond to the opportunity described in the Policy Research Organization draft proposal." It is telling that he linked the Division of Social Sciences, GSA, and PPRO.[92]

Meanwhile, Aldrich was musing about how well the proposed PPRO fit within the framework of a land-grant institution. His marginal annotations on Archibald's PPRO proposal give insight into his thought in a way that more formally prepared communications might not. In discussing the need to change the university's faculty incentive structure in order to promote policy research, Archibald wrote that "in many cases success in applied research is actually given a negative valuation, and is interpreted as an index of, at best, lack of scientific respectability and, at worst, lack of creativity. Thus the incentives for doing interdisciplinary policy research are in most departments on most campuses at best absent and at worst negative." Aldrich jotted in the margin: "not in Agric[ultural] Exp[eriment] Station—perhaps AES should be used as model." When Archibald wrote that "the distinctive nature of policy research means that it is both complementary to and *in conflict with* the main purposes of the University: teaching and basic research," Aldrich noted: "Not the land-grant university."[93] To Aldrich, PPRO was exactly the kind of endeavor that a revamped land-grant university should pursue. He cited "considerable precedent within the Division of Agricultural Sciences" for PPRO. There were "staff members holding appointment to the Agricultural Experiment Station only," who did research but not teaching. "It should be possible," he concluded, "to set up a similar arrangement in every field of inquiry within the University."[94] This model became increasingly common in American research universities; as it did, the percentage of university resources allocated to persons unconnected with any teaching department increased.

Aldrich's argument won the day with UC dean of academic planning Robert D. Tschirgi, the UCLA physiology professor who assumed control of the PPRO planning committee when Revelle left for Harvard. Tschirgi had come to UCLA's new medical school in 1953 from the University of Chicago, where he had worked with James G. Miller's behavioral science group, especially with fellow physiologist Ralph W. Gerard. By 1964, Gerard was the first dean of the graduate school at UC Irvine and working with March on strengthening the role of computers in social science education. The roles played by Tschirgi and Gerard in forming the Irvine program illustrate the impact of the behavioral science movement. The ideal of direct service motivated Tschirgi too. He told Kerr, "the proposed *Institution* [PPRO] would apply its resources to answering real-world questions generated by outside clients. This is most similar to the Agriculture Experiment Stations within the University . . . I am personally favorably disposed toward this philosophy as consonant with the increasing role of the University as an agency for direct public service."[95] Tschirgi also told Kerr that PPRO "might fit most appropriately at Irvine where similar concepts have already been considered. Roger Revelle fears it would not attract the best people at Irvine. I tend to disagree." In the margin, Kerr wrote "favor Irvine" in his usual green pen.[96]

Despite Kerr's favor, PPRO staggered out of the starting blocks at Irvine. Administrators made Archibald assistant director and she moved to Irvine, but she was the only academic person on the PPRO payroll for two years and even so devoted much of her time to teaching social science classes for March.[97] In the late 1960s, she left Irvine and worked for the Public Service Commission of Canada and RAND.[98] Negotiations with Rowen advanced far enough for a memo to cite "the pending appointment of Henry S. Rowen as Director . . . effective January 1, 1966," but Rowen ultimately declined.[99] For a variety of reasons, the UC central administration did not adequately support the fledgling PPRO. To be sure, Kerr and his colleagues were distracted by the series of events from the Free Speech Movement at the time of PPRO's founding, through Kerr's brief resignation the following spring, to his firing in January 1967 (discussed below). They were also planning the Graduate School of Public Policy at UC Berkeley, which opened in 1969 as the country's first full-fledged school of this type and competed with PPRO for attention and resources within the UC system.[100] Revelle was no longer around the UC system offices to advocate for PPRO. UC budget officials questioned the exorbitant salaries that planners proposed to attract nationally renowned figures to PPRO.[101] In addition, the UC Academic Senate rejected a PPRO request to create a new series of faculty ranks designated for policy researchers, perhaps exhibiting faculty resistance to one structural feature of the instrumental university.[102]

The arrival of Alexander Mood as PPRO's first director in November 1967 helped to make it at least a moderately functioning ORU, though it fell well short of the founders' aspirations.[103] Mood had taken his PhD at Princeton and studied there with Samuel Wilks, one of the leading figures in the development of mathematical statistics, then took a position in the "Stat Lab" at Iowa State University, where he met George Brown. The two moved together to RAND, where Mood worked with John von Neumann on game theory before leaving to found the General Analysis Corporation as a competitor. In 1965, Mood joined the US Office of Education as founding director of the National Center for Educational Statistics and hired James Coleman to conduct what became the famous "Coleman Report" on equality of educational opportunity.[104] By then Brown was dean of the Graduate School of Administration at UC Irvine and chair of the campus advisory committee for PPRO, and he invited Mood to join forces once again. Yet even the advent of such a

senior, pedigreed scholar as Mood did not launch PPRO to the heights originally envisioned. It did not develop a significant faculty of its own, but instead
functioned much like a research arm of GSA, relying heavily on Fagin and
Kraemer. It remained small and beset by continued self-criticism about its perceived failure into the 1970s, and never did the kind of foreign policy work that
its planners envisioned.[105] PPRO garnered twenty grants between April 1967
and April 1972. Only two exceeded $67,000: $180,000 from combined Carnegie
and Ford sources to Mood for a "Survey of Knowledge and Research Pertain-
ing to Effective Use of Resources in Higher Education" and $123,852 from
the US Public Health Service to Fagin as part of a joint project with the
Orange County Health Planning Council (which received over 80 percent of
the total project funds). PPRO also had two separate state appropriations annually beginning in 1966–1967, "General Support" and "General Research,"
despite UC's difficulties in funding the unit. The General Support budget
ranged from $43,300 to $69,006. The General Research budget hovered
around $20,000 most years. For the first three years (through 1968–1969),
however, PPRO expended almost none of the General Research budget, perhaps because it was not conducting sufficient activity to require the money.[106]

After several years of unsuccessful attempts at large-scale projects, PPRO
changed course in 1973. A special university-wide faculty committee returned
a resoundingly negative review, criticizing the unit's intellectual quality and
recommending its elimination.[107] Around the same time, however, PPRO succeeded in two grant proposals related to municipal information systems, totaling $180,000.[108] This success, along with the ramifications of the internal
review, spurred PPRO in a new direction, toward a tighter and primary focus
on information technology policy.[109] It eventually merged into an ORU dedicated solely to that topic in 1992.[110] Thus the notion of a land-grant university based on social science, despite the failure of the more grandiose projects
it inspired, did create a space in which the information technology emphasis
that ultimately characterized UC Irvine's policy research could flourish.

None of the luminaries who attended the Sausalito meeting or talked with
Archibald on her eastern trip ended up coming to PPRO, perhaps in part
because the special salaries and faculty ranks that the planners envisioned never
materialized. The planners still had Wohlstetter penciled in as their top senior
scholar as of a November 1964 document, but he joined the University of
Chicago's political science department shortly after that and stayed there
until his retirement in 1980.[111] He did head PPRO's national advisory committee, which included Calkins and Hitch, but UC Irvine officials disbanded
it in the mid-1970s because of perceived ineffectiveness.[112]

Charles Hitch did join the university in summer 1965, but not in PPRO. He became one of Kerr's top lieutenants, initially as vice president–finance and then, tellingly, as vice president–administration. His story is notable because of the national reputation he achieved for a style of ultraquantitative, systems analysis–based administration through his work at RAND and then as comptroller of the Department of Defense, where he radically overhauled its budgetary procedures. The hiring of a university vice president rarely prompts articles in *Newsweek* and *Science*, but Hitch's did. The closing paragraph in *Newsweek* is instructive: "Nor does Hitch himself see any fundamental change in his own function between his government and academic posts. 'The military always want about 30 per cent more than they really need,' he said with a disarming wink. 'I know that's true of industry and I'll probably find the same thing at the University of California.'"[113] Hitch believed in a generalized administration that could be applied to organizations with different value frameworks, the same belief that powered UC Irvine's Graduate School of Administration.

PPRO played a role in Hitch's assumption of such a prominent position at UC. Years later, Kerr presented a simple story of how Hitch came to the post. Hitch's brother Tom, a longtime friend of Kerr, called Kerr to say his brother "might be interested" in the finance position. Kerr's "initial reaction was entirely favorable. And Charlie really was interested. I never asked him why. Did he see the Vietnam imbroglio on the horizon? . . . For whatever reason, Charlie was interested and we were delighted, and the Regents agreed with enthusiasm."[114] The reality was more complex. In their earliest discussions, PPRO planners envisioned Hitch as a candidate for director. Revelle's initial memo to Kerr proposing PPRO, dated March 29, 1964, stated that Hitch "may be available in about a year, but that a salary of $30,000 or more might be required to enlist him." On the memo, Kerr wrote "please proceed" and placed check marks by each paragraph, including the one about Hitch.[115] Kerr thus approved the plan to recruit Hitch for PPRO, a year before the vice president–finance opening and the phone call from Hitch's brother. Archibald communicated UC's desire to place Hitch in charge of PPRO to candidates for the ad hoc committee as she canvassed them to get their reaction to the proposed organization. On her typed memo summarizing one meeting, she wrote in by hand that the candidate "was also concerned about the proposed higher salary scale, commenting on the suggested $30,000 for Hitch, that it might be higher than the current salary of a Chancellor."[116] Some UC faculty, then, were skeptical of the plan to change academic norms to institutionalize policy research.

At the same time, another related part of the university was making entreaties to Hitch, at least for a short visit, if not as an entrée for a longer stay. UC Berkeley had accepted a gift from System Development Corporation to establish the H. Rowan Gaither Lectures in System Science. The Graduate School of Business Administration and the Center for Research in Management Science, in charge of arranging the lectures, asked Hitch in 1964 to deliver the inaugural lectures in April 1965. He accepted, and later published his lectures under the revealing title *Decision-Making for Defense*.[117] Although it is unreasonable to assume that any university president knows the details of lectures being planned in his institution, it is reasonable to assume that Kerr would have known about the effort to bring Hitch, given his close relations with the UCB entities arranging the lecture and his own personal relationship with Gaither.

Kerr's presidency came to a stunning end in January 1967, when newly inaugurated Republican governor Ronald Reagan orchestrated Kerr's firing. Reagan had campaigned on a promise to "clean up the mess at Berkeley," a reference to the fallout from student unrest beginning with the Free Speech Movement, which had pressured Kerr from both the political left and right. Upon taking office, Reagan moved to abolish the free in-state tuition that Kerr defended. Kerr had a longtime nemesis in Regent Ed Pauley, now remembered largely for his donation of UCLA's basketball arena, Pauley Pavilion. A Democrat who served Harry Truman as a reparations negotiator after World War II, Pauley tried for years to get Kerr dismissed and seized his opportunity with Reagan's election. After the election, Reagan appointees changed the balance of the Board of Regents, and several regents privately told Kerr that his job was in jeopardy. Kerr refused to step down during the academic year under gubernatorial pressure, but offered to resign the following summer. Reagan never spoke with Kerr one-on-one, twice canceling appointments Kerr had made. At the January 1967 regents meeting, Reagan—who as governor was a regent—and his allies mustered a 14 to 8 vote to dismiss Kerr. They did so even after hearing from the chair of the system-wide Academic Council that Kerr had overwhelming faculty support. Kerr's ouster provoked an outcry. Three days later, a *New York Times* editorial proclaimed the "Twilight of a Great University." The *Daily Californian* called the firing "one of the great blunders of the history of this State."[118]

In September 1967, the regents announced that Hitch would succeed Kerr. Letters sent to Hitch at the time revealed polarized opinions about him. Herman Lindauer of Kemper Military School (Missouri), Hitch's alma mater, where he served as board chairman, wrote, "I know you will restore the type of discipline you underwent as a boy at Kemper."[119] A woman portraying herself as a concerned citizen of California wrote, "I am interested to know the mind of a man who is facing the presidency of a great university like U.C. with a background like yours. A background in which you are credited with 'introduction of modern "systems analysis" into the development of the new U.S. weapons' & subsequently their use in the horror that is Vietnam."[120] It is striking that the regents hired Hitch as president in the political and cultural climate of 1967. Apparently their faith in his methods and vision—in the "high modernist" strain of American modernity—was undiminished.

Meanwhile, Kerr continued to think about how to adjust the land-grant tradition. On October 18, he delivered a lecture at City College of New York, "The Urban-Grant University: A Model for the Future," which the popular press reported widely. He extolled the land-grant concept as "one of the great ideas in the history of the United States and of higher education throughout the world." He argued for its enlargement to something he called the urban-grant university, "which would have an aggressive approach to the problems of the city, where the city itself and its problems would become the animating focus, as agriculture once was and to some extent still is of the land-grant university." He boldly "propose[d] that we create, to stand beside the 67 land-grant universities, some 67 urban-grant universities, at least one for each city of over a quarter of a million and several for the very large cities." He believed urban-grant universities would be "fully useful to the modern society" and that the federal government should aid these institutions. Such a university "might parallel the land-grant institution not only via city-oriented curricula and on-campus research studies but also by setting up experiment stations to work on the problems of the city as they once worked on the problems of the land, and by setting up intensified urban extension services like agricultural extension." Urban extension was an idea that had motivated some policy and programs since the late 1950s. Kerr was familiar with the Ford Foundation's urban extension program of 1959–1966, and Title I of the Higher Education Act of 1965 provided funding for urban extension. Kerr believed the urban-grant university would be "a positive approach to some of the greatest of our national problems" and allow students to participate in "new approaches to our social problems."[121] As he had in the preliminary announcement for Irvine, then, Kerr continued to portray the university as a problem-solving instrument.

By 1973, UC Irvine had abandoned the bulk of its pioneering efforts to make social science the new heart of a land-grant university. March departed for Stanford in 1970, which led to a new dean and a revamped program for the School of Social Sciences (renamed from Division of Social

Sciences during March's tenure), although the school continued not to be organized into traditional departments until the early 1980s.[122] The Graduate School of Administration became a largely standard business school. PPRO abandoned its national and international aspirations and settled into a role as a minor player on local and regional policy and information technology issues.

Nevertheless, the founding vision remains important for several reasons. First, it exhibited the vitality and flexibility of the land-grant concept, which inspired capacious thinkers like Kerr to imagine how land-grant universities might move in new and more fruitful directions while exemplifying land-grant ideals. Second, these early programs at UC Irvine provide a window into a brief period in the mid-1960s when "high modern" ideas about relations between academic knowledge and social order reached their apex. It is instructive to note the activities of those (such as the UC Irvine planners) who control prestige and resources, especially when they have the opportunity to build something from scratch. In this case, their proposals revealed the influence among elite American academics of belief in an instrumental university to administer American modernity. The Irvine planners' overweening faith in mathematical, theoretical, interdisciplinary social science was part of an important moment in American history, a hinge of massive cultural change. Furthermore, even as a general decline in the prestige of high modern social science might have contributed to the waning of the original UC Irvine vision, many of that vision's ideas about the university's role in shaping public policy (albeit in less extreme or idealistic forms) have only gained a stronger hold across many sectors of American higher education since that time. Finally, the grand ambitions and meager results of UC Irvine's initial programs provide a cautionary tale about the difficulties involved in effecting major structural change in American universities and in using large-scale university programs to engineer social change in the wider world.

Epilogue
Critics of the Instrumental University

Despite the instrumental university's rise to prominence in the quarter-century after World War II, it had internal critics. Their insights enlarge our understanding of the instrumental university and its continuing consequences. The sociologist Robert Nisbet penned the most powerful critique of postwar academia, *The Degradation of the Academic Dogma* (1971). He coined the term "academic capitalism" to describe organized research, which he identified as the central factor reshaping the university. He analyzed how academic capitalism changed the social structures of universities. Yet Nisbet was not the only one who believed organized research was corrupting the university's soul.

A 1960 exchange between Penn State University professor of physics Ray Pepinsky, a world-renowned crystallographer, and President Eric Walker highlighted one key conflict over the instrumental university. Walker, a leading champion of organized research, presented a paper that fall at the Fourteenth Annual Conference on the Administration of Research at the University of Michigan.[1] He founded the conference in 1947, inspired by his wartime experience as associate director of Harvard's Underwater Sound Lab, a leading unit for organized military-related research.[2] The date and inspiration for the conference's founding suggest when and why organized research expanded. A decade later, the new *Administrative Science Quarterly* spotlighted administered research, with its third issue "wholly devoted" to the topic, including how wartime research had spurred the practice.[3]

Walker held that since research had become "an economic and political necessity," many scientists "must accept a certain measure of direction" because "a large amount of uncoordinated, undirected research" would not "add up to a significant assault against the massive problems we face today." In order for universities to "satisfy the legitimate claims made upon them for research," the scientific community needed to accept "the imposition of some aims . . . beyond the personal interests and desires of individual scientists." Much of the needed research required coordination of interdisciplinary teams "under the direction of a project leader," who functioned more as an "administrator than [a] scientist."

Walker also cited land-grant universities' agricultural experiment stations as a model for administered research in other fields. The federal government had funded these stations continuously since 1887, which enabled station directors "to plan their programs years in advance." Walker's belief that the agricultural experiment station should be a model for organized research was part of a larger trend to that effect, as suggested by the University of California's Public Policy Research Organization (chapter 6). The postwar university's move toward organized, instrumental research meant that the land-grant model extended its influence beyond land-grant institutions to elite universities while the German research university model waned in influence, as Walker mentioned.[4]

Pepinsky, enraged by Walker's paper, fired off a scathing letter and a twenty-page treatise outlining his view of university research to his president. The crystallographer reported that Walker's paper had "been discussed already at two national meetings of physicists" with "much concern." Pepinsky charged that Walker had "abandoned several long-standing principles," including the university's independence, the ideal of pursuing knowledge for its own sake, and the individual investigator's complete freedom in selecting and executing research projects. The physicist argued that "when 'outside direction' enters the scholarly realm of the university, the society in which this desecration is permitted has already begun to fail."[5] In his view, "the man and his ideas . . . are of prime importance in science; machines and team efforts take a second place." "Organization" endangered the source of new ideas and thus the advance of technology. "Administration of research" was "a dangerous concept."[6] Pepinsky cited two important contemporary sociological works, David Riesman et al.'s *The Lonely Crowd* and William Whyte's *The Organization Man*, as diagnosing a kind of "groupism" and "worship" of organization in American society that he believed had infected the university. He quoted three passages where Whyte discussed how the rise of "organization" meant the decline of the individual researcher pursuing fundamental knowledge.

Others also questioned the new dominance of organized research. Clark Kerr's collaborator Walter Galenson, despite his own participation in coordinated research (including taking direction from Kerr), argued for the superiority of research performed by individuals (see chapter 2). Some leading university presidents opposed organized research as well. The University of Michigan's new ORUs of the late 1940s that came to constitute its Institute of Social Research arose despite the critical attitude of President Alexander Ruthven, who retired in 1950. At Yale, President Charles Seymour allowed the Institute of Human Relations to expire in 1949 by not seeking additional funding. His successor, A. Whitney Griswold, was more dramatic. Griswold abolished the Rockefeller-funded Institute of International Studies, which fled to Princeton, and other smaller units. Griswold "believed strongly that the best academic work was accomplished by individual scholars working within disciplinary traditions," which made him a foremost defender of the older vision in the face of the trend toward organization.[7]

Nisbet published his critique after spending forty years at the University of California. A native Californian, he took bachelor's, master's, and doctoral degrees at Berkeley.[8] Late in his life, Nisbet portrayed the Berkeley of those years in a memoir. Its title, *Teachers and Scholars*, aptly summarized his view of what a university should be.[9] After completing his doctorate in the Department of Social Institutions in 1939, he immediately joined its faculty. The nature and extent of Nisbet's relationship with Kerr is a subject of great interest but some mystery. In his memoir, *The Gold and the Blue*, Kerr said that he "greatly admired Nisbet" and called him a "friend."[10] They interacted as faculty colleagues after Kerr returned to Berkeley as a professor in 1945, but might have known each other when both were graduate students there a decade earlier.

Both became administrators in the early 1950s. When Kerr was named chancellor at Berkeley in 1952, Nisbet wrote him a congratulatory letter expressing great pleasure at the news.[11] The next year, Nisbet left to begin a decade-long term as the first dean of the College of Letters and Science at the new UC campus in Riverside, which had been UC's Citrus Experiment Station. Initially, Provost Gordon Watkins (see chapter 1) shaped the new campus into an elite liberal arts college with an enrollment of 1,500, which some surveys considered a top ten national liberal arts college and others called "the Amherst of the West."[12] When Watkins retired in 1956, the faculty "submitted only one name" as his successor: Nisbet, who also enjoyed strong student support. But President Robert G. Sproul instead chose Herman Spieth, chair

FIGURE 10.   Robert Nisbet (third from left), dean of the College of Letters and Science, looks over plans for the University of California's new Riverside campus with fellow administrators, including Provost Gordon Watkins (far right), May 1953. University of California, Riverside photographs (UA 282), box 14, item 1067. Used by permission of Special Collections and University Archives, University of California, Riverside.

of the division of life sciences. In conjunction with Kerr, who became president in 1958 and changed Spieth's title from provost to chancellor, Spieth led Riverside away from the elite liberal arts college model to become a general campus. Spieth did make Nisbet vice-chancellor (while still dean) from 1960 to 1963, after which Nisbet returned to the faculty.[13] When Kerr was named UC president, Nisbet wrote him another glowing congratulatory letter, praising his work as chancellor.[14] But it appears that perhaps Nisbet's attitude toward UC soured in the 1960s. A year after publishing *Degradation*, Nisbet left UC Riverside for a brief stint at the University of Arizona, then concluded his academic career by serving as Albert Schweitzer Professor of Humanities at Columbia University.

Kerr lauded Nisbet's *Teachers and Scholars* as "the best available description of Berkeley as a teaching university of the 1930s . . . [and] thus a prelude to [Kerr's] *Uses of the University*, which describes the rise of the research university of the 1960s that took its place." Yet Kerr also suggested what he believed were the limitations of Nisbet's view of the university. Kerr claimed to "share the nostalgia of Robert Nisbet and members of his generation of which I was one . . . for a campus community of close-knit friends engaged in collegiate activities," but insisted that it was "no longer a practical alternative" and that nostalgia was "not for those navigating the swift-flowing currents of life."[15]

Nisbet's long experience in the UC system might have sparked his critique of the American university. In the preface to *Degradation*, Nisbet wrote that he began developing its analysis during the final years of his deanship at Riverside, and it is plausible to think that his being passed over for provost and the subsequent demise of the liberal arts college model that he helped to build motivated some of the book. But throughout *Degradation*, he mentioned conditions at Berkeley most frequently—and Berkeley led American universities in developing ORUs. Like Kerr and Gaylord Harnwell, Nisbet depicted the university as changing dramatically—with a "Reformation-like intensity"—after World War II. Yet his position diametrically opposed theirs on the source and necessity of that change, as well as on whether the change was good. Perhaps Nisbet had Kerr in mind when he noted that traditional scholars who believed "labor organizations [were] the place for labor-relations consulting" were now "towered over by those who" believed such activities belonged in the university.[16] At the least, this comment recognized the role of industrial relations in shaping the instrumental university.

More important was Nisbet's denunciation of the tendency to place the university in a progressive philosophy of history. (Nisbet did not name Kerr or Harnwell, but they often took this approach.) Nisbet argued that the key step in the rehabilitation of the American university was the "repudiation of historicism." Here he drew on Karl Popper's notion of historicism as "some imagined trajectory of development." Nisbet asserted that the greatest danger facing the university was "the habit of assuming that some indwelling pattern of development exists and that planning for the university must be in accord with this pattern." Such "preposterous" thinking, he said, *a priori* downplayed traditional practices and labeled new university activities widely considered good as "inevitable or modern." A true appreciation of history, Nisbet insisted, enabled one to recognize that believing history proceeded along a single track led to "follies and knaveries."[17] At the time Nisbet wrote, Kerr had not yet made the phrase "higher education cannot escape history" the title of a 1990 article and a 1994 book.[18] Yet in *Uses* he had already advocated what Nisbet would call a historicist position. There Kerr argued that the university "has a reality rooted in the logic of history. It is an imperative rather than a reasoned choice." When Kerr asked "what is the justification of the modern American multiversity?" he said "history is one answer."[19] Even if Nisbet did not specifically have Kerr in mind, then, he made a top priority of criticizing a position that was one of Kerr's important and long-held beliefs about the university.

According to Nisbet, university activity traditionally occurred under "a kind of social contract." Society allowed professors "the freedom to indulge . . . in the aristocratic pleasures of seeking knowledge for its own sake and then teaching [it] to [their] students." In return, the university and its professors stayed "as far as possible out of politics, out of economic enterprise, and, generally, out of the areas of society where partisan feelings are endemic, where passionate moralism is of the essence." Under that contract, "it would never have occurred to even the most radical (or conservative) [professor] to seek to convert the university into a kind of political engine. Or, for that matter, an economic engine."[20] But Nisbet believed that the rise of organized research in the postwar university had shattered this social contract, leading to the instrumentalizing of the university as an "engine" for political and economic projects.

Nisbet coined the term "academic capitalism" to describe a new set of practices that he believed was eroding the university's traditional character. They centered on externally funded research in large ORUs, and all of its implications throughout the university's social structure. For Nisbet, "the first million dollars given to a university for project research was far too much." The key point was that "for the first time in Western history, professors and scholars were thrust into the unwonted position of entrepreneurs in incessant search for new sources of capital." Nisbet did not blame the influence of businessmen outside the university. Rather, academic capitalism was "a force that arose within the university and that has had as its most eager supporters the members of the professoriate."[21] For Nisbet, capitalism was not defined by a quest for personal profit. Drawing on Adolf Berne and Gardiner Means's *The Modern Corporation and Private Property*, Nisbet argued that status and power were major motivators of capitalists, whether businessmen or "the research titan[s] who began in the late 1940s to govern the American university campus."[22]

While the new research economy was the context for the university's transformation, Nisbet argued that the primary change agent was not money itself but the structural changes that universities made in order to attract such funds. The rise of the ORU caused the degradation of the academic dogma. He believed "direct grants from government and foundation" to ORUs were "the single most powerful agent of change that we can find in the university's long history." The ORU became "the characteristic agency of the new money." The most unfortunate consequence of "the new, vast, highly organized and bureaucratized research" was that it separated research from teaching, thus tearing asunder what he conceived as a coherent fabric of academic practice.[23]

ORUs employed many PhDs who did no teaching. Nisbet argued that even those who did some teaching were often "institute-oriented" rather than "department-oriented." Here, ironically, Nisbet applied the distinction between "cosmopolitans" and "locals" that Alvin Gouldner articulated in two early issues of *Administrative Science Quarterly*. According to Nisbet, the spread of ORUs created a new status hierarchy within the faculty, elevating "cosmopolitan" institute-oriented professors over "local" department-oriented ones.[24]

A more subtle understanding of Nisbet's take on why the ORU was such a problem comes from an analogy he used to begin a chapter on "The Higher Capitalism." The chapter contains an epigraph from Rousseau's *A Discourse on the Origin of Inequality*, in which Rousseau argued that the first person who enclosed a piece of ground and claimed ownership of it was the founder of civil society. Nisbet followed the epigraph with his own analogy: "The first man who, having enclosed a piece of the university, bethought of himself of saying 'This is my institute,' and found members of the faculty simple enough to believe him, was the real founder of the university's higher capitalism." According to Nisbet, ORU directors flouted traditional university standards of community and authority by setting up their own shops and raising money to do what they wanted within them, without reference to other elements of the university. In the past, the smaller sums available for research had come to faculty members through a dean or research committee. This "system of intermediate authority that had been designed, so to speak, to protect academic man from the market place, now seemed to many enterprising research titans an unwarranted invasion of their right to get to the market place."[25]

In a chapter titled "The New Men of Power" (nodding to C. Wright Mills's book on labor leaders), Nisbet elaborated on how the rising prestige of ORU directors altered the distribution of authority in the university, particularly with respect to the place of departments. This political outcome, he believed, was "in the long run the most shattering" impact of academic capitalism on "the traditional academic community." The stature of the department mattered because it symbolized the interdependence of research and teaching, which Nisbet believed was essential to the academic enterprise. He argued that the pre-1945 structure of authority, centered on departments, was "the product of the universally conceived function of the university in society: the indirect service to society that flowed directly from the academic dogma with its twin responsibilities of acquiring knowledge and of disseminating it in classroom and seminar." Now in the era of direct service, however, the ORU—with its immediate access to external patrons and overwhelming focus on research to the exclusion of teaching—surpassed the department in authority and thus in prestige. The status of the department chair, formerly an "honored" and "coveted" position, reflected this change, as scholars now shunned its duties. In this shift, prestige followed the money. Whereas once funds came primarily through deans and department chairs, now much greater sums were available through ORU directors. As a result, the latter gained prestige at the expense of the former. Writing in the era of widespread student protest, Nisbet punctuated his argument by claiming that "the first real revolt against academic authority was not that of the students but of faculty members who by their own prowess managed to draw large sums of money" from external sources and then insisted on their immunity from traditional university authority structures.[26]

According to Nisbet, as academic capitalism diminished the authority of traditional academic administrators, it paradoxically spurred a new managerialism. It "converted scholars into managers of research enterprises—with *research*, as a word, gradually succeeding scholarship in prestige." The sheer size of the new research enterprises and the grants that funded them led to increased managerialism. One reason was that some ORUs became "large-scale organizations," which inherently had "managerial demands" and in practice often featured "large managerial staffs, complete with workers and technicians." Another reason was that as a result of the new money, "overnight a whole sector of administration, that concerned with finances . . . assumed unwonted importance in the academic-administrative hierarchy. The business and the managerial mind became increasingly vital." Moreover, presidents, deans, and department chairs were no longer chosen for their academic vision or curricular expertise, "but because they had something called 'administrative' ability," which frequently boiled down to "salesmanship." Academic capitalism also generated managerialism less directly, by breaking down academic community. As a result, "formalized, more or less bureaucratized, ways of proceeding," overseen by a growing army of administrators, replaced traditional "highly informal modes of consensus" for determining academic matters. The logic of this process sought a "new specialist" for every university activity, whose "very existence invite[d] more duties." The result was that "staffs and retinues of secretaries, technicians, clerks, specialists of all kinds enlarged constantly."[27]

Despite this appraisal, Nisbet did not believe the university should be isolated from society. He even called the notion of the university as an ivory tower "repugnant." For him, "The university [was] properly concerned with service to society" and had been since its medieval beginning. Yet he identified and critiqued the shift from indirect to direct service that characterized the instrumental university. He argued that "the university's service to society has always tended to be indirect; [preparing] the students, to go forth and directly serve the . . . needs of the social order." But "few things [were] more spectacular about the [postwar] American university than its plunge into direct service to society." This "deluge of humanitarianism" was "among the greatest" causes of the degradation of the academic dogma. The problem with direct service, despite its noble aims, was that faculty members "cannot help valiantly and at the same time . . . effectively . . . teach and engage in scholarship, [and] in the preparation of students" who will go on to solve social problems. Nisbet feared that the university would be overwhelmed and fail in trying to solve numerous social problems directly. Such failure would diminish its overall prestige, thus undermining public trust in its capability to carry out its core mission of teaching and scholarship. He also argued that since "some ascendant political interest" typically motivated "the university's venture into a new humanitarian sphere," direct attention to social problems put universities "at the mercy of the politician and the interest group with political pressure," which was sure to change frequently. Each interest group's particular problem, when taken up by the university, "tends to leave its ineradicable bureaucratic framework, rarely if ever adaptable to" the next big issue. The resulting "piling up of bureaucratic frameworks" encumbers the university more greatly with the passage of time. Ultimately, then, "the university cannot hope to be its own master in this politically charged area."[28]

Nisbet's critique, then, took a different tack than Pepinsky's. Both reacted against what they perceived to be increased managerialism within the university, spurred by the expansion of research funded by external patrons. They wanted to preserve the freedom of the individual scholar in an age of administered research, but they differed on how specific funding policies affected this situation and in how they portrayed authority. Pepinsky seemed to make the individual professor all-powerful, whereas Nisbet emphasized the professor's (at least partial) subordination to a traditional academic hierarchy of department chairs and deans.

While there is no evidence that he drew on Pepinksy, Nisbet honed his ideas about the university in conversation with Russell Kirk. A history professor at Michigan State College, Kirk resigned in 1953 to protest what he believed was MSC's deliberate lowering of academic standards in order to increase enrollment. He became a high-profile independent man of letters, speaking and writing widely on higher education. Kirk and Nisbet corresponded over the period of at least 1955 to 1963 (probably longer) and even vacationed together.[29] Kirk included several pages on Nisbet's thought in the second and subsequent editions of The Conservative Mind (1953), which went to a seventh edition.[30] In Academic Freedom (1955), Kirk quoted one letter from Nisbet, on the medieval roots of academic freedom, and possibly another, from "a professor with personal experience" of the loyalty oath controversy in California.[31] Around that time, he visited Nisbet and praised the small liberal arts college version of UC Riverside as "boldly original."[32] Nisbet reviewed *Academic Freedom* for *The Western Political Quarterly*, praising Kirk as a "brilliant young scholar . . . who has already established himself as an intellectual leader of philosophical conservatism in the contemporary world."[33] Like Nisbet, Kirk was concerned with how the university defined its service to society. Kirk disapproved of the prevailing emphasis on teaching everything "in relation to present needs."[34] He criticized Kerr as "the architect of gigantism in California's higher learning."[35] He also implicitly critiqued the concept of the university as a community service institution by emphasizing that the Academy's greatest allegiance—that for which Socrates died—was to "Truth," not to community.[36] Service to society was only a byproduct of the university's central pursuit, "the discussion of the most important questions."[37] For Kirk, the university's instrumental turn imperiled its independence and its true mission.

Two central elements in *The Degradation of the Academic Dogma* might owe something to Kirk. The first is the punchy title. Nisbet's official explanation is that it took after the collection of Henry Adams's writings published posthumously by his brother Brooks, *The Degradation of the Democratic Dogma*.[38] Yet Kirk referred to "degradation of the democratic dogma" in *Academic Freedom* and again in "Rebellion Against Boredom" (1969).[39] Perhaps Kirk's use of the phrase in conjunction with academic matters sparked Nisbet to alter it for his title. Unsurprisingly, Kirk also credited the Adams brothers when he defined the phrase as meaning "the extension of political forms to the realm of spirit and intellect." Kirk argued that this degradation of the democratic dogma caused what he called one of the major "fallacies" of postwar American higher education—"the notion that everybody, or practically everybody, ought to attend college."[40] In his view, this fallacy led to a lowering of academic standards that enervated true higher learning and its ability to provide talented students with an excellent education for democratic political leadership.

The other area where Nisbet might have built on Kirk's fragmentary insights is more subtle. While Nisbet depicted academic capitalism as the central villain that degraded the academic dogma, Kirk wrote in a more tentative vein about the university's market behavior. He rejected the phrase "free trade in ideas" as a descriptor of academic freedom, because "scholars and teachers are not traffickers in a market." Instead, their greatest concern should be what Burke called "the contract of eternal society," which is far above an ordinary contract for trading some commodity of "low concern." Despite Kirk's limited references to universities' market behavior, he gave it a prominent placement in the last sentence of *Academic Freedom*, with the admonition that "if the Academy is bent . . . upon reforming itself after the model of the market-place, not all the eloquence of the prophets can save it."[41] Many recent histories of postwar American conservatism have focused on businessmen and libertarians, with some even addressing their impact on the university.[42] Nisbet's and Kirk's critiques of capitalism in the university remind us that some of the most influential postwar conservative thinkers, traditionalists such as Kirk and Nisbet, opposed the extension of market logic into social institutions like universities.

The Instrumental University Today

The vehemence of their commentary is an important historical fact. It also underscores the seriousness of more recent debates over the structure, the operation, and the purposes of the contemporary research university. Even though participants in those debates do not reference Nisbet or similar voices, some do share their concerns. At stake is the capacity of research universities to promote intellectual, moral, or even spiritual goods.

Today's discussions on the influence in universities of capitalism, managerialism, and their cultures fall into two groupings: a social scientific approach centered on academic capitalism, and a focus on the dangers of corporatization that comes mostly from humanists.[43] The latter, who view corporate logics and practices as now dominant in university life, are often intensely critical. They frequently suggest that such trends have been detrimental to teaching and scholarship—particularly by leading universities to diminish or neglect the humanities and undergraduate liberal education.[44] These works are extremely valuable. Yet one aspect of their analysis is chronologically shortsighted—they often trace the phenomena they describe to the 1970s, especially to the growing strength of neoliberalism at that time.

This book has shown that academic capitalism and corporatizing, managerializing tendencies in the university have roots that extend much further back than the 1970s, planted more deeply in technocratic progressivism than in neoliberalism. The postwar vision of American modernity, rooted in technocratic progressivism, held that organized scientific research on social problems was an essential task for universities. This belief and its associated structural imperatives led to a boom in the creation of ORUs, which Nisbet blamed for spawning academic capitalism and destroying the university as a community of teachers and scholars that he idealized.

From the perspective of almost fifty years, Nisbet looks like a seer. Public trust in universities has declined; the ranks of administrators have swelled unceasingly; the pressure on individual professors to win external grants is greater than ever; universities compete for students by constructing luxury accommodations. On this last point, Nisbet wrote that one sign of the new wealth produced by academic capitalism was that "dormitories not seldom resembled luxury hotels"—and this in 1971![45] Competition for students is not strongly connected to the instrumental turn, but the other trends are at least partially products of how ingrained the instrumental model has become. The two most notable markers of the instrumental university's persistence today are ORUs and the quest to promote economic development.

In the half century since Nisbet published his critique, ORUs have proliferated all the more wildly, and not just at elite research universities. Almost every college or university has a collection of "centers" and "institutes," often independent from academic departments. As of 2012, there were more than ten thousand such entities in American universities. The top twenty-five research universities each hosted an average of 119 ORUs.[46] To be sure, many of them are not particularly instrumental, at least not on a level with units described in this book, such as Berkeley's Institute of Industrial Relations or Michigan's Center for Research on Economic Development. Their very presence in the university structure, however, carries some of the costs that Nisbet elaborated.

Nevertheless, some believe ORUs have brought benefits that Nisbet overlooked, even ones that resonate with his core beliefs. For all his admiration of hierarchical authority in the university, he was a relentless critic of the centralizing state, and a Tocquevillian promoter of a pluralistic society constituted by small communities and voluntary associations. ORUs provide an opportunity for a similar kind of pluralism in the university. They allow small groups of faculty (sometimes even a single professor), in partnership with donors outside the university, to establish beachheads for intellectual traditions and projects that are generally marginalized within the university or specific disciplines. In 2015, for instance, *The Chronicle of Higher Education* reported on the trend of donor-funded university centers and institutes focused on ideas (often considered conservative) stereotyped as unwelcome in academic disciplines. These efforts, such as Clemson University's Institute for the Study of Capitalism or the University of Texas's Thomas Jefferson Center for Core Texts and Ideas, are not in the same league as attempts to manage society through rational control via ORUs.[47] Yet they still represent a more limited instrumentalism, in that they function as instruments through which external patrons can use the university for particular purposes. Nisbet, a professed conservative, might approve of the ideas being studied in some of these centers, but he would likely view the structures as participating in the academic capitalism he disdained.

Belief in another pillar of technocratic progressive American modernity, that a university should be an instrument for promoting economic development, is now more fervent than ever. The longest serving Ivy League president in recent years, the economist Richard Levin, who led Yale from 1993 to 2013, frequently framed the university as an engine of economic development. One brief statement of his accomplishments noted that the university "had designed innovative partnerships to advance economic development . . . in New Haven."[48] Teresa Sullivan, president of the University of Virginia from 2010 to 2018, delivered a September 2011 address on "Higher Education as the Engine of the American Economy," a title that nicely sums up the widespread current belief about the university's purpose among university leaders and elites outside the university.[49] A recent overview of the University of Virginia on its website emphasizes the endurance of the instrumental vision of multidisciplinary organized research to solve social problems. Three of the four "recent achievements" chosen to epitomize the university are along those lines: "a pan-university Brain Institute," "a unique cross-disciplinary effort to end childhood diabetes," and the Data Science Institute, which "works as an accelerator across disciplines, developing a blueprint for a future in which data science will play an increasing role in our ability to solve complex societal challenges."[50] There is no word of theoretical advances in disciplines. These comments are remarkable because among elite research universities today, Virginia is probably one of the least instrumental. The fact that even a university like Virginia highlights such initiatives to market itself suggests how thoroughly the instrumental mindset has permeated American higher education. Yet more evidence of that mindset is the current national fad of using the acronym STEM to lump together areas of the university concerned with science, technology, engineering, and mathematics. Using this acronym implicitly downplays the role of mathematics and the natural sciences as liberal disciplines, highlighting instead that they are valuable because they produce technology.

Making the university an instrument for promoting economic development and solving social problems might have material benefits, but it has intellectual, moral, and spiritual costs. Evaluating university activities in terms of their economic impact or their success in addressing perceived present needs might undermine the historic disposition of the university as a place that protects scholars from pressures for immediate relevance so that they can pursue their curiosity and take the long view. If the university is primarily an instrument for economic development, there is little room for questions about truth and the good life, or for forming students to participate in civic activity. Material prosperity becomes the ultimate good, which degrades the special character of the university as a place set apart for deeper thought and contemplation.

Institutions draw from a stock of moral dispositions that have accrued over time. As the instrumental trend continues, universities risk exhausting the moral capital that made them so special in the first place.

ACKNOWLEDGMENTS

More than twelve years have passed since I began this book. During that time, many people and institutions have assisted me, and it is my pleasure to acknowledge them. Several faculty members at the University of Pennsylvania head this list. Bruce Kuklick, an extraordinary teacher and thinker, provided stellar guidance in the project's early stages and has continued to supply timely feedback as it has moved toward completion. Sarah Igo also shaped this project when it began, and more recently helped me complete it with her detailed readings of almost-final versions of several chapters. Warren Breckman helped me to see American ideas in a larger frame. Michael Katz and Rob Kohler showed me ways to think about the history of academic institutions. Walter Licht and Tom Sugrue also assisted with early ideas for this project, and Walter McDougall and Kathy Peiss provided institutional support while I taught at Penn. Many graduate student colleagues contributed to my intellectual formation while writing this book, most notably Dan Amsterdam, Brian Daniels, Matt Gaetano, Leah Gordon, Matt Karp, Drew Lipman, Clinton Ohlers, Karen Tani, and Sarah Van Beurden. Outside the department, Matt Allison, Zac and Joanna Brooks, Kevin Funderburk, and David Skeel helped to sustain this project.

This book also has roots at Wheaton College in Illinois. Mark Noll taught me how to be a historian, and particularly how to construct a historical argument in writing. He has continued to be a valued mentor, and he provided key insight as I prepared final versions of the introduction and epilogue. I am grateful for his example in scholarship and life. Hank Allen introduced me to the work of Clark Kerr, Herbert Simon, and James March. In an independent study with him on the sociology of higher education, I first read *The Uses of the University* and began to ask questions about the university as an engine of economic growth. I thank him for his inspiration and dedication to university ideals. Among other faculty, Jeffry Davis and David Setran helped steer me on the course leading to this book, while Kathryn Long and Gregory Morrison facilitated research support. Two graduate student colleagues at Wheaton, Daniel Gabelman and Luke Harlow, have been important friends during our journeys into academia. I especially thank Luke for helping me get this book's introduction into final form. In the Wheaton area, Daniel Benyousky, Ryan Earley, Robert Hanna, Scott Linhart, Jacquie Gall Martino, and Jon Penner all provided essential support. Matt Sterenberg and Anthony and Megan Tongen, friends from my days at Northwestern, have helped me greatly. Lastly, I extend thanks to two mentors from elsewhere in Illinois, Fred Beuttler and Paul Bushnell, who played key roles in my becoming a historian.

I am grateful to Cornell University Press and its series editors, Brian Balogh and Jon Zimmerman, for their encouragement and patience. I thank Brian for showing the initial interest in my project for what was then called the American Institutions and Society series and for helpful insights along the way. We did not know then that I would later join him at the University of Virginia, where he welcomed me as an honorary member of the Miller Center community. I am thankful for Jon's consistent responsiveness, willingness to help, and questions and suggestions that have improved this book. Senior editor Michael McGandy has made this book much better by forcing me to sharpen how I communicate my argument and to cut words when I did not want to. I also thank Meagan Dermody and Bethany Wasik for production assistance, and two anonymous readers, whose feedback both encouraged me and helped me to refine the manuscript.

Other scholars have helped me to improve this book. Dan Amsterdam, Chris Nichols, and Andrea Turpin have been valuable friends and gave feedback at many stages. Andrew Jewett, Tim Lacy, and Chris Loss have helped me think through the intellectual history of American academia. David Ekbladh, David Engerman, Hunter Heyck, and Stephen Macekura provided comments on chapter drafts, while David Hollinger offered insight during my archival research in Berkeley. I am grateful for the comments I received while presenting parts of this book at the Ecole Normale Supérieure de Cachan, the Institute for Advanced Studies in Culture, and Penn State University. I thank Philippe Fontaine for inviting me to Cachan and Prakash Kumar for inviting me to Penn State. Roger Geiger at Penn State, with his voluminous knowledge of the history of American higher education, has helped my career since before I began this book. I am thankful for the many ways he has aided this project.

This book goes deep in archival material, which means I have accrued many debts to archives and archivists. Mark Frazier Lloyd, who has ably stewarded the University Archives and Records Center at the University of Pennsylvania for more than thirty-five years, has done much to support this project. His colleagues have helped me a great deal, particularly Nancy R. Miller during my research phase and Tim Horning as I prepared the book for production. At the Bancroft Library of the University of California, Berkeley, I thank Michael Lange, Kathi Neal, Susan Snyder, and the rest of the staff for help over more than a decade. The Rockefeller Archive Center and the University of Michigan's Bentley Historical Library supported this project with fellowships, and I thank their staffs for assistance. I am also grateful to the staffs of university archives at Penn State, UC Irvine, UCLA, and UC Riverside, as well as to archivists at the Architectural Archives of the University of Pennsylvania and the National Archives in College Park. Several subjects of my book allowed me to interview them: Clifford Jones, Kenneth Kraemer, James March, and Governor William Scranton. I am grateful to Marian Gade, Clark Kerr's longtime research assistant, for sharing her experience of Kerr's life and work.

I extend special gratitude for permission to republish parts of three articles. Portions of chapter 2 are adapted from "'To 'Administer the Present': Clark Kerr and the Purpose of the Postwar American Research University," *Social Science History* 36 (Winter 2012): 499–523, republished by permission of the Social Science History Association. Portions of chapters 1 and 2 are adapted from "Clark Kerr's Early Career, Social Science, and the American University," *Perspectives on the History of Higher Education* 28 (2011): 193–222, and portions of chapters 2 and 6 are adapted from "Social Science over Agriculture: Re-imagining the Land-Grant Mission at the University of California-Irvine in the 1960s," *Perspectives on the History of Higher Education* 30 (2013): 311–333, both republished by permission of Transaction Publishers.

The Institute for Advanced Studies in Culture at the University of Virginia, an exemplary and intentionally non-instrumental organized research unit, provided a postdoctoral fellowship that aided the completion of this book. James Davison Hunter, Tony Lin, and Josh Yates provided crucial support during my time there, and I also thank Stephen Assink, Brent Cebul, Joe Davis, Samantha Jordan, Philip Lorish, Murray Milner, John Owen, Chad Wellmon, and Susan Witzel for their contributions. Across Grounds, Lauren Turek and the rest of the diplomatic history group offered an important reading of chapter 4 and parts of the introduction. Elsewhere in beautiful Charlottesville, one of the greatest towns in America, a host of wonderful people—including Cindy and Jim Anderson, Anne and Malcolm Hughes, Becca and Matt Puffer, and Drew and Marie Trotter—made an extraordinary community. We miss it so much.

I completed this book as a faculty member at Azusa Pacific University, which has provided release time and financial support. I am grateful to Mark Eaton, Diane Guido, Don Isaak, Dan Palm, Mark Stanton, and Jennifer Walsh, as well as to the Faculty Research Council, for this assistance. Two of my best students, Penelope Edmondson Marx and Jacqueline Summers, also helped this book toward completion. My colleagues in the Department of History and Political Science provided support during this time. Across APU, I particularly thank Brad Hale, David Weeks, and David Williams for the advice and opportunities they have given me as a liberal arts educator. I have had the privilege of being a reader at the Huntington Library, where I have done most of the finishing work on this book in the Rothenberg Reading Room, a true scholar's haven. I am grateful to Christopher Adde for providing desk space.

Family and friends have sustained me during this journey. Kevin and Pat Gray have been wonderful parents-in-law. I particularly thank Pat for helping with child care during a critical stretch that allowed me to get the manuscript ready for external review. I am grateful to Andrew Nyren for helping me study educational institutions and their campuses from a young age, to Kristoffer Popp, and to Morse Tan. My father, Doug Schrum, and my mother, Laurie Schrum, deserve much credit for this book. They poured love into me from the time I was an incessantly questioning little boy and supported all my educational endeavors. My own children, Bartholomew and Maia, were born during the latter phases of work on this book. Their smiles lift my spirits, and I now enjoy answering their many questions. They have involved me in reading different kinds of books and thinking about moral formation in new ways. My greatest thanks goes to my wife, Kara, who blesses me with the fruits of her deep reading, thinking, and writing. I am finishing this manuscript within days of our fifth anniversary, which means that the last five years of working on this book have been the best years of my life. She is truly a special companion. I dedicate this book to her.

NOTES

Abbreviations Used in Notes

People

CK	Clark Kerr
CKS	Carroll K. Shaw
EED	Edmund E. Day
GA	Gardner Ackley
GPH	Gaylord P. Harnwell
HES	Harold E. Stassen
JGM	James G. March
JHW	Joseph H. Willits
NDP	Norman D. Palmer
RGS	Robert G. Sproul
SPH	Samuel P. Hayes Jr.

Archival Collections

AR	Office of Alumni Records Biographical Records, UPF 1.9 AR, University Archives and Records Center, University of Pennsylvania
BPAR	Bureau of Public Administration Records, CU-46, The Bancroft Library, University of California, Berkeley
CKP	Clark Kerr Personal and Professional Papers, CU-302, The Bancroft Library, University of California, Berkeley
CLSAR	College of Literature, Science, and the Arts Records, Bentley Historical Library, University of Michigan
CRED	Center for Research on Economic Development Papers, Bentley Historical Library, University of Michigan
DCES	Department of Commerce Records, RG 40, Office of the Secretary, Executive Secretariat's Subject File, 1953–1974, Finding Aid A1 Entry 78, National Archives at College Park, College Park, Maryland
DCST	Department of Commerce Records, RG 40, Office of Science and Technology, Assistant Secretary for Science and Technology Subject File 1962–1970, Finding Aid A1 Entry 19, National Archives at College Park, College Park, Maryland
DER	Department of Economics (University of Michigan) Records, 1915–1980, Bentley Historical Library, University of Michigan

EWP   Eric Walker Papers, Group #106, Box 13, Folder: President (Office of the): President (The): Publications 1960, Penn State University Archives

FADR   School of Fine Arts Office of the Dean Records, UPB 8.4, University Archives and Records Center, University of Pennsylvania

FFA   Ford Foundation Archives, Rockefeller Archive Center

GHPC   G. Holmes Perkins Collection, Architectural Archives, University of Pennsylvania

GPHP   Gaylord P. Harnwell Papers, UPT 50 H 289, University Archives and Records Center, University of Pennsylvania

KPR   Wharton School Special Programs Karachi Project Records, 1954–1959, UPB 5.95 K, University Archives and Records Center, University of Pennsylvania

NPAR   University Relations News and Public Affairs Records, 1912–1997, UPF 8.5, University Archives and Records Center, University of Pennsylvania

RFA1   Rockefeller Foundation Archives, RG 1.1, Series 200, Rockefeller Archive Center

RFA3   Rockefeller Foundation Archives, RG 3 Program and Policy, Series 910, Rockefeller Archive Center

SCMOH Samuel C. McCulloch Oral Histories, AS-033, Special Collections and Archives, The UC Irvine Libraries, Irvine, California

UCBCR Records of the Office of the Chancellor, University of California, Berkeley, 1952– [ongoing], CU-149, The Bancroft Library, University of California, Berkeley

UCICR Central Records Unit Records, AS-004, Special Collections and Archives, The UC Irvine Libraries, Irvine, California

UCOP2 Office of the President Records, CU-5 Series 2, The Bancroft Library, University of California, Berkeley

UCOP3 Office of the President Records, CU-5 Series 3, The Bancroft Library, University of California, Berkeley

UCOP4 Office of the President Records, CU-5 Series 4, The Bancroft Library, University of California, Berkeley

UCOP5 Office of the President Records, CU-5 Series 5, The Bancroft Library, University of California, Berkeley

UCOP8 Office of the President Records, CU-5 Series 8, The Bancroft Library, University of California, Berkeley

UPOPR Office of the President Records, UPA 4, University Archives and Records Center, University of Pennsylvania

VPLMC Van Pelt Library microfilm collection, University of Pennsylvania (nonarchival)

WSODR Wharton School Office of the Dean Records, UPB 5.4, University Archives and Records Center, University of Pennsylvania

Introduction

1. Clark Kerr, *The Uses of the University* (Cambridge, MA: Harvard University Press, 1963), 1–2, v–vi, 6, 20, 87.

2. Instrumental rationality (or procedural rationality) concerns the means or procedures to achieve some goal, in contrast to value or substantive rationality, which concerns the nature of things or the establishment of values.

3. Despite agreement that Kerr was the most important university president in the past sixty years, historians have yet to craft a full account of his work and its significance. The best existing attempt to take stock of Kerr's thought is Paddy Riley, "Clark Kerr: From the Industrial to the Knowledge Economy," in *American Capitalism: Social Thought and Political Economy in the Twentieth Century*, ed. Nelson Lichtenstein (Philadelphia: University of Pennsylvania Press, 2006), 71–87. As I show in chapter 2, however, his title is misleading. Other interpretations include Nils Gilman, *Mandarins of the Future: Modernization Theory in Cold War America* (Baltimore: Johns Hopkins University Press, 2003), 107–112; Mary Soo and Cathryn Carson, "Managing the Research University: Clark Kerr and the University of California," *Minerva* 42 (2004): 215–236; Paul Mattingly, "Clark Kerr: The Unapologetic Pragmatist," *Social Science History* 36, no. 4 (2012): 481–497; and several pieces by Sheldon Rothblatt: "Clark Kerr and the Pursuit of Excellence in the Modern University," *Minerva* 33, no. 3 (1995): 265–277; "Views from the Acropolis and the Agora: Clark Kerr's Industrial Society," in *The Benefit of Broad Horizons: Intellectual and Institutional Preconditions for a Global Social Science*, ed. Hans Joas and Barbro Klein (Leiden, NL: Brill, 2010), 339–353; Rothblatt, "Clark Kerr: Two Voices," in *Clark Kerr's World of Higher Education Reaches the 21st Century: Chapters in a Special History*, ed. Rothblatt (Dordrecht, NL: Springer, 2012), 1–42. Except Mattingly, these scholars have a connection with Kerr's home campus, UC Berkeley. The most voluminous work on Kerr's career is his own two-volume memoir of the University of California. Clark Kerr, *The Gold and the Blue: A Personal Memoir of the University of California, 1949–1967*, 2 vol. (Berkeley: University of California Press, 2001, 2003). Kerr is featured in books that address some of the most significant episodes of the University of California's postwar history, which had national ramifications: the loyalty oath controversy, the Master Plan for Higher Education, the Free Speech Movement, and student radicalism in general. See, respectively, Bob Blauner, *Resisting McCarthyism: To Sign or Not to Sign California's Loyalty Oath* (Stanford, CA: Stanford University Press, 2009); John Aubrey Douglass, *The California Idea and American Higher Education: 1850 to the 1960 Master Plan* (Stanford, CA: Stanford University Press, 2000); Robert Cohen and Reginald E. Zelnik, eds., *The Free Speech Movement: Reflections on Berkeley in the 1960s* (Berkeley: University of California Press, 2002) and Robert Cohen, *Freedom's Orator: Mario Savio and the Radical Legacy of the 1960s* (New York: Oxford University Press, 2009); Seth Rosenfeld, *Subversives: The FBI's War on Student Radicals, and Reagan's Rise to Power* (New York: Farrar, Straus and Giroux, 2012).

4. Clark Kerr, "The Schools of Business Administration," May 1957, CKP, Carton 6, Folder 42.

5. John F. Kennedy, quoted in Franklin Foer, "The Story of How The New Republic Invented Modern Liberalism," *New Republic*, November 9, 2014, https://newrepublic.com/article/120193/how-new-republic-was-founded, accessed October 6, 2018.

6. The term first appeared in David R. Deener, "On the Causes of the Present Discontents between Campus and Society," *Loyola Law Review* 15 (1968–69): 243–254, but it has rarely been used since then.

7. Historians have written very little about organized research units. The essential piece is Roger L. Geiger, "Organized Research Units—Their Role in the Development

of University Research," *Journal of Higher Education* 61, no. 1 (1990): 1–19. Geiger interprets ORUs as providing the university with a buffer from external pressures, helping to preserve the intellectual independence of academic departments, whereas I see the postwar profusion of ORUs as leading universities in a more instrumental direction. Earlier, Laurence R. Veysey wrote that the rise of ORUs was the only major structural change to American research universities after 1910. *The Emergence of the American University* (Chicago: University of Chicago Press, 1965), 338.

8. Raymond M. Hughes, "Research in American Universities and Colleges," in National Resources Committee, *Research: A National Resource, Part I: Relation of the Federal Government to Research* (Washington, DC: US Government Printing Office, 1938), 176, quoted in Joel Genuth, "Groping Towards Science Policy in the United States in the 1930s," *Minerva* 25 (Autumn 1987): 257.

9. Rebecca S. Lowen, *Creating the Cold War University: The Transformation of Stanford* (Berkeley: University of California Press, 1997).

10. My argument that patron-driven interdisciplinary organized research oriented toward social problems became prominent in the postwar university challenges accounts that claim that disciplines became more central during that time. Thomas Bender and Carl E. Schorske, eds., *American Academic Culture in Transformation: Fifty Years, Four Disciplines* (Princeton, NJ: Princeton University Press, 1997) made academic disciplines its primary lens, and asserted that the postwar university saw a return to disciplinary purity and a shrinking from civic responsibility. This pro-discipline argument returned fifteen years later in two short pieces not based on archival research. Theodore M. Porter, "Foreword: Positioning Social Science in Cold War America," in *Cold War Social Science: Knowledge Production, Liberal Democracy, and Human Nature*, ed. Mark Solovey and Hamilton Cravens (New York: Palgrave Macmillan, 2012), ix–xv, claimed that postwar social science became more oriented toward disciplines and less oriented toward patrons. Philip Mirowski, "A History Best Served Cold," in *Uncertain Empire: American History and the Idea of the Cold War*, ed. Joel Isaac and Duncan Bell (New York: Oxford University Press, 2012), 61–74, argued that the federal research economy strengthened disciplinary structures in such a way that interdisciplinary efforts struggled to gain a foothold in the university and thus institutionalized in think tanks instead. The most important opposition to the pro-discipline approach is Roger Backhouse and Philippe Fontaine, "Toward a History of the Social Sciences," in *The History of the Social Sciences since 1945*, ed. Backhouse and Fontaine (Cambridge, UK: Cambridge University Press, 2010), 184–235. This piece, a prospectus for writing the history of postwar social science, argues that cross-disciplinary efforts were definitive for postwar social science and thus merit more attention from historians. My approach is in line with this suggestion and an earlier essay that made the point about cross-disciplinary work less emphatically and less programmatically: Hunter Crowther-Heyck, "Patrons of the Revolution: Ideals and Institutions in Postwar Behavioral Science," *Isis* 97, no. 3 (2006): 420–446. Another recent work that correctly describes patrons as more important than disciplines during this time is Mark Solovey, *Shaky Foundations: The Politics-Patronage-Social Science Nexus in Cold War America* (New Brunswick, NJ: Rutgers University Press, 2013).

11. Roger L. Geiger, *Research and Relevant Knowledge: American Research Universities since World War II* (New York: Oxford University Press, 1993), 58.

12. The instrumental university model thus helps to explain the decline of institutional diversity in the postwar era. For an earlier account of the decline, see Richard M. Freeland, *Academia's Golden Age: Universities in Massachusetts, 1945–1970* (New York: Oxford University Press, 1992).

13. My argument is about the elite research university, even though I often say "research university" or "university" to vary diction and save space.

14. Michigan also became a system, but the campuses at Dearborn and Flint were not intended as research universities.

15. This book revamps our understanding of technocratic progressivism by showing how it persisted into the postwar period as the cornerstone of the new edifice of American modernity. Existing accounts of technocratic progressivism as an intellectual tradition focus on the 1910–1940 period. Guy Alchon coined the term for a movement that emerged in the 1910s and flourished during World War I, "focused on organizational solutions to economic and social problems" and "part of a larger impulse toward organizational and associational activity." Alchon, *The Invisible Hand of Planning: Capitalism, Social Science, and the State in the 1920s* (Princeton, NJ: Princeton University Press, 1985), 9. David A. Hollinger has described the importance of technocratic progressivism as a vision for 1930s universities in "Two NYUs and 'The Obligation of Universities to the Social Order' in the Great Depression," in *Science, Jews, and Secular Culture: Studies in Mid-Twentieth-Century American Intellectual History* (Princeton, NJ: Princeton University Press, 1996), 60–79. Two major discussions of technocratic progressivism use alternate terminology. John M. Jordan, *Machine-Age Ideology: Social Engineering and American Liberalism, 1911–1939* (Chapel Hill: University of North Carolina Press, 1994), primarily uses "social engineering." Hunter Heyck has argued for "liberal managerialism" as a better term to describe the technocratic progressives gathered around Charles Merriam. Hunter Crowther-Heyck, *Herbert A. Simon: The Bounds of Reason in Modern America* (Baltimore: Johns Hopkins University Press, 2005), 43. Jordan and Heyck intentionally focus on the relationship between liberalism and the technocratic impulse. Alan Dawley, *Struggles for Justice: Social Responsibility and the Liberal State* (Cambridge, MA: Harvard University Press, 1991), dubbed these figures "managerial liberals," a terminology later employed in Andrew Jewett, *Science, Democracy, and the American University: From the Civil War to the Cold War* (New York: Cambridge University Press, 2012) to describe those who believed social science was value-neutral and thus could be used for technocratic management.

16. On the federal research economy, see Kerr, *Uses*, chap. 2; Geiger, *Research and Relevant Knowledge*. Kerr emphasized this influence so much that another of his monikers for the postwar university was "the federal grant university." The notion of the "Cold War university"—an institution characterized by military-related research in the physical sciences and area studies in the social sciences—has been the dominant framework for understanding the university's role in the postwar United States. The wave of scholarship that established this framework included Stuart W. Leslie, *The Cold War and American Science: The Military-Industrial-Academic Complex at MIT and Stanford* (New York: Columbia University Press, 1993); Lowen, *Creating the Cold War University*; Noam Chomsky et al., *The Cold War & the University: Toward an Intellectual History of the Postwar Years* (New York: New Press, 1997); Christopher Simpson, ed., *Universities and Empire: Money and Politics in the Social Sciences During the Cold War* (New York: New

Press, 1998). Among subsequent works, Margaret Pugh O'Mara, *Cities of Knowledge: Cold War Science and the Search for the Next Silicon Valley* (Princeton, NJ: Princeton University Press, 2005) retained the Cold War framework, but others have been cautious about attributing too much influence to the Cold War. See David C. Engerman, "Rethinking Cold War Universities: Some Recent Histories," *Journal of Cold War Studies* 5, no. 3 (2003): 80–95 and "Bernath Lecture: American Knowledge and Global Power," *Diplomatic History* 31, no. 4 (2007): 599–622. More recently, Christopher P. Loss, *Between Citizens and the State: The Politics of American Higher Education in the Twentieth Century* (Princeton, NJ: Princeton University Press, 2011) interpreted the twentieth-century university without emphasizing a Cold War framework. Loss, however, focuses less on university research and more on the ways that the federal government used universities to acclimate students and other citizens to the bureaucratic state.

17. On the notion of "high modern," see James C. Scott, *Seeing Like a State: How Certain Schemes to Improve the Human Condition Have Failed* (New Haven, CT: Yale University Press, 1998), which has influenced my understanding of modernity and attempts to solve social problems with administered research.

18. My definition of American modernity is more specific than that of David Steigerwald, who has done some of the best work on the subject. He gave little attention to universities, however. David Steigerwald, *The Sixties and the End of Modern America* (New York: St. Martin's, 1995). Dorothy Ross, "American Modernities, Past and Present," *American Historical Review* 116, no. 3 (2011): 702–714, reviews how the concept of modernity has figured in historical writing about the United States. In describing modernity, Ross de-emphasizes two notions that I highlight: technocratic governance and science as a privileged way of knowing.

19. On the teachers see Jonathan Zimmerman, *Innocents Abroad: American Teachers in the American Century* (Cambridge, MA: Harvard University Press, 2006).

20. Robert A. McCaughey, *International Studies and Academic Enterprise: A Chapter in the Enclosure of American Learning* (New York: Columbia University Press, 1984); Bruce Cummings, "Boundary Displacement: Area Studies and International Studies After the Cold War," in *Universities and Empire*, ed. Simpson; Robert Vitalis, "International Studies in America," *Social Science Research Council Items and Issues* 3 (Summer 2002).

21. Mainstream historians of the United States have written little about the four modern ideals, especially in relation to one another. Histories of industrial relations and city planning tend to be written in isolation by specialists in those fields. The best among such works are Bruce E. Kaufman, *The Origins and Evolution of the Field of Industrial Relations in the United States* (Ithaca, NY: Cornell University Press, 1993), and Anthony Alofsin, *The Struggle for Modernism: Architecture, Landscape Architecture, and City Planning at Harvard* (New York: Norton, 2002). Jennifer S. Light's books that place city planning in a larger context are the major exception: *From Warfare to Welfare: Defense Intellectuals and Urban Problems in Cold War America* (Baltimore: Johns Hopkins University Press, 2003) and *The Nature of Cities: Ecological Visions and the American Urban Professions, 1920–1960* (Baltimore: Johns Hopkins University Press, 2009).

22. This argument challenges several existing accounts, which claim that domestic opportunities for applied social science to implement a New Deal vision became more limited beginning around 1950, prompting frustrated applied social scientists to engage in such efforts overseas instead. Howard Brick, "The Reformist Dimension of

Talcott Parsons' Early Social Theory," in *The Culture of the Market: Historical Essays*, ed. Thomas L. Haskell and Richard F. Teichgraeber III (Cambridge, UK: Cambridge University Press, 1996), 357–396; Jordan, *Machine-Age Ideology*; Gilman, *Mandarins of the Future*; Nicole Sackley, "Passage to Modernity: American Social Scientists, India, and the Pursuit of Development, 1945–61," (PhD diss., Princeton University, 2004); Leah N. Gordon, *From Power to Prejudice: The Rise of Racial Individualism in Midcentury America* (Chicago: University of Chicago Press, 2015).

23. A number of economists and economic historians have written on the subfield of development economics as part of the economic development impulse. See Gerald M. Meier, *Biography of a Subject: An Evolution of Development Economics* (New York: Oxford University Press, 2005), and chapter 5 in this book. Several works address bodies of knowledge affiliated with the administration ideal: Stephen P. Waring, *Taylorism Transformed: Scientific Management Theory Since 1945* (Chapel Hill: University of North Carolina Press, 1991); Crowther-Heyck, *Herbert A. Simon*; Hunter Heyck, *Age of System: Understanding the Development of Modern Social Science* (Baltimore: Johns Hopkins University Press, 2015); William Thomas, *Rational Action: The Sciences of Policy in Britain and America, 1940–1960* (Cambridge, MA: MIT Press, 2015). On administration as a central concept in business schools, I build on Rakesh Khurana, *From Higher Aims to Hired Hands: The Social Transformation of American Business Schools and the Unfulfilled Promise of Management as a Profession* (Princeton, NJ: Princeton University Press, 2007) and William P. Bottom, "Organizing Intelligence: Development of Behavioral Science and the Research Based Model of Business Education," *Journal of the History of the Behavioral Sciences* 45, no. 3 (2009): 253–283. None of these works, however, treat the institutionalization of the administration ideal to the extent this book does. There is a large literature on the administrative state, but it is generally unconcerned with the impact of research universities. The major exception here is Brian Balogh, *Chain Reaction: Expert Debate and Public Participation in American Commercial Nuclear Power, 1945–1975* (Cambridge, UK: Cambridge University Press, 1991). Balogh traces the increasing importance of research and of university-certified experts for the federal state's administrative capacity after World War II and argues that this trend created a proministrative state characterized by a distinct kind of politics. Balogh's work does not, however, give much coverage to universities as institutions.

24. The emphasis on these fields suggests a new way for scholars to understand postwar social science, in contrast to the all-encompassing Cold War framework that has dominated a burgeoning literature on the subject. The Cold War framework has inclined scholars to concentrate on area studies and contributions (from fields such as psychology and communication science) to psychological warfare, intelligence, and counterinsurgency, as well as on military patronage and challenges to academic freedom. See Chomsky et al., *The Cold War & the University*; Simpson, ed., *Universities and Empire*; Ron Robin, *The Making of the Cold War Enemy: Culture and Politics in the Military-Industrial Complex* (Princeton, NJ: Princeton University Press, 2001); Matthew Farish, *The Contours of America's Cold War* (Minneapolis: University of Minnesota Press, 2010). Even scholars who have suggested how to move away from this framework use "Cold War" in their titles. See Joel Isaac, "The Human Sciences in Cold War America," *Historical Journal* 50, no. 3 (2007): 725–746; two essays in a special section of *Isis* 101, no. 2 (2010) on science and the Cold War: Paul Erickson, "Mathematical Models, Rational

Choice, and the Search for Cold War Culture," 386–392, and David C. Engerman, "Social Science in the Cold War," 393–400; Peter Mandler, "Deconstructing 'Cold War Anthropology,'" in *Uncertain Empire*, ed. Isaac and Bell, 245–266. The most promising recent attempts to counter the Cold War framework include Backhouse and Fontaine, "'Toward a History of the Social Sciences," which notes how Cold War projects merely continued trends toward cross-disciplinary social science that were established by the late 1940s, and Joel Isaac, *Working Knowledge: Making the Human Sciences from Parsons to Kuhn* (Cambridge, MA: Harvard University Press, 2012). Isaac argues that an epistemological perspective that developed in peculiar institutional spaces at Harvard from roughly 1920 to 1970 strongly shaped mid-twentieth-century American social science. I agree with Isaac's periodization and the importance of some of the intellectual developments he describes, but I also point to other forces that shaped twentieth-century social science. In the face of these works, historians who see the Cold War as definitive for postwar social science are trying to hold their ground, especially insistent on the need to study military patronage. See Joy Rohde, "Gray Matters: Social Scientists, Military Patronage, and Democracy in the Cold War," *Journal of American History* 96 (June 2009): 99–122, and *Armed with Expertise: The Militarization of American Social Research during the Cold War* (Ithaca, NY: Cornell University Press, 2013). The most vocal among such scholars is Philip Mirowski, who wants to "restor[e] our appreciation for the ways in which [the Cold War] pervaded most scientific thought in that era." Mirowski goes so far as to call Engerman and Isaac revisionists, perhaps the first time that term has been applied to this historiographical issue. "A History Best Served Cold," 61–74 (quote on 64). Other scholars are ambivalent. Mark Solovey, in his monograph *Shaky Foundations*, highlights how the Cold War shaped postwar social science, speaks of "the Cold War funding system" (194), and has a chapter on military patronage. Yet in a lucid methodological essay on "Cold War Social Science" that headlines an edited collection with the same title, Solovey expresses caution about the concept. "Cold War Social Science: Specter, Reality, or Useful Concept?" in *Cold War Social Science*, ed. Solovey and Cravens, 1–22.

25. On Cold War concerns in industrial relations, see chapter 2; on city planning, see Light, *From Warfare to Welfare*.

26. "Economic development" and "economic growth" were often used interchangeably. Strictly speaking, "economic growth" refers to quantitative change in per capita GDP whereas "economic development" has a broader, more qualitative connotation and can even be seen to include quantitative economic growth. I use "economic development" for that reason and because states, foundations, and universities seemed to prefer it.

27. Few scholars have analyzed the relation of economic development ideology to universities, but many have reflected on its centrality to beliefs about the nature and destiny of the United States. Daniel Bell argued that "for some of the liberals of the West, 'economic development' has become a new ideology," and Arthur Schlesinger Jr. noted that "'economic growth' . . . was the catchword of our national economic philosophy" in the 1950s. Daniel Bell, *The End of Ideology: On the Exhaustion of Political Ideas in the Fifties*, rev. ed. (New York: Free Press, 1962 [1960]), 403; Arthur M. Schlesinger Jr., *The Vital Center: The Politics of Freedom*, with a new introduction (Boston: Houghton Mifflin, 1962 [1949]), xvi. Later scholars explored the subject in more

detail. Alan Wolfe argued that in 1946 liberals and conservatives at an impasse formed a bipartisan coalition that made economic growth "the rationale of the political system"; in so doing they "created a whole new approach to government, one that would not so much exercise political power to make choices as it would manage expansion and empire to avoid choice." Alan Wolfe, *America's Impasse: The Rise and Fall of the Politics of Growth* (New York: Pantheon Books, 1981), 10. More recently Robert Collins has traced the appearance of economic growth on the center stage of American political discourse to Franklin Roosevelt's presidency, and David Engerman has argued that scholars have underestimated the extent to which a "romance of economic development" shaped the Cold War. Robert M. Collins, *More: The Politics of Economic Growth in Postwar America* (New York: Oxford University Press, 2000); David C. Engerman, "The Romance of Economic Development and New Histories of the Cold War," *Diplomatic History* 28, no. 1 (2004): 23–54. Margaret O'Mara's work on how some postwar universities began programs to spur science-based economic development strategies for their regions marked a turn to scholarship that examines more seriously the relationship between universities and ideas about economic development in the postwar era. She focused on how federal and municipal urban policy—as well as ideas about physical space more generally—shaped these university activities. O'Mara, *Cities of Knowledge*.

28. The main exception is Henry S. Etzkowitz, who has advanced the notion of the "entrepreneurial university," an institution that added a third mission of economic development to its earlier goals, teaching and research. He traced the origins of this model from the interwar period and showed how in the 1930s, MIT president Karl Compton became perhaps the first university leader to articulate and act on the central insight of the knowledge economy concept—that knowledge produced by universities could replace raw materials as the backbone of an economy. See "Entrepreneurial Scientists and Entrepreneurial Universities in American Academic Science," *Minerva* 21 (1983): 198–233; "The Making of an Entrepreneurial University: The Traffic Among MIT, Industry, and the Military, 1860–1960," in *Science, Technology, and the Military*, ed. Everett Mendelsohn, Merritt Roe Smith, and Peter Weingard, *Sociology of the Sciences: A Yearbook* 12, no. 2 (1988): 515–540; "Enterprises from Science: The Origins of Science-Based Regional Economic Development," *Minerva* 31, no. 3 (1993): 326–360; *MIT and the Rise of Entrepreneurial Science* (London: Routledge, 2002). Etzkowitz is correct that research universities have become more entrepreneurial since the mid-twentieth century and that this trend is rooted partially in the rise of organized research. However, the rise of what Etzkowitz calls "an economic development mission" is better framed as one element of a wider instrumental orientation that characterizes research universities, rather than as the central element in an entrepreneurial orientation. Elizabeth Popp Berman, *Creating the Market University: How Academic Science Became an Economic Engine* (Princeton, NJ: Princeton University Press, 2012) addresses similar issues but does not use the term "knowledge economy." Instead, she focuses on the related concept of "innovation" and how its prominence among policymakers from the late 1960s through the early 1980s shaped what she calls "the market university."

29. For an example of the claim that Kerr was thinking in terms of a transition to a postindustrial society circa 1960, see Lowen, *Creating the Cold War University*, 2.

30. Howard Brick, "Optimism of the Mind: Imagining Postindustrial Society in the 1960s and 1970s," *American Quarterly* 44, no. 3 (1992): 348–380; "The Postcapitalist Vision in Twentieth-Century American Social Thought," in *American Capitalism*, ed. Lichtenstein; *Transcending Capitalism: Visions of a New Society in Modern American Thought* (Ithaca, NY: Cornell University Press, 2006). Brick briefly mentions Kerr, correctly stating that Kerr remained firmly in the industrial imagination even as he advanced some ideas that postindustrial theorists shared. "Optimism of the Mind," 354–355.

31. The behavioral science movement has also suffered from Cold War myopia in the literature. Behavioral science, however, was a bona fide intellectual revolution with definitive prewar roots that transformed existing disciplines, sparked new interdisciplinary configurations, and encouraged methods that came to be applied to many fields. Isaac, *Working Knowledge*, especially chapter 5, is the best account of the pre–Cold War roots of behavioral science.

32. Isaac, *Working Knowledge*, 164–165, 159, 176.

33. Ibid., 63, 164, 179, 24 (quote).

34. G. A. Swanson, "James Grier Miller," International Society for the Systems Sciences, http://projects.isss.org/James_Grier_Miller, accessed 8 June 2009 (site discontinued).

35. Isaac, *Working Knowledge*, 63.

36. On these intellectual movements, see Heyck, *Age of System*; Thomas, *Rational Action*.

37. Crowther-Heyck, *Herbert A. Simon*, 119, 2.

38. Ibid., 9.

39. Daniel A. Wren, *The Evolution of Management Thought* (New York: Ronald Press, 1972), 340–341, 464–466.

40. Crowther-Heyck, *Herbert A. Simon*, 323–324; Waring, *Taylorism Transformed*, 24–25.

41. On Wilson's prominence as a university president, see James Axtell, "The Educational Vision of Woodrow Wilson," in *The Educational Legacy of Woodrow Wilson: From College to Nation*, ed. Axtell (Charlottesville: University of Virginia Press, 2012), 9–48; on the relation of these speeches to Wilson's body of educational writings, see Adam R. Nelson, "Woodrow Wilson on Liberal Education for Statesmanship, 1890–1910," in Axtell, *The Educational Legacy of Woodrow Wilson*, 49–73.

42. Woodrow Wilson, "Princeton in the Nation's Service," October 21, 1896, in *The Papers of Woodrow Wilson*, ed. Arthur S. Link, vol. 10 (Princeton, NJ: Princeton University Press, 1971), 23, 30.

43. Woodrow Wilson et al., "A Memorial to the Princeton Trustees," December 2, 1896, in *Papers*, ed. Link, vol. 10, 69; see also Willard Thorp et al., *The Princeton Graduate School: A History*, 2nd ed. (Princeton, NJ: Association of Princeton Graduate Alumni, 2000).

44. Woodrow Wilson to Andrew Carnegie, quoted in Axtell, "The Educational Vision of Woodrow Wilson," 26.

45. Wilson, "Princeton in the Nation's Service," 29–30.

46. Charles R. Van Hise, "Inaugural Address of President Charles Richard Van Hise," *Science* 20, no. 502 (1904): 193–205.

47. Veysey, *The Emergence of the American University*, 108.

48. Historians of American universities have paid little attention to Ely's structural innovation, though they have mentioned his importance for social science and the development of academic freedom protocol. Ely's institute is mentioned briefly in Roger L. Geiger, *To Advance Knowledge: The Growth of American Research Universities, 1900–1940* (New York: Oxford University Press, 1986), 154.

49. Benjamin G. Rader, *The Academic Mind and Reform: The Influence of Richard T. Ely in American Life* (Lexington: University of Kentucky Press, 1966), 160.

50. Ibid., 205–208.

51. Emil Oliver Jorgensen, *False Education in Our Colleges and Universities: An Expose of Prof. Richard T. Ely and His "Institute for Research in Land Economics and Public Utilities"* (Chicago: Manufacturers and Merchants Federal Tax League, 1925).

52. Rader, *The Academic Mind and Reform*, 209–212, 227–228, 233; Geiger, *To Advance Knowledge*, 154. This narrative raises the question of whether ORUs would have proliferated before 1945 if the Depression and World War II had not occurred, which has numerous implications for the role of World War II, the Cold War, and attitudes toward capitalism in forming the instrumental university.

53. Minutes of the Executive Committee, University of Michigan College of Literature, Science, and the Arts, May 25, 1960, Bentley Historical Library, University of Michigan.

54. Robert Nisbet, *The Degradation of the Academic Dogma: The University in America, 1945–1970* (New York: Basic Books, 1971).

1. The Progressive Roots of the Instrumental University

1. Donald Fisher, *Fundamental Development of the Social Sciences: Rockefeller Philanthropy and the United States Social Science Research Council* (Ann Arbor: University of Michigan Press, 1993); John M. Jordan, *Machine-Age Ideology: Social Engineering and American Liberalism, 1911–1939* (Chapel Hill: University of North Carolina Press, 1994).

2. Brian Balogh, *The Associational State: American Governance in the Twentieth Century* (Philadelphia: University of Pennsylvania Press, 2015). While state universities were in one sense units of the state, the management of society through universities was distinct from management through government agencies. Furthermore, many private universities participated in the same kind of associational government as state universities.

3. Barry D. Karl, *Executive Reorganization and Reform in the New Deal: The Genesis of Administrative Management, 1900–1939* (Cambridge, MA: Harvard University Press, 1963), 38–39.

4. See Gabriel Almond, "Who Lost the Chicago School of Political Science?" *Perspectives on Politics* 2, no. 1 (2004): 91–93 and other articles in the same special section, Forum on the Chicago School of Political Science.

5. Karl, *Executive Reorganization*, 60.

6. Ibid., 61.

7. Andrew Jewett, *Science, Democracy, and the American University: From the Civil War to the Cold War* (New York: Cambridge University Press, 2012), 177.

8. Fisher, *Fundamental Development*, 29; Charles E. Merriam, "The Present State of the Study of Politics," *American Political Science Review* 15, no. 2 (1921): 85; Barry

D. Karl, *Charles E. Merriam and the Study of Politics* (Chicago: University of Chicago Press, 1974), 105.

9. Karl, *Charles E. Merriam*, 107–108.

10. William Fielding Ogburn and Alexander Goldenweiser, eds., *The Social Sciences and Their Interrelations* (Boston: Houghton Mifflin, 1927); Fisher, *Fundamental Development*, 68.

11. http://rockefeller100.org/exhibits/show/social_sciences/laura-spelman -rockefeller-memo, accessed 16 September 2015 (site discontinued).

12. Fisher, *Fundamental Development*.

13. http://rockefeller100.org/exhibits/show/social_sciences/laura-spelman -rockefeller-memo, accessed 16 September 2015 (site discontinued).

14. Quoted in Fisher, *Fundamental Development*, 85.

15. Karl, *Executive Reorganization*, 39, 77.

16. Fisher, *Fundamental Development*, 109.

17. Ibid., 156, 157.

18. Karl, *Executive Reorganization*, 76.

19. Ibid., 78.

20. Shirley Anne Warshaw, *Guide to the White House Staff* (Washington, DC: CQ Press, 2013), 56.

21. Brian J. Cook, *Bureaucracy and Self-Government: Reconsidering the Role of Public Administration in American Politics* (Baltimore: Johns Hopkins University Press, 1996), 118, 105.

22. Franklin D. Roosevelt, "New Conditions Impose New Requirements upon Government and Those Who Conduct Government," Campaign Address on Progressive Government at the Commonwealth Club, San Francisco, California, September 23, 1932, in *The Public Papers and Addresses of Franklin D. Roosevelt*, vol. 1 (New York: Random House, 1938), 752.

23. Cook, *Bureaucracy and Self-Government*, 105.

24. Ibid., 92, 117–118, 118.

25. Ibid., 105.

26. Cook, *Bureaucracy and Self-Government*, 98; Sidney M. Milkis, *The President and the Parties: The Transformation of the American Party System Since the New Deal* (New York: Oxford University Press, 1993), 110, emphasis original, quoted in Cook, *Bureaucracy and Self-Government*, 112.

27. Cook, *Bureaucracy and Self-Government*, 106.

28. Milkis, *The President and the Parties*, 145, quoted in Cook, *Bureaucracy and Self-Government*, 107.

29. Cook, *Bureaucracy and Self-Government*, 107, 113, emphasis original.

30. In Germany, the closest precedent was "state administration" (*Staatswirthschaft*) and particularly what some considered its subdiscipline, "police science" (*Policeywissenschaft*), which arose within cameralism, a particularly German form of mercantilism, taught at the University of Göttingen in the mid-1700s. Göttingen was a newly founded university considered distinctly modern at the time, in part because it aimed to serve "the needs of the state and society." Chad Wellmon, *Organizing Enlightenment: Information Overload and the Invention of the Modern Research University* (Baltimore: Johns Hopkins University Press, 2015), 50, 51; Andre Wakefield, *The Disordered Police State: German Cameralism as Science and Practice* (Chicago: University of Chicago Press, 2009).

31. John M. Gaus, *A Study of Research in Public Administration*, report prepared for the Advisory Committee on Public Administration of the Social Science Research Council (New York, 1930), 1.

32. Woodrow Wilson, "The Study of Administration" (1887), quoted in Cook, *Bureaucracy and Self-Government*, 90.

33. Cook, *Bureaucracy and Self-Government*, 94.

34. Jewett, *Science, Democracy, and the American University*, 177.

35. Gaus, *A Study of Research in Public Administration*, 8, 93, 67, 68, 86.

36. Ibid., 89, 115.

37. Barton Gellman and Beth English, *In the Nation's Service: Seventy-Five Years at the Woodrow Wilson School* (Princeton: Woodrow Wilson School, 2005), 14, 22–23.

38. Quoted in ibid., 21.

39. Ibid., 21; Gaus, *A Study of Research in Public Administration*, 95; Marcia G. Synott, "Dodds, Harold Willis," *American National Biography*, http://www.anb.org/view/10.1093/anb/9780198606697.001.0001/anb-9780198606697-e-0900974, accessed August 2018; Karl, *Executive Reorganization*, 1–2.

40. Organizing Committee for the Bureau of Urban Research, "A Proposal for the Establishment of the Bureau of Urban Research within Princeton University, Princeton, N.J.," n.d. [1940], RFA1, Box 388, Folder 4603.

41. Warshaw, *Guide to the White House Staff*, 56.

42. "Guide to the Charles E. Merriam Papers 1893–1957," https://www.lib.uchicago.edu/ead/rlg/ICU.SPCL.MERRIAMCE.pdf, accessed August 2018; "Clarence A. Dykstra papers, 1930–1950 bulk 1930–1945," http://www.oac.cdlib.org/findaid/ark:/13030/tf6n39p0wq/entire_text/, accessed August 2018.

43. Gerald R. Ford School of Public Policy, University of Michigan, http://fordschool.umich.edu/timeline, accessed August 2018.

44. Gaus, *A Study of Research in Public Administration*, 112.

45. S. C. May to E. M. Sait, December 18, 1921, and S. C. May to David Barrows, September 18, 1922, BPAR, Box 1, Folder 15; Mary Sisson to Kathlyn Malloy, September 15, 1954, BPAR, Box 1, Folder 16; quote is from the latter.

46. Gaus, *A Study of Research in Public Administration*, 112.

47. Minutes of the Board of Trustees, 27 November 1928, Laura Spellman Rockefeller Memorial Collection, Series I, Box 5, Folder 44, Rockefeller Archive Center.

48. Robert G. Sproul to C. B. Lipman, June 28, 1929; S. C. May to Raymond G. Gettell, August 30, 1930; May to Gettell, March 10, 1931, BPAR, Box 1, Folder 15. Despite BPA's administrative autonomy and separation from teaching, May wanted to keep alive the feeling that it was connected with the political science program.

49. W. W. Campbell to Beardsley Ruml, June 10, 1929, BPAR, Box 1, Folder 16.

50. S. C. May to E. E. Jensen, October 31, 1929, BPAR, Box 1, Folder 15; Agenda, 1st meeting of the Council of the BPA, April 12, 1930, BPAR, Box 1, Folder 16.

51. Gaus, *A Study of Research in Public Administration*, 89, 112, 113.

52. Ibid., 125.

53. Hunter Crowther-Heyck, *Herbert A. Simon: The Bounds of Reason in Modern America* (Baltimore: Johns Hopkins University Press, 2005), 76.

54. Harriet Nathan, quoted in Ewald T. Grether, *Dean of the UC Berkeley Schools of Business Administration, 1943–1961; Leader in Campus Administration, Public Service, and Marketing Studies; and Forever a Teacher*, vol. 2, an oral history conducted 1975–1987 by

Harriet Nathan (Regional Oral History Office, The Bancroft Library, University of California, Berkeley, 1993), 675.

55. Karl, *Executive Reorganization*, 139.

56. Ibid., 150–151; Gaus, *A Study of Research in Public Administration*, 70.

57. Leonard D. White, "The Local Community Research Committee and the Social Science Research Building," in *Chicago: An Experiment in Social Science Research*, ed. T. V. Smith and L. D. White (Chicago: University of Chicago Press, 1929), 21.

58. Fisher, *Fundamental Development*, 74, 119, 123, 118. Day was the representative of the American Statistical Association to the SSRC.

59. Ibid., 122–123; Gaus, *A Study of Research in Public Administration*, 1.

60. Gaus, *A Study of Research in Public Administration*, 117, 135, 126, 68. Gaus did not cite works involved in this debate, but Jordan, *Machine Age Ideology*, referred to similar discussions.

61. Gaus, *A Study of Research in Public Administration*, 124.

62. Balogh, *The Associational State*, 36.

63. Fisher, *Fundamental Development*, 123, 137–139, 112, 136.

64. This paragraph draws from Morton Keller and Phyllis Keller, *Making Harvard Modern: The Rise of America's University* (New York: Oxford University Press, 2001), 130–133.

65. Ibid., 130.

66. Quoted in ibid.

67. Ibid., 132.

68. "Social Sciences Appropriations Classified 1929–1938," RFA3, Box 2, Folder 14. Other records at the Rockefeller Archive Center suggest that the GSPA probably received RF funding at least through 1946.

69. Stephen A. Sass, *The Pragmatic Imagination: A History of the Wharton School, 1881–1981* (Philadelphia: University of Pennsylvania Press, 1982), 221.

70. University of Pennsylvania Board of Business Education minutes [hereafter BBE minutes], January 15, 1943, VPLMC. Emphasis added.

71. Trustees of the University of Pennsylvania Executive Board minutes [hereafter EB minutes], October 28, 1942, VPLMC.

72. Quoted in Sass, *Pragmatic Imagination*, 245.

73. Trustees of the University of Pennsylvania minutes, February 1, 1943, VPLMC.

74. Sass, *Pragmatic Imagination*, 221, 268.

75. "History of NYU," New York University, https://www.nyu.edu/about/news-publications/history-of-nyu.html, accessed August 2018.

76. Anthony Alofsin, *The Struggle for Modernism: Architecture, Landscape Architecture, and City Planning at Harvard* (New York: W.W. Norton, 2002), 42, 64.

77. Patrick D. Reagan, "Creating the Organizational Nexus for New Deal National Planning," in *Voluntarism, Planning, and the State: The American Planning Experience, 1914–1946*, ed. Jerold E. Brown and Patrick D. Reagan (New York: Greenwood Press, 1988), 90.

78. *Report of a Conference on a Project for Research and Instruction in City & Regional Planning Held at Columbia University, May 3, 1928* (New York: 1928).

79. Henry V. Hubbard to EED, November 30, 1928, RFA1, Box 346, Folder 4114.

80. Alofsin, *The Struggle for Modernism*, 70–71.

81. Hubbard to EED, 30 November 1928.

82. Alofsin, *The Struggle for Modernism*, 40, 13, 44, 46.

83. Bremer W. Pond to EED, December 12, 1928, RFA1, Box 346, Folder 4114.

84. A. Lawrence Lowell to Rockefeller Foundation, May 16, 1929, RFA1, Box 346, Folder 4115.

85. Cross-reference sheet, RFA1, Box 346, Folder 4115, RAC.

86. Rockefeller Foundation board docket excerpt, May 22, 1929, RFA1, Box 346, Folder 4114.

87. Alofsin, *The Struggle for Modernism*, 72.

88. EED to Henry V. Hubbard, September 20, 1935, RFA1, Box 346, Folder 4119.

89. Henry V. Hubbard to EED, August 20, 1929, RFA1, Box 346, Folder 4115.

90. Henry V. Hubbard to EED, December 30, 1935, RFA1, Box 346, Folder 4119.

91. William R. Castle to EED, April 24, 1936, RFA1, Box 346, Folder 4120.

92. Alofsin, *The Struggle for Modernism*, 129–130.

93. Ibid., 65.

94. EED to Alfred Bettman, May 25, 1936, RFA1, Box 346, Folder 4120.

95. EED to Stacy F. May, n.d. [April–May 1936], RFA1, Box 346, Folder 4120.

96. Fisher, *Fundamental Development*, 134.

97. Stacy May, Memorandum upon Harvard Application for Support of Regional Planning Project, May 6, 1936, RFA1, Box 346, Folder 4120.

98. "Social Sciences Appropriations Classified 1929–1938."

99. Alofsin, *The Struggle for Modernism*, 112–130, 128, 129, 144, 173–174, 201.

100. Sherley W. Morgan to JHW, October 14, 1940, RFA1, Box 388, Folder 4600.

101. "A Proposal for the Establishment of the Bureau of Urban Research."

102. *The Rockefeller Foundation Annual Report 1940*, https://assets.rockefellerfoun dation.org/app/uploads/20150530122139/Annual-Report-1940.pdf, accessed September 29, 2018.

103. Harold Dodds to JHW, November 8, 1940, November 27, 1940, RFA1, Box 388, Folder 4600.

104. Harold Willis Dodds, "Procedure in State Legislatures" (PhD diss., University of Pennsylvania, 1917).

105. Dodds to JHW, November 8, 1940.

106. *Princeton's War Program and Post-War Plans: The President's Annual Report*, January 20, 1944, Official Register of Princeton University.

107. "Social Sciences Grant in Aid No RA SS 4119 Princeton University—Bureau of Urban Research," April 3, 1941, RFA1, Box 388, Folder 4600.

108. Melville C. Branch Jr., to JHW, February 10, 1943, RFA1, Box 388, Folder 4601.

109. Sherley W. Morgan to JHW, November 27, 1940, RFA1, Box 388, Folder 4600.

110. "Proposal for Bureau of Urban Research," n.d. [1940], RFA1, Box 388, Folder 4600.

111. "The Bureau of Urban Research," n.d. [1941], RFA1, Box 388, Folder 4600.

112. National Resources Committee, *Our Cities: Their Role in the National Economy* (Washington, DC: United States Government Printing Office, 1937), 83, 84.

113. "A Proposal for the Establishment of the Bureau of Urban Research."

114. Princeton University, *Report of the President for the Academic Year 1940–1941*, 97.

115. Princeton University Bureau of Urban Research, *Local Planning Activity in the United States* (Princeton, NJ: Bureau of Urban Research, 1941).

116. Princeton University Bureau of Urban Research, *Urban Planning and Public Opinion: A Pilot Study* (Princeton, NJ: Bureau of Urban Research, 1942), quote on 1.

117. Reviewer comments attached to Morgan to JHW, 27 November 1940.

118. JHW memo, February 5, 1941, RFA1, Box 388, Folder 4600.

119. J. Douglas Brown to JHW, February 20, 1941, and G. A. Brakeley to JHW, March 25, 1941, RFA1, Box 388, Folder 4600.

120. "Social Sciences Grant in Aid No RA SS 4119 Princeton University—Bureau of Urban Research."

121. Roger F. Evans, "Bureau of Urban Research—Princeton," March 2, 1942, RFA1, Box 388, Folder 4601.

122. Melville C. Branch Jr., *Planning and the Human Condition: Conceptual Development, Prospective Conclusions* (San Jose, CA: Writer's Showcase, 2002), 8, 9.

123. A Guide to the Papers of Melville C. Branch Jr., 1914–2004, http://ead.lib.virginia.edu/vivaxtf/view?docId=vcu-cab/vircu00111.xml, accessed August 2018.

124. George Brakeley to JHW, June 25, 1941, RFA1, Box 388, Folder 4600.

125. George Brakeley to JHW, March 30, 1942, RFA1, Box 388, Folder 4601.

126. "The Bureau of Urban Research."

127. Jean Labatut Papers, Princeton University Library, http://findingaids.princeton.edu/collections/C0709, accessed August 2018; "Jean Labatut Is Dead; Taught at Princeton," *New York Times*, http://www.nytimes.com/1986/11/29/obituaries/jean-labatut-is-dead-taught-at-princeton.html, accessed August 2018; Princeton University, *The President's Report 1951–52*, 18.

128. JHW to Walter W. Stewart, March 24, 1942, RFA1, Box 388, Folder 4601.

129. "Memorandum Concerning the Plans of the Bureau of Urban Research, Princeton University," March 28, 1944, RFA1, Box 388, Folder 4602; Roger F. Evans to JHW, April 11, 1944, RFA1, Box 388, Folder 4602.

130. "Memorandum Concerning the Plans of the Bureau of Urban Research."

131. *The Rockefeller Foundation Annual Report 1945*, https://assets.rockefellerfoundation.org/app/uploads/20150530122149/Annual-Report-1945.pdf, accessed September 29, 2018, 285; J. Douglas Brown to JHW, June 9, 1945, RFA1, Box 388, Folder 4602.

132. JHW to J. Douglas Brown, June 15, 1945, RFA1, Box 388, Folder 4602.

133. Melville C. Branch Jr., to JHW, December 6, 1945, RFA1, Box 388, Folder 4602.

134. Princeton University School of Architecture Biography and History, http://findingaids.princeton.edu/names/f46d996ed4edf56fe5934f7ebb968773, accessed August 2018.

135. Official Register of Princeton University.

136. James Axtell, *The Making of Princeton University: From Woodrow Wilson to the Present* (Princeton: Princeton University Press, 2006), chap. 2; quotes on 88 and 86.

137. This paragraph and the two following it draw heavily on Bruce E. Kaufman, *The Origins and Evolution of the Field of Industrial Relations in the United States* (Ithaca, NY: Cornell University Press, 1993), chap. 1.

138. Benjamin G. Rader, *The Academic Mind and Reform: The Influence of Richard T. Ely in American Life* (Lexington: University of Kentucky Press, 1966), 167.

139. Thomas S. Adams and Helen Sumner, *Labor Problems: A Text Book* (New York: Macmillan, 1905); John R. Commons, ed., *Trade Unionism and Labor Problems* (Boston:

Ginn and Company, 1905). See also Malcolm Rutherford, "Wisconsin Institutionalism: John R. Commons and His Students," *Labor History* 47, no. 2 (2006): 161–188.

140. Mary O. Furner, "Knowing Capitalism: Public Investigation and the Labor Question in the Long Progressive Era," in *The State and Economic Knowledge: The American and British Experiences*, ed. Furner and Michael J. Lacey (Cambridge: Cambridge University Press, 1990), 241–286.

141. Kaufman, *Origins and Evolution*, 10.

142. Ibid., 45.

143. JHW, *Philadelphia Unemployment, with Special Reference to the Textile Industries* (Philadelphia: City of Philadelphia Department of Public Works, 1915).

144. Sass, *Pragmatic Imagination*, 178–179.

145. "Pioneer in Academic Business Research: Anne Bezanson, Professor," *Wharton Alumni Magazine*, Spring 2007, https://www.wharton.upenn.edu/wp-content/uploads/125anniversaryissue/bezanson.html, accessed August 2018.

146. Sass, *Pragmatic Imagination*, 178, 246; Mary Ann Dzuback, "Creative Financing in Social Science," in *Women and Philanthropy in Education*, ed. Andrea Walton (Bloomington: Indiana University Press, 2005), 119, 126n26; BBE minutes, 23 October 1940; EB minutes, 15 December 1944.

147. One exception was an $11,000 Rockefeller grant in 1939 for two specific projects. Dzuback, "Creative Financing in Social Science," 126n28.

148. Fisher, *Fundamental Development*, 54–55.

149. Quoted in Kaufman, *Origins and Evolution*, 12.

150. Fisher, *Fundamental Development*, 121–122, 164.

151. Sass, *Pragmatic Imagination*, 246, 301.

152. University of Pennsylvania Board of Graduate Education and Research minutes, October 19, 1942, VPLMC.

153. Edward B. Shils, "George W. Taylor: Industrial Peacemaker," *Monthly Labor Review* (December 1995): 29–34 (quote on 29); Sass, *Pragmatic Imagination*, 211–213, 223.

154. Kaufman, *Origins and Evolution*, 45–47, 211n5; James L. Cochrane, *Industrialism and Industrial Man in Retrospect: A Critical Review of the Ford Foundation's Support for the Inter-University Study of Labor* (New York: Ford Foundation, 1979), 11.

155. Clarence J. Hicks, *My Life in Industrial Relations: Fifty Years in the Growth of a Profession* (New York: Harper & Brothers, 1941), 144, 141.

156. Harold W. Dodds, *The President's Report 1954–1955* (Princeton: Princeton University Press, 1955), 16.

157. John V. Van Sickle, report on Sixth Conference Course in Industrial Relations, Graduate College, Princeton University, September 21–26, 1936, RFA1, Box 388, Folder 4588.

158. Dodds, *The President's Report 1954–1955*, 16.

159. *Annual Report 1937–38, Industrial Relations Section*, Princeton University, RFA1, Box 388, Folder 4588.

160. Thomas W. Ennis, "Dr. J. Douglas Brown, a Dean and Social Security Architect," *New York Times*, January 21, 1986, http://www.nytimes.com/1986/01/21/obituaries/dr-j-douglas-brown-a-dean-and-social-security-achitect.html, accessed August 2018; Dodds, *The President's Report 1954–1955*, 15.

161. Axtell, *The Making of Princeton University*, 88.

162. Ennis, "Dr. J. Douglas Brown."

163. *Annual Report 1937–38, Industrial Relations Section*, Princeton University.

164. Untitled document, RFA1, Box 388, Folder 4588.

165. *Annual Report 1937–38, Industrial Relations Section*, Princeton University.

166. Rockefeller Foundation Executive Committee resolution, May 19, 1944, RFA1, Box 387, Folder 4585; "Memorandum on the Needs of the Industrial Relations Section of Princeton University," [March 1944], RFA1, Box 387, Folder 4585.

167. JHW, memorandum on Industrial Relations Section, Princeton University, March 24, 1944, RFA1, Box 387, Folder 4585.

168. UC Riverside biographical sketch of Gordon Watkins, https://www.ucr.edu/about/history, accessed August 2018.

169. Paul A. Dodd, "Financial Policies in the Aviation Industry" (PhD diss., University of Pennsylvania, 1933).

170. Ethan Schrum, "Establishing a Democratic Religion: Metaphysics and Democracy in the Debates Over the President's Commission on Higher Education," *History of Education Quarterly* 47, no. 3 (2007): 277–301.

171. For one of the only pieces to address the unusually large impact of academic industrial relations on universities, see Ronald W. Schatz, "What's Wrong with Industrial Relations?" *Reviews in American History* 23, no. 4 (1995): 693–698.

172. Elaine Gruenfeld Goldberg, ed., Robert B. McKersie, et al., comp., *The ILR School at Fifty: Voices of the Faculty, Alumni, and Friends* (Ithaca, NY: Cornell University, 1996).

173. Paul Dodd to RGS, February 17, 1944, UCOP2, 1944:454.

174. Paul Dodd to RGS, October 31, 1944, UCOP4, Box 18, Folder 14.

175. Baldwin Woods to E. T. Grether, August 24, 1944, UCOP2, 1944:454; Woods to RGS, September 28, 1944, UCOP4, Box 18, Folder 13.

176. Earl Warren, *The Memoirs of Earl Warren* (New York: Doubleday, 1977), 39–40.

177. Jim Newton, *Justice for All: Earl Warren and the Nation He Made* (New York: Riverhead, 2006), 209–210.

178. RGS to Earl Warren, December 27, 1944, UCOP4, Box 18, Folder 14.

179. Excerpt from California Assembly Daily Journal, January 8, 1945, UCOP4, Box 18, Folder 14.

180. Unreleased press release, n.d. [around January 10, 1945], UCOP4, Box 18, Folder 14.

181. E. T. Grether to RGS, December 26, 1944, UCOP4, Box 18, Folder 14.

182. Untitled note, n.d. [Summer 1945], UCOP4, Box 18, Folder 14.

183. Kaufman, *Origins and Evolution*, 63.

184. CK, "Report to the President from the Institute of Industrial Relations (Northern Division)," October 18, 1946, UCOP4, Box 18, Folder 14.

185. Charles E. McAllister, *Inside the Campus: Mr. Citizen Looks at His Universities* (New York: Fleming H. Revell, 1948), chap. 6.

186. Kaufman, *Origins and Evolution*, 69–71; W. H. McPherson to CK, September 10, 1947 and October 28, 1947, CKP, Carton 10, Folder 33; CK, "A Perspective on Industrial Relations Research—Thirty-six Years Later," in *Proceedings of the Thirty-sixth Annual Winter Meeting, Industrial Relations Research Association* (Madison, WI: IRRA, 1983), 14–21.

187. Quoted in Kaufman, *Origins and Evolution*, 72.

188. Monroe Deutsch, Memorandum of Conversation with Dean E. T. Grether, May 29, 1945, UCOP4, Box 18, Folder 14.

189. "Report of the Coordinating Committee on the Institute of Industrial Relations," n.d. [September 1945]; Harry R. Wellman to RGS, September 25, 1945, UCOP4, Box 18, Folder 14.

190. CK, quoted in Ronald W. Schatz, "From Commons to Dunlop: Rethinking the Field and Theory of Industrial Relations," in *Industrial Democracy in America: The Ambiguous Promise*, ed. Nelson Lichtenstein and Howell John Harris (Cambridge, UK: Cambridge University Press, 1993), 101. The bracketed parts are Kerr's words—in order to render his text accurately, I here depart from the standard format of this book wherein bracketed entities within quotes are my interpolations.

191. I gained this insight from one of the external reviewers for Cornell University Press.

192. On the last point see Roger L. Geiger, *The History of American Higher Education: Learning and Culture from the Founding to World War II* (Princeton, NJ: Princeton University Press, 2015), 349.

2. Clark Kerr

1. I will call the project the Inter-University Study throughout the chapter, even though it had different names at the beginning and end of its lifespan. Inter-University Study is the main name by which the project is known in scholarly literature.

2. Minutes of Board Meeting, March 1, 1954 in Room 1135, Waldorf-Astoria Hotel, New York City, CKP, Carton 10, Folder 3.

3. John T. Dunlop, Frederick H. Harbison, CK, and Charles A. Myers, *Industrialism and Industrial Man Reconsidered: Some Perspectives on a Study over Two Decades of the Problems of Labor and Management in Economic Growth* (Princeton, NJ: The Inter-University Study of Human Resources in National Development, 1975).

4. Milton Katz to Joseph M. McDaniel Jr., March 6, 1953, Grant PA 54-19 (preliminary grant), Reel 0127, Section 4, FFA.

5. CK et al., "The Labor Problem in Economic Development: A Comparative Analysis; Report of the Four-University Group," n.d. [winter 1953–1954], CKP, Carton 10, Folder 1.

6. Ronald W. Schatz, "From Commons to Dunlop: Rethinking the Field and Theory of Industrial Relations," in *Industrial Democracy in America: The Ambiguous Promise*, ed. Nelson Lichtenstein and Howell John Harris (Cambridge, UK: Cambridge University Press, 1993), 101–102; Bruce E. Kaufman and John Dunlop, "Reflections on Six Decades in Industrial Relations: An Interview with John Dunlop," *Industrial and Labor Relations Review* 55, no. 2 (2002): 324–348. For more detail on this topic and many others in the next section, see Ethan Schrum, "Clark Kerr's Early Career, Social Science, and the American University," *Perspectives on the History of Higher Education* 28 (2011): 193–222.

7. Morton Keller and Phyllis Keller, *Making Harvard Modern: The Rise of America's University* (New York: Oxford University Press, 2001); Judith Block McLaughlin and David Riesman, *Choosing a College President: Opportunities and Constraints* (Princeton, NJ: Carnegie Foundation for the Advancement of Teaching, 1990), xxvii n8.

8. On the Master Plan, see John Aubrey Douglass, *The California Idea and American Higher Education: 1850 to the 1960 Master Plan* (Stanford, CA: Stanford University Press, 2000).

9. Roger L. Geiger, *Research and Relevant Knowledge: American Research Universities since World War II* (New York: Oxford University Press, 1993), 75.

10. For a detailed account of Grether's rationale for hiring Kerr, see Schrum, "Clark Kerr's Early Career."

11. Geiger, *Research and Relevant Knowledge*, 80–81; Reinhard Bendix, *From Berlin to Berkeley: German-Jewish Identities* (New Brunswick, NJ: Transaction, 1986), 230.

12. Bruce E. Kaufman, "Clark Kerr and the Founding of the Berkeley IIR: A Celebratory Remembrance," *Industrial Relations* 44, no. 3 (2005): 407.

13. CK, *The Gold and the Blue: A Personal Memoir of the University of California, 1949–1967*, vol. 1 (Berkeley: University of California Press, 2001), 136–137.

14. Ibid., 34.

15. CK, Memorandum for the Files: Re: <u>Director of Institute of Industrial Relations</u>, June 1, 1954, UCBCR, Box 43, Folder 34.

16. Reinhard Bendix to E. T. Grether, January 5, 1954, CKP, Carton 2, Folder 28.

17. CK, "Memorandum of Appt. with Harry Wellman," March 18, 1954, CKP, Carton 2, Folder 28; Arthur M. Ross, memorandum, October 25, 1954, UCBCR, Box 43, Folder 30.

18. Kaufman, "Clark Kerr," 407.

19. CK, "Memorandum of Appt. with Harry Wellman."

20. Robert A. McCaughey, *Stand, Columbia: A History of Columbia University in the City of New York, 1754–2004* (New York: Columbia University Press, 2003), 379.

21. Seymour Martin Lipset to CK, May 4, 1953, CKP, Carton 9, Folder 15.

22. CK to Frank Stanton, April 9, 1954, CKP, Carton 9, Folder 37.

23. Malcolm Waters, *Daniel Bell* (London: Routledge, 1996); Howard Brick, *Daniel Bell and the Decline of Intellectual Radicalism* (Madison: University of Wisconsin Press, 1986).

24. Minutes of Board Meeting, Stockholm, Sweden, July 20–26, 1955, CKP, Carton 10, Folder 6.

25. Arthur Ross to Statewide Coordinating Committee, May 19, 1955, UCBCR, Box 43, Folder 34.

26. E. T. Grether, Report on the Statewide Coordinating Committee of the Institute of Industrial Relations, May 29, 1957, UCBCR, Box 43, Folder 34.

27. CK, "Establishment of the Institute of International Studies," n.d., CKP, Carton 2, Folder 16.

28. Gene M. Lyons and Louis Morton, *Schools for Strategy: Education and Research in National Security Affairs* (New York: Praeger, 1965), 166–167.

29. CK to RGS, September 30, 1954, UCOP3, Box 50, Folder 13.

30. CK, "Reorganization of International Studies on the Berkeley Campus," September 30, 1954, UCOP3, Box 50, Folder 13.

31. Robert A. McCaughey, *International Studies and Academic Enterprise: A Chapter in the Enclosure of American Learning* (New York: Columbia University Press, 1984), 191, 194.

32. Paul S. Taylor, Chairman, Institute of International Studies, "The University's proper discharge of its share of the national responsibility . . ."—A report to the Academic Advisory Committee, June 3, 1959, UCBCR, Box 15, Folder 20.

33. Mary O. Furner, *Advocacy and Objectivity: A Crisis in the Professionalization of American Social Science, 1865–1905* (Lexington: University Press of Kentucky, 1975); Edward T. Silva and Sheila A. Slaughter, *Serving Power: The Making of the Academic Social Science Expert* (Westport, CT: Greenwood Press, 1984); Robert C. Bannister, *Sociology and Scientism: The American Quest for Objectivity, 1880–1940* (Chapel Hill: University of North Carolina Press, 1987); Dorothy Ross, *The Origins of American Social Science* (Cambridge, UK: Cambridge University Press, 1991); Mark C. Smith, *Social Science in the Crucible: The American Debate over Objectivity and Purpose, 1918–1941* (Durham, NC: Duke University Press, 1994). Quote is from Furner, *Advocacy and Objectivity*, 8.

34. Rakesh Khurana, *From Higher Aims to Hired Hands: The Social Transformation of American Business Schools and the Unfulfilled Promise of Management as a Profession* (Princeton, NJ: Princeton University Press, 2007), 282; see also Marion Fourcade, *Economists and Societies: Discipline and Profession in the United States, Britain, and France, 1890s to 1990s* (Princeton, NJ: Princeton University Press, 2009), 70.

35. William Korey, *Taking on the World's Repressive Regimes: the Ford Foundation's International Human Rights Policies and Practices* (New York: Palgrave Macmillan, 2007), 4–14.

36. Robert M. Hutchins, quoted in James L. Cochrane, *Industrialism and Industrial Man in Retrospect: A Critical Review of the Ford Foundation's Support for the Inter-University Study of Labor* (New York: Ford Foundation, 1979), 26.

37. Cochrane, *Retrospect*, 24–27, 31.

38. Ibid., 78, 80.

39. Robert M. Hutchins to CK, June 21, 1951, and Virginia Taylor to Hutchins, June 25, 1951, Grant PA 52-153, Reel 0127, Section 4, FFA.

40. CK et al., "Labor Relations and Democratic Policy," [1951], Grant PA 52-153, Reel 0127, Section 4, FFA.

41. Paul Hoffman to James Killian, August 30, 1951, Grant PA 52-153, Reel 0127, Section 4, FFA.

42. Cochrane, *Retrospect*, 33–34.

43. Richard M. Bissell Jr., *Reflections of a Cold Warrior: From Yalta to the Bay of Pigs* (New Haven, CT: Yale University Press, 1996).

44. Ibid., 11.

45. Charles Myers to CK, March 3, 1952, CKP, Carton 9, Folder 13.

46. Richard M. Bissell Jr. to Joseph M. McDaniel Jr., March 6, 1952, Grant PA 52-153, Reel 0127, Section 4, FFA.

47. Joseph M. McDaniel Jr. to Richard M. Bissell Jr., March 11, 1952, Grant PA 52-153, Reel 0127, Section 4, FFA.

48. Joseph M. McDaniel Jr. to Milton Katz, n.d. [spring 1952], Grant PA 52-153, Reel 0127, Section 4, FFA.

49. Chester C. Davis, memo to files of conversation with Milton Katz, June 10, 1952, Grant PA 53-214 (B-18), Reel 0053—Bissell project, Section 4, FFA.

50. CK et al., "Proposal for a Research Project on <u>Utilization of Human Resources: A Comparative Analysis</u>," CKP, Carton 9, Folder 49; Cochrane, *Retrospect*, 80. The concept of "human resources" came into common usage during the 1940s.

51. Richard M. Bissell Jr. to H. Rowan Gaither, May 13, 1952, Grant PA 52-153, Reel 0127, Section 4, FFA.

52. Joseph M. McDaniel Jr. to Richard M. Bissell Jr., May 22, 1952, Grant PA 52-153, Reel 0127, Section 4, FFA; Cochrane, *Retrospect*, 76–80.

53. [Richard M. Bissell Jr.], Excerpt from Economic Workshop Report, June 13, 1952, Grant PA 52-153, Reel 0127, Section 4, FFA.

54. Richard M. Bissell Jr. to Oliver May, July 18, 1952, Grant PA 52-153, Reel 0127, Section 4, FFA.

55. "Statement prepared by Dr. Kerr for presentation at Regents' Finance Committee meeting November 13, 1952: Proposed Ford Foundation Grant—Institute of Industrial Relations, Berkeley," CKP, Carton 9, Folder 49.

56. Cochrane, *Retrospect*, 31–32; Dwight Macdonald, *The Ford Foundation: The Men and the Millions* (New York: Reynal, 1956), 146–153; "Ford Fund Allots $17,695,000 Grants," *New York Times*, March 2, 1953.

57. Cochrane, *Retrospect*, 86.

58. "Dyke Brown, Founder of the Athenian School in Danville, California, Passes Away," 20 December 2006, http://www.athenian.org/about/documents/mediaadvisory-DykeBrownpasses_000.pdf, accessed 18 March 2009 (site discontinued).

59. Cochrane, *Retrospect*, 90.

60. CK et al., "The Utilization of Human Resources: A Comparative Analysis, Interim Report of the Four-University Group," February 17, 1953, CKP, Carton 9, Folder 48.

61. Joseph M. McDaniel Jr. to file, May 6, 1953, Grant PA 54-19 (preliminary grant), Reel 0127, Section 4, FFA.

62. Cochrane, *Retrospect*, 32; Richard E. Neustadt, "Don K. Price (23 January 1910–9 July 1995)," *Proceedings of the American Philosophical Society* 142, no. 1 (1998): 155–160.

63. Francis X. Sutton, "The Ford Foundation: The Early Years," *Daedalus* 116, no. 1 (1987): 81.

64. [Thomas H. Carroll], "Confidential Working Paper for Advisory Group Conference, October 16–17, 1953," EDA Office Files 1952–1957, Box 1, Folder: Advisory Group: Working Paper and Comments, FFA.

65. Donald T. Critchlow, "Think Tanks, Antistatism, and Democracy: the Nonpartisan Ideal and Policy Research in the United States, 1913–1987," in *The State and Social Investigation in Britain and the United States*, ed. Michael J. Lacey and Mary O. Furner (Cambridge, UK: Cambridge University Press, 1993), 291.

66. CK to Thomas H. Carroll, n.d., Grant PA 54-19 (preliminary grant), Reel 0127, Section 4, FFA; CK to Charles Myers, Frederick Harbison, and John Dunlop, September 17, 1953, CKP, Carton 9, Folder 48.

67. Thomas H. Carroll to Donald David, November 12, 1953, Grant PA 54-19 (preliminary grant), Reel 0127, Section 4, FFA.

68. CK to John Dunlop, December 7, 1953, CKP, Carton 10, Folder 1.

69. John Dunlop to CK, Charles Myers, and Frederick Harbison, January 15, 1954, CKP, Carton 10, Folder 1.

70. Thomas H. Carroll to CK, January 11, 1954, CKP, Carton 10, Folder 1.

71. Thomas H. Carroll to CK, February 23, 1954, CKP, Carton 10, Folder 3.

72. Docket Excerpt, Meeting of the Trustees, February 19–20, 1954, Grant PA 54-19 (preliminary grant), Reel 0127, Section 1, FFA.

73. CK to John Dunlop, February 4, 1955, CKP, Carton 10, Folder 4.

74. Minutes of Board Meeting, Biltmore Hotel, NY, January 4–6, 1956, UCOP3, Box 41, Folder 32.

75. John Dunlop to CK, April 21, 1956, UCOP3, Box 41, Folder 32.

76. Economics 250-B course description, Spring 1953, CKP, Carton 9, Folder 27.

77. Walter Galenson, "Labor Theory and Inductive Method," in *Labor, Management, and Economic Growth: Proceedings of a Conference on Human Resources and Labor Relations in Underdeveloped Countries*, ed. Robert L. Aronson and John P. Windmuller (Ithaca, NY: Cornell University, 1954), 230–231.

78. CK to RGS, December 10, 1950, UCOP3, Box 41, Folder 28.

79. University of California Regents, finance meeting minutes, September 28, 1950, UCOP3, Carton 33, Folder 6.

80. James G. Miller to CK, November 16, 1953, CKP, Carton 9, Folder 44.

81. Schrum, "Clark Kerr's Early Career."

82. Minutes of the Fifth Meeting of the Board of Directors, Center for Advanced Study in the Behavioral Sciences, January 2, 1954, CKP, Carton 9, Folder 37; untitled document, CKP, Carton 14, Folder 18.

83. For a more detailed account of the debacle and how it provides insight into Kerr's ideas, see Schrum, "Clark Kerr's Early Career."

84. Harold E. Jones to William R. Dennes, August 8, 1951, UCOP3, Box 41, Folder 28.

85. Joel Isaac, *Working Knowledge: Making the Human Sciences from Parsons to Kuhn* (Cambridge, MA: Harvard University Press, 2012), 179–188.

86. CK to RGS, January 21, 1954, UCOP3, Box 33, Folder 6.

87. Geiger, *Research and Relevant Knowledge*, 80.

88. CK to RGS, March 14, 1955, UCOP3, Box 33, Folder 6.

89. H. Rowan Gaither to RGS, July 10, 1956, UCOP3, Box 33, Folder 6.

90. Hunter Heyck, *Age of System: Understanding the Development of Modern Social Science* (Baltimore: Johns Hopkins University Press, 2015), 131.

91. Paul Erickson et al., *How Reason Almost Lost its Mind: The Strange Career of Cold War Rationality* (Chicago: University of Chicago Press, 2013), 46.

92. Andrew Abbott, *The System of Professions: An Essay on the Division of Expert Labor* (Chicago: University of Chicago Press, 1988), 236–237.

93. Stephen P. Waring, "Cold Calculus: The Cold War and Operations Research," *Radical History Review* 63 (1995): 28–51; Bruce Kuklick, *Blind Oracles: Intellectuals and War from Kennan to Kissinger* (Princeton, NJ: Princeton University Press, 2006), 19; Philip M. Morse and George E. Kimball, *Methods of Operations Research* (Cambridge: Technology Press of Massachusetts Institute of Technology and New York: Wiley, 1951).

94. Stephen P. Waring, *Taylorism Transformed: Scientific Management Theory Since 1945* (Chapel Hill: University of North Carolina Press, 1991), 20–25 (quote on 20).

95. C. West Churchman c.v., http://www.cnr.berkeley.edu/~schultz/people/churchman_cv.html, accessed November 15, 2008 (site discontinued); William Thomas, *Rational Action: The Sciences of Policy in Britain and America, 1940–1960* (Cambridge, MA: MIT Press, 2015), 243–255. Quote is from c.v.

96. [C. West Churchman?], untitled proposal, n.d., UCBCR, Box 43, Folder 32.

97. Ewald T. Grether, *Dean of the UC Berkeley Schools of Business Administration, 1943–1961; Leader in Campus Administration, Public Service, and Marketing Studies; and Forever a Teacher*, vol. 2, an oral history conducted 1975–1987 by Harriet Nathan (Regional Oral History Office, The Bancroft Library, University of California, Berkeley, 1993), 733, 676.

98. Ibid., 734–735.

99. Ibid., 736.

100. Ibid., 735; [Churchman?], untitled proposal; Arthur M. Ross to Glenn T. Seaborg, July 12, 1960, UCBCR, Box 43, Folder 32.

101. Edward W. Strong to CK, April 14, 1961, UCBCR, Box 43, Folder 32.

102. Grether, *Dean of the UC Berkeley Schools of Business Administration*, 737.

103. Fred Balderston, quoted in ibid., 739.

104. Schrum, "Clark Kerr's Early Career."

105. Robert C. Alberts, *Pitt: The Story of the University of Pittsburgh 1787–1987* (Pittsburgh: University of Pittsburgh Press, 1986), 247–249; Geiger, *Research and Relevant Knowledge*, 147; Nicholas J. Demerath, William J. McEwen, Robert W. Avery, Donald R. Van Houten, and William A. Rushing, "James D. Thompson: A Memorial," *Administrative Science Quarterly* 19, no. 1 (1974): 1–5.

106. James D. Thompson, "Editorial," *Administrative Science Quarterly* 1, no. 1 (1956): 1.

107. *Administrative Science Quarterly* 1, no. 1 (1956).

108. Alberts, *Pitt*, 244.

109. Ibid.; Geiger, *Research and Relevant Knowledge*, 146–155; "Pitt's Big Thinker," *Time*, September 7, 1962.

110. Both men had recently been among a small group involved in the founding activities of Walter Isard's Regional Science Association in 1955, another exemplary activity of the instrumental university (see chapter 3). Walter Isard, *History of Regional Science and the Regional Science Association International: The Beginnings and Early History* (Berlin: Springer, 2003), 91.

111. CK to Robert Calkins, May 3, 1957, CKP, Carton 12, Folder 20.

112. Robert Calkins, "The Economy and the University," manuscript of speech given at the Wharton School, University of Pennsylvania, March 5, 1957, CKP, Carton 12, Folder 20.

113. Robert Calkins, *The Art of Administration and the Art of Science* (Bloomington: Indiana University School of Business, 1959).

114. E. T. Grether to CK, March 29, 1957, CKP, Carton 12, Folder 20.

115. Grether, *Dean of the UC Berkeley Schools of Business Administration*, 677.

116. Grether to Kerr, March 29, 1957.

117. RGS to Robert Calkins, August 31, 1940, and Robert Calkins to RGS, October 1, 1940, UCOP 4, Box 8, Folder 4.

118. Grether to Kerr, March 29, 1957.

119. CK to William Whyte, August 12, 1957, CKP, Carton 12, Folder 20.

120. Mary Soo and Cathryn Carson, "Managing the Research University: Clark Kerr and the University of California," *Minerva* 42 (2004): 230.

121. CK, "The Schools of Business Administration," address given at the University of Pittsburgh, May 1957, CKP, Carton 6, Folder 42.

122. Ibid., 5. Emphasis added. Kerr had used the image similarly in *Business Leadership and Economic Development* (Berkeley: University of California, 1956).

123. CK, *The Uses of the University* (Cambridge, MA: Harvard University Press, 1963), 47.

124. Kerr, "The Schools of Business Administration," 7.

125. Heyck, *Age of System*, 131.

126. Peter Drucker to CK, February 9, 1955, CKP, Carton 6, Folder 25.

127. CK to Peter Drucker, February 21, 1955, CKP, Carton 6, Folder 25.

128. CK, *Uses*, 89–90.

129. Ibid., 85. Heyck, *Age of System*, 35, explains how for Parsons, "the goal is the continuous management of society to maintain social equilibrium."

130. CK, John T. Dunlop, Frederick H. Harbison, and Charles A. Myers, *Industrialism and Industrial Man: The Problems of Labor and Management in Economic Growth* (Cambridge, MA: Harvard University Press, 1960), 21, 15, 33.

131. Nils Gilman, *Mandarins of the Future: Modernization Theory in Cold War America* (Baltimore: Johns Hopkins University Press, 2003), 108.

132. CK et al., *Industrialism and Industrial Man*, 33, 15, 284.

133. Ibid., 37.

134. CK to Henry Luce, July 17, 1956, UCOP3, Box 41, Folder 32.

135. CK et al., *Industrialism and Industrial Man*, 137, 136, 36, 37.

136. CK et al., *Industrialism and Industrial Man*, 28. Marx and Engels had said that "the place of manufacture was taken by the giant, Modern Industry"; ibid., 318n22.

137. Ibid., 33, 47, 19, 20, 47, 20.

138. Ibid., chap. 10.

139. Gilman, *Mandarins of the Future*, especially 107–112 on Kerr's relationship to modernization theory; Michael E. Latham, *Modernization as Ideology: American Social Science and "Nation-Building" in the Kennedy Era* (Chapel Hill: University of North Carolina Press, 2000).

140. CK et al., *Industrialism and Industrial Man*, 17, 8.

141. CK and Abraham Siegel, "The Structuring of the Labor Force in Industrial Society: New Dimensions and New Questions," *Industrial and Labor Relations Review* 8, no. 2 (1955): 151–168.

142. Theodore Schultz to CK, July 15, 1955, CKP, Carton 6, Folder 40.

143. CK et al., *Industrialism and Industrial Man*, 290, 287, 41.

144. Heyck, *Age of System*, 128.

145. CK, "The Distribution of Authority and its Relation to Policy," in *Problems and Policies of Dispute Settlement and Wage Stabilization during World War II*, ed. W. E. Chalmers, M. Derber, and W. H. McPherson (Washington, DC: US Bureau of Labor Statistics, 1950).

146. CK, "The Executive—The New Educational Requirements of the New Society," speech delivered at Lake Arrowhead, California, 1958, CKP, Carton 12, Folder 28.

147. CK et al., *Industrialism and Industrial Man*, 42.

148. CK, "The Distribution of Authority and its Relation to Policy," 313.

149. CK et al., *Industrialism and Industrial Man*, 36, 34, 37, 11.

150. See chapter 3 and Rebecca S. Lowen, *Creating the Cold War University: The Transformation of Stanford* (Berkeley: University of California Press, 1997), 15.

151. CK et al., *Industrialism and Industrial Man*, 146, 185.

152. Frederick Harbison and Charles A. Myers, *Education, Manpower, and Economic Growth: Strategies of Human Resource Development* (New York: McGraw-Hill, 1964), v, vi.

153. Ushma Patel, "William G. Bowen, 17th president of Princeton University, dies at age 83," https://www.princeton.edu/news/2016/10/21/william-g-bowen-17th-president-princeton-university-dies-age-83, accessed September 17, 2018.

154. CK et al., *Industrialism and Industrial Man*, 36, 289.

155. Minutes of Board Meeting, Accra, Ghana, February 12–15, 1958, UCOP3, Box 41, Folder 34; CK to John Dunlop, April 26, 1958, CKP, Carton 11, Folder 17.

156. CK, "Education for the Twenty-First Century," inaugural address at UC Riverside, October 1, 1958, CKP, Carton 12, Folder 39.

157. Ibid.

158. Kerr, "The Executive."

159. Minutes of Board Meeting, June 29, 1956, Waldorf-Astoria, UCOP3, Box 41, Folder 32.

160. Minutes of Board Meeting, Cambridge, MA, May 12–14, 1957, UCOP3, Box 41, Folder 33.

161. Document summarizing trip, CKP, Carton 12, Folder 51. Kerr's home was technically located in El Cerrito, a municipality adjoining the city of Berkeley but sharing the Berkeley hills.

162. University of California Special Leave of Absence, CKP, Carton 18, Folder 8.

163. Myrdal was living in New Delhi while his wife served as Sweden's ambassador to India. CK to Charles Myers, December 8, 1958, CKP, Carton 18, Folder 8.

164. Robert M. Collins, "Growth Liberalism in the Sixties: Great Societies at Home and Grand Designs Abroad," in *The Sixties: From Memory to History*, ed. David R. Farber (Chapel Hill: University of North Carolina Press, 1994), 15–16.

165. President's Commission on National Goals, *Goals for Americans* ([Englewood Cliffs, NJ]: Prentice Hall, 1960), 10–11, 27.

166. Robert M. Collins, *More: The Politics of Economic Growth in Postwar America* (New York: Oxford University Press, 2000), chap. 1.

167. Collins, "Growth Liberalism," 17–18, 25.

168. CK, *The Gold and the Blue: A Personal Memoir of the University of California, 1949–1967*, vol. 2 (Berkeley: University of California Press, 2003), 278–279.

169. On this discussion, see Collins, "Growth Liberalism," 16–17. Important publications emerging from this discussion include Rockefeller Brothers Fund, *Prospect for America: the Rockefeller Panel Reports* (Garden City, NY: Doubleday), 1961; John K. Jessup et al., *The National Purpose* (New York: Holt, Rinehart and Winston, 1960).

170. CK, *Uses*, 87.

171. Harold Stoke, *The American College President* (New York: Harper, 1959), 164, 166.

172. CK, *Uses*, 36; Stoke, *The American College President*, 15, 124.

173. Quotes are from Bruce E. Kaufman, *The Global Evolution of Industrial Relations* (Geneva: International Labour Office, 2004), 261; also see Cochrane, *Retrospect*, 137, 141–142; George Strauss and Peter Feuille, "Industrial Relations Research in the United States," in *Industrial Relations in International Perspective: Essays on Research and Policy*, ed. Peter B. Doeringer (New York: Holmes and Meier, 1981), 83.

174. CK, *Uses*, 122.

175. Christopher Newfield, *Unmaking the Public University: the Forty-Year Assault on the Middle Class* (Cambridge, MA: Harvard University Press, 2008), 221.

3. The Urban University as Community Service Institution

1. City of Philadelphia mayoral proclamation, April 9, 1970, NPAR, Box B61, Folder 2.

2. GPH, *University of Pennsylvania: An Instrument of National Purpose. The President's Message, February 1964* (Philadelphia: University of Pennsylvania President's Office, 1964), 12.

3. Greater Philadelphia Movement, January 28, 1965 news release on Philadelphia Award, 3, NPAR, Box B60, Folder 14.

4. GPH, address at opening convocation, September 25, 1953, NPAR, Box B63, Folder 3.

5. Ethan Schrum, "Establishing a Democratic Religion: Metaphysics and Democracy in the Debates Over the President's Commission on Higher Education," *History of Education Quarterly* 47, no. 3 (2007): 277–301.

6. GPH, remarks at Trustees Luncheon, May 13, 1966, NPAR, Box B63, Folder 8. John L. Puckett and Mark Frazier Lloyd's *Becoming Penn: The Pragmatic American University, 1950–2000* (Philadelphia: University of Pennsylvania Press, 2015), while generally recognizing the outsize influence of Harnwell on the university and on his successors, attributes to them this view about how a problem-centered approach could unify the university, which Harnwell clearly articulated.

7. GPH, remarks at University of Pennsylvania Founder's Day convocation, January 18, 1964, NPAR, Box B63, Folder 6.

8. GPH, address to National Council (of Penn) Metro New York, September 17, 1963, NPAR, Box B63, Folder 6.

9. John Dewey, *Problems of Men* (New York: Philosophical Library, 1946), 17.

10. GPH to JHW, October 19, 1953, JHW Papers, Box 18, Folder 135, Rockefeller Archive Center. The priority that Harnwell placed on the social sciences indicates their high profile in the postwar university, even among some elite physical scientists like Harnwell, contrary to the depiction in Andrew Jewett, *Science, Democracy, and the American University: From the Civil War to the Cold War* (New York: Cambridge University Press, 2012).

11. Ethan Schrum, "The Reluctant President: Gaylord P. Harnwell and American University Leadership after World War II," *Pennsylvania Magazine of History and Biography* 141 (October 2017): 329–359.

12. Stephen A. Sass, *The Pragmatic Imagination: A History of the Wharton School, 1881–1981* (Philadelphia, University of Pennsylvania Press, 1982), 246, 301, 282–283.

13. University of Pennsylvania, *School of Fine Arts Announcement 1934–35* (Philadelphia, 1934); George Simpson Koyl to G. Holmes Perkins, October 30, 1950, FADR, Box 82, Folder 4A.

14. Russell F. Weigley, ed., *Philadelphia: A 300 Year History* (New York: Norton, 1982), 646.

15. Kirk R. Petshek, *The Challenge of Urban Reform: Policies and Programs in Philadelphia* (Philadelphia: Temple University Press, 1973), 20–21.

16. Biographical sketch of Edward Hopkinson Jr., November 18, 1957, AR, Box 1189, Folder "Hopkinson, Edward, Jr. #2."

17. Ann L. Strong and George E. Thomas, *The Book of the School: 100 Years: The Graduate School of Fine Arts of the University of Pennsylvania* (Philadelphia: University of Pennsylvania Graduate School of Fine Arts, 1990), 162; Steven J. Diner, *Universities and their Cities: Urban Higher Education in America* (Baltimore: Johns Hopkins University Press, 2017), 49.

18. Robert Mitchell c.v., October 1968, NPAR, Box 100, Folder 27.

19. "Courses Relating to City Planning Offered at the University of Pennsylvania 1943," FADR, Box 84, Folder: City and Regional Planning.

20. Charles C. Rohlfing and Stephen B. Sweeney, "Requested Memorandum on Curriculum Suggestions," February 8, 1944, FADR, Box 84, Folder: City and Regional Planning.

21. Alexander Garvin, *The American City: What Works, What Doesn't*, 2nd ed. (New York: McGraw-Hill, 2002), 526.

22. University of Pennsylvania Trustees minutes, October 27, 1947, Van Pelt Library microfilm collection, University of Pennsylvania.

23. As Mitchell explained to G. Holmes Perkins in 1950, "I have been trying to find a copy of the last memorandum I made for Hopkinson on the creation of an institute for urban studies at Pennsylvania." That memo apparently does not survive, but an earlier draft dated May 21, 1947 is extant. Robert B. Mitchell to G. Holmes Perkins, November 13, 1950, 054.216, GHPC.

24. [Robert B. Mitchell], Philadelphia City Planning Commission, untitled memo, May 21, 1947, 054.216, GHPC.

25. MIT Institute Archives and Special Collections, "History of the Department of Urban Studies and Planning," https://libraries.mit.edu/mithistory/, accessed September 17, 2018; Anthony Alofsin, *The Struggle for Modernism: Architecture, Landscape Architecture, and City Planning at Harvard* (New York: W. W. Norton, 2002), 302.

26. Mel Scott, *American City Planning Since 1890: A History Commemorating the Fiftieth Anniversary of the American Institute of Planners* (Berkeley: University of California Press, 1969), 365.

27. [Mitchell], untitled memo, May 21, 1947.

28. University of Pennsylvania Architectural Society to HES, March 29, 1949, UPOPR, Box 32, Folder: Fine Arts, School of (Special Advisory Committee—James Kellum Smith, Chairman) [hereafter SAC]—I 1945–1950.

29. Francis Henry Taylor to HES, May 9, 1949, UPOPR, Box 32, Folder: SAC III. On Wurster, see Marc Treib, ed., *An Everyday Modernism: The Houses of William Wurster* (Berkeley: University of California Press, 1996).

30. Wurster's new wife, the influential city planner and public housing advocate Catherine Bauer, also took a position at Berkeley and worked closely with Clark Kerr on a proposed western development project. On her life, see H. Peter Oberlander, *Houser: The Life and Work of Catherine Bauer* (Vancouver: UBC Press, 1999).

31. Taylor to HES, May 9, 1949.

32. Sydney Martin to HES, June 9, 1949, UPOPR, Box 32, Folder: SAC V.

33. George S. Koyl to HES, December 12, 1949, UPOPR, Box 32, Folder: Fine Arts, School of (General)—II 1945–1950.

34. HES to James Kellum Smith, March 21, 1950, UPOPR, Box 32, Folder: SAC VI.

35. Gilmore D. Clarke to HES, November 7, 1949, UPOPR, Box 32, Folder: SAC V.

36. James Kellum Smith to HES, May 11, 1950, UPOPR, Box 32, Folder: SAC VI.

37. James Kellum Smith to HES, June 6, 1950, UPOPR, Box 32, Folder: SAC VII.

38. Alofsin, *The Struggle for Modernism*, 134, 199–200.

39. HES to James B. Conant, telegram, n.d. [June 1950], UPOPR, Box 32, Folder: SAC VII.

40. G. Holmes Perkins c.v., UPOPR, Box 32, Folder: SAC VII.

41. G. Holmes Perkins to HES, July 7, 1950, UPOPR, Box 50, Folder: Fine Arts, School of (Deanship) 1950–55.

42. G. Holmes Perkins to Edwin B. Williams, October 13, 1950, FADR, Box 82, Folder 4A.

43. Edwin B. Williams to Paul Musser, November 13, 1950, FADR, Box 82, Folder 1B.

44. John M. Gaus to James C. Charlesworth, October 30, 1950, FADR, Box 82, Folder 2U.

45. G. Holmes Perkins to Edwin B. Williams, December 28, 1950, FADR, Box 82, Folder 4A.

46. G. Holmes Perkins to Paul Musser, April 5, 1951, FADR, Box 82, Folder 1B; Alofsin, *The Struggle for Modernism*, 293n10.

47. Robert B. Mitchell to G. Holmes Perkins, March 20, 1951, FADR, Box 85, Folder: Williams, Edwin B. (Provost) 1951–52.

48. Strong and Thomas, *The Book of the School*, 168.

49. Paul Musser to G. Holmes Perkins, April 16, 1951, FADR, Box 82, Folder 1B.

50. Alofsin, *The Struggle for Modernism*, 230; Catherine Bauer Wurster to Coleman Woodbury, copy to G. Holmes Perkins, July 31, 1951, FADR, Box 85, Folder: Urban Redevelopment Study 1951–52.

51. Mitchell to Perkins, March 20, 1951.

52. G. Holmes Perkins to HES, May 15, 1951, FADR, Box 82, Folder 1.

53. G. Holmes Perkins to Robert McCracken, October 17, 1951, FADR, Box 84, Folder: Institute for Urban Studies 1951–52.

54. University of Pennsylvania, "Request to the Ford Foundation for a Grant-in-Aid for City Planning," 1957, UPOPR, Box 81, Folder: Ford Foundation (Grant—City Planning, Department of, and Institute for Urban Studies).

55. Martin Meyerson and Edward C. Banfield, *Politics, Planning, and the Public Interest: The Case of Public Housing in Chicago* (Glencoe, IL: Free Press, 1955).

56. Strong and Thomas, *The Book of the School*, 168; William L.C. Wheaton c.v. November 1961, AR, Box 2941, Folder: Wheaton, William L.C. Faculty.

57. Alofsin, *The Struggle for Modernism*, 303.

58. Martin Meyerson, *Gladly Learn and Gladly Teach: Franklin and His Heirs at the University of Pennsylvania, 1740–1976* (Philadelphia: University of Pennsylvania Press, 1978), 216, 221–222.

59. Schrum, "The Reluctant President."

60. University of Pennsylvania Board of Graduate Education and Research [BGER] minutes, November 21, 1938, December 18, 1939, and January 15, 1940, VPLMC, University of Pennsylvania. This effort invites further examination of Margaret O'Mara's assertion that although Penn had "a long history of close ties to industry," Penn administrators in the 1940s "felt quite strongly that commercial interests jeopardized the integrity of the basic research and education functions of the university." Margaret Pugh O'Mara, *Cities of Knowledge: Cold War Science and the Search for the Next Silicon Valley* (Princeton, NJ: Princeton University Press, 2004), 148.

61. University of Pennsylvania Board of Liberal Arts minutes, May 23, 1939, VPLMC, University of Pennsylvania.

62. BGER minutes, November 17, 1941.

63. GPH, address to Annual Correspondent Bank Meeting of the First Pennsylvania Banking and Trust Company, October 3, 1956, NPAR, Box B63, Folder 4.

64. GPH, excerpts from March 20, 1954 speech to Philadelphia chapter of American Institute of Banking, NPAR, Box B63, Folder 3.

65. I do not intend "macrothought" as a synonym for worldview as some scholars have. See James E. Grunig and Jon White, "The Effect of Worldviews on Public Relations Theory and Practice," in *Excellence in Public Relations and Communications Management*, ed. Grunig (Hillsdale, NJ: Lawrence Earlbaum Associates, 1992), 33.

66. David Kaiser, "Cold War Requisitions, Scientific Manpower, and the Production of American Physicists after World War II," *Historical Studies in the Physical and Biological Sciences* 33, no. 1 (2002): 131–159.

67. "Reclaiming Engineers," *New York Times*, March 8, 1942.

68. "Report of the National Research Council," in *Report of the National Academy of Sciences 1950–51* (Washington, DC: US Government Printing Office, 1955), 36–37.

69. GPH, excerpts from speech to American Institute of Banking.

70. GPH, address to University of Pennsylvania Club of New England, May 4, 1956, AR, Box 1053, Folder: Speeches 1954–1960.

71. GPH, notes for Baltimore Alumni Club speech, April 20, 1956, AR, Box 1053, Folder: Speeches 1954–1960.

72. On the belief in complexity see Hunter Heyck, *Age of System: Understanding the Development of Modern Social Science* (Baltimore: Johns Hopkins University Press, 2015), 139.

73. GPH, speech to National Council (of Penn) Metro New York.

74. GPH, remarks at Trustees' announcement luncheon for new capital program, November 20, 1964, NPAR, Box B63, Folder 6.

75. Press release on Harnwell Chair, May 9, 1963, NPAR, Box B60, Folder 13.

76. Schrum, "The Reluctant President."

77. GPH, speech to Phi Delta Kappa and Pi Lambda Theta, April 21, 1955, NPAR, Box B63, Folder 3.

78. GPH, notes for Baltimore.

79. GPH, remarks at luncheon for new capital program.

80. Sass, *Pragmatic Imagination*, 248–260.

81. GPH, address in New England.

82. GPH, *Instrument of National Purpose*, 12–13.

83. Clark Kerr, *The Uses of the University* (Cambridge, MA: Harvard University Press, 1963), 87.

84. Various documents, GPHP, Box 7, Folder 31.

85. GPH, remarks at commencement, May 20, 1963, NPAR, Box B63, Folder 6.

86. For instance, GPH, remarks to Philadelphia Public Relations Association Award presentation, April 20, 1967, AR, Box 1053, Folder: Speeches 1961–1970.

87. GPH, "A Higher Educational Program," prepared for delivery at the Convocation on Higher Education, Forty-Second Annual Education Congress, Harrisburg, PA, October 2, 1963, NPAR, Box B63, Folder 6.

88. GPH, *Instrument of National Purpose*.

89. Drucker emphasized this point as the central element of the knowledge economy in Peter F. Drucker, *The Age of Discontinuity: Guidelines to Our Changing Society* (New York: Harper and Row, 1969), chap. 12, "The Knowledge Economy," to which scholars attribute the popularization of the term "knowledge economy."

90. Fritz Machlup, *The Production and Distribution of Knowledge in the United States* (Princeton, NJ: Princeton University Press, 1962); Benoît Godin, "The Knowledge Economy: Fritz Machlup's Construction of a Synthetic Concept," Project on the History and Sociology of S&T Statistics, Working Paper No. 37, 2008, http://www.csiic.ca/PDF/Godin_37.pdf, accessed September 17, 2018; Kerr, *Uses*, 87–91.

91. Peter F. Drucker, *Landmarks of Tomorrow* (New York: Harper, 1957), 122; Nils Gilman, "The Prophet of Post-Fordism: Peter Drucker and the Legitimation of the Corporation," in *American Capitalism: Social Thought and Political Economy in the Twentieth Century*, ed. Nelson Lichtenstein (Philadelphia: University of Pennsylvania Press, 2006), 110.

92. Theodore Schultz, "Investment in Human Capital," *American Economic Review* 51 (March 1961): 1–17; Schultz, *The Economic Value of Education* (New York: Columbia University Press, 1963); Gary S. Becker, *Human Capital: A Theoretical and Empirical Analysis, with Special Reference to Education* (New York: Columbia University Press, 1964). On Schultz, Becker, and their milieu at the University of Chicago, see Johan Van Overtveldt, *The Chicago School: How the University of Chicago Assembled the Thinkers Who Revolutionized Economics and Business* (Chicago: Agate, 2007), chap. 4.

93. GPH, address to annual meeting of the Corporate Fiduciaries Association, June 3, 1965, NPAR, Box B63, Folder 7.

94. O'Mara, *Cities of Knowledge*.

95. Harnwell, address to Corporate Fiduciaries Association. The article he cited is Gilbert Burck, "Knowledge: The Biggest Growth Industry of Them All," *Fortune*, November 1964, 128–131, 267–270.

96. Puckett and Lloyd, *Becoming Penn*, chaps. 3 and 4; O'Mara, *Cities of Knowledge*, 159–166.

97. Leo Molinaro, manuscript of address delivered at luncheon in honor of Harnwell's retirement as chairman of the West Philadelphia Corporation, March 29, 1978, AR, Box 1054, Folder: President of the University.

98. Puckett and Lloyd, *Becoming Penn*, chap. 3.

99. GPH to John Moore, June 15, 1959, UPOPR, Box 73, Folder: Community Relations, West Philadelphia Corporation I.

100. O'Mara, *Cities of Knowledge*, 166–172.

101. GPH, address to Corporate Fiduciaries Association, 14–15.

102. GPH, "The University and Society," address to "Inside Pennsylvania" for the media, Wistar Auditorium, November 1, 1965, NPAR, Box B63, Folder 8.

103. "Report on the Campus," *First Pennsylvania Bank Report*, July 1968, 12, NPAR, Box B62, Folder 1. Harnwell was a director of the First Pennsylvania Bank, and its chairman, William L. Day, was chairman of Penn's Board of Trustees.

104. O'Mara, *Cities of Knowledge*, 168, 176; Puckett and Lloyd, *Becoming Penn*, chap. 4.

105. GCST notes, GPHP, Box 17, Folder 25.

106. William Warren Scranton, interview by author, July 15, 2008, Scranton, PA.

107. Clifford L. Jones, interview by author, August 17, 2007, Mechanicsburg, PA.

108. GPH, "Governor's Council on Science and Technology," March 25, 1963, GPHP, Box 18, Folder 10.

109. Quoted in Elizabeth Popp Berman, *Creating the Market University: How Academic Science Became an Economic Engine* (Princeton, NJ: Princeton University Press, 2012), 1.

Indeed, Berman argues that states "certainly had not tried to leverage science for the purposes of economic development" (p. 16) prior to the late 1970s. My account of GCST and how the knowledge economy framework motivated Harnwell's leadership of it suggests otherwise.

110. GPH to John Tabor, April 5, 1963, GPHP, Box 18, Folder 10.

111. Roy Nichols to Jonathan Rhoads, June 28, 1957, Office of the Provost General Files, UPA 6.4, Box 76, Folder 33, University Archives and Records Center, University of Pennsylvania.

112. Walter Isard, *History of Regional Science and the Regional Science Association International: The Beginnings and Early History* (Berlin: Springer, 2003); quote is on p. 7. Perkins actually worked for the Housing and Home Finance Agency.

113. GPH, address to Lancaster Chamber of Commerce, January 24, 1967, NPAR, Box B63, Folder 9.

114. Governor's Council of Science and Technology, *Science and Technology: Generators of Economic Well-Being* (Harrisburg: Commonwealth of Pennsylvania, 1964). Draft materials for the report can be found in GPHP, Box 18, Folders 2, 4.

115. GPH, "Potential Benefits to Philadelphia's Industry and Commerce as a Result of Current Research at the University of Pennsylvania," speech to Greater Philadelphia Chamber of Commerce, May 17, 1966, NPAR, Box B63, Folder 8.

116. Elizabeth Popp Berman dates universities' widespread self-identification as economic engines to around 1980. *Creating the Market University*, 3, 30.

117. GCST, *Science and Technology: Generators of Economic Well-Being*, 5.

118. GPH, "The Expansion of Academic Research and the External Services of Universities," 3.

119. Nathan Ostroff to Luther H. Hodges, August 7, 1961, DCES, Box 11, Folder: Science, ASST; National Academy of Sciences, *Role of the Department of Commerce in Science and Technology* (Washington, DC: Government Printing Office, 1960).

120. Dorothy Nelkin, *The Politics of Housing Innovation: The Fate of the Civilian Industrial Technology Program* (Ithaca, NY: Cornell University Press, 1971), 30.

121. Luther H. Hodges to Senator Warren G. Magnuson, chairman of the Committee on Interstate and Foreign Commerce, February 20, 1961, DCES, Box 11, Folder: Science, ASST.

122. Robert E. Giles to Luther H. Hodges, February 6, 1962, DCES, Box 23, Folder: Science, ASST.

123. Nelkin, *The Politics of Housing Innovation*, 31; Matthew Wisnioski, *Engineers for Change: Competing Visions of Technology in 1960s America* (Cambridge, MA: MIT Press, 2012), 151.

124. Wisnioski, *Engineers for Change*, 31, 132.

125. Nelkin, *The Politics of Housing Innovation*, 16–21.

126. Ibid., 34–39.

127. Legislative History State Technical Services Act of 1965 [February 1966?], DCST, Box 6, Folder: Legislative History Furnished.

128. Civilian Industrial Technology—Statement by J. Herbert Hollomon, Assistant Secretary of Commerce for Science and Technology, Department of Commerce Records, RG 40, Office of Science and Technology, Science and Technology Research File, 1962–1970, Finding Aid A1 Entry 18, Box 1, Folder: Civilian Industrial Technology Program, National Archives at College Park, College Park, MD.

129. PL 89-182 89th Congress S. 949.

130. Nelkin, *The Politics of Housing Innovation*, 102.

131. J. Herbert Hollomon to David R. Baldwin, February 2, 1967, DCST, Box 4, Folder: Feb.

132. List of State Designated Agencies [for STS], March 15, 1967, DCST, Box 6, Folder: Office of State Technical Services—General; Berman, *Creating the Market University*, 28.

133. OSTS Support of Technical Services in Fiscal Year 1967 by States and Participating Institution or Agency, DCST, Box 6, Folder: Office of State Technical Services—General.

134. J. Herbert Hollomon to Jason R. Lemon, March 29, 1967, DCST, Box 4, Folder: March.

135. Outline of Remarks by Dr. J. H. Hollomon for the Evaluation Committee for State Technical Services, July 26, 1967, DCST, Box 6, Folder: OSTS.

136. Results of Questionnaire on State Technical Services Act, Prepared by National Association of State Universities and Land-Grant Colleges, September 15, 1967, DCST, Box 6, Folder: Office of State Technical Services—General.

137. Nelkin, *The Politics of Housing Innovation*, 102.

138. Wisnioski, *Engineers for Change*, 154.

139. GPH, *Instrument of National Purpose*, 3.

140. CK, *Uses*, 36.

141. GPH, "The University and Society."

142. GPH, "Potential Benefits to Philadelphia's Industry and Commerce."

143. GPH, remarks at Opening Exercises, September 7, 1966, NPAR, Box B63, Folder 8.

144. O'Mara, *Cities of Knowledge*, 171.

145. Ibid., 163.

146. Glenn T. Seaborg, "Third Revolution," *Science News-Letter* 82 (October 6, 1962): 221–223.

147. When Harnwell used "revolution" to characterize the urban situation, he did not primarily mean what many Americans began to call the "urban crisis" during these years—the racial tensions that first exploded into the public eye during the Watts riots of 1965—although it was a piece of the larger picture he referred to. He did give a November 1966 speech at cross-town institution LaSalle University on that topic. GPH, "The Urban Crisis," November 11, 1966, NPAR, Box B61, Folder 6.

148. GPH, address to Lancaster Chamber of Commerce.

149. GPH, "The Future of University City," speech to Philadelphia Chapter of American Society of Appraisers, January 17, 1967, NPAR, Box B63, Folder 8.

150. GPH, Remarks to Annual Meeting, National Association of Principals of Schools for Girls, February 27, 1968, NPAR, Box B63, Folder 9.

151. GPH, *Instrument of National Purpose*, 1, 3.

152. David A. Hollinger, "Two NYUs and 'The Obligation of Universities to the Social Order' in the Great Depression," in *Science, Jews, and Secular Culture: Studies in Mid-Twentieth-Century American Intellectual History* (Princeton, NJ: Princeton University Press, 1996), 61. Many urban universities did alter their activities somewhat to meet special concerns of the city. Penn and fourteen other institutions founded the Association of Urban Universities in 1914. Yet the prewar AUU concerned itself primarily

with topics such as how to adjust faculty salaries for the higher cost of living in cities, rather than with the kinds of postwar endeavors Harnwell would embrace.

153. William Rainey Harper, "The Urban University" (1902), in Harper, *The Trend in Higher Education* (Chicago: University of Chicago Press, 1905), 158–159.

154. My reading of Harper's Columbia address differs from that offered in Lee Benson, Ira Harkavy, and John Puckett, *Dewey's Dream: Universities and Democracies in an Age of Education Reform* (Philadelphia: Temple University Press, 2007), which curiously portrays Harper's mention of "problems" as referring to a belief that universities should "consciously work to solve the central problems confronting their society" and omits from its quotation of Harper the actual problems (coeducation, student life, larger-scale finances, and personnel) that he gave as examples of how the urban university must address unique problems because of its urban setting. These authors impute the Dewey/Harnwell view of the urban university back onto Harper.

155. One area of the city's life to which Harper did give great attention was its schools, chiefly through his influence in the university's Department of Pedagogy.

156. Martin Bulmer, *The Chicago School of Sociology: Institutionalization, Diversity, and the Rise of Sociological Research* (Chicago: University of Chicago Press, 1984), 15–22; Robin F. Bachin, *Building the South Side: Urban Space and Civic Culture in Chicago, 1890–1919* (Chicago: University of Chicago Press, 2004), 100–101; Roger L. Geiger, *To Advance Knowledge: The Growth of American Research Universities, 1900–1940* (New York: Oxford University Press, 1986), 36–37.

157. Bachin, *Building the South Side*, 123, 100–101.

158. Bulmer, *The Chicago School of Sociology.*

159. University of Chicago School of Social Service Administration, http://www.ssa.uchicago.edu/about-ssa, accessed January 6, 2018.

160. GPH, Remarks to Principals of Schools for Girls.

161. GPH, Address to Lancaster Chamber of Commerce.

162. GPH, *Instrument of National Purpose*, 8.

163. GPH, Speech to National Council (of Penn) Metro New York. GPH used an almost identical argument a few months later in *Instrument of National Purpose*, 5, where he added business to the list of academic fields.

164. GPH, Remarks to Principals of Schools for Girls.

165. GPH, "The Expansion of Academic Research and the External Services of Universities."

166. GPH, Remarks to Principals of Schools for Girls, emphasis added.

167. University of Pennsylvania press release on CURE, NPAR, Box B62, Folder 1.

168. Carnegie Foundation for the Advancement of Teaching, "Carnegie Selects Colleges and Universities for 2015 Community Engagement Classification," January 7, 2015, http://www.carnegiefoundation.org/newsroom/news-releases/carnegie-selects-colleges-universities-2015-community-engagement-classification/, accessed September 17, 2018.

169. Carnegie Foundation for the Advancement of Teaching, "All Classified Community Engagement Institutions (2006, 2008, and 2010)," http://www.nerche.org/images/stories/projects/Carnegie/2006_2008_2010_CE_Institutions.pdf, accessed 21 May 2016 (site discontinued).

170. O'Mara, *Cities of Knowledge*, 179; http://www.sciencecenter.org/our-facilities/research-parks, accessed 15 May 2009 (site discontinued).

4. "Instruments of Technical Cooperation"

1. GPH to Donald McDonald, 8 March 1961, GPHP, Box 1, Folder 29.

2. On the Kanazawa relationship, see Martin Bronfenbrenner, *Academic Encounter: The American University in Japan and Korea* (New York: Free Press of Glencoe, 1961), 143–148. Kanazawa inquired with nine American universities about forming such a relationship, and Penn showed the most interest, "probably because President Gaylord P. Harnwell is an enthusiast on international education." Ibid., 144.

3. Honorary degree citation for the shah of Iran, April 18, 1962, GPHP, Box 4, Folder 28.

4. To be sure, sporadic efforts had existed in the past. For example, President William S. Clark of Massachusetts Agricultural College (now UMass) spent 1876–77 in Japan establishing Sapporo Agricultural College, now Hokkaido University. Bronfenbrenner, *Academic Encounter*, 11–16. Such enterprise, however, became widespread only after World War II.

5. Inderjeet Parmar, *Foundations of the American Century: The Ford, Carnegie, and Rockefeller Foundations in the Rise of American Power* (New York: Columbia University Press, 2012), especially 135–142.

6. This extensive literature has three foundational monographs: Michael E. Latham, *Modernization as Ideology: American Social Science and "Nation-Building" in the Kennedy Era* (Chapel Hill: University of North Carolina Press, 2000); Nils Gilman, *Mandarins of the Future: Modernization Theory in Cold War America* (Baltimore: Johns Hopkins University Press, 2003); and David C. Engerman, *Modernization from the Other Shore: American Intellectuals and the Romance of Russian Development* (Cambridge, MA: Harvard University Press, 2004), an especially important comparative work that addresses Soviet modernity. Later works with a longer chronological sweep include David Ekbladh, *The Great American Mission: Modernization and the Construction of an American World Order* (Princeton, NJ: Princeton University Press, 2010); and Latham, *The Right Kind of Revolution: Modernization, Development, and U.S. Foreign Policy from the Cold War to the Present* (Ithaca, NY: Cornell University Press, 2011). While the foundational works by Latham and Gilman do acknowledge the importance that modernization theorists placed on institutions, these books do not treat the role of institutions in modernization systematically or give much attention to institution building and public administration. For exceptions on the latter point, see Latham, *Modernization as Ideology*, 86, 181. Gilman does focus on the role of (academic) institutions in the formation of modernization theory, but does not treat the role of institutions in the actual American practices of modernization in other countries. Other relevant pieces that do not cover American universities' overseas institution building include Edward H. Berman, *The Influence of the Carnegie, Ford, and Rockefeller Foundations on American Foreign Policy: The Ideology of Philanthropy* (Albany: SUNY Press, 1983) and "Rockefeller Philanthropy and the Social Sciences: International Perspectives," in *The Development of the Social Sciences in the United States and Canada: The Role of Philanthropy*, ed. Theresa Richardson and Donald Fisher (Stamford, CT: Ablex, 1999). The only substantial historical account that does so is Richard Garlitz, *A Mission for Development: Utah Universities and the Point Four Program in Iran* (Logan: Utah State University Press, 2018). There is a brief, general, not archivally based account of US government-sponsored university work overseas in Vernon W. Ruttan, *United States Development Assistance Policy: The Domestic Politics of Foreign Economic Aid* (Baltimore: Johns Hopkins University Press, 1996), 204–220.

There is also a brief treatment of a UC Berkeley program in Indonesia in Parmar, *Foundations of the American Century*, 135–142. James M. Carter's book on American state building in South Vietnam takes administration seriously and describes Michigan State University's contribution to the project but does not center on university institution building. *Inventing Vietnam: The United States and State Building, 1954–1968* (Cambridge, UK: Cambridge University Press, 2008). Another recent work that gives some attention to institution building and briefly mentions the role of universities is Gregg Brazinsky, *Nation Building in South Korea: Koreans, Americans, and the Making of a Democracy* (Chapel Hill: University of North Carolina Press, 2007). A sociological approach to similar material can be found in Eunhye Yoo, "Globalization, Power, and Knowledge Production in South Korea: The University of Minnesota-Seoul National University Educational Cooperation Project from 1954 to 1962" (PhD diss., University of Minnesota, 2012). My argument about the importance of public administration provides a corrective to the tendency in recent literature to emphasize the centrality of agriculture and of social scientific thinking about poverty in forming development policy and practices. Agriculture played an important role in launching the US government's university contracts abroad program but was far from its only focus. See Nicole Sackley, "Passage to Modernity: American Social Scientists, India, and the Pursuit of Development, 1945–61" (PhD diss., Princeton University, 2004); Paul Burnett, "The Visible Land: Agricultural Economics, US Export Agriculture, and International Development, 1918–1965" (PhD diss., University of Pennsylvania, 2008); Sheyda Jahanbani, "'A Different Kind of People': The Poor at Home and Abroad, 1935–1968" (PhD diss., Brown University, 2009); Nick Cullather, *The Hungry World: America's Cold War Battle against Poverty in Asia* (Cambridge, MA: Harvard University Press, 2010). Even the best contemporaneous account of the university contract program erroneously claimed that "projects were exclusively oriented toward agricultural and rural development" through mid-1953, ignoring the public administration work that began in 1952. John M. Richardson Jr., *Partners in Development: An Analysis of AID-University Relations 1950–1966* (East Lansing: Michigan State University Press, 1969), 10, cf. 32. Daniel Immerwahr, *Thinking Small: The United States and the Lure of Community Development* (Cambridge, MA: Harvard University Press, 2015), recovers the communitarian strain in postwar US development programs but also does not address public administration.

7. On Point Four, see Stephen Macekura, "The Point Four Program and U.S. International Development Policy," *Political Science Quarterly* 128 (Spring 2013): 127–160.

8. Harry S. Truman, inaugural address, January 20, 1949.

9. Quoted in Amanda Kay McVety, *Enlightened Aid: U.S. Development as Foreign Policy in Ethiopia* (New York: Oxford University Press, 2012), 97, 99, 103.

10. On the debate over writing Point Four into law see McVety, *Enlightened Aid*, 96–104.

11. Ibid., 112–114; Richardson, *Partners in Development*, 30; Richard D. McKinzie, Oral History Interview with Stanley Andrews, October 31, 1970, Harry S. Truman Library and Museum, http://www.trumanlibrary.org/oralhist/andrewss.htm, accessed September 17, 2018, 29; Mutual Security Act of 1951.

12. McVety, *Enlightened Aid*, 128.

13. Department of State, Office of the Historian, http://history.state.gov /departmenthistory, accessed September 17, 2018.

14. 1956 ICA staff telephone directory, KPR, Box 4.

15. Dean Rusk, "Observations on Foreign Relations of American Universities," in *Education Without Boundaries: Addresses and Summary of Proceedings of the Conference on University Contracts Abroad, Washington, D.C., November 13–14, 1958*, ed. Richard A. Humphrey (Washington, DC: American Council on Education, 1959), 27. Richardson commented that "it is impossible to say whether or not one man first envisioned a program involving the university as an instrument of technical assistance." *Partners in Development*, 13.

16. Richardson, *Partners in Development*, 14.

17. McKinzie, Oral History Interview with Stanley Andrews, 134; John A. Hannah, "Universities Expectations of Government," in *University Projects Abroad: Papers Presented at the Conference on University Contracts Abroad, Michigan State University, November 17–18, 1955*, ed. Richard A. Humphrey (Washington, DC: American Council on Education, 1956), 51.

18. Henry G. Bennett, "The Human Side of Point Four," in *Proceedings of the Association of Land-Grant Colleges and Universities*, Sixty-Fifth Annual Convention, Houston, Texas, November 13–15, 1951, 69.

19. Hannah, "Universities Expectations of Government," 51.

20. Richardson, *Partners in Development*, 15.

21. Ibid., 29.

22. McKinzie, Oral History Interview with Stanley Andrews, 1–34.

23. "Panama and University of Arkansas Strengthening Ties," February 19, 2010, http://www.thepanamadigest.com/2010/02/panama-and-university-of-arkansas-strengthening-ties/, accessed September 17, 2018; McVety, *Enlightened Aid*, 127; John A. Hannah, *A Memoir* (East Lansing: Michigan State University Press, 1980); Edward Danforth Eddy Jr., *Colleges for Our Land and Time: The Land-Grant Idea in American Education* (New York: Harper, 1956), 252; Edward W. Weidner et al., *The International Programs of American Universities* (East Lansing: Michigan State University Institute of Research on Overseas Programs, 1958).

24. Richardson, *Partners in Development*, 17–25.

25. Edward W. Weidner, *Technical Assistance in Public Administration Overseas: The Case for Development Administration* (Chicago: Public Administration Service, 1964), 40.

26. Richardson, *Partners in Development*, 34–35; HES, "Technical Service Overseas," in *Proceedings of the Association of Land-Grant Colleges and Universities*, Sixty-Seventh Annual Convention, Columbus, Ohio, November 10–12, 1953, 52–57.

27. Stassen, "Technical Service Overseas," 55. On modernization theorists' analogies to American history see Latham, *Modernization as Ideology*; Gilman, *Mandarins of the Future*.

28. Richardson, *Partners in Development*, 37. The quote is from unnamed FOA officials.

29. Ibid., 41.

30. Ibid., 35.

31. Ibid., 37.

32. ICA reported sixty-six contracts in operation as of June 30, 1955 (Stassen actually resigned in March), but Richardson claims there were eighty-one contracts at the end of Stassen's tenure. ICA *Operations Report*, data as of June 30, 1961, 26;

Richardson, *Partners in Development*, 43. The dramatic expansion of the university contract program under Stassen abets the interpretation in Macekura, "The Point Four Program," which even without mentioning university contracts, correctly argues against other scholars that the development impulse did not wither when technical assistance became administratively combined with military and economic aid under MSA and then FOA auspices. For example, Stassen's push for university contracts contradicts the judgment of Darlene Rivas, who claimed that "technical assistance programs in particular suffered on administrator Harold Stassen's watch." *Missionary Capitalist: Nelson Rockefeller in Venezuela* (Chapel Hill: University of North Carolina Press, 2002), 202.

33. D. A. FitzGerald, "Government Expectations of Universities," in *University Projects Abroad*, ed. Humphrey, 44.

34. ICA *Operations Report*, data as of June 30, 1961, 26; Richardson, *Partners in Development*, 43.

35. ICA, "University Contracts in Operation by Country as of Sept. 30, 1957," KPR, Box 4.

36. ICA, "Quarterly Summary Statements: ICA-Financed University Contracts in Operation as of September 30, 1957," KPR, Box 4. India's prominence in the university contracts program undermines Dennis Merrill's claim that by the mid-1950s "the American undertaking in India continued to be an extremely limited one. Low-level funding prevented the expansion of American activities beyond the agricultural sector." Merrill, *Bread and the Ballot: The United States and India's Economic Development, 1947–1963* (Chapel Hill: University of North Carolina Press, 1990), 122. In fact, five of the ten university contracts in India focused outside agriculture: two with the Ministry of Education and three to build engineering programs in institutions of higher learning. On US attempts to balance aid to India and Pakistan, see Robert J. McMahon, *The Cold War on the Periphery: The United States, India, and Pakistan* (New York: Columbia University Press, 1994).

37. "US Foreign Policy Briefing for University Officials Participating in Technical Assistance Program," April 18, 1956, UPOPR, Box 69, Folder: American Council on Education (Institutional Projects Abroad, Committee on)—I 1955–60.

38. "Basic FOA Policy on University Contracts," June 13, 1955, KPR, Box 4. This list was similar to what Stassen had laid out when proposing the expanded program to ALGCU in November 1953: "agriculture . . . medicine, home economics, engineering, administrative and business services . . . water resources and related activities." Stassen, "Technical Service Overseas," 55.

39. *Handbook of Training in the Public Service* (New York: United Nations, 1966), 4–5.

40. *A Handbook of Public Administration: Current Concepts and Practice with Special Reference to Developing Countries* (New York: United Nations, 1961), 1.

41. Herbert Emmerich, *Administrative Roadblocks to Co-ordinated Development* (New York: United Nations, 1961).

42. Bronfenbrenner, *Academic Encounter*, 42.

43. Arthur S. Adams, "Foreword," in *University Projects Abroad*, ed. Humphrey, v; Brooks Hays, "Educational Cooperation, Instrument of National Policy," *Educational Record* 37 (July 1956): 192–195.

44. "Summary of a Research Project on Overseas Programs of American Universities," Institute of Research on Overseas Programs, Michigan State University, 1957,

KPR, Box 3, Folder: Michigan State—Research on Overseas Programs. Emphasis added. The Carnegie project produced books such as Bronfenbrenner, *Academic Encounter*; Weidner et al., *The International Programs of American Universities*; Richard N. Adams and Charles C. Cumberland, *United States University Cooperation in Latin America: A Study Based on Selected Programs in Bolivia, Chile, Peru and Mexico* (East Lansing: Michigan State University Institute of Research on Overseas Programs, 1960); Henry C. Hart, *Campus India: An Appraisal of American College Programs in India* (East Lansing: Michigan State University Press, 1961); Edward W. Weidner, *The World Role of Universities* (New York: McGraw-Hill, 1962); Walter Adams and John A. Garraty, *Is the World Our Campus?* (East Lansing: Michigan State University Press, 1960). The last title is the most discerning and critical work in the literature that proliferated around 1960 on universities' overseas institution building.

45. "Blueprint and Experience: Universities as Instruments of Technical Cooperation," Conference on University Contracts Abroad, November 14–15, 1957, KPR, Box 2, Folder: Committee on Institutional Projects Abroad.

46. Committee on the University and World Affairs, *The University and World Affairs* (New York: Ford Foundation, n.d. [1960?]), 46, emphasis original.

47. Ibid. 13.

48. Ibid., 1.

49. Walter H. C. Laves, "Some Educational Issues Involved in the Contract Program," in *University Projects Abroad*, ed. Humphrey, 3.

50. Roland R. Renne, "Integration of the Contract Program into Future Academic Programs," in *University Projects Abroad*, ed. Humphrey, 39.

51. Committee on the University and World Affairs, *The University and World Affairs*, 52.

52. *The Almanac*, March 1957, clipping in AR, Box 2003, Folder: "Palmer, Norman." Unusually among American universities, Wharton housed Penn's departments of economics, political science, and sociology until the mid-1970s.

53. University of Pennsylvania News Release, September 14, 1947, NPAR, Folder: "Palmer, Norman D."

54. Statement of Norman D. Palmer . . . before the Subcommittee on Technical Assistance Programs of the Senate Committee on Foreign Relations, February 24, 1955, KPR, Box 3, Folder: Correspondence—General (1954–1955) [hereafter CG54].

55. Norman Dunbar Palmer and Howard C. Perkins, *International Relations; the World Community in Transition* (Boston: Houghton Mifflin, 1953).

56. Joan Woollcott, "The Palmers Bring Tokens of the Orient to Suburbia, U.S.A." *Philadelphia Inquirer*, November 16, 1958, clipping in AR, Box 2003, Folder: "Palmer, Norman."

57. On United States–Pakistan relations see R. C. Gupta, *U.S. Policy Towards India and Pakistan* (Delhi: B. R. Publishing, 1977); McMahon, *The Cold War on the Periphery*; Dennis Kux, *The United States and Pakistan 1947–2000: Disenchanted Allies* (Washington, DC: Woodrow Wilson Center Press, and Baltimore: Johns Hopkins University Press, 2001); Lubna Saif, *Authoritarianism and Underdevelopment in Pakistan 1947–1958: The Role of the Punjab* (Oxford: Oxford University Press, 2010).

58. Merrill, *Bread and the Ballot*, 103.

59. Quoted in ibid., 104.

60. Ibid., 104–105. Quote is on 104.

61. USOM/Pakistan monthly report, March 1954, KPR, Box 2, Folder: Correspondence—ICA (General) #1; "Wharton Sends Staff to Pakistan," *Collegiate News and Views*, December 1954, clipping in WSODR, Box 23, Folder: Karachi Project.

62. Foreign Operations Administration, *American Universities in Technical Cooperation* (1954), 13–15, UPOPR, Box 50, Folder: Fine Arts, School of (General)—II 1950–55 [hereafter SFA50].

63. NDP, "Partial list of Persons Consulted in Karachi, April 12–24 . . ." KPR, Box 3, Folder: CG54.

64. NDP to C. Canby Balderston, April 24, 1954, KPR, Box 3, Folder: CG54; NDP to Philip Newman, June 18, 1954, KPR, Box 3, Folder: CG54.

65. Philip Newman to NDP, July 20, 1954; Philip Newman to NDP, n.d. [early 1955], KPR, Box 3, Folder: CG54.

66. Winfield P. Niblio to NDP, June 8, 1954, KPR, Box 3, Folder: CG54.

67. L. A. Wilson to G. Wright Hoffman, July 15, 1954, KPR, Box 3, Folder: CG54.

68. NDP to Balderston, 24 April 1954.

69. ICA, *Technical Cooperation in Education* (Washington, DC: 1960), 6.

70. C. Canby Balderston to E. B. Williams, May 7, 1954, KPR, Box 3, Folder: CG54.

71. GPH to Ben Selfon, May 27, 1954, UPOPR, Box 66, Folder: Wharton School (General)—IV 1950–1955.

72. Contract between the Foreign Operations Administration and the Trustees of the University of Pennsylvania, September 24, 1954, WSODR, Box 23, Folder: Karachi Project.

73. It appears that not all ICA university contracts provided for overhead, but in some it was a significant incentive for the university. For examples, see Bronfenbrenner, *Academic Encounter*, 174, 196.

74. Adams and Garraty, *Is the World Our Campus?* 111.

75. Donald S. Murray to GPH, July 29, 1957, UPOPR, Box 114, Folder: Wharton School (Karachi Project)—III 1955–1960 [hereafter KP III].

76. Contract, September 24, 1954.

77. GPH to Deficit Budget Administrators, January 7, 1954, WSODR, Box 25, Folder: Budget Information 1953–4; Memorandum from the President to Budget Administrators, March 5, 1954, WSODR, Box 26, Folder: Preliminary Discussions Budget 1954–5.

78. Untitled document, n.d., WSODR, Box 25, Folder: Budget Information—Spring—1954.

79. "Chronology of Budget Crisis Spring 1954," WSODR, Box 25, Folder: Budget Information—Spring—1954.

80. C. Canby Balderston, "Long-Range Policy for the Wharton School, March 4, 1954," WSODR, Box 26, Folder: Budget Information.

81. Untitled document, n.d., WSODR, Box 25, Folder: Budget Information—Spring—1954.

82. HES to NDP, June 11, 1954, KPR, Box 2, Folder: Correspondence—ICA (General) #1.

83. Richardson, *Partners in Development*, 45; Statement of Norman D. Palmer, February 24, 1955.

84. Adams and Cumberland, *United States University Cooperation in Latin America*, 228.

85. Ibid., 226–234.

86. "Summary—Ankara Project," May 11, 1955, UPOPR, Box 50, Folder: SFA50; Nancy Thorne, Transcribed Interview with G. Holmes Perkins, July 26, 2002, 13, 054.517a, GHPC.

87. Thorne, Transcribed Interview with G. Holmes Perkins, 13–14.

88. HES to GPH, November 23, 1954, UPOPR, Box 50, Folder: SFA50.

89. G. Holmes Perkins to Edwin B. Williams, December 15, 1954, UPOPR, Box 50, Folder: SFA50.

90. For a similar account of Stassen using his connections to establish an FOA contract (with the University of Minnesota, his alma mater, which he supervised for a period as Minnesota's governor), see Bronfenbrenner, *Academic Encounter*, 173.

91. "Wharton to set up Karachi Business School," *Daily Pennsylvanian*, September 30, 1954; "University of Karachi Announcement, Two-Year Graduate Programme, Institute of Public and Business Administration," UPOPR, Box 114, Folder: Wharton School (Karachi Project)—I 1955–1960 [hereafter KP I]; "Wharton Sends Staff to Pakistan"; A. B. A. Haleem to G. Wright Hoffman, December 19, 1954, WSODR, Box 23, Folder: Karachi Project.

92. NDP to CKS, April 30, 1958, KPR, Box 2, Folder: Correspondence—ICA (Shaw).

93. T. W. Schultz, "Critical Appraisal of the Main Strengths and Weaknesses of the Program," in *University Projects Abroad*, ed. Humphrey, 36.

94. Contract, September 24, 1954.

95. Thomas A. Budd to Harvey Sherman, January 14, 1955, and Anne I. Spock to NDP, February 24, 1955, KPR, Box 1, Folder: Personnel—Wixon; C. Canby Balderston to Edwin B. Williams, July 6, 1954, WSODR, Box 25, Folder: Budget Correspondence 1953–54.

96. "Long-Range Policy for the Wharton School, March 4, 1954," WSODR, Box 26, Folder: Budget Information.

97. "Institute of Public and Business Administration, University of Karachi, Announcement," April 1956, UPOPR, Box 114, Folder: KP I.

98. Roger F. Evans to Marion Pond, August 1, 1956, UPOPR, Box 114, Folder: KP I.

99. Rufus Wixon to NDP, October 31, 1955, KPR, Box 1, Folder: Personnel—Wixon.

100. ICA Airgram, "USOM/P Evaluation of the University of Pennsylvania Contract," April 11, 1957, KPR, Box 2, Folder: Correspondence—ICA (General) #1.

101. McMahon, *The Cold War on the Periphery*, 211.

102. CKS to NDP, September 20, 1957, KPR, Box 2, Folder: Correspondence—ICA (Shaw).

103. NDP to CKS, September 24, 1957, KPR, Box 2, Folder: Correspondence—ICA (Shaw).

104. NDP, "Evaluation of the Policy Statement of the Committee on Institutional Projects Abroad," in *University Projects Abroad*, ed. Humphrey, 26.

105. John B. Fox to NDP, December 6, 1955, KPR, Box 3, Folder: CG54. The coordinator of research at Cornell University also praised Palmer along similar lines; John W. Hastie to NDP, December 12, 1955, KPR, Box 3, Folder: CG54.

106. GPH to C. A. Kulp, May 31, 1957, UPOPR, Box 114, Folder: Wharton School (Karachi Project)—II 1955–1960 [hereafter KP II].

107. GPH to Jonathan Rhoads, May 14, 1957, UPOPR, Box 114, Folder: KP II.

108. CKS to GPH, March 3, 1958, UPOPR, Box 114, Folder: KP III.

109. GPH to Jonathan Rhoads, Willis J. Winn, and NDP, March 7, 1958, UPOPR, Box 114, Folder: KP III.

110. NDP to GPH, March 17, 1958, UPOPR, Box 114, Folder: KP III.

111. CKS to NDP, April 25, 1958, UPOPR, Box 114, Folder: KP III.

112. Palmer, "Evaluation of the Policy Statement of the Committee on Institutional Projects Abroad," 20.

113. ACE Office on Institutional Projects Abroad, "A Summary of Institutional Views on the University Contract Program," KPR, Box 2, Folder: Committee on Institutional Projects Abroad.

114. Committee on the University and World Affairs, *The University and World Affairs*, 36, 34.

115. Project Proposal & Approval Summary (PPA) FY 1959, November 7, 1958, KPR, Box 2, Folder: Correspondence—ICA (General) #2 [hereafter ICA2].

116. ICA Washington, ICA Airgram to USOM Karachi, January 7, 1959, KPR, Box 2, Folder: ICA2.

117. [James S. Killen?], ICA Airgram to CKS, January 16, 1959, KPR, Box 2, Folder: ICA2. It is difficult to determine the actual author or share of contributions to ICA documents like this one. It was "drafted" by R. W. Reinhold, "authorized" by G. St. Louis, and "signed" by Killen. Presumably, Killen as USOM director had final authority over the contents.

118. NDP to Charles W. Fredriksen, January 27, 1959, KPR, Box 2, Folder: ICA2.

119. Willis J. Winn to G. W. Lawson Jr., February 2, 1959, KPR, Box 2, Folder: ICA2.

120. Norman D. Palmer to G. W. Lawson Jr., March 9, 1959, KPR, Box 2, Folder: ICA2.

121. GPH to Arthur S. Adams, March 18, 1959, UPOPR, Box 114, Folder: Wharton School (Karachi Project)—IV 1955–1960 [hereafter KP IV].

122. Willis J. Winn to G. W. Lawson Jr., April 13, 1959, KPR, Box 2, Folder: ICA2.

123. NDP to Arthur Adams, March 18 1959, KPR, Box 2, Correspondence—General (1959); Harnwell to Adams, March 18, 1959.

124. GPH to Sen. Joseph S. Clark, April 27, 1959, UPOPR, Box 114, Folder: Wharton School (Karachi Project)—V 1955–1960 [hereafter KP V].

125. Willis J. Winn to Ross M. Trump, May 20, 1959, KPR, Box 2, Correspondence—General (1959).

126. G. W. Lawson Jr. to Willis J. Winn, March 23, 1959, UPOPR, Box 114, Folder: KP IV.

127. Draft of public protest by University of Pennsylvania, n.d. [written between April 20–27, 1959], KPR, Box 2, Correspondence—General (1959).

128. Lawson to Winn, March 23, 1959.

129. NDP to G. W. Lawson Jr., March 21, 1959, KPR, Box 2, Folder: ICA2.

130. Winn to Lawson, April 13, 1959.

131. GPH to G. W. Lawson Jr., April 14, 1959, KPR, Box 2, Folder: ICA2; Winn to Trump, May 20, 1959.

132. GPH to Clark, April 27, 1959.

133. Ibid.; Edward Kunze to GPH, April 20, 1959, KPR, Box 2, Folder: ICA2.

134. GPH to Lawson, April 14, 1959.

135. Winn to Lawson, April 13, 1959. On his deaning, also see Winn to Trump, May 20, 1959.

136. Kunze to GPH, April 20, 1959.

137. Winn to Trump, May 20, 1959.

138. GPH to Clark, April 27, 1959.

139. Sen. Joseph S. Clark to GPH, August 20, 1959, UPOPR, Box 114, Folder: KP V.

140. GPH to Sen. Joseph S. Clark, August 28, 1959, UPOPR, Box 114, Folder: KP V.

141. GPH to Edward Kunze, draft not sent, KPR, Box 2, Folder: ICA2.

142. Winn to Trump, May 20, 1959.

143. GPH to President Mohammad Ayub Khan, May 6, 1959, UPOPR, Box 114, Folder: KP V.

144. G. Wright Hoffman to James S. Killen, May 14, 1959, UPOPR, Box 114, Folder: KP V.

145. Harnwell to Clark, April 27, 1959.

146. Draft of public protest.

147. Willis J. Winn to CKS, May 12, 1959, UPOPR, Box 114, Folder: KP V.

148. Winn to Trump, May 20, 1959.

149. NDP to O. B. Conway, July 8, 1959, KPR, Box 2, Correspondence—General (1959).

150. Wesley E. Bjur, *Institution Building in an Emerging Nation: Pakistan* (Los Angeles: University of Southern California, 1968), 70–71.

151. Ibid., 66, 71.

152. Contract No. AIDc-1690, quoted in Ibid., 24.

153. Bjur, *Institution Building*, 35.

154. Weidner, *Technical Assistance in Public Administration Overseas*, 40.

155. Wesley E. Bjur, "Technical Assistance and Institution Building: A University Experience in Brazil" (PhD diss., Claremont Graduate University, 1967).

156. Bjur, *Institution Building*, 21.

157. Ibid., 22.

158. Ibid., 33.

159. Bjur, "Technical Assistance and Institution Building," 62, 73.

160. M. W. Abbasi, "Civil Services," in *Introducing Pakistan*, ed. Muzaffar Qadir and Iftikhar Ahmad (Lahore, PAK: National Institute of Public Administration, 1966), 108–109, quoted in Bjur, *Institution Building*, 21.

161. Abbasi, "Civil Services," 110 [not quoted by Bjur].

162. Bjur, *Institution Building*, 22, 25.

163. Ibid., 20.

164. Ibid., 51–54.

165. Qadir and Ahmad, eds., *Introducing Pakistan*, 90n5.

166. Bjur, *Institution Building*, 25, 56, 44.

167. Ibid., 44–48.

168. Ibid., 37.

169. Ibid., 39.

170. Ibid., 40.

171. Ibid.; Philip Selznick, *Leadership in Administration: A Sociological Interpretation* (Evanston, IL: Row, Peterson, 1957).

172. Selznick, *Leadership in Administration*, 5, emphasis original.

173. Charles Perrow, *Complex Organizations: A Critical Essay*, 3rd ed. (New York: McGraw-Hill, 1986), chap. 5; see especially 157n2 on the trajectory of Selznick's publications.

174. For surveys of the literature on institution building, see Hans C. Blaise, *The Literature on Institution Building (A Bibliographic Note)* (Pittsburgh: University of Pittsburgh, 1964); and especially Melvin G. Blase, *Institution Building: A Source Book*, rev. ed. (Columbia: University of Missouri Press, 1986 [1972]).

175. On Cleveland's career, see David Ekbladh, *The Great American Mission: Modernization and the Construction of an American World Order* (Princeton, NJ: Princeton University Press, 2010), 168–171. Ekbladh notes that Cleveland believed "it was less important what task a modernization project performed so long as it built institutions to administer various aspects of social life" (p. 169), but he does not systematically trace Cleveland's thought about institution building.

176. Harlan Cleveland, *The Theory and Practice of Foreign Aid* (Syracuse, NY: Syracuse University, 1956).

177. Ibid., 43, 45.

178. Harlan Cleveland and Gerard J. Mangone, eds., *The Art of Overseasmanship: Americans at Work Abroad* (Syracuse, NY: Syracuse University Press, 1957), vii, viii.

179. Harlan Cleveland, "Institution-Building: Some Lessons from Foreign Aid," in *The Art of Overseasmanship*, ed. Cleveland and Mangone, 105.

180. Ibid., 112.

181. Harlan Cleveland, Gerard J. Mangone, and John Clarke Adams, *The Overseas Americans* (New York: McGraw-Hill, 1960).

182. Bjur, "Technical Assistance and Institution Building."

183. Committee on the University and World Affairs, *The University and World Affairs*, 56.

184. Latham, *Modernization as Ideology*, 86.

185. *A Handbook of Public Administration*, 3.

186. Arthur Goldschmidt, "Technology in Emerging Countries," *Technology and Culture* 3 (Autumn 1962): 581–600. On Goldschmidt's career, see Ekbladh, *The Great American Mission*, 206–209.

187. Goldschmidt, "Technology in Emerging Countries," 592.

188. Ibid., 592–593.

189. Ibid., 594.

190. Bjur, *Institution Building*, 39.

191. Richard L. Duncan and William S. Pooler, *Technical Assistance and Institution Building* (Pittsburgh: University of Pittsburgh, 1967).

192. Bjur, *Institution Building*, 45.

193. Ibid., 66. This new director replaced Killen's replacement.

194. Ibid., 46.

195. Ibid., 46, 67.

196. Joseph B. Robinson, Richard J. Isadore, and Humayun Khan, "Report on Present Status and Future Prospects of National Institutes of Public Administration," quoted in Bjur, *Institution Building*, 70.

197. Ibid., 80.

198. AID *Operations Report* for December 31, 1966, June 30, 1970, and June 30, 1973; Report of the Comptroller General of the United States, "Strengthening and Using Universities as a Resource for Developing Countries," n.d. [1976], 2, https://www.gao .gov/assets/120/115849.pdf, accessed October 2, 2018.

199. "Strengthening and Using Universities," 5.

200. Ibid., iv.

201. Ibid., 2.

202. Ibid., 46.

203. U.S. Agency for International Development, "Contracts and Grants and Co-operative Agreements with Universities, Firms and Non-Profit Institutions Active During the Period October 1, 1995—September 30, 1996. Fiscal Year 1996," http://pdf .AID.gov/pdf_docs/pnacf508.pdf, accessed 23 May 2012 (site discontinued). A more detailed account of AID-university contract activity through 1996 is available in Ruttan, *United States Development Assistance Policy*.

5. A Use of the University of Michigan

1. George Sullivan, *The Story of the Peace Corps* (New York: Fleet Publishing, 1964), 28, 31.

2. This account is taken from James Tobin, "JFK at the Union: The Unknown Story of the Peace Corps Speech," *Michigan Today*, January 15, 2008.

3. Sargent Shriver, quoted in ibid.

4. Harris Wofford, *Of Kennedys and Kings: Making Sense of the Sixties* (Pittsburgh: University of Pittsburgh Press, 1992 [1980]), chap. 8.

5. Sullivan, *The Story of the Peace Corps*, 29–31; SPH, *An International Peace Corps: The Promise and the Problems* (Washington, DC: Public Affairs Institute, 1961).

6. Hayes, *An International Peace Corps*, 39

7. Sullivan, *The Story of the Peace Corps*, 31.

8. Hayes, *An International Peace Corps*, 10, 27.

9. On the Peace Corps, modernity, and social engineering, see Michael E. Latham, *Modernization as Ideology: American Social Science and "Nation Building" in the Kennedy Era* (Chapel Hill: University of North Carolina Press, 2000).

10. On the relationship of behavioral science and economics, see Jefferson Pooley and Mark Solovey, "Marginal to the Revolution: The Curious Relationship between Economics and the Behavioral Sciences Movement in Mid-20th Century America," in *The Unsocial Social Science? Economics and Neighboring Disciplines since 1945*, ed. Roger E. Backhouse and Philippe Fontaine (Durham, NC: Duke University Press, 2010).

11. Gerald M. Meier, *Biography of a Subject: An Evolution of Development Economics* (New York: Oxford University Press, 2005), 41.

12. H. W. Arndt, "Development Economics Before 1945," in *Development and Planning: Essays in Honor of Paul Rosenstein-Rodan*, ed. Jagdish Bhagwati (Cambridge, MA: MIT Press, 1973), 124.

13. Ibid., 125.

14. Institute of Social Studies, "Paul Rosenstein-Rodan," https://www.iss.nl/en /about-iss/honorary-fellows/paul-rosenstein-rodan, accessed October 2, 2018; Sukhamoy

Chakravarty, "Paul Rosenstein-Rodan: An Appreciation," *World Development* 11, no. 1 (1983): 73–75.

15. Gerald M. Meier, "From Colonial Economics to Development Economics," in *From Classical Economics to Development Economics*, ed. Meier (New York: St. Martin's, 1994), 174.

16. Pranab Bardhan and Christopher Udry, eds., *Readings in Development Economics Volume I, Micro-Theory* (Cambridge, MA: MIT Press, 2000), ix.

17. Meier, "From Colonial Economics to Development Economics," 175.

18. Kurt Mandelbaum, *The Industrialisation of Backward Areas* (Oxford: Basil Blackwell, 1945), iii.

19. Martin Jay, *The Dialectical Imagination: A History of the Frankfurt School and the Institute of Social Research, 1923–1950* (Boston: Little, Brown, 1973).

20. Mandelbaum, *The Industrialisation of Backward Areas*, iii.

21. Ibid., 3.

22. Albert O. Hirschman, "The Rise and Decline of Development Economics," in *The Theory and Experience of Economic Development: Essays in Honor of Sir W. Arthur Lewis*, ed. Mark Gersovitz et al. (London: Allen & Unwin, 1982), 375–376; see also Tamas Szentes, "Development in the History of Economics," in *The Origins of Development Economics: How Schools of Economic Thought Have Addressed Development*, ed. Jomo K.S. and Erik S. Reinert (London: Zed Books, 2005).

23. George Stathakis and Gianni Vaggi, eds., *Economic Development and Social Change: Historical Roots and Modern Perspectives* (London: Routledge, 2006), 19.

24. Hirschman, "The Rise and Decline of Development Economics," 377.

25. W. Arthur Lewis, "Economic Development with Unlimited Supply of Labour," *Manchester School of Economic and Social Studies* 22 (May 1954): 134–191; Lewis, *The Theory of Economic Growth* (London: Allen & Unwin, 1955).

26. P. F. Leeson, "Kurt Martin 1904–1995," *Manchester School of Economic and Social Studies* 64, no. 1 (1996): 112–113.

27. Ronald Findlay, "On W. Arthur Lewis's Contributions to Economics," in *The Theory and Experience of Economic Development*, ed. Gersovitz et al., 3.

28. Robert L. Tignor, *W. Arthur Lewis and the Birth of Development Economics* (Princeton, NJ: Princeton University Press, 2005).

29. Manning Nash, ed., *Essays on Economic Development and Cultural Change* (Chicago: University of Chicago Press, 1977), v. For more on Hoselitz, see Nicole Sackley, "Passage to Modernity: American Social Scientists, India, and the Pursuit of Development, 1945–1961" (PhD diss., Princeton University, 2004), 143–149.

30. "Editorial," *Economic Development and Cultural Change* 1, no. 2 (1953): 83–86; Bert F. Hoselitz, "Non-Economic Barriers to Economic Development," *Economic Development and Cultural Change* 1, no. 1 (1952): 8–21.

31. "Hoselitz, Bert F.," in *Who's Who in Economics*, 3rd ed., ed. Mark Blaug (Cheltenham, UK: Edward Elgar, 1999), 550.

32. Nils Gilman, *Mandarins of the Future: Modernization Theory in Cold War America* (Baltimore: Johns Hopkins University Press, 2003), 160.

33. SPH, "Voters Attitudes Toward Men and Issues" (PhD diss., Yale University, 1934).

34. Guide to the Samuel P. Hayes Personal Papers (#101), John F. Kennedy Library, https://www.jfklibrary.org/Asset-Viewer/Archives/SPHPP.aspx?f=1, accessed October 2, 2018.

35. SPH, "Point Four in United States Foreign Policy," *Annals of the American Academy of Political and Social Science*, vol. 268, "Aiding Underdeveloped Areas Abroad" (March 1950): 27–35.

36. SPH, *The Beginning of American Aid to Southeast Asia: The Griffin Mission of 1950* (Lexington, MA: Heath Lexington, 1971); SPH [published anonymously], "Foreign Technical Assistance in Economic Development in a Newly Independent Country: Some Observations in Indonesia," *Economic Development and Cultural Change* 1, no. 1 (1952): 73–80. This publication is notable because it appeared in the first issue of this journal, the significance of which is described above.

37. This account of Hayes's government service draws heavily on Richard D. McKinzie, Oral History Interview with Samuel P. Hayes, Harry S. Truman Library and Museum, http://www.trumanlibrary.org/oralhist/hayessp.htm, accessed September 17, 2018.

38. Jean Converse, *Survey Research in the United States: Roots and Emergence 1890–1960* (Berkeley: University of California Press, 1987), 493n15.

39. CK to RGS, December 10, 1950, UCOP3, Box 41, Folder 28.

40. Roger L. Geiger, *Research and Relevant Knowledge: American Research Universities since World War II* (New York: Oxford University Press, 1993), 53.

41. David A. Hollinger, "Academic Culture at the University of Michigan, 1938–1988," in *Science, Jews, and Secular Culture: Studies in Mid-Twentieth-Century American Intellectual History* (Princeton, NJ: Princeton University Press, 1996), 121–154; Ron Robin, *The Making of the Cold War Enemy: Culture and Politics in the Military-Industrial Complex* (Princeton, NJ: Princeton University Press, 2001), chap. 1.

42. Floris Heukelom, *Behavioral Economics: A History* (Cambridge, UK: Cambridge University Press, 2014), 4.

43. Irving Morrissett, "Business and Behavior Research," *Journal of Marketing* 20, no. 1 (1955): 59–61; http://www.icos.umich.edu/content/the-likert-prize, accessed 8 December 2008 (site discontinued).

44. Rensis Likert and SPH, eds., *Some Applications of Behavioural Research* (Place de Fontenoy, FR: 1957).

45. Ibid., 9.

46. Ibid., 10.

47. SPH, "Relating Behavioural Research to the Problems of Organizations," in *Some Applications of Behavioural Research*, ed. Likert and Hayes, 316.

48. Ibid., 317.

49. "Draft proposal to the Office of Education," n.d. [probably November 1959], 15–16, CRED, Box 2, Folder: CRED—Administration—History—1956 to 1992 [hereafter CRED].

50. Kenneth E. Boulding, SPH, Charles F. Remer, and Wolfgang F. Stolper, "Proposal for a Center for Economic Development at the University of Michigan," December 21, 1956, CRED, Box 2, Folder: CRED. Hayes wrote this document with advice from the others; the names were listed alphabetically.

51. CK to RGS, 14 March 1955, UCOP3, Box 33, Folder 6.

52. Kenneth E. Boulding, "Evidences for an Administrative Science: A Review of the Administrative Science Quarterly, Volumes 1 and 2," *Administrative Science Quarterly* 3, no. 1 (1958): 1–22.

53. Maochun Yu, *OSS in China: Prelude to Cold War* (New Haven, CT: Yale University Press, 1996), 10–11.

54. Ralph A. Sawyer to Ronald Freeman, October 21, 1960, CLSAR, Box 128, Folder: Department of Economics 1960–61.

55. "Memorandum of Discussion at the first meeting of the Executive Committee, Center for Research on Economic Development, Friday, October 27, 1961," DER, Box 3, Folder: Center for Econ. Development Research [hereafter CEDR].

56. Richard Musgrave, Wolfgang F. Stolper, SPH, and Charles F. Remer, Memorandum to the Executive Committee [Department of Economics], n.d. [late 1956/early 1957], DER, Box 3, Folder: CEDR.

57. Boulding, SPH, et al., "Proposal for a Center for Economic Development."

58. SPH, "Summary of Conversations—May 23, 1958," CRED, Box 2, Folder: CRED.

59. Musgrave et al., Memorandum to the Executive Committee.

60. GA to Economics Department Staff, July 29, 1958, DER, Box 3, Folder: CEDR.

61. Roger W. Heyns to Burton D. Thuma, June 27, 1958, CLSAR, Box 113, Folder: Department of Economics, 1957–58.

62. GA, "Outline of an Expanded Program in Economic Development," June 26, 1958, DER, Box 3, Folder: CEDR.

63. SPH, "Summary of Conversations—May 23, 1958," CRED, Box 2, Folder: CRED.

64. GA, "Outline of an Expanded Program"; GA to Leland C. Divinney, October 9, 1958, DER, Box 3, Folder: CEDR.

65. SPH, "Summary of Conversations—May 23, 1958."

66. SPH, "Proposal for a Center for Economic Development at the University of Michigan," May 22, 1958, CLSAR, Box 123, Folder: Department of Economics, 1959–60.

67. GA, "Outline of an Expanded Program."

68. SPH, Memorandum of Luncheon Conversation with George Cameron and Bill Schorger, May 28, 1958, CRED, Box 2, Folder: CRED.

69. GA, "Outline of an Expanded Program."

70. "Richard Musgrave, renowned pioneer of public finance, dies at 96," UC Santa Cruz press release, January 17, 2007, https://news.ucsc.edu/2007/01/1026.html, accessed October 2, 2018; Mary Williams Walsh, "Richard A. Musgrave, 96, Theoretician of Public Finance, Dies," *New York Times*, January 20, 2007; "Architect of the Public Household," *economicprincipals.com: An Independent Weekly*, February 15, 2004, http://www.economicprincipals.com/issues/2004.02.15/83.html, accessed October 2, 2018.

71. Richard A. Musgrave to GA, August 18, 1958, DER, Box 3, Folder: CEDR.

72. "Musgrave, Richard Abel," in *Who's Who in Economics*, ed. Blaug, 811.

73. GA to College of Literature, Science, and the Arts Executive Committee, July 14, 1959, CLSAR, Box 123, Folder: Department of Economics, 1959–60.

74. GA to Roger Heyns, June 30, 1959, CLSAR, Box 118, Folder: Department of Economics, 1958–59.

75. SPH to Roger Heyns, October 16, 1959, CLSAR, Box 123, Folder: Department of Economics, 1959–60. It is not clear why the department deviated from its plans and suddenly began a doctoral program. The National Defense Fellowship program was already in its second year of applications, so it is not as if the department's action merely responded to the start of the fellowship program. There is no evidence that the department applied unsuccessfully in the fellowship program's first year, and it is likely that they knew about the program at that time.

76. "The National Defense Graduate Fellowship Program is unique among Federal fellowship programs in that it makes no restriction as to field of study and sets no priority among the various fields in the award of fellowships. Its primary purpose is to encourage students to prepare for college teaching in all fields." US Office of Education, *Report on the National Defense Education Act, Fiscal Year Ending June 30, 1960: A Summary of Programs Administered by the Office of Education Submitted Under Public Law 85-864* (Washington, DC: US Government Printing Office, 1961), 15.

77. US Office of Education, *Report on the National Defense Education Act, Fiscal Year 1963: A Summary of Programs Administered by the Office of Education Submitted Under Public Law 85-864* (Washington, DC: US Government Printing Office, 1964), 27. For an example of the erroneous statement, see Hugh Davis Graham and Nancy Diamond, *The Rise of American Research Universities: Elites and Challengers in the Postwar Era* (Baltimore: Johns Hopkins University Press, 1997), 43.

78. US Office of Education, *Report on the National Defense Education Act, Fiscal Year Ending June 30, 1959: A Summary of Programs Administered by the Office of Education Submitted Under Public Law 85-864* (Washington, DC: US Government Printing Office, 1960), 23.

79. "Draft proposal to the Office of Education."

80. US Office of Education, *Report on the National Defense Education Act, Fiscal Year 1963*.

81. GA to Kenneth Boulding, February 19, 1960, DER, Box 3, Folder: CEDR. The other $3,500 went to the university central administration due to its policy of retaining 20 percent overhead from such funds. SPH, Memo of Conversation—July 19, 1960 with Roger Heyns and GA, CRED, Box 2, Folder: CRED.

82. "Memorandum of Discussion at the first meeting of the Executive Committee, Center for Research on Economic Development." It is not clear what Hayes's salary was for 1960–1961 or whether part of it came from another source.

83. "Center for Research on Economic Development Revised Budget for the Fiscal Year Ending June 30, 1962," December 5, 1961, DER, Box 3, Folder: CEDR.

84. SPH to Amado A. Castro, August 14, 1961, DER, Box 3, Folder: Center for Research on Economic Development.

85. "Memorandum of Discussion at the first meeting of the Executive Committee, Center for Research on Economic Development."

86. Roger Heyns to SPH, June 8, 1961, CLSAR, Box 128, Folder: Department of Economics 1960–61.

87. SPH, "Preliminary Statement," October 1961, CRED, Box 2, Folder: CRED.

88. "Functions and Staffing of CRED," n.d. [probably fall 1961], DER, Box 3, Folder: Center for Research on Economic Development.

89. "Center for Research on Economic Development," n.d. [around 1965], CRED Records, Box 2, Folder: CRED. On the origins of the Nigerian project, first suggested by Stolper and then outlined by Hayes, see Wolfgang F. Stolper, memorandum to GA and others, August 19, 1960, and SPH to Wolfgang F. Stolper, August 11, 1961, DER, Box 3, Folder: Center for Research on Economic Development.

6. Founding the University of California at Irvine

1. Dick Turpin, "Former School Teacher Johnson Dedicates Vast Irvine UC Campus," *Los Angeles Times*, June 21, 1964; Claudia Anderson [LBJ Library archivist], email message to author, 16 December 2008.

2. Johnson came twice; in addition to the Irvine appearance, he spoke at UCLA Charter Day in spring 1964 along with Mexican president Lopez Mateos. Robert G. Neumann to CK, March 16, 1964, UCOP5, Box 81, Folder 22. He declined Kerr's request to address the university as part of his fall election campaign; CK to Lyndon Baines Johnson, September 28, 1964, UCOP5, Box 83, Folder 8.

3. David Harvey, *The Condition of Postmodernity: An Enquiry into the Origins of Cultural Change* (Oxford: Blackwell, 1989); James C. Scott, *Seeing Like a State: How Certain Schemes to Improve the Human Condition Have Failed* (New Haven, CT: Yale University Press, 1998); Hunter Heyck, *Age of System: Understanding the Development of Modern Social Science* (Baltimore: Johns Hopkins University Press, 2015).

4. Bruce Kuklick, *Blind Oracles: Intellectuals and War from Kennan to Kissinger* (Princeton, NJ: Princeton University Press, 2006) 23, 35–36.

5. During construction of the Berkeley campus buildings from 1869 to 1873, the university operated from the Oakland campus of the College of California.

6. On the history of the University of California, see John Aubrey Douglass, *The California Idea and American Higher Education: 1850 to the 1960 Master Plan* (Stanford, CA: Stanford University Press, 2000); Patricia A. Pelfrey, *A Brief History of the University of California*, 2nd ed. (Berkeley: University of California Press, 2004); Verne A. Stadtman, *The University of California 1868–1968* (New York: McGraw Hill, 1970); CK, *The Gold and the Blue: A Personal Memoir of the University of California*, 2 vol. (Berkeley: University of California Press, 2001, 2003).

7. Ann Forsyth, *Reforming Suburbia: The Planned Communities of Irvine, Columbia, and The Woodlands* (Berkeley: University of California Press, 2005).

8. *Preliminary Announcement University of California, Irvine Academic Program 1965–1966* (Irvine: University of California, 1965).

9. Office of the President, "Need for Additional Facilities for Education in Architecture and Planning," May 12, 1961, UCICR, Box 65, Folder: Academic Planning, Irvine, 1961–1962.

10. Records of UC Irvine Academic Senate Committee on Preliminary Planning for a School of Architecture and Environmental Planning, Fall 1967, Representative Assembly of the Academic Senate, AS-005, Box 1, Folder: 1967 Jun–Dec, UCI Archives.

11. Robert J. Kett and Anna Kryczka, *Learning by Doing at the Farm: Craft, Science, and Counterculture in Modern California* (Chicago: Soberscove Press, 2014).

12. Daniel Aldrich c.v., January 1962, UCOP5, Box 84, Folder 4.

13. Jan Erickson, Transcription of an Oral History Interview with Ivan and Birk Hinderaker, June 5, 1998, http://www.ucrhistory.ucr.edu/pdf/hinderakeri.pdf, accessed September 17, 2018. Quote is on 21.

14. [Daniel G. Aldrich], "Comments on the Academic Plan, 1964–1975, of the University of California dated September 1964," enclosure in letter to R. D. Tschirgi, October 5, 1964, UCICR, Box 58, Folder: University Academic Plan 1965–1975 correspondence.

15. Hunter Crowther-Heyck, *Herbert A. Simon: The Bounds of Reason in Modern America* (Baltimore: Johns Hopkins University Press, 2005), 170–171.

16. JGM, interview by author, 8 February 2008, Palo Alto, CA.

17. Erickson, Transcription of an Oral History Interview with Ivan and Birk Hinderaker, 25–30.

18. JGM, "Making Artists Out of Pedants," in *The Process of Model-Building in the Behavioral Sciences*, ed. Ralph M. Stodgill (New York: Norton Library, 1972 [1970]), 59.

19. Samuel C. McCullough, oral history interview with JGM, August 8, 1973, 1, SCMOH, Box 5, Folder: JGM, 1973 August 8, UCI Archives.

20. JGM to Ivan Hinderaker, November 1, 1963, SCMOH, Box 5, Folder: JGM, 1973 August 8, UCI Archives.

21. Kenneth L. Kraemer, interview by author, January 8, 2008, Irvine, CA.

22. JGM to Hinderaker, November 1, 1963.

23. JGM, "General Perspectives for the Social Science Division," enclosure in JGM to Hinderaker, November 1, 1963.

24. JGM to Hinderaker, November 1, 1963.

25. Quoted in Donncha Kavanagh, "Reviewing March's Vision," paper submitted to the 28th Standing Conference on Organisational Symbolism (SCOS), Lille, July 2010, 8, http://epubs.surrey.ac.uk/2450, accessed October 4, 2018.

26. Quoted in Kavanagh, "Reviewing March's Vision," 15.

27. JGM to Hinderaker, November 1, 1963.

28. Minutes, Social Science Conference, April 25–26, 1955, UCBCR, Box 17, Folder 8.

29. "Remarks of President Clark Kerr at the Inauguration of Daniel G. Aldrich, Jr., as Chancellor of the Irvine Campus of the University of California, May 20, 1966," CKP, Carton 29, Folder 119.

30. JGM, "Making Artists Out of Pedants," 54, 65, 59, 60, 61.

31. Ibid., 60, 61, 63–64, 64–65, 67–69.

32. Charles A. Lave and JGM, *An Introduction to Models in the Social Sciences* (New York: Harper and Row, 1975).

33. JGM, "Making Artists Out of Pedants," 65, 66.

34. Mary S. Morgan, "Economics," in *The Cambridge History of Science: Volume 7, The Modern Social Sciences* (Cambridge, UK: Cambridge University Press, 2003), 286–288; Willy Sellekaerts, ed., *Economic Development and Planning: Essays in Honour of Jan Tinbergen* (London: Macmillan, 1974).

35. Michael A. Bernstein, "Academic Research Protocols and the Pax Americana: American Economics During the Cold War Era," in *Re-Thinking the Cold War*, ed. Allen Hunter (Philadelphia: Temple University Press, 1998), 260.

36. Crowther-Heyck, *Herbert A. Simon*, 9–10.

37. Herbert A. Simon, *Models of Man, Social and Rational: Mathematical Essays on Rational Human Behavior in a Social Setting* (New York: Wiley, 1957), viii.

38. Herbert A. Simon, *Models of My Life* (New York: Basic Books, 1991); Mie Augier and JGM, eds., *Models of a Man: Essays in Memory of Herbert A. Simon* (Cambridge, MA: MIT Press, 2004).

39. Erickson, Transcription of an Oral History Interview with Ivan and Birk Hinderaker, 32.

40. Earl C. Bolton to CK, October 14, 1960, UCOP5, Box 3, Folder 4. Kerr's planners explicitly drew on Martin Meyerson's concept of "The Opportunity Area for

Planning" from Martin Meyerson and Edward C. Banfield, *Politics, Planning, and the Public Interest: The Case of Public Housing in Chicago* (Glencoe, IL: Free Press, 1955).

41. Rakesh Khurana, *From Higher Aims to Hired Hands: The Social Transformation of American Business Schools and the Unfulfilled Promise of Management as a Profession* (Princeton, NJ: Princeton University Press, 2007), chap. 6.

42. Ivan Hinderaker, "The Study of Administration: Interdisciplinary Dimensions," *Western Political Science Quarterly* 16, no. 3, Supplement (1963): 7.

43. Lloyd D. Musolf, presentation at Western Political Science Association, March 1966, UCOP8, Box 74, Folder 1.

44. Hinderaker, "The Study of Administration," 10.

45. Ibid., 11.

46. Samuel C. McCullough, *Instant University: The History of the University of California, Irvine, 1957–1993* (Irvine: University of California, 1996), 30.

47. Stephen J. Wayne, Mary T. Hanna, Glenn D. Paige, James A. Robinson, Joseph F. Zimmerman, and Martin Edelman, "In Memoriam," *PS: Political Science and Politics* 31, no. 2 (1998): 240–243.

48. Lyman W. Porter, "An Unmanaged Pursuit of Management," http://www.siop.org/presidents/Porter.aspx, accessed September 17, 2018; Porter, "Personal Reflections on the Birth of the OB Field" (2006), http://obweb.org/index.php/awards/scholarship-awards/2006-lifetime-achievement-award-address-by-lyman-porter, accessed September 17, 2018.

49. Kraemer, interview.

50. Henry Fagin, "Urban Transportation Criteria," *Annals of the American Academy of Political and Social Science* 352 (March 1964): 141.

51. Kraemer, interview.

52. Ibid.

53. Hinderaker, "The Study of Administration," 10.

54. Kraemer, interview; Kenneth L. Kraemer and James L. Perry, "Camelot Revisited: Public Administration Education in a Generic School," in *Education for Public Service 1980*, ed. Guthrie S. Birkhead and James D. Carroll (Syracuse, NY: Maxwell School of Citizenship and Public Affairs, Syracuse University, 1980), 87–102.

55. Camilla Stivers, *Bureau Men, Settlement Women: Constructing Public Administration in the Progressive Era* (Lawrence: University Press of Kansas, 2000); Brian R. Fry and Jos C. N. Raadschelders, *Mastering Public Administration, From Max Weber to Dwight Waldo*, 2nd ed. (Washington, DC: CQ Press, 2008).

56. Alice O'Connor, *Poverty Knowledge: Social Science, Social Policy, and the Poor in Twentieth-Century U.S. History* (Princeton, NJ: Princeton University Press, 2001), 217.

57. Aaron Wildavsky, "The Once and Future School of Public Policy," *Public Interest* 79 (Spring 1986): 25–41; Hugh Davis Graham, "The Stunted Career of Policy History: A Critique and an Agenda," *Public Historian* 15, no. 2 (1993): 28; Julian Zelizer, *Governing America: The Revival of Political History* (Princeton, NJ: Princeton University Press, 2012), 41.

58. Daniel S. Appleton, Henry Fagin, and Kenneth L. Kraemer, *Policy Research at UCI* (Irvine: University of California, 1973), 23.

59. James Allen Smith, *The Idea Brokers: Think Tanks and the Rise of the New Policy Elite* (New York: Free Press, 1991); Bruce Kuklick, "The Rise of Policy Institutes in the United States, 1943–1971," *Orbis* (Fall 2011): 685–699. Hugh Davis Graham has argued

that the rise of policy analysis was related to the emergence by the early 1970s of a new regulatory state, "far more pervasive and complex" than its predecessors. "The Stunted Career of Policy History," 23.

60. Bill Turque, *Inventing Al Gore: A Biography* (Boston: Houghton Mifflin, 2000), 58–59, 234–237.

61. CK, *The Gold and the Blue*, vol. 1, 248–250; Sarah L. Sharp, *Director of Scripps Institution of Oceanography, 1951–1964*, oral history interviews with Roger Revelle, vol. 3, The Bancroft Library, University of California, Berkeley, quotes on 112.

62. Kathleen Ann Archibald, "The Utilization of Social Research and Policy Analysis" (PhD diss., Washington University, 1968). Strangely, the dissertation does not mention her experience with planning PPRO. On Gouldner, see Steven Shapin, *The Scientific Life: A Moral History of a Late Modern Vocation* (Chicago: University of Chicago Press, 2008), 118.

63. Kathleen Archibald, memorandum, "Meeting with [Raymond G.] Bressler on Policy Research Organization, April 10," April 14, 1964, UCICR, Box 128, Folder: Ad Hoc Committee on Public Policy Research Organization 1963–1965 [hereafter AHC PPRO].

64. Jerome B. Wiesner, "A Memoir: How Roger Revelle Became Interested in Population and Development Problems," n.d., http://ic.media.mit.edu/projects/JBW/ARTICLES/REVELLE/REVELLE.HTM, accessed September 17, 2018.

65. Pauline Wyckoff to Gloria Copeland, January 20, 1963, UCOP5, Box 115, Folder 29.

66. Sharp, *Director of Scripps Institution of Oceanography*, 112–113.

67. CK to Daniel G. Aldrich [same letter to several others], May 21, 1964, UCICR, Box 128, Folder: AHC PPRO. For Revelle's authorship of the draft, see Roger Revelle to CK, May 8, 1964, UCOP5, Box 111, Folder 10.

68. "Minutes of the Meeting of the Ad Hoc Committee on Policy Research, June 20, 1964, Hilton Inn, San Francisco International Airport," UCICR, Box 128, Folder: AHC PPRO.

69. Kuklick, *Blind Oracles*, 60–64.

70. http://www.albertwohlstetter.com/, accessed November 23, 2008 (site discontinued).

71. Fred Kaplan, *The Wizards of Armageddon* (New York: Simon & Schuster, 1982), 348; Alex Abella, *Soldiers of Reason: The Rand Corporation and the Rise of American Empire* (Orlando: Harcourt, 2008), 196.

72. Richard N. Rosecrance, ed., *The Dispersion of Nuclear Weapons: Strategy and Politics* (New York: Columbia University Press, 1964).

73. Albert Wohlstetter, "Intelligence and the Avoidance of Surprise," presentation, Institute of International Studies, University of California, Berkeley, May 15, 1964, A Register of the Albert J. and Roberta Wohlstetter Papers, Hoover Institution Archives, http://www.oac.cdlib.org/findaid/ark:/13030/kt1489q8rg, accessed September 17, 2018; Kathleen Archibald, ed., *Strategic Interaction and Conflict: Original Papers and Discussion* (Berkeley: Institute of International Studies, University of California, 1966); Paul Erickson, *The World the Game Theorists Made* (Chicago: University of Chicago Press, 2015).

74. Kathleen Archibald, "Institute vs. Institution," n.d. [likely late 1964], UCICR, Box 128, Folder: AHC PPRO.

75. Kathleen Archibald to Ad Hoc Committee on Policy Research, "Summary of memorandum on Eastern trip (June 21—July 3, Washington, D.C.—Cambridge, Mass.)," UCICR, Box 128, Folder: AHC PPRO.

76. [Kathleen Archibald], "Draft Proposal for a University-wide Policy Research Organization," June 8, 1964, 8, 9–10, UCICR, Box 128, Folder: AHC PPRO.

77. Ibid., 13–19 (quotes on 13 and 19).

78. Ibid., 16–17.

79. Peter Galison and Bruce Hevly, eds., *Big Science: The Growth of Large-Scale Research* (Stanford, CA: Stanford University Press, 1992).

80. [Archibald], "Draft Proposal for a University-wide Policy Research Organization," 19.

81. Archibald, "Summary of memorandum on Eastern trip."

82. Robert Calkins to CK, August 12, 1964, UCOP5, Box 111, Folder 10.

83. Archibald, "Summary of memorandum on Eastern trip."

84. Kuklick, *Blind Oracles*, 153.

85. "Minutes of the Meeting of the Ad Hoc Committee on Policy Research, June 20, 1964."

86. For the description of the Kennedy School in this and the previous paragraph, see Kuklick, *Blind Oracles*, chap. 8.

87. E. T. Grether to CK, March 29, 1957, CKP, Carton 12, Folder 20.

88. "Minutes of the Meeting of the Ad Hoc Committee on Policy Research, June 20, 1964."

89. Office of the University Dean of Research, "Draft—Tentative Agenda for Proposed Weekend Meeting," August 14, 1964, UCOP5, Box 111, Folder 10.

90. JGM to Kathleen Archibald, September 14, 1964, UCICR, Box 128, Folder: AHC PPRO.

91. JGM to Daniel G. Aldrich, July 28, 1964, UCICR, Box 128, Folder: AHC PPRO.

92. Daniel G. Aldrich to JGM, August 11, 1964, UCICR, Box 128, Folder: AHC PPRO.

93. [Archibald], "Draft Proposal for a University-wide Policy Research Organization," 6, 9.

94. Aldrich to JGM, August 11, 1964.

95. Quoted in Archibald, "Institute vs. Institution." Emphasis original.

96. R. D. Tschirgi to CK, September 29, 1964, UCOP5, Box 111, Folder 11.

97. Appleton et al., *Policy Research at UCI*; March, interview.

98. Kathleen Archibald, *Sex and the Public Service* (Ottawa: Queen's Printer for Canada, 1970), iii; K. A. Archibald et al., *Factors Affecting the Use of Competition in Weapon System Acquisition* (Santa Monica, CA: RAND Corporation, 1981).

99. J. G. Wilson to C. J. Coury, November 9, 1965, UCOP8, Box 104, Folder 15; March, interview.

100. Jeanne Nienaber Clarke and Helen M. Ingram, "A Founder: Aaron Wildavsky and the Study of Public Policy," *Policy Studies Journal* 38, no. 3 (2010): 565–579.

101. Office of the Vice President to CK, Analysis of 1966–67 Target Budget Request Irvine Campus, n.d., UCOP5, Box 19, Folder 2.

102. Appleton et al., *Policy Research at UCI*, 15.

103. For a more detailed account of the operations of PPRO sketched in this paragraph, see Ethan Schrum, "Social Science over Agriculture: Re-imagining the Land-

Grant Mission at the University of California–Irvine in the 1960s," *Perspectives on the History of Higher Education* 30 (2013): 311–333.

104. Alexander M. Mood, "Miscellaneous Reminiscences," *Statistical Science* 5, no. 1 (1990): 35–43.

105. Kraemer, interview; Public Policy Research Organization, *Research Programs*, January 1978, UCICR, Box 128.

106. Appleton et al., *Policy Research at UCI*, 14.

107. Review Committee Report of the PPRO, January 19, 1973, UCOP8, Box 104, Folder 16.

108. Appleton et al., *Policy Research at UCI*, 65–70.

109. Public Policy Research Organization, *Research Programs* (Irvine: University of California, 1978), UCICR, Box 128, Folder: "Public Policy Research Organization, *Research Programs*, Jan 1978 (booklet)."

110. Kraemer, interview.

111. Daniel G. Aldrich to CK, November 4, 1964, UCICR, Box 128, Folder: AHC PPRO.

112. Appleton et al., *Policy Research at UCI*, iii.

113. "What a Whiz Kid Did," *Newsweek*, July 19, 1965, 21.

114. Remarks by CK, Charles J. Hitch memorial service, September 24, 1995, CKP, Carton 59, Folder 34.

115. Roger Revelle to CK, March 29, 1964, UCOP8, Box 104, Folder 16.

116. Kathleen Archibald, "Report on Meeting with Dean Ellberg re: Policy Research Organization, April 13, 1964," UCICR, Box 128, Folder: AHC PPRO.

117. Charles J. Hitch, *Decision-Making for Defense* (Berkeley: University of California Press, 1965).

118. This account is drawn from CK, *The Gold and the Blue*, vol. 2.

119. Herman Lindauer to Charles J. Hitch, September 22, 1967, UCOP5, Box 66, Folder 14.

120. Christine Agur to Charles J. Hitch, September 22, 1967, UCOP5, Box 66, Folder 14.

121. CK, *The Urban-Grant University: A Model for the Future* (New York: City College: 1968), 5, 6, 7, 14, 9.

122. Kavanagh, "Reviewing March's Vision," 17.

Epilogue

1. Elliott C. Kulakowski and Lynne U. Chronister, *Research Administration and Management* (Sudbury, MA: Jones and Bartlett, 2006), 18.

2. *Proceedings of the Tenth National Conference on the Administration of Research*, September 5–7, 1956 (University Park: Pennsylvania State University Press, 1957), 1, 2, 46.

3. Steven Shapin, *The Scientific Life: A Moral History of a Late Modern Vocation* (Chicago: University of Chicago Press, 2008), 117–118 (quotes on 117).

4. Eric A. Walker, "Implications of Environmental Demands for Educational Institutions," paper presented at the Fourteenth Annual Conference on the Administration of Research, University of Michigan, September 20, 1960, EWP.

5. Ray Pepinsky to Eric A. Walker, November 4, 1960, EWP.

6. Ray Pepinsky, "Some Views of Scientific Research in a University," [1960], EWP.

7. Roger L. Geiger, *Research and Relevant Knowledge: American Research Universities Since World War II* (New York: Oxford University Press, 1993), 107, 359n28, 88.

8. On Nisbet's career, see Robert G. Perrin, "Robert Alexander Nisbet," *Proceedings of the American Philosophical Society* 143, no. 4 (1999): 695–710.

9. Robert Nisbet, *Teachers and Scholars: A Memoir of Berkeley in Depression and War* (New Brunswick, NJ: Transaction, 1992).

10. CK, *The Gold and the Blue: A Personal Memoir of the University of California*, vol. 1 (Berkeley: University of California Press, 2001), 316.

11. R. A. Nisbet to CK, January 26, 1952, CKP, Carton 10, Folder 19.

12. Kerr, *The Gold and the Blue*, vol. 1, 314; John R. Thelin, *A History of American Higher Education* (Baltimore: Johns Hopkins University Press, 2004), 296.

13. Kerr, *The Gold and the Blue*, vol. 1, 316. Archival material on this episode is in UCOP3, Box 9.

14. R. A. Nisbet to CK, October 21, 1957, CKP, Carton 26, Folder 6.

15. CK, *The Gold and the Blue: A Personal Memoir of the University of California*, vol. 2 (Berkeley: University of California Press, 2003), 118, 21, 22.

16. Robert Nisbet, *The Degradation of the Academic Dogma: The University in America, 1945–1970* (New York: Basic Books, 1971), xii, 83.

17. Ibid., 212, 213.

18. CK, "Higher Education Cannot Escape History: The 1990s," in *An Agenda for the New Decade*, ed. Larry W. Jones and Franz A. Nowotny (San Francisco: Jossey-Bass, 1990): 5–17; CK, *Higher Education Cannot Escape History: Issues for the Twenty-First Century* (Albany: SUNY Press, 1994).

19. CK, *The Uses of the University* (Cambridge, MA: Harvard University Press, 1963), 5, 33.

20. Nisbet, *Degradation*, 199, 200. Nisbet's mention of an "economic engine" suggests that this terminology was in use by 1971.

21. Ibid., 73, 72, 73. He did not mention Thorstein Veblen's *The Higher Learning in America: A Memorandum on the Conduct of Universities by Business Men* (1918), probably the most famous attack on business influence on the university.

22. Nisbet, *Degradation*, 83.

23. Ibid., 72–73, 77, 80.

24. Ibid., 78; Alvin W. Gouldner, "Cosmopolitans and Locals: Toward an Analysis of Latent Social Roles—I," *Administrative Science Quarterly* 2, no. 3 (1957): 281–306; Gouldner, "Cosmopolitans and Locals: Toward an Analysis of Latent Social Roles—II," *Administrative Science Quarterly* 2, no. 4 (1958): 444–480.

25. Nisbet, *Degradation*, 71, 76.

26. Ibid., 89, 97, 93, 96, 95, 98.

27. Ibid., 81, 80, 76, 77, 146, 150–151.

28. Ibid., 188, 127, 128, 129, 135, 124, 193, 189, 190, 193.

29. "Russell A. Kirk," Russell Kirk biographical file, Michigan State University archives; Bradley J. Birzer, "Seven Conservative Minds," *The American Conservative*, December 3, 2013, http://www.theamericanconservative.com/articles/seven-conservative-minds/, accessed September 17, 2018; Birzer, *Russell Kirk: American Conservative* (Lexington: University Press of Kentucky, 2015); Russell Kirk Collection finding aid, Clarke Historical Library, Central Michigan University; Russell Kirk, *The Sword of Imagination: Memoirs of a Half-Century of Literary Conflict* (Grand Rapids, MI: Eerd-

mans, 1995), 153–155; Russell Kirk, "Academic Freedom and Educational Standards," in *Collier's 1954 Year Book: Covering National and International Events of the Year 1953*, ed. W. T. Couch (New York: P. F. Collier, 1954), 1–5.

30. Birzer, *Russell Kirk*, 194.

31. Russell Kirk, *Academic Freedom: An Essay in Definition* (Chicago: Henry Regnery, 1955), 2, 149.

32. Russell Kirk, *Decadence and Renewal in the Higher Learning: An Episodic History of American University and College since 1953* (South Bend, IN: Gateway Editions, 1978), 212; Kirk, *Academic Freedom*, 36.

33. R. A. Nisbet, review of *Academic Freedom* by Russell Kirk, *Western Political Quarterly* 9, no. 1 (1956): 216–217.

34. Kirk, *Academic Freedom*, 176.

35. Kirk, *Decadence and Renewal*, 101.

36. Kirk, *Academic Freedom*, 11.

37. Ibid., 15, quoting Robert Maynard Hutchins.

38. Nisbet, *Degradation*, 3.

39. Kirk, *Academic Freedom*, 57; Kirk, "Rebellion Against Boredom," in *Seeds of Anarchy: A Study of Campus Revolution*, ed. Frederick Wilhelmsen (Dallas: Argus Academic Press, 1969), 33.

40. Kirk, *Decadence and Renewal*, xv, xiv, xv.

41. Kirk, *Academic Freedom*, 122, 122–123, 191.

42. Kim Phillips-Fein, *Invisible Hands: The Businessmen's Crusade Against the New Deal* (New York: W. W. Norton, 2009); Jennifer Burns, *Goddess of the Market: Ayn Rand and the American Right* (New York: Oxford University Press, 2009); Daniel Stedman-Jones, *Masters of the Universe: Hayek, Friedman, and the Birth of Neoliberal Politics* (Princeton, NJ: Princeton University Press, 2012); Angus Burgin, *The Great Persuasion: Reinventing Free Markets since the Depression* (Cambridge, MA: Harvard University Press, 2012); Elizabeth Tandy Shermer, *Sunbelt Capitalism: Phoenix and the Transformation of American Politics* (Philadelphia: University of Pennsylvania Press, 2013).

43. On the former, see Edward J. Hackett, "Science as a Vocation in the 1990s: The Changing Organizational Culture of Academic Science," *Journal of Higher Education* 61, no. 3 (1990): 241–279; Sheila Slaughter and Larry L. Leslie, *Academic Capitalism: Politics, Policies, and the Entrepreneurial University* (Baltimore: Johns Hopkins University Press, 1997); Sheila Slaughter and Gary Rhoades, *Academic Capitalism and the New Economy: Markets, State, and Higher Education* (Baltimore: Johns Hopkins University Press, 2004); Roger L. Geiger, *Knowledge and Money: Research Universities and the Paradox of the Marketplace* (Stanford, CA: Stanford University Press, 2004); Elizabeth Popp Berman, *Creating the Market University: How Academic Science Became an Economic Engine* (Princeton, NJ: Princeton University Press, 2012). These scholars do not mention Nisbet's work on academic capitalism.

44. Benjamin Ginsberg, *The Fall of the Faculty: The Rise of the All-Administrative University and Why it Matters* (New York: Oxford University Press, 2011); Gaye Tuchman, *Wannabe U: Inside the Corporate University* (Chicago: University of Chicago Press, 2009); Frank Donoghue, *The Last Professors: The Corporate University and the Fate of the Humanities* (New York: Fordham University Press, 2008); Jennifer Washburn, *University, Inc.: The Corporate Corruption of Higher Education* (New York: Basic Books, 2005); Eric Gould, *The University in a Corporate Culture* (New Haven, CT: Yale University Press,

2003). This literature also resonates with Nisbet's analysis, especially on structural change and managerialism, without recognizing him.

45. Nisbet, *Degradation*, 86.

46. Jerry A. Jacobs, *In Defense of Disciplines: Interdisciplinarity and Specialization in the Research University* (Chicago: University of Chicago Press, 2013), 91.

47. Peter Schmidt, "Big Gifts and Low Profiles Help Conservative Centers Spread to Campuses," *The Chronicle of Higher Education*, February 6, 2015, http://chronicle.com/article/Big-GiftsLow-Profiles/151701, accessed September 17, 2018.

48. http://elsinore-test.its.yale.edu/about/levin.html, accessed 3 June 2016 (site discontinued).

49. Teresa A. Sullivan, "Higher Education as the Engine of the American Economy," lecture delivered at the Miller Center, University of Virginia, September 7, 2011, available on video at https://millercenter.org/news-events/events/higher-education-engine-american-economy.

50. University of Virginia, http://www.virginia.edu/overview, accessed September 17, 2018.

Index

CPSIA information can be obtained
at www.ICGtesting.com
Printed in the USA
BVHW031219200519
547915BV00012B/15/P